VAMPIRES, RACE, AND TRANSNATIONAL HOLLYWOODS

Traditions in American Cinema
Series Editors Linda Badley and R. Barton Palmer

Titles in the series include:

The "War on Terror" and American Film: 9/11 Frames Per Second
by Terence McSweeney

American Postfeminist Cinema: Women, Romance and Contemporary Culture
by Michele Schreiber

Film Noir
by Homer B. Pettey and R. Barton Palmer (eds)

In Secrecy's Shadow: The OSS and CIA in Hollywood Cinema 1941–1979
by Simon Willmetts

Indie Reframed: Women's Filmmaking and Contemporary American Independent Cinema
by Linda Badley, Claire Perkins, and Michele Schreiber (eds)

Vampires, Race, and Transnational Hollywoods
by Dale Hudson

www.edinburghuniversitypress.com/series/tiac

VAMPIRES, RACE, AND TRANSNATIONAL HOLLYWOODS

Dale Hudson

EDINBURGH
University Press

Edinburgh University Press is one of the leading university presses in the UK. We publish academic books and journals in our selected subject areas across the humanities and social sciences, combining cutting-edge scholarship with high editorial and production values to produce academic works of lasting importance. For more information visit our website: edinburghuniversitypress.com

© Dale Hudson, 2017

Edinburgh University Press Ltd
The Tun—Holyrood Road
12 (2f) Jackson's Entry
Edinburgh EH8 8PJ

Typeset in 10/12.5pt Sabon by
Servis Filmsetting Ltd, Stockport, Cheshire

A CIP record for this book is available from the British Library

ISBN 978 1 4744 2308 3 (hardback)
ISBN 978 1 4744 2309 0 (webready PDF)
ISBN 978 1 4744 2310 6 (epub)

The right of Dale Hudson to be identified as author of this work has been asserted in accordance with the Copyright, Designs and Patents Act 1988 and the Copyright and Related Rights Regulations 2003 (SI No. 2498).

CONTENTS

List of Illustrations	viii
Acknowledgments	x
Introduction: Migrations and Mutations	1
Why Vampires Matter	6
Overview of the Book	8
How Hollywood is Transnational and Race has Afterlives	13
Chapter Outlines	17
1. Blood, Bodies, and Borders	21
The Moment of Count Dracula	24
Count Dracula Refashioned as "Vampire Ayatollah"	31
An Iranian American Feminist Screens a Vampire Film at Sundance	34
The Figure of the Vampire as Object and Method	40
2. "Making" Americans from Foreigners	45
Masquerading US Landscapes as Foreign Locales	47
Comedies of Contained Assimilation and Segregation	51
Romance and Literacy as Alternatives to Unionized Labor	55
Romantic Assimilation to Productive Citizenship	58
Melodrama and Miscegenation	61
Locating Borders on the Body	66

3. Classical Hollywood Vampires: The Unnatural Whiteness of America ... 68
   - Hollywood's Unnaturally White Stars ... 71
   - Accented Arrivals and Deadly Departures ... 75
   - Scarred Bodies, Scared Nations ... 80
   - Hollywood's "Broken Spanish" ... 85
   - Ethnicity after Assimilation ... 89
   - Postwar Parodies of Intrawhite Racism ... 92
   - The Vampire as Frontier Fighter ... 96

4. International Hollywood Vampires: Cosmopolitanisms of "Foreign Movies" ... 100
   - Feeling American through "Cheap Foreign Movies" ... 103
   - Hollywood Finances an "English Gothic" ... 106
   - Sequels and Parodies of an Anglo-Saxon Homeland ... 109
   - Silencing through Dubbing, Interpreting through Subtitling ... 114
   - Making "Mexicans" in Miami: Mexi-Gothic for US Television ... 116
   - Undead, Unidentified, Unacknowledged: "Made For America" in the Philippines ... 123
   - Distributing Childlike Images ... 130

5. Vampires of Color: A Critique of Multicultural Whiteness ... 134
   - Diverse Hollywood, Familiar Habits ... 136
   - National Passing: Difference Disappearing into Diversity ... 140
   - Black Vampires, from Disqualified Immigration to Qualified Citizenship ... 143
   - "Getting Civilized" ... 149
   - Transient and Unsettled Whiteness ... 152
   - Miscegenation and Multiculturalism ... 155
   - Historicizing Multiculturalism ... 158

6. Terrorist Vampires: Religious Heritage or Planetary Advocacy ... 163
   - Humanism's Limiting Empathy ... 166
   - A Heritage of Christian Crusades ... 170
   - Vampires in Post-NAFTA Borderlands ... 173
   - The Difference between Slayers and Daywalkers ... 179
   - The "Twilight" of Indigenous Nations and Other Exterminations ... 184
   - Genetically Engineered Species and Neoliberal Wars ... 188

7. Other Vampires, Other Hollywoods: Serialized Citizenship and Narrowcast Difference ... 193
   - Media Convergence and Conglomerations ... 196
   - Canada as Hollywood's Home Market ... 199

Asian America, Made for Television	202
Slaying without a Feminist Role Model, Walking while Black	205
Vampires in the New South	209
Recognizing Difference: Miami, Toronto, Dublin	215
Web Series and Queer Feminism	221
Adapting to (and from) Videogames	225
Conclusion: History and Hollywood, Mashed-up	229
Filmography	240
Bibliography	245
Index	264

ILLUSTRATIONS

Figure I.1	Béla Lugosi as Count Dracula in publicity still for "The Strangest Love Story Ever Told." *Dracula*	4
Figure I.2	PBS's nonthreatening and nonviolent vampire Count von Count teaches empathy and intelligence. *Sesame Street*	15
Figure 1.1	Gary Oldman as an orientalized Count Dracula welcomes Keanu Reeves as Jonathan Harker at the start of another excellent adventure. *Bram Stoker's Dracula*	32
Figure 1.2	The Girl encounters Arash, lost under a streetlamp and dressed like a classical Hollywood vampire. *A Girl Walks Home Alone at Night*	36
Figure 2.1	Ivan Orloff whips wife and mule in eastern Europe. *Making an American Citizen*	53
Figure 2.2	Rudolf Valentino carries away a docile white female body. *The Sheik*	65
Figure 3.1	Hollywood Gothic's armadillos in the Castle Dracula. *Dracula*	77
Figure 3.2	The terrifying mark of interracial romance on the female white body. *The Cheat*	82
Figure 3.3	Inspecting the stylized mark of the vampire on the female white body. *Dracula*	83

ILLUSTRATIONS

Figure 4.1	The haunted hacienda as adaptation of Hollywood's southern (Alta) California Gothic. *El Vampiro/The Vampire*	118
Figure 4.2	Parody of dubbing becomes judgment of a "goofy country." Mystery Science Theater 3000 broadcast of *Samson versus the Vampire Women*	122
Figure 4.3	Doña Consuelo Escodero de Victoria returns from the grave to visit her daughter Leonore. *The Curse of the Vampires*	127
Figure 4.4	Prehistoric cave people from *Tagani* refashioned as vampires. *Horror of the Blood Monsters*	129
Figure 5.1	David Niven in blackface as Count Dracula after "mixing" of blood. *Old Dracula*	146
Figure 5.2	Beyond blaxploitation: the educated and affluent African American man as the vampire Dr. Hess Green. *Ganja and Hess*	147
Figure 5.3	Grace Jones as the voiceless foreign vampire Katrina, trapped under Keith Haring's makeup. *Vamp*	153
Figure 5.4	NYU doctoral student in philosophy, Kathleen Conklin, shocked by her own ignorance of US military massacre of women and children in Viet Nam. *The Addiction*	160
Figure 6.1	Menacing crescent shadow of the Muslim Turks over Christian Europe. *Bram Stoker's Dracula*	171
Figure 6.2	Aztec ruins littered with consumer goods in an archeology of successive conquests. *From Dusk till Dawn*	175
Figure 6.3	Skulls as trophies within terrorism of privatized border control via vigilante vampire hunters. *Vampires*	177
Figure 7.1	Buying TruBlood at a convenience store as the first image of "mainstreaming" vampires. *True Blood*	211
Figure 7.2	Nan Flanagan advocating for vampire rights on television. *True Blood*	213
Figure 7.3	Laura Hollis and friends capture her crush, the vampire Carmilla Karnstein, for a university journalism project. *Carmilla*	224
Figure C.1	Internet mashup of Edward Cullen from *Twilight* pursued by Abraham Lincoln from *Abraham Lincoln: Vampire Hunter*	231

ACKNOWLEDGMENTS

My thinking about the figure of the vampire began with a course that I taught in graduate school. Francis Ford Coppola's adaptation of Bram Stoker's novel *Dracula*, along with the novel itself, allowed for a different point of entry into critical understandings of colonial binaries, such as "good and evil" and "east and west," and an opening to postcolonial realities of complex understandings of power and difference At the time, *Buffy the Vampire Slayer* was popular on television. The perspectives of vampires often seemed delegitimized by the overriding confidence of slayers, who killed without asking questions. I found vampires more compelling and later noticed that I was not alone.

Anticolonial and postcolonial thinkers from Frantz Fanon to Alberto Memmi and Achille Mbembe, alongside other critics of oppressive ideologies and epistemologies, including Gilles Deleuze and Félix Guattari, Michael Hardt and Antonio Negri, turned to supernatural figures—vampires, zombies, werewolves—to describe insights from the perspectives of postcolonies and diasporas; experiences of statelessness, exile, and alternative modernities; and ways to contest neoliberal forms of capitalism. I found that the figure of the vampire also offered filmmakers an opportunity to address social difference, particularly as it was rendered meaningful through racialization in social conventions and legal systems. The vampire, I thought, was the ideal figure for thinking through the process of democratization in a former settler colony that had become an empire.

This book would not have come into being without the enthusiastic support, insightful advice, and superb guidance of Gillian Leslie and Richard Strachan

ACKNOWLEDGMENTS

at Edinburgh University Press, where it further benefited from Eddie Clark and Rebecca Mackenzie in production and design, and from Stephanie Pickering's copyediting. I am tremendously grateful to the series editors, Linda Badley and R. Barton Palmer, for their support—and their prompt reviews of proposals and manuscripts. I am thrilled to have my book on Hollywoods in the plural as part of their series on traditions in American cinema, and I thank them for identifying anonymous readers, whose suggestions improved the book's structure and arguments. I thank Lisa Rivero for indexing this book, and I thank the New York University Abu Dhabi Institute for a grant to support this work.

My ideas have benefited over the years by the support of Daniel Bernardi, Carla Feccero, Claire Jean Kim, and Harry Benshoff, who supported my research and offered helpful comments on articles they included in edited volumes. I am also grateful to Gwendolyn Audrey Foster for her enthusiastic review of a chapter that I contributed to one of these volumes. Although we have never met, I look forward to thanking her in person for encouraging me to continue this research when others sometimes dismissed it. I also look forward to one day thanking in person Donald Pease for his encouragement of this research.

I am forever indebted to Catherine Portuges for helping me conceive and shape the initial ideas that would come together into this book. Her mentorship was invaluable, and I still aspire to follow her model of rigorous academic research in stylish prose. In many ways, her argument that a Hollywood of European exiles unsettled presumptions that classical Hollywood films were unequivocally "American" allowed me a way into thinking about transnational dimensions within nationalist narratives and industries. I am also indebted to Anne Ciecko for helping me develop the critical and theoretical frameworks that contributed, not only to this book, but to my first print publication, which appeared without my acknowledgments. Her suggestions on my early thoughts on transnational stardom inform my thinking about migratory movements. I also want to give a special thanks to Anita Mannur for suggesting I look at *Bram Stoker's Dracula* and to Doreen Lee for *A Girl Walked Home Alone at Night*.

My thinking has additionally benefited from the opportunity to work within so many vibrant intellectual circles in western Massachusetts, central New York, and now ones between Abu Dhabi and New York. I am grateful to Wendy Bergoffen, Stephanie Dunson, Justine Dymond, Elizabeth Fitzpatrick, Enrique García, Nina Ha, Sally Lawall, Don Levine, Sura Levine, Sunaina Maira, Dawn Lundy Martin, Anita Mannur, Patricia Matthew, Bridget Matthews-Kane, Corinne Oster, Alix Paschkowiak, Cathy Schlund-Vials, Sejal Shah, and Jennifer Stone for inspiring conversations and gracious comments on early drafts of writing that developed into articles, chapters, and parts of this book. I thank Grace An, Renate Ferro, Gina Marchetti, Monika Mehta, Timothy Murray, Anna Siomopoulos, Lisa Patti, Patricia Zimmermann for welcoming me into another intellectual community when I taught at Ithaca College. Returning to western Massachusetts, I joined yet another such community with colleagues Jack Cameron, Rhonda Cobham-Sander, Judy Frank, Leah Hewitt, Marisa Parham, Andrew Parker, and Helen von Schmidt and our Dean of Faculty, Gregory Call, at Amherst College, as well as Five Colleges colleagues Robin Blaetz, Jenny Perlin, Ajay Sinha, and Elizabeth Young at Mount Holyoke College, Alexandra Keller at Smith College, and Baba Hillman, Penny Lane, Susana Loza, and Abraham Ravett at Hampshire College.

Leaving the United States for a start-up institution in the United Arab Emirates was an opportunity to rethink terms of comparison, so I thank Hilary Ballon, Ron Robin, and Mariët Westermann for bringing me into the project of New York University Abu Dhabi and to Al Bloom and Fabio Piano for its realization. The opportunity to work with students from more than 200 different countries at an institution where no one group dominates has been transformative to my thinking and renewed my commitment to unsettling canonical assumptions in academic research. I have also gained the opportunity to join a vibrant intellectual community that spans campuses in Abu Dhabi, New York, and Shanghai, as well as other universities in Abu Dhabi and New York, offering me the opportunity for ongoing conversations with friends and colleagues, including Amir Al Islam, Richard Allen, Awam Amkpa, Nezar Andary, Wendy Bednarz, Saglar Bougdaeva, Gwyneth Bravo, Özge Calafato, Catherine Corey, Virginia Danielson, Jonny Farrow, Reindert Falkenburg, Toral Gajarawala, Gayatri Gopinath, Radha Hegde, Leonard Retel Helmrich, Jason King, Martin Klimke, Jill Magi, Pascal Menoret, Amir Minsky, Lauren Minsky, Mia Mochizuki, Sana Odeh, Robert Parthesius, Mary Poovey, Gunja SenGupta, Ella Shohat, Robert Stam, Mark Swislocki, Helga Tawil-Souri, Yasser Tabbaa, Denise-Marie Teese, James Toth, Robert J. C. Young, Alia Yunis, and Zhen Zhang. My thinking has also benefited from discussions with Tamu Al Islam, Hannah Brückner, and Alta Mauro on issues of inclusion and equity in academia.

I thank Mark Quigley at the UCLA Film and Television Archive for allowing me to screen a few immigration comedies and melodramas not available elsewhere. I thank Rebecca Touger, who worked as my research assistants at Amherst College. I have also been incredibly fortunate to have wonderful friends, who opened their homes and couches to me when I would return to Manhattan and Westchester from Amherst and Ithaca for weekends. I drafted early version of ideas with Joanna Langada and Alfred Korn, who even drove me to a midtown cinema to see a few of these films, and with Joan Peters, who even took the subway downtown with me to see a few others.

I especially thank Doreen Lee for her comments and suggestions over the years. An awesome friend and confidant, we met in Ithaca, taught together in Amherst, and unwittingly vex Sheetal with our Sagittarian whims no matter where we are. I also want to give special thanks to my friend and coauthor Patty Zimmermann for her advice on publishers and academia in general—and for helping me to reinvigorate my prose with zesty verbs. I have never known anyone in academia more generous than Patty, not just with me, but with so many friends and colleagues. She is a driving force towards making our field a better one.

I thank my family and extended family for their emotional support. I am extremely grateful to my parents, Mary and Dale Hudson, for allowing me to pursue interests and a career in academia. I owe a huge debt to my maternal grandparents, Jane and Thomas Thurlow, for teaching me how to unsettle my own assumptions. I thank my parents-in-law, Meenakshee and Narendra Majithia, for adopting me into their family. I thank my sisters and brothers-in-law, especially Snehal Majithia, Hetu Parakh, Jane Hudson Eaker, Jeff Eaker, Stephanie Hudson Forsberg, Steve Forsberg, and my nieces and nephews Anand, Kylie, Kendall, Nile, Caleb, and Josh—along with Atticus, Radley, Malaika, and Kishmish for providing a feline counterpoint to a world that often seems so anthropocentric.

More than anyone, I thank Sheetal Majithia, who willingly screened many vampire films and series with me. The book's focus on immigration and globalization reflects our story as we migrated from the United States to the United Arab Emirates. Before us, members of our families emigrated from France to the United States, from India to East Africa, from the United States to England and back again, from Tanzania to India to Uganda and Kenya to India again and then to the United States. Most moved more than once for financial to political reasons, often beyond our control. Sheetal has taught me better ways of being in this ever-moving world, which contributed in unexpected ways to the arguments that I develop in this book. Without her, this book would have been a very diminished one, as would be my life.

Sections of Chapter 5 originally appeared as "Vampires of Color and the Performance of Multicultural Whiteness," in *The Persistence of Whiteness: Race and Contemporary Hollywood Cinema*, ed. Daniel Bernardi (New York: Routledge, 2007): 127–56. Sections of Chapter 7 appeared as "'Of Course There are Werewolves and Vampires': *True Blood* and the Right to Rights for Other Species," *American Quarterly* 65.3 special issue on Species/Race/Sex, ed. Carla Feccero and Claire Jean Kim (September 2013): 661–83.

INTRODUCTION: MIGRATIONS AND MUTATIONS

A defining feature of vampires is their ability to mutate and migrate. Evoking the black-and-white mise-en-scène of classical Hollywood, Ana Lily Amirpour's *A Girl Walks Home Alone at Night* (2014) introduced a female vampire who rides a skateboard in hijab. The vampire's chador rejects typical post-9/11 suspicions about Muslims, racialized by their clothing. Instead, it shields her from unwanted attention of predatory human men. The film self-consciously references the visual ambiance of Hollywood's first vampire films, Universal Pictures' *Dracula* (1931) and *Drácula* (1931), but marks a different historical moment and cultural politics. Count Dracula and Conde Drácula's flowing black capes may have seemed foreign to audiences during the 1930s, but the open black chador of Amirpour's vampire is relatively familiar today, if sometimes reductively as a sign of patriarchal oppression or foreign menace. Amirpour reworks Hollywood conventions of male vampires, attacking female victims, into a feminist vampire, protecting women. Marshaling the chador's power against male terrors of the night—and a skateboard for enhanced female mobility, Amirpour's vampire also subverts conventional thinking about difference and belonging, guiding us through worlds that have always folded into one another.

Vampires may be historically rooted in eastern European folklore, but their progeny proliferates unbound. They mutate and migrate between melodrama, romance, horror, comedy, soap opera, and science fiction. They adapt freely to codes and conventions as diverse as Latin American *lucha libre* and *telenovela*, South Asian *masala*, East Asian *wuxia* and *anime*, and industrial contexts as different as Hollywood, Lollywood, Bollywood, Nollywood, and Hallyuwood.[1] Our fascination with vampires is undying; their popularity, inexhaustible. Since vampires are diverse and unruly as a category, vampire media is sometimes dismissed as having little to say. *Vampires, Race, and Transnational Hollywoods* argues that vampires have something to say precisely because they are so diverse and unruly as a category. The book proposes that vampire films and series constitute a different way of understanding Hollywood by investigating two twinned trajectories in the context of production, distribution, and exhibition: *what* vampire films and series depict on the screen, and *how* they produce affect in audiences that ranges from affiliation and empathy to repulsion and suspicion. Vampires allow us to refocus on Hollywood as *plural*, US history as *transnational*, and race as having *afterlives*. The vampire's figurative and discursive significance addresses ongoing debates that are not always addressed in more realist modes.

The figure of the vampire thus serves as both object and mode of analysis for more than eight decades of Hollywood film, television, and web production. The vampire's popularity has swelled, emerging as a millennial favorite. Vampire films once arrived in waves. Classical Hollywood reinvented vampires as part of its black-and-white horror cycle with sequels to *Dracula* and *Drácula* in *Dracula's Daughter* (1936) and *Son of Dracula* (1943), then postwar comedic "monster mashes," such as *Bud Abbott and Lou Costello Meet Frankenstein* (1949). Comedic vampires appeared on weekly television, *The Addams Family* (1964–6) and *The Munsters* (1964–6), and as hosts of syndicated movie-of-the-week programming. During the 1960s and 1970s, Hollywood imported vampire films from Europe, Latin America and Southeast Asia that appeared in color, full of sex and violence, notably Hammer Films' *Horror of Dracula* (1958), inspiring Hollywood's blaxploitation cycle with hits such as *Blacula* (1972). Since the 1990s, vampire films have attracted A-list stars in films such as *Bram Stoker's Dracula* (1992) and *Interview with the Vampire* (1994). Vampire films now arrive in multipicture franchises like *Underworld* (2003–16) and *Twilight* (2008–12), distributed globally in theaters, on television, DVD, and Blu-ray, via streaming and download by a Hollywood that is no longer located entirely in the United States. Vampire television series such as *True Blood* (2008–14) and *The Vampire Diaries* (2009–present) have also exploded after decades of relatively isolated hit shows such as *Dark Shadows* (1966–71) and *Buffy the Vampire Slayer* (1997–2003). Vampires move between equally compelling television formats of teen dramas, sci-fi thrillers, telenovelas, and children's television. Some series are embedded in alternative-reality games (ARGs) that engage audiences through social media and mobile phones. These mutations and migrations indicate the need for an approach that does not segregate vampire media into a subgenre of horror, dismiss it as apolitical entertainment, or understand it as unequivocally American.

Hollywood comes to resemble a vampire that shifts shape, moves at unnatural speeds, and multiplies. Like a vampire, Hollywood mutates and migrates, sometimes escaping recognition. Like a vampire, Hollywood has an insatiable appetite and will likely also never die. It mutates and migrates in site-specific overseas versions of its films since the 1910s. It renews itself by consuming foreign styles and talent, much as vampires renew themselves by drinking blood from victims/lovers. Studio heads learned that recruiting foreign talent into Hollywood production helped diminish potential competition (Miller et al. 2005: 130). Hollywood shifts shape and location from east-coast entrepreneurs bypassing the Edison Company's restriction of technologies to southern California's Big Five (Paramount, Metro-Goldwyn-Mayer, Warner Bros., RKO, and 20th Century Fox), Little Three (Universal, Columbia, United Artists), and Poverty Row (Republic, Monogram, Producers Releasing Corp.) studios, then shifts from independent production with freelancers into transnational media conglomerations with outsourced production. It also shifts from producing content for, or leasing content to, the Big Three free-to-air networks (NBC, CBS, ABC) to transmitting it on its own networks such as CW, cable networks such as HBO and FX, or streaming platforms such as Netflix and Hulu. This book locates the movement of Hollywood's vampires between low-budget quickies and high-budget franchises, between unpretentious soap operas and spotlight cable series. It considers Hollywood's appropriation of visual styles from German, Mexican, and Hong Kong cinemas at different historical junctures. Representations also move in film and television production from southern California and urban New York to Canada, Europe, México, and the Philippines, as well as other parts of the United States, at different political and economic junctures. While consuming foreign styles and talent, it also penetrates foreign markets. Vampire media thus offers opportunities to think about Hollywood as a transnational system.

Vampires also tell us something about the idea of America and the realities of the United States. Hollywood's vampire stories are deeply transnational, as are their modes of production and distribution. Vampires have a capacity to negotiate competing expectations about foundational and revisionist myths. Universal's first vampire films consolidated several centuries of folkloric, literary, and dramatic figures of the vampire into the cinematic character of Count Dracula. From this moment onwards, vampires were associated with elegant dress, mysterious accents, mesmerizing seductions, and undead travels. They were visualized in the iconic pale skin and dark hair of actor Béla Lugosi. With Hollywood's special lighting and makeup, the vampire was white but not quite white. Lugosi's Count Dracula appears unquestionably white to audiences today, but he was Hungarian at a time when Hungarian immigrants

Figure I.1 Béla Lugosi as Count Dracula in publicity still for "The Strangest Love Story Ever Told." *Dracula* (USA 1931; dir. Tod Browning).

were not necessarily considered white-upon-arrival or fit for citizenship. Hungarians bore the mark of race. Hollywood's ever-shifting depictions of vampires reveal the ever-shifting contours of race in/and the United States. Hungarians eventually no longer bore the mark of race. They were assimilated into the so-called new race of the Melting Pot. Moreover, the immigrant histories of eastern Europeans were subsumed into a US national history. Vampires became African American, Filipino, Mexican, Chinese American, and Mexican American when these groups were often considered unfit for citizenship at home or even incapable of self-rule abroad. The vampire's unnatural whiteness, thus, unsettles our assumptions about race. Moreover, the vampire's ever-shifting racial identities allow us to see racism, not as isolated acts by individuals, but as part of a broader system of inequality that sustains itself by remaining largely unmarked. White skin and its privileges are not "primary issues," explains bell hooks, since "white supremacist ways of thinking and acting [. . .] are expressed by folks of all skin colors" (hooks 2013: 6). Such contradictions also help us understand how racial inequality affects an underclass of white people, notably in pitting landless "poor whites against freed slaves" after the Civil War (Isenberg 2016: 176). Vampire media can contest such systems, modeling "transformative learning and practical change" needed for empathy, accountability, and equity.

Unlike most volumes in the field that analyze vampire media as a subgenre of horror, this book examines about 200 films, television and web series to recover a history that has not been widely told because it requires thinking about narrative text and political economy as mutually constitutive. The book foregrounds Hollywood's latent transnational and transmedia vectors through analysis of a particular category of production and distribution often dismissed as unimportant because it does not conform to traditional categories of Hollywood historiography or critical analysis, such as genres, studios, film directors, television producers, or periods. Vampire films and television series are not necessarily classified as horror. Nor are they classified entirely as science fiction, romance, or melodrama. If anything, they are a *transgenre*. To complicate definition further, Hollywood vampire media is not always produced in southern California or even in the United States. The films enrich our understanding of Hollywood. Despite its pop-culture manufactured phantasmatics, Hollywood is itself notoriously difficult to define. Usually understood as an exception, Hollywood is not precisely a national cinema. It does not necessarily conform to non-national frameworks, such as international cinema, regional cinema, or world cinema. Although promoted as value-free entertainment, Hollywood film and television has exhibited nationalist, internationalist, and universalist orientations at different historical conjunctures. Vampire media allows fresh insights into our understanding of history, identity, geography, and ourselves. Transnational Hollywood's vampires accompany us through the decades, sometimes wearing a black cape and flashing white fangs like Count Dracula, at other times wearing a black chador and riding a skateboard.

A film with an Iranian American perspective, *A Girl Walks Home Alone at Night* exemplifies how vampire stories migrate and mutate to convey ever-shifting identities and orientations in a world where the United States and Iran might not be as distant or as different as once imagined. Its story is set in the fictional Iranian town of Bad City, whose desolate landscapes of oil wells, smoke stacks, and power cables resemble actual oil-and-gas towns in California, where the film was shot, despite the Farsi-language signage. The soundscape of post-punk and underground Iranian rock evokes "Tehrangeles," a part of Los Angeles that is home to world's largest Iranian exilic population. The film conveys how cultures co-contaminate to produce the political idea of becoming something else through endless re-combinations, much like vampires engender new communities through infection. Iran and the United States are bound by transnational histories. The mutations and migration of vampires invite us to notice. They also invite us to notice how definitions of race in the United States shift from social company to nativity/

nationality to skin color—and how these definitions are tied to belonging. Rather than an Islamic terrorist, Amirpour gives us a Muslim feminist. Her film offers nuanced and ethical models for understanding social difference by reconfiguring the vampire's supernatural difference from potentially destructive to productive and even radical.

Why Vampires Matter

The sheer abundance of Hollywood vampire films and series conveys the vampire's ever-renewing popularity with audiences and relevance for scholars. "More than our heroes or pundits," suggested Nina Auerbach in the mid-1990s, "our Draculas tell us who we are" (1995: 112). As a university student during the 1960s, she explains: "Vampires were supposed to menace women, but to me at least, they promised protection against a destiny of girdles, spike heels, and approval" (4). She locates potentially feminist moments in films that male critics found socially conservative from the standpoint of class. "I loved vampires before I hated Republicans," she explains; "not only as a citizen, but as a woman" (3). For her, vampires offered a respite from patriotic certainty of the George Bush presidency (1988–92), along with attacks on women's rights over their own bodies. By the late 1980s and early 1990s, fear turned inward, she argues, permeating into a culture "stripped of its heroes and villains, shorn of a script for its national morality play," resulting in "a mounting backlash against the social gains of the 1970s" (2). Vampires offered Auerbach opportunities to *imagine* other possibilities. She reclaimed vampires from masculinist scholars, who guarded them as a "boy's game," for feminist scholars, who often dismissed them as less significant than "real fears" such as physical and sexual abuse.

Comparably, folklorist Nadine Dresser found university students understood vampires as liberating and affirming for different reasons. They associated vampires with materialism and narcissism, which they understood in *positive* terms during the 1980s. "American vampires," she concluded, "adapted to the soil to which they have been transplanted, reflecting the individualism of the American people" (1989: 200). Students learned what they knew about vampires from media and advertising, a cultural knowledge that Madison Avenue marketing firms had exploited after Count von Count appeared on the children's television series *Sesame Street* (1969–present) and boxes of Count Chocula breakfast cereal. From a different critical orientation, Rob Latham (2002) argued that the appeal of vampires by the 1990s lay in consumption through and by consumerism. Vampires became as unremarkable as suburban mall culture and, like malls, were alluring and seductive to some yet repulsive and garish to others. Vampires, then, tell us things about ourselves as individuals and as a society. They imagine scenarios for aspirations and anxieties that are sometimes so honest that they could not otherwise be depicted according to Hollywood realism.

Many audiences enjoy vampire films and series for the fantasies that they offer of empowerment and justice. Vampirism allows for stories about social control and social critique. As folklorist Bruce McClelland (2008) notes, vampires emerged alongside the figure of the vampire hunter or slayer. Taking its cue from Hammer's films, starring Christopher Lee as virile Count Dracula and Peter Cushing as an athletic Professor van Helsing, Hollywood began to emphasize vampires and vampire hunters as potentially *equally compelling* to audiences. By the 1990s, vampire hunting was no longer an enterprise restricted to men. Conceived as a self-conscious parody of slasher films, *Buffy the Vampire Slayer* (1992) transformed the vampire hunter from a patriarchal figure into the vampire slayer as a postfeminist figure. The film had little immediate cultural impact, but its adaptation as a television series (1997–2003) developed a large base of devoted fans, some of whom inserted feminism into storylines by appropriating characters in their own fan fiction, then sharing and discussing it in online communities. Some scholars praised the series for its empowerment of a universalized category of young women—white, cisgender, middle-class, Christian and/or Jewish, queer-friendly, and thus all-American; others criticized this empowerment as complicit with non-intersectional (white) feminism and, more broadly, white nationalism. The varied critical and popular responses to the series point to the capacity for Hollywood vampires and vampire hunters to support multiple interpretations, ranging from predictably reactionary to surprisingly revolutionary. The supernatural figure of the vampire allows for a narrative freedom to address controversial questions in indirect ways that might not ensure the needed ratings points for broadcast media, box office for theatrical media, or engagement for digital media.

Vampire media engages our relationships to society. A self-defined "black man from Texas" looked to the fantasy of being a vampire to negotiate the pain of racism. He transformed the *experience* of being watched suspiciously by white women because he was a black man into the *fantasy* of being feared by them because he was a vampire (Marcus 1997: 9–10). *Becoming* a supernatural figure—feared because powerful—was a means of negotiating the social realities of *being* stigmatized as unquestionably criminal and minoritized as politically powerless.[2] Audiences produce complex responses, often reconfiguring meaning in an aspirational mode from films and series that might otherwise exclude their perspectives. Relationships between humans and supernatural species suggest ways for all of us to negotiate—and even contest—naturalized social inequalities, yet they can also serve as a way to ignore discursive and material legacies of these inequalities, including the anthropocentrism that imagines humans as the basis upon which all other forms of life are evaluated. By considering vampirism as a trope for *relationships* that unfold in different historical and cultural contexts—rather than a trope for *representations* of difference in the figure of the monster or Other—we can begin to understand how and why vampire films and series are able to elicit different responses, as well as why and how film and television producers return again and again to stories of vampires. By challenging some of the conventional frameworks by which we think about vampire media, we can challenge the ways that we think about Hollywood, the United States, and ourselves.

This book proposes a reading strategy that releases vampires from the detention center of a horror genre, Hollywood from limiting vision of national and world cinemas, and US history from the self-destructive amnesia of national exceptionalism. The book looks transnationally to where vampires emerge. They infect an imagined unity of America, opening it to a productive disunity of the United States. Hollywood's vampires reveal a complex history that moves from the stigmatization of so-called hyphenated Americans (e.g., Italian-Americans, German-Americans) through the 1920s to the recovery of transnational histories and political agency in intersectional identities (e.g., African America, Asian America, Native America) in the 1980s. Vampire stories concern the "afterlives" of race in the United States. They reveal points of fracture and contention in the illusion of sameness. Vampires matter because they make clear that difference, particularly race, cannot be rejected ("we're all human," "all lives matter") or minimized ("more unites that divides us," "common humanity") by well-intentioned liberal and conservative thinking alike. As we will see, vampires refuse to obey top-down appeals for tolerance and consensus that typically work to reject or minimize dissent. Vampire stories reveal that dissent might seem aggressive to the dominant groups, but tolerance and consensus feel violent to non-dominant groups. Vampires invite us to consider that sometimes perspectives and experiences cannot be translated. They are insurgent and untamable. They invite us to understand difference through *versatility* in thinking and through intercultural and interspecies *empathy*.[3]

Overview of the Book

Most scholarship argues that vampires are simultaneously monstrous and human, repulsive and seductive, overpowering and empowering. Some trace movements from Old World to New World sensibilities or from misogynist to postfeminist themes.[4] This book opens thinking on how vampire media can model for transformational approaches for understanding Hollywood, the United States, and race. Part of its innovation is to consider Hollywood according to frameworks typically reserved for non-Hollywood. It extends transnational frameworks, raised earlier in edited volumes and increasingly in monographs, to an analysis of vampire media to rethink what is at stake in asserting "the national" or "the universal" within much of our present thinking about Hollywood, the United States, and perhaps ourselves.[5] The book acknowledges and complicates premises in past scholarship to propose three overlapping contributions: (1) reconfiguring Hollywood historiography and traditions as *transnational* in terms of film, television, and web production, distribution, and exhibition/transmission; (2) offering fresh interpretations of vampire film and television as a *transgenre* and *transmedia* site for political contestation; and (3) situating constructions of *race* in/and the United States as constitutive of nation.

First, the book defines Hollywood more broadly than its southern California studio system and New York executive offices to include films produced independently or abroad because they benefit directly and indirectly from Hollywood. So-called independent films and foreign movies are produced through Hollywood's networks of distributors, exhibitors, and reviewers. Hollywood has a long history of transnational orientations that weave together narrative text and industrial context. Hollywood offshores film production and postproduction to the Czech Republic, México, New Zealand, Romania, and South Africa—and television production to Australia, Canada, and Ireland for tax incentives. Yet this process is not new. It simply continues a longer history. During the 1950s, Hollywood developed vampire films through international financing in Europe and runaway productions in Southeast Asia. By the 1960s and 1970s, it was re-editing and dubbing films from México and the Philippines for US television and drive-in markets. Vampire films and series pull into sharper focus this repressed transnational history of Hollywood.

Considering Hollywood as transnational acknowledges *nationalism* and *national exceptionalism* within its stories. Bound to nation, professional exceptionalism is part of industry mythologies by which Hollywood imagines itself. It claims to lure foreign stars, in the words of Will Hays. Another interpretation suggests that Hollywood produces itself as a so-called global standard by emphasizing lower production values or allegedly poorly crafted stories in films produced outside the studio system during the classical era or outside the control of transnational media corporations today. Hollywood is transnational in ways that exceed the incorporation of European émigrés, escaping fascism and the Holocaust during the 1930s and 1940s, and the corporate conglomerations during the 1990s. Its films incorporate aspects of the visual style and cinematography of Mexican films and kinetic fight sequences of Hong Kong films. During the 1960s and 1970s, Hollywood produced vampire films abroad as foreign alternatives to domestic product. Hollywood's transnational reach stretches across oceans and continents in the form of pre-production financing, runaway production, post-production computer graphics, and a pantheon of foreign-born stars that date to "America's Sweetheart," Canadian-born Mary Pickford. Early cinema may have been "made American" (Abel 1999) between 1900 and 1910, but Hollywood never was fully constrained by this national framework.

Another Hollywood myth is that television comprised competition for audiences. Scholars note historical collaboration and symbiosis between the mediums, which has increased with deregulation and corporate mergers. Television is sometimes called the "other Hollywood." Although early television production was based in New York and rooted in national projects, especially in live broadcast, it has become increasingly transnational. Resulting from changes in tax laws in Canada and the United States during the 1980s and 1990s, Toronto and Montréal became major sites for runaway Hollywood television production, masquerading as "Anytown, USA" or "Nowheresville, USA." So much of Hollywood's television series production moved to British Columbia that Vancouver became "Hollywood North." Europe now offers tax incentives for employment relocation (run-away) for television, such as Showtime's *Penny Dreadful* (2014–16). To qualify for European support, Hollywood's productions pass cultural tests, demonstrating cultural and economic benefit to Europe. Nonetheless, such productions still reflect potential cultural domination. This book also engages with new media, including authorized streaming services and sponsored web series alongside unauthorized file sharing and user-generated content (UGC) that contest, not only copyright, but also Hollywood's attempts to "own" meaning through copyright.

Second, the book departs from conventional paradigms that locate root meaning for vampires in Romantic poetry, Gothic novels, and European horror films. Without denying these connections, it uncovers lateral and rhizomatic relationships with other genres, complicating any linear historical narrative. Vampire films borrow codes and conventions from immigration comedies, assimilation romances, and miscegenation melodramas of early cinema (1890s–1900s) and early Hollywood (1910s–20s). These genres link national belonging and citizenship to a perceived capacity for self-governance (often visualized in terms of race/ethnicity, class, or religion) and defense of territory (often visualized in terms of women's bodies). They develop visual and narrative strategies that later shape vampire films. Rather than a subgenre of horror, vampire films are a *transgenre* across comedy, horror, melodrama, and science fiction—and part of a *transmedia* across theatrical and television features, television and web series, novels, comics, and videogames—allowing for a multiplicity in responses to different iterations of content. Vampire media serves as a site for questions overlooked by industry-determined models of earlier generations of scholarship that largely understood Hollywood according to its own terms.

Multiple genres come into play when we consider how vampires negotiate social difference. Melodrama, for example, serves "as a safety-valve for ideological contradictions" (Mulvey 1989: 39). Comedy often performs a ritual function of celebrating social integration, whereas Westerns uphold social order (Schatz 1981: 29). If genre theory suggests vampire hunters provide a symbolic function in eradicating a community of difference, what risks getting occluded is that vampires are often figures of affiliation, emancipation, and empathy. The vampire's difference is sometimes received with ambivalence; other times, by desire or repulsion. Hollywood billed the English-language version of its first vampire film as a mystery—as "The Strangest Love Story Ever Told"—which premiered near Valentine's Day to minimize associations with horror. A transgenre approach rethinks a Hollywood Gothic (Skal 1990) by considering what were formerly dismissed as continuity errors, low-budget gaffes, or camp as significant aspects of discursive meaning. By reading vampire media without conventional restraints from genre theory, meaning unfolds across and between codes and conventions, thereby opening the films and series to overlooked questions.

Scholarship in film, television, and media studies has increasingly looked to transnational frameworks to address inaccuracies in conclusions drawn from national cinemas and world cinema without dismissing their importance. Comparably, (North) American Studies has increasingly focused its attention on ways that immigrants and indigenous peoples alongside intersectional identities have been silenced and erased from US national histories (Zinn [1980] 2005, Dunbar-Ortiz 2015).[6] This book situates its analysis of relationships between cinematic and political representation within the political economies of media industries and social assumptions about difference. It considers Hollywood ancillary products—spinoffs and tie-ins that range from cable series, direct-to-video features, and videogames—as metrics for evaluating "success" shift from box office and ratings to engagement. Web series develop from promotional material for films and series to additional content and free-standing series, opening the scope of perspectives without the financial risk of blockbusters or broadcast series.

Third, the book considers race as constitutive of US transnational histories, which have been largely erased to mount the fantasy of singular national history. Produced through transnational exchanges dating to the seventeenth century, relationships between vampires and vampire hunters become historical indices of unequal access to citizenship. They signify transnational relationships within US experiences that become most apparent in stories of immigration and invasion. The conspicuous absence of Native America in Hollywood vampire media is significant in this regard. A mix of reality effects and special effects, anchored to cultural codes deemed "American," produces Hollywood realism across genres that work to prioritize white-identified-ness as an unmarked guarantor of uncontested belonging.[7] The vampire's deathly pallor is a white-but-not-quite-ness that reminds us the afterlives of race can return at any time. During the early 1930s, the fright of vampires from eastern and southern Europe in *Dracula* and *Drácula* was rooted in implicit suspicions of European Jews and Catholics as incapable of national loyalty. Southern and eastern Europeans needed to "work" towards whiteness since racism of the time saw them as closer to blackness. By tracing definitions of race that historically shifted between social differentiation based on nativity/nationality, religion, class, social company, skin color, and other features and behaviors, the book examines the conditional nature of assimilation due to afterlives of race. Descendants of legally white immigrants from México continue to be subjected to racist epithets such as "border hoppers," from the War on Drugs (1971–2011) into the War on Terror (2003–present).

Imani Perry suggests that contemporary racism is "post-intentional" (2011). By loosening racism's ties to past assumptions about race, we notice processes of racialization that ensure domination yet exceed how race has allegedly been defined in law, biology, or faith. Vampires disrupt what bell hooks calls the "interlocking systems that work together to uphold and maintain cultures of domination" (2013: 4), which is why they—like talking about race—make some people feel uncomfortable and get dismissed as no longer relevant. Vampires inhabit spaces that evoke the borderlands/la frontera that Gloria Anzaldúa (1987) theorized as multivocal and invisible. In such places, contradictions abound through encounters with difference. As Ella Shohat argues, "genders, sexualities, races, classes, nations, and even continents exist not as hermetically sealed entities but, rather, as part of a set of permeable, interwoven relationships," and relationality "is particularly significant in a transnational age typified by the global traveling of images, sounds, goods, and populations" (2001: 1269). Vampires highlight intersectionality. Kimberlé Crenshaw (1991) argues that attacks on so-called identity politics fail to acknowledge that multiple vectors of difference, such as race and sex in the case of women of color, combine to affect opportunities and access to rights. Caste, religion, ability, and species are other vectors of intersectional difference that not only affect access to social belonging and political agency but continually recombine, shifting like the shape of the vampire.

The vampire's migrations and mutations allow us to consider race as a highly unstable yet historically sustained aspect of daily life, partculary as we think of the state (i.e., United States) as a nation (i.e., "America"). The historical dimensions within interlockings of race and nation become highly visible and audible in the recent explosion of television series set in the New South. Although the Old South functioned as colonizer through slavery, servitude, dispossession, and secession, it considered itself colonized after the Civil War.[8] Postcolonial theory offers multiple concepts to describe such conditions. Using one on supernaturalism developed in the context of a former US colony, the Philippines, deprovincializes US exceptionalism. Bliss Lim develops the concept of "immiscible times" to describe "a translation of thorny and disreputable supernaturalisms into the terms of a modern, homogeneous, disenchanted time" with a simultaneous "persistence of supernaturalism [that] often insinuates the limits of disenchanted chronology," which may be understood by the metaphor of water and oil comingling without yielding a "true solution" (2009: 12, 32). Vampires mark where histories comingle—where they are multiple rather than singular, particular rather than universal, and transnational rather than national. Vampire media augments voices often excluded in realist genres.

Thinking about racism, sexism, speciesism, and other forms of social oppression might not be what initially entices audiences to become fans—whether emphatic or reluctant—of Hollywood vampires; however, this book demonstrates that vampires help raise important questions about structural inequality that might ordinarily make Hollywood producers feel uncomfortable. The book reconsiders Hollywood vampires for the intellectual and political pleasures that they offer rather than confining them to the realm of so-called guilty pleasures. It focuses on films and series for the *unresolved questions* that they raise rather than celebrating films and series for self-affirming answers they offer within the (privileged and self-infantilizing) rebellion of so-called fanboys and girl power. It looks for *critical pleasures* in some of Hollywood's most commercial and ostensibly anti-intellectual and apolitical films and series. It also looks for critical pleasures that often emerge alongside and within the visceral pleasures of fright and delight.

How Hollywood is Transnational and Race has Afterlives

Hungarian actor Béla Lugosi portrayed Hollywood's first vampire in the English-language *Dracula*; Spanish actor Carlos Villarías, in the Spanish-language *Drácula*. Both actors' foreign-accents were incorporated into the stories. In later decades, Hollywood's vampire stories drew upon the racial/ethnic identities of actors cast as vampires, who appear African American, Mexican American, or Chinese American. By contrast, the first vampires in *The Originals* (2013–present) were born in Virginia yet are played by Australian, Canadian, English, and Welsh actors. They speak in non-US-accented English, yet no one notices. Hollywood's vampire film and television series acknowledge social difference and inequality yet do not necessarily address them directly. Their stories evoke ambivalences, anxieties, and aspirations about migration, invasion, assimilation, and nativism, defining a US transnational history. Understanding vampire films and series as nodes within systems of competing meanings allows repressed and often invisible facets of complex traditions in Hollywood film and television production to come into focus.

Conceiving of Hollywood as transnational foregrounds what is at stake in asserting a fantasized and constructed nation. In media, nation operates explicitly in *patriotism* and *nativism* and implicitly in *universality* and *national exceptionalism*. Since we encounter vampires at such an early age, we tend to ignore how vampires are entangled in nationalism's web. Vampire television series aimed at children remain popular long after the original broadcast runs. Sometimes belittled as a teen trend, vampires are with us to stay. It is difficult to underestimate effects of the vampire's proliferation and popularity. Children sometimes say that they want to become a vampire when they grow up, pointing to how vampires have permeated US popular culture and claimed a position, at least for children, akin to doctors, lawyers, and even the president. At the same time, internet memes recast US politicians—George W. Bush, Dick Cheney, Hillary Clinton, Barack Obama, Condoleezza Rice—as vampires to express dissent, associating them with Vlad Țepeș and Elizabeth Báthory, who impaled enemies on stakes and bathed in the blood of virgins. Politicians are accused of not representing people or protecting nation—of draining lifeblood.

Dramatic conflicts in most vampire stories hinge upon racialization in transnational world. Race continues to structure social relations in the United States, determining where we live, how much we earn, whom we marry, and whether we are likely to be incarcerated in prisons, detained in rendition centers, or shot dead by police. Despite their palpability as everyday realities, races and nations are as supernatural as vampires.[9] Neither biological nor divine fact, race and nation function as social facts. Likewise, vampires are simultaneously unreal and real: unreal as determined by science and religion, but real as marked by culture. As Bram Stoker conceived it in his novel *Dracula* (1897), vampires are neither living nor dead but "undead." By extension, race is neither living nor dead but undead. Race persists; it never fades entirely or dies completely. It appears to disappear then resurfaces with an infinite and often unpredictable succession of afterlives that expose always-present traces of slavery and servitude, undying vestiges of colonialism and genocide, and under-acknowledged structural inequalities within US democracy. Arab immigrants from Lebanon and Syria (including non-Christian ones), for example, were considered white for decades yet more recently have sometimes been racialized as potential terrorists. Even earlier South Asian immigrants were categorized as "Aryan" but determined not to be "Caucasian" in the 1923 landmark case *United States* v. *Bhagat Singh Thind*. Race allows us to trace historical dimensions of inclusion and exclusion in relation to broader events. Race determines access to citizenship, not only in nineteenth-century empires but also in twenty-first-century democracies.

Looking at the historical "intimacies of four continents," Lisa Lowe connects disparate continental threads that have not always been woven into a transnational US history. She identifies race as "a mark of colonial difference" and "enduring remainder of the process through which the human is universalized and freed by liberal forms" of universalizing thought, including reason, civilization, and freedom (2015: 7). She locates the precarious place of belonging and enfranchisement within a national project that aspires towards diversity, inclusion, and equity. Vampire films and television series concern shifting racialized social relationships that the supernatural figure of the vampire makes apparent, as debates on racial profiling and border regulation continue to dominate political discussions. Comparable social tensions find expression—or are displaced—in the antirealist tropes of vampire media. Groups of humans plot to exterminate vampires in films and series, such as *Buffy the Vampire Slayer* and *Underworld*. Vampires advocate for citizenship in *True Blood*.

Although some films and series evoke casual and explicit racism, they typically include an element of hope for a future in which racism and other prejudices might be eradicated. Many audiences first encounter vampires on children's television, most notably Count von Count, who debuted on PBS's *Sesame Street* (1969–present) in 1972. His pink skin departs from the white makeup worn by Lugosi yet blends into the multicolored and multispecies Muppets—and multiracial and multilingual human cast—of *Sesame Street*, which inspired learning among underserved and disadvantaged audiences through innovative formats and experimental pedagogies. When Kermit the Frog sings, "it's not easy being green," he inspires children to self-acceptance—and to listen to minoritized perspectives, not only literally of amphibians, but symbolically of people of color. The series emphasizes

Figure I.2   PBS's nonthreatening and nonviolent vampire Count von Count teaches empathy and intelligence. *Sesame Street* (USA 1969–present; cr. Joan Ganz Cooney and Lloyd Morrisett).

productive aspects of Lugosi's vampire. Count von Count does not seduce and murder; instead, he teaches children how to count, playing upon eastern European folklore of the compulsion of vampires to count. A rare example of US television serving the public interest within a predominantly commercial industry, *Sesame Street*'s newest resident is Zara, promoted as a feminist hijabi from Afghanistan. The figure of the vampire, thus, can also teach us how to live with difference rather than submit to top-down notions of consensus or tolerance.

Not surprisingly, vampire media appeals to socially and politically marginalized audiences—and ones who witness acts of oppression and violence. Vampires may first look powerful, but they are usually revealed as vulnerable. Vampire films and series serve as productive nodes for reflection on marginalized groups, including immigrant and indigenous groups, who are often stigmatized as social problems and seldom recognized for their contributions. Because Hollywood's vampire films resist the transparencies of realism, they respond imaginatively to complexities of race and allow audiences to speculate about possibilities rather than draw conclusions. This book is concerned with *how* and *why* Hollywood can be understood as transnational by analyzing *how* and *why* audiences find vampires both alluring and frightening—and vampire hunters both heroic and homicidal—and *what* debates and discussions these film and series can encourage. It explores complexities in *how* film and television affect us in tandem with *what* they depict to us. The figure of the vampire allows us to consider social and political context from historical and intercultural perspectives—transhuman and transspecies—that are nearby but not necessarily our own. Many vampires look human. But unlike humans, they are immortal. Vampires inhabit our anthropocentric world in such a way that their stories position us for greater understandings of social processes.

Vampire film and television reveal a version of Hollywood that is *doubly* transnational: they narrate stories about migrations that affect our sense of nation, and the political economies of their production and distribution go beyond national borders. They reveal how Hollywood constructs different images of the US national imaginary for different audiences at different times. They map how Hollywood negotiates US relationships with Native America, African and Caribbean America, México, the Philippines, Europe, the Middle East, North Africa, and South Asia (MENASA) regions, and beyond. Vampire media reveals how race is produced through the political economies of film production and distribution in national and racial/ethnic stereotypes, as it is produced through labor practices from slavery and indentured servitude to freelancing and outsourcing. At the intersection of migration and commerce, vampire films and series contribute to a doubled transnational analytic: *textual meaning* of stories, characters, styles, and performance and *political economies* that determine production, distribution, and exhibition.

INTRODUCTION

CHAPTER OUTLINES

Chapter 1, "Blood, Bodies, and Borders," starts with an analysis of Stoker's novel *Dracula* (1897) within the context of literary traditions and political realities. Vampires negotiate social contradictions within emerging democracies and fading empires, particularly around issues of mobility. The chapter compares two films that reinterpret Stoker's vampire in different ways. Francis Ford Coppola's *Bram Stoker's Dracula* (1992) parodies a nostalgic and orientalist perspective on debates about the place of the Middle East in the formation of US transnational identity and history, whereas Ana Lily Amirpour's *A Girl Walks Home Alone at Night* (2014) moves towards this history's radical revision. Coppola imagines a "vampire ayatollah" during the first US invasion of Iran's neighbor Iraq; Amirpour, as a feminist hijabi in the sonic space of Tehrangeles.[10] The filmmakers' familial trajectories underscore Hollywood's transnational constitution as linked to US policy. Like Coppola's, Amirpour's family emigrated in response to transnational political and economic conditions. The comparison develops a critical approach for how vampires serve as both object and mode of analysis throughout the book. Stoker's tropes of blood, bodies, and borders map onto US laws concerning race, immigration, and assimilation.

Although conventional studies look to the earliest surviving vampire film, Prana-Films' *Nosferatu* (1922), as source for visual codes and narrative conventions, Chapter 2, "'Making' Americans from Foreigners," locates them in segregation comedies, immigration romances, and miscegenation melodramas.[11] These films establish conventions that facilitate or inhibit foreigners being americanized. Since citizenship for women was derivative from fathers or husbands, foreign women were considered less threatening. Consequently, male immigrants in Edison Company shorts (1895–6), industrial and state recruitment films, and commercial entertainments, such as Alice Guy-Blaché's *Making an American Citizen* (1912), Cecil B. DeMille's *The Cheat* (1915), D. W. Griffith's *Broken Blossoms* (1919), and George Melford's *The Sheik* (1921), serve as cinematic prototypes for classical Hollywood's vampires. Within these narratives of americanizing foreigners, the afterlives of race emerge in relation to sex and nativity around issues of universal citizenship and sovereign territory.

Chapter 3, "Classical Hollywood Vampires: The Unnatural Whiteness of America," explores how these conventions enter into Hollywood's first vampire films. It examines ambivalence towards immigration and imperatives to assimilate to an Anglo-American mythical norm in films including *Dracula* (1931), *Drácula* (1931), *Mark of the Vampire* (1935), *Dracula's Daughter* (1936), *Son of Dracula* (1943), *House of Frankenstein* (1944), and *House of Dracula* (1945). In early films, southern California masquerades as

Transylvania, replete with (non-European) armadillos and scorpions. These films are implicitly set in the United States; others are explicitly set there. The Melting Pot myth of unidirectional assimilation into the *unnatural whiteness of America* negotiates policies and programs during the 1920s that regulated immigration from eastern and southern Europe and crossings from Canada and México. The chapter concludes by examining how vampire films rework colonial conventions from Westerns.

After belated awareness of racism, specifically anti-Semitism within European fascism, not only did postwar US immigration policies change but so too did Hollywood's vampire films. Chapter 4, "International Hollywood Vampires: Cosmopolitanisms of 'Foreign Movies'," probes Hollywood's international financing of films in the United Kingdom, runaway productions in Europe and the Philippines, and Mexican and Philippine films that were re-edited and dubbed for US markets. Deterritorialized from Los Angeles, Hollywood produces categories of foreign movies alongside domestically shot studio and independent films, evident in *Horror of Dracula* (1958), *Samson Versus the Vampire Women* (1962/1963), and *Horror of the Blood Monsters* (1970). Other films within this analytic parody an imperial-inflected cosmopolitanism of foreign movies, notably *The Fearless Vampire Killers, or Pardon Me, Your Teeth Are in My Neck* (1967) and *Blood for Dracula* (1974). Since film circulation operates according to ethnic/racial and national hierarchies in immigration and naturalization law, postwar films unsettle assumptions.

Chapter 5, "Vampires of Color: A Critique of Multicultural Whiteness," explores whiteness's purported expansion through multiculturalism after Civil Rights and the Immigration Act of 1965. By yoking the inclusivity of multiculturalism and exclusivity of whiteness, *multicultural whiteness* sustains white privilege without acknowledging it, granting conditional or provisional inclusion to select nonwhite groups. It becomes a performative category ("white-identified-ness") questioned in films like *Blacula* (1972), *Ganja and Hess* (1973), *Martin* (1976), *Fright Night* (1985), *The Lost Boys* (1987), *Near Dark* (1987), *Interview with the Vampire* (1994), and *The Addiction* (1995). Classical Hollywood whiteness is transformed by greater emphasis on so-called national values—individualism, consumerism, patriotism, secularism, and willful amnesia—that sustain foundational myths of a nation of immigrants, land of opportunity, and beacon of democracy. Within the proliferation of representations of a multicultural United States, films question limitations on political representation for anyone not identifying—or being identified—with whiteness, including so-called white trash.

Chapter 6, "Terrorist Vampires: Religious Heritage or Planetary Advocacy," unpacks depictions of US foreign policy in Hollywood blockbusters, franchises, and series, whose content was repurposed and production was often offshored. Vampire hunters perform the racialized warfare of the failed War on Drugs and ongoing War on Terror. Vampires advocate for planetary consciousness after neoliberalism's ascendancy. *Bram Stoker's Dracula* (1992), *From Dusk till Dawn* (1995), and *Vampires* (1998) organize fears of so-called Islamic fundamentalists and Mexican border hoppers. Deterritorialized biological warfare also manifests in films that return to the historical trauma of mixed blood via stories of mixed species in franchises such as *Blade* (1998–2004) and *Underworld* (2003–16) and series such as *True Blood* (2008–14), *The Vampire Diaries* (2009–present), and *The Originals* (2013–present). Others examine resilience through multiple conquests, as in *Cronos* (1992), set in México's federal district and released on the quincentennial of Columbus's conquest. Meanwhile, the *Twilight* franchise (2008–12) christianizes the figure of the vampire and, by extension, the concept of the US secular democracy, but also evokes indigenous rights to land. Films ask us to find a space for empathy amidst the terror of economic and military violence.

Chapter 7, "Other Vampires, Other Hollywoods: Serialized Citizenship and Narrowcast Difference," explores an explosion of serialized vampires after television's deregulation. Like newspapers and newscasts, serialized television can produce national audiences around topical issues about citizenship and difference. What cinema often excludes due to the financial risk, television can include by offshoring production and narrowcasting transmission. Although *Buffy the Vampire Slayer* (1997–2003) ushered in "girl power" and a place for same-sex relationships, it was criticized for its racial insensitivity. With greater racial/ethnic diversity, *True Blood*, *The Vampire Diaries*, and *The Originals* explore legacies of racial oppression. Transnational Hollywood largely masks locations, prioritizing economic over cultural consideration. Some series are produced in southern California, others elsewhere—*Gabriel, amor inmortal* (2008) in Florida, *The Vampire Diaries* and *The Originals* in Georgia, *True Blood* in Louisiana, *From Dusk till Dawn: The Series* (2014–present) in Texas, *The Strain* (2014–present) in Ontario, and *Penny Dreadful* (2014–16) in Ireland. Web series emerge as a means of narrative and economic experimentation, ranging from UGC in *The Hunted* (2001–present) to cross-platform marketing and narrative experiments of *Valemont* (2009) and *Carmilla* (2014–present) to videogames.

The conclusion, "History and Hollywood, Mashed-up," pulls into focus the interplay of aspirations about democratizing media and realities of democratizing the United States as they coalesce on race and the presidency by focusing on the viral video *Barackula: The Musical* (2008) and theatrical feature *Abraham Lincoln: Vampire Hunter* (2012). In them, US presidents or future-presidents are represented as vampire hunters and enduring icons of US exceptionalism. Amateur and astroturfed grassroots internet memes demonize the first and only nonwhite president of the United States by employing the animalistic and dehumanizing iconography of *Nosferatu*, thus signaling afterlives of race in self-authorized acts of racism that can now be distributed via social media to larger audiences than classical Hollywood ever dared imagine.

Notes

1. Colloquial expressions include Lollywood for Lahore's Urdu-language industry, Bollywood for Mumbai's Hindi-language industry, Nollywood for Nigeria's English-, Yoruba-, Hausa-, Igbo-, and Edo-language industries, and Hallyuwood for the South Korean industry. (See Hudson 2014.)
2. Daughter of Nigerian immigrants to Britain, Melissa Anyiwo found Stoker's *Dracula* invited her on a "strange journey through identity, race, and marginalization" (2015: 1).
3. This framework understands six steps—ignorance, rejection, approximation, awareness, acceptance, versatility—towards intercultural understanding (Salyer 1993).
4. See: Frayling (1991), Gelder (1994 and 2012), Auerbach (1995), Rickels (1995), Grant (1996), Gordon and Hollinger (1997), Latham (2002), Abbott (2007), McClelland (2008), Picart and Browning (2009), Mutch (2012), Weinstock (2012), Khair and Höglund (2013), and Stephanou (2014).
5. Edited volumes include Dennison and Lim (2006), Ezra and Rowden (2006), Marciniak et al. (2007), Marciniak and Bennett (2016); monographs include Lu (1997), Higbee (2014), and Teo (2015).
6. Also see: King (2000) and Singh and Schmidt (2000). Grewal (2005), Fluck et al. (2011), and Hebel (2012) make transnational critiques of the field's original mandate to promote "America" at home and abroad.
7. Hollywood dominates overseas markets by "consent" based on formal and industrial features: continuity editing for transparent narrative flow, emphasis on technological developments, and use of contracted stars (Stafford 2014: 29).
8. Comparably, the myth of US independence from Britain confuses infighting among colonizers with anticolonial struggle by indigenous populations.
9. About spectral presence of indigenous nations in US literature, Bergland (2000) argues that ghosts' ability to signal asymmetrical power relations was thwarted when ghosts are internal and psychological.
10. I thank Doreen Lee for bringing this film to my attention.
11. An earlier adaptation of Stoker's novel was *Drakula halála/The Death of Dracula* (Hungary 1921; dir. Károly Lajthay). No surviving prints are known (Heiss 2009: 296–300).

1. BLOOD, BODIES, AND BORDERS

Ana Lily Amirpour's black-and-white *A Girl Walks Home Alone at Night* seduced audiences with a skateboard-riding, feminist hijabi vampire. It reimagined the socially and emotionally isolated female vampires in classical Hollywood's *Dracula's Daughter* and later art-house films, such as Michael Almereyda's *Nadja* and Abel Ferrara's *The Addiction*. Amirpour promoted her film as "the first Iranian vampire western," playfully reworking national and generic assumptions. She purposefully confuses and deliberately fuses spaces of national histories, identities, and geographies into transnational ones. She challenges nationalist certainties within the political theatrics by US and Iranian leaders, which extend from the US-backed Pahlavi monarchy (1925–79) through the Iranian Revolution and hostage crisis (1979–81) into political disagreements between Iranian president Mahmoud Ahmadinejad (2005–13) and US president George W. Bush (2001–9) over nuclear programs that resurface today in debates on lifting the US trade embargo and normalizing relationships. *A Girl Walks Home Alone at Night* asks us to think about—and to feel—what it is like to inhabit this history across space. Amirpour's film does not tell the story of a vampire, who migrates from one place to another, infecting humans with vampirism, so they mutate into vampires. Instead, she tells a story of a world that has mutated due to human migrations, where things might not be what they appear—and where systems of human relations may themselves be vampire-like. Vampires appear where histories meet.

Like classical Hollywood's first vampire films, Amirpour's film raises questions about immigration and belonging through motifs of blood, bodies, and borders. These motifs can be traced both to literary sources, such as Bram Stoker's novel *Dracula* (1897), and to cinematic ones, such as early films on immigration and assimilation. The figure of the vampire accumulates meaning, as it moves from folklore and literature to theatrical stage and cinematic screen. Supernatural qualities in vampire stories allow social assumptions to find overt expression, whereas other kinds of stories demand that they remain hidden in covert agendas. Vampire hunters murder vampires—and are seldom arrested. Although scenes of violence, sexuality, and interspecies coupling were discreetly hidden behind the vampire's black cape—yet exploited in stills for advertising and promotion—Béla Lugosi's portrayal of Count Dracula excited imaginations with his sexually predatory and socially destabilizing suggestiveness in *Dracula*. He departs from the animalized-cadaverous vampire in *Nosferatu, eine Symphonie des Grauens/Nosferatu: A Symphony of Horror* (Germany 1922; dir. F. W. Murnau). Count Orlok looks and moves like a cadaver. Murnau's close-ups of his rat-like teeth and long shots of shadows cast by his talon-like hands as they grasp the tender throats of victims were abandoned for classical Hollywood's medium shots of fangless vampires in tuxedos. Over nearly nine decades, Hollywood's stars become increasingly recognizable as *sexually desirable* even when portraying vampires stigmatized as *socially undesirable*.

Hollywood's most humanized and domesticated vampire, *Twilight*'s Edward Cullen, is nonviolent until sexual. He is a native-born American from the Midwest. He does not wear a black cape like Count Dracula because he does nothing to hide. Nor does he wear a black chador like Amirpour's vampire because he embodies white-male privilege. Count Dracula is deathly pale under his whiteface makeup, but Edward is positively sparkly under his glamour lighting and special effects. If Count Dracula passes as human in ways that Count Orlok cannot, then Edward passes as a citizen in ways that Count Dracula—and many people of color today—cannot. Count Dracula and Edward Cullen represent different moments in a transnational US history. One vampire encounters the first decade of regulated immigration and border; the other, several decades in transnational economic integration. In Stoker's novel, Count Dracula can only rest peacefully in a box lined with soil from his native Transylvania, a convention that remains in countless vampire films. His mobility is limited. Edward does not require sleep but nonetheless has bedrooms inside a family house in the Pacific Northwest and a holiday-getaway home in Brazil. He can come and go where and when he pleases. His mobility is virtually unlimited. He claims access to powers of belonging unimaginable to earlier generations of Hollywood vampires.[1] Count Dracula and Edward, however, are able to pass as white, male, human, and perhaps even as citizens. It is precisely this recognizable—if not legally recognized—quality of Hollywood's vampires that makes them evocative of shifting perceptions of national belonging in the United States. Edward Cullen's uncontested right to feel American suggests a different configuration of history, identity, and geography than the contested rights of vampires in Amirpour's film or Stoker's novel.

Despite their differences, vampire stories generally involve *bloods* that mix, *bodies* that migrate, and *borders* that mutate. Vampires drain lives by sucking blood and reanimate bodies by giving blood. They pollute or contaminate bloodlines and transform identities. They take multiple wives and reproduce endemically. They are sometimes seen as nonproductive in terms of capital but over-reproductive in terms of children. Vampires resist control and containment by loving outside social norms, yet must rest in coffins lined with soil from their homeland and cannot enter a house without the owner's invitation. They might be deathly pale but are not quite white. They seduce and frighten us with erotically charged spectacles of mixed blood, unruly bodies, and ever-shifting borders—all of which move alongside shifting definitions for the "us" in the United States. The erotically and nationally charged spectacle of vampires has been interpreted in relation to sexually transmitted diseases (syphilis and HIV) and the ascendancy of secularism and modern technologies over religion and superstition. It can also be contextualized in relation to social and legal discourses of blood (e.g., quantum theories, anti-miscegenation, *jus sanguinis*), bodies (e.g., phenotypes, skin color, biometrics), and borders (e.g., *jus soli*, criminalized vagrancy, illegal immigration) that define citizenship and territory. Vampires "pass" as one of us—and sometimes "trespass" against us. Vampire stories facilitate critical examination of nativism that targets immigrant and indigenous groups with outrageous claims that they "drain" the economy and should "go home" or, in the case of indigenous nations, should "disappear."

Vampires also question US national exceptionalism that can delegitimize and discredit dissenting voices in democratic debate, especially ones of minoritized groups who may identify as women, LBGTQ, disabled, homeless, or stateless. In social life, citizenship is performed and contested along intersecting vectors of difference—race/ethnicity, sex and gender, sexuality, class, religion, nationality/nativity, ability, and species, among other "styles of the flesh," as Judith Butler (1986: 48) might call them. The figure of the vampire unearths these buried dimensions of history identity and geography through tropes of blood, bodies, and borders. This book argues that vampires are not necessarily feared or desired because they will drain the blood of nation; instead, they may be feared or desired because they threaten or promise to populate the nation with progeny of so-called mixed blood. The constant and unpredictable shape-shifting and flight of vampires point to unresolved anxieties over, and unrealized aspirations about, America. Since vampires are often nonhuman characters, vampire films and series push us to think beyond interracial communities to interspecies ones. Because they transcend rational and empirical categories of knowledge, supernatural species become apt figures for showing us something about our relationship with others, including nonhuman animals and nonanimal species. Supernatural species like vampires, zombies, and werewolves dare us to look beyond the visual and auditory evidence, beyond technologies of vision and hearing that record audiovisual images in ways that seem invisible, silent, and unbiased.

The Moment of Count Dracula

Developed in eastern European folklore during the seventeenth century, the term *vampire* was appropriated into western European literature.[2] Folkloric vampires were reanimated corpses who stayed close to home and familiar, but literary vampires became aristocratic antiheroes who travelled afar to embrace the foreign and faraway. They passed as human and transgressed social norms in poetry by Samuel Taylor Coleridge and Charles Baudelaire, stories by John Polidori and James Malcolm Rymer, plays by James Planché and Charles Nodier.[3] Abbreviated, the term *vamp* designated sexualized women including the earliest cinematic vampires played by Theda Bara and Musidora.[4] Most cinematic vampires follow conventions of aristocratic Lord Ruthven from Polidori's *The Vampyre* (1819), who served as a prototype for Count Dracula. Countess Karnstein from Joseph Sheridan LeFanu's *Carmilla* (1871–2) produced a model for female vampires, including Amirpour's. Unlike Ruthven, Carmilla was bound to her father's colonial property and, like European women, could not travel freely or even count as a citizen. Bram Stoker's *Dracula* reconfigured vampires from intimate friends into the deadly outsiders that dominate what we think about vampires (Auerbach 1995).

The moment of Count Dracula is one of social contradictions and transformations. European states expanded overseas empires while announcing democratic principles at home. They championed universal rights and humanism while enslaving, indenturing, and dispossessing on a scale hitherto unimagined. Science allegedly confirmed and visualized prejudices that criminalized deviances from invented norms. Vampires emerge within this moment. Stoker narrates anxieties and aspirations that anticipate US experiences. *Dracula* consolidates conventions that lend themselves to adaptation for stage and screen. Ordinary props like crucifixes and coffins become extraordinary objects to injure or protect vampires. There may be no literal connections to race and immigration, but there are affective ones. Audiences *feel* that they cannot see or know enough. The world is not what it may have once seemed.

The novel supports a range of interpretations. Carol Senf (1982) saw *Dracula* as a reactionary response to the New Woman, who claimed independence and sometimes autonomy from men. During the HIV panic, Christopher Craft

(1997) related vampirism to sexually transmitted diseases such as syphilis and gonorrhea. Other critics read *Dracula* in relation to Darwin's theory of evolution and Freud's theory of the unconscious. Still others understand the novel as a critique of modernity and of capitalism.[5] Stephen Arata finds reactionary panic in fears of "reverse colonialism" via vampires invading "the space of their knowledge" before bodies or land (1997: 470). "[Count] Dracula imperils not simply his victims' personal identities, but also their cultural, political, and racial selves," he explains; "miscegenation leads, not to the mixing of the races, but to the biological and political annihilation of the weaker race by the stronger" (465–6). He situates *Dracula* in relation to England's occupation of Ireland, which was later reproduced around the world.

In recent decades, the novel is understood less literally. Joseph Valente reads it as social satire of British culture, explaining Stoker was "an interethnic Anglo-Celt and hence a member of a conquering and conquered race, a ruling and a subject people, and imperial and an occupied nation" (2002: 4). For David Glover, *Dracula* is an Irish novel about Ireland rather than an English one about England. Faraway Transylvania is described in terms of nearby Ireland, and vampire-hunting protagonists are not heroes (1996: 33). Stoker was himself Anglo-Irish—part of the colonizing English, who often felt like the colonized Irish. Feeling foreign as a son of a Catholic Italian within Protestant England, Polidori's relationship to nation is also vexed.[6] Given their ambivalent experiences of British colonialism, their interpretation of the figure of the vampire lends itself to both postcolonial and posthuman critique. Rather than internalizing racism to become model colonial subjects—or ignoring it altogether to pose as cosmopolitan citizens, Polidori and Stoker imagined vampires to contest racism, sexism, and speciesism within humanism.

Dracula opens questions on mobility in relation to history, identity, and geography. Part travelogue and part mystery, it foregrounds historical intersections of blood, bodies, and borders upon which contemporary ones develop. Vampire stories concern travellers, responses to whom are riddled with curiosity and apprehension. Initially recounted through epistles by individual characters, *Dracula*'s narrative coheres as a relay of different accounts of crossing borders; disciplining undisciplined bodies with taxonomies (e.g., race/ethnicity, class, gender and sex, species); fretting and fighting over blood's overdetermined meaning. The plot concerns different migrations that precede the mutations of humans into vampires—and vampires in any number of other forms: (1) Jonathan Harker relocates temporarily from England to Transylvania to work for Count Dracula, (2) Count Dracula attempts to relocate permanently from Transylvania to England, (3) Harker returns to England after being nursed to health by Christian nuns, (4) Count Dracula flees England for Transylvania after being targeted by bloodthirsty vampire hunters, (5) vampire hunters chase Count Dracula to Transylvania, where they assassinate him, and (6) Harker returns to visit Transylvania with his wife after vanquishing vampires.

The moment of Count Dracula suggests a reconfiguring of social relations through emerging mobilities. Before immigrating to England, Count Dracula purchases property and acculturates himself to its foreign society. He hires Harker to prepare legal documents. The exact reason for his emigration is unknown. He is the only major character whose voice is excluded. Incomplete evidence becomes reason for the vampire hunters' irrational suspicions that find expression in terms of blood, bodies, and borders. The novel's epistolary form shifts between letter and newspaper stories to diary entries that evoke conventions of travel writing. We learn what characters *feel* as they travel between different geopolitical contexts. In the first diary entry, "3 May Bistritz," Harker records a memo to get a recipe for "*paprika hendl*" (1997: 9) for his fiancée Mina. Travel writing conveys a sense of ownership, notes Mary Louise Pratt, even in "anti-conquest" forms, by engaging "strategies of representation whereby European bourgeois subjects seek to secure their innocence in the same moment as they assert European hegemony" (2008: 3, 9). Harker's personal profiteering parodies this hegemony through his colonial arrogance and ignorance evident. He legally facilitates Count Dracula's mobility, but Count Dracula financially facilitates his mobility.

Like travel writing, *Dracula*'s characters convey ownership of land through the possessive language of military, religious, and economic campaigns over foreign lands. Although not mentioned in its epistles, part of the novel's broader historical context was the so-called scramble for Africa, culminating in the Berlin Conference (1884–5). European colonization of Africa coincided with the US colonization of the western plains (1825–80). Territory was visualized on illustrated maps and narrativized in exploration stories in images of primitivized and animalized female bodies, awaiting colonizers to conquer their unruly and assumed natural ways (Shohat and Stam 1994). Count Dracula appears suspicious for having three wives and for seducing men and women alike. In addition to prejudices against Muslims as polygamists with harems of sex slaves, Count Dracula's too-many wives parody colonizers' displaced awareness of their own avarice in annexing so many foreign lands. While the deranged English character of Renfield might quote Christian biblical verse—"the blood is the life"—other characters imply that the possession of land is the only kind of life worth living.

The hyper-visibility of bloods mixing in Stoker's novel lampoon anxieties over distinct racial/ethnic and national types, which legitimized regulation of immigration while obscuring its economic and political causes. Stoker parodies associations of blood with soil—two key elements in determining rights to citizenship according to *jus sanguinas* (right of blood) and *jus soli* (right of soil). Blood becomes more than a vessel for diseases such as syphilis. It allegedly confirms faith that identities are bound to geographies. Blood's significance moves from biological and medical to cultural and political. Describing a conversation on the "story of his race," Harker records that Count Dracula identifies as Székely, one of the "four distinct nationalities" in Transylvania. He is "descended from Attila and the Huns" (Stoker 1997: 10), adding that Székelys have veins inside of which "flows the blood of many brave races" within the "whirlpool of European races" (33). He claims that "there is hardly a foot of soil in all this region that has not been enriched by the blood of men, invaders and patriots" (27) within a tumultuous history of battles among Wallachians, Saxons, and Turks to control Transylvania. The soil with which Count Dracula travels—his "earth-boxes," usually rendered as coffins—is presumably sodden with Balkanism's divisive violence, an antithesis to unifying purity and coherence of the modern nation-state and a terrifying omen that geopolitical borders cannot tame and contain historical borderlands.

For Britons, the Balkans existed as a site for cultural conflicts between a so-called Christian civilization and its Islamic orient, replete with nomadic Jews and Roma (i.e., gypsies or "counterfeit Egyptians"). Cultural differences are mapped onto geopolitical divisions of land and remapped onto bodies and behaviors. Vampires evoke an orientalized Europe that bordered on becoming Asia or—perhaps worse in British minds—an Islamic world. The Balkans may not have been important as a terrestrial passage from Britain to its most important colony India, but they were important within larger geopolitics. The Treaty of Berlin (1878) decided the fate of the Balkans with Britain's effort as "maintaining the Ottoman presence in Europe as a counterbalance to Russia," which it saw as "a possible threat to Britain's control of India" (Gibson 2006: 71). As borderlands between European Christianity and European Islam, they posed a problem for Enlightenment conceptions of secular modernity. Vampire hunters act in the name of rationality and humanity but combine spiritual and political concepts, not unlike practices that Partha Chatterjee (1993) finds among anticolonial nationalists in British India. In *Dracula*, Christian civilization is no longer able to mask itself as secular. Its basis in religion emerges in highly visible ways, notably crucifixes as weapons against vampires. The novel asks us to notice blind spots.

Stoker parodies nativist anxieties as Britain became increasingly less homogeneous than the nation-state's imaginary amalgamation of nation and state demands. At the turn of the century, London became not only metropolitan, but multinational. Fears of cultural submersion and possible racial/ethnic or national extinction abounded. Jews from eastern Europe became second only to the Irish as the largest immigrant community in England.[7] Nineteenth-century laws collapsed racialized groups, notably Roma, into what David Mayall describes as the "larger vagrant problem" within the "context of the needs of an industrialising urbanising society" wherein "itinerancy served merely as a cloak for a deviant range of predatory, parasitic and criminal activities," thereby defining "the superiority of the settled over the nomadic culture" and facilitating fears and prejudices against "immigrants, nomads, and other minority groups" (1992: 8). Laws sustained illusions of racial superiority of settled over nomadic peoples.[8] Bodies became legally visible; borders, legible; blood, territorialized. Itinerant and nomadic bodies were criminalized or stigmatized as premodern, savage, and animalistic, all of which was mapped anatomically onto the figure of the vampire. For readers today, vampires are more often emancipatory. Novelist Anne Rice allowed them to speak in *Interview with the Vampire* (1976).

Count Dracula's immigration is portrayed not only as what he might *take* from, or *diminish* within, England but also as what he might *bring* to, or *augment* within, England. Fears over his draining the national body of blood do not produce nativist anxieties; fears over his blood mixing into the national body—changing its composition and appearance—do. Count Dracula's body becomes an obsession, with Harker repeatedly noting the "very marked physiognomy" of his Transylvanian host. Maria Todorova argues that it was not until the late eighteenth century that "an awareness that the European possessions of the Ottoman Empire had a distinct physiognomy of their own that merited separate attention" took place, shattering the "unitary character of the oriental world" (1997: 62). The terrifying idea of orientalized Europeans suggests why Stoker's characters describe Count Dracula's body in terms of animals and corpses. "[Count] Dracula is seen as a metaphor for the Balkan condition and for the Western rejection of Balkan Europeanness as 'impure'," explains Vesna Goldsworthy; he "is threatening precisely because he is European," and the Balkans are perceived as "a contagious disease, an infectious sore in the soft underbelly of Europe, best left to fester in isolation" with its conflicts as "revolting departures from the ideal of cosmopolitanism" (1998: 83, xi).[9] Her analysis evokes stories about Janissaries, young Christian men who were kidnapped and enslaved to the Ottoman Sultan, which circulated as Europe began to imagine itself as a separate continent, rather than mere subcontinent of Asia.[10]

The novel's tropes of blood, bodies, and borders raise questions about territory-bound identities. The concept of nation-states made sovereignty territorial after the Peace of Westphalia in 1648. Empires, however, made sovereignty extraterritorial through colonialism and imperialism. Access to citizenship is infinitely deferred or abridged for racialized citizens. Some bodies are discursively bound to land, appearing as rightful occupants; others, discursively unbound, criminalized as illegal immigrants. Bodies are marked when they cross borders or are perceived to have crossed them even generations earlier. The etymology of territory from *terra* (earth) and *terrere* (to frighten) points to why Count Dracula's immigration and purchase of fifty properties (i.e., plots of English land) represents terrorism to vampire hunters. He is required to repose in, and travel with, "earth-boxes" filled with soil from his native land. They pathologize his "earth-home," "coffin-home," and "hell-home" (212). Isomorphic notions of restricted movement—place moving with people—evoke the nineteenth-century German expression "blood and soil" (*Blut und Boden*) to suggest "blood and soil become mixed in national perceptions," implying unchanging notions of descent within a homeland that has existed since time immemorial (Connor 1999: 205).[11]

If Count Dracula's blood drinking is an indirect way of describing sexual relations, then it promises to manifest itself in subsequent generations of so-called mixed-blood children. Vampirism spreads by infection and contagion, producing impure thoughts and progeny, altering perceptions of social coherence and demographic statistics that allegedly confirm it and legitimize political representation. Count Dracula becomes a radical figure in disrupting primordial notions of nation in an era of nation-states. Blood functions in discourses on racial purity and public health, which are mapped onto bodies to locate them within geopolitical systems of relational power. Miscegenation and degeneration are visualized in caricatures with animalistic features and behaviors, reflecting social and institutional prejudices—or in cadaverous creatures, reflecting fears of illness. Angela Smith argues that eugenics replaced superstitions about stillbirths, difficult births, and birth defects with genetic determinism (2011: 40). The pseudoscience maintained irrational fears of "illegitimate offspring of two illegitimate persons," she argues, citing a phrase from Emily Gerard's study on folklore, which Stoker read as part of his research. Count Dracula's blood mixes into the English bodies of Renfield, Lucy, and Mina, destabilizing their gender, sexuality, and allegiance. Their blood becomes impure; their bodies and minds, unstable and degenerate. Once-white bodies are racialized when vampirized, as are once-all-white bodies politic. It is not until 1864, a few years after Charles Darwin's *On the Origin of Species* (1859), that the term "miscegenation" replaced amalgamation for "the fertile fusion and merging of two races," notes Robert Young, with constructions of race functioning according to evolutionary structures with "computation of normalities" and "degrees of deviance" measured against an idealized white norm with none more demonized than "mixed race" (1995: 7, 170).[12] Vampires, however, refuse all forms of racism. For Donna Haraway, the vampire "insists on the nightmare of racial violence behind the fantasy of purity in the rituals of kinship" (1996: 322–3). Considered more monstrous than partially assimilated immigrants were native-born persons whose racial/ethnic identities could not be fully determined. If conservative British readers got chills over images of blood, bodies, and borders affected by vampires, then so too did Hollywood's conservative US audiences. Others, however, took comfort in seeing imperial patriarchy contested.

Stoker's novel questions ambivalence about nativist notions that some immigrants never fully assimilate because they might incite a degeneration of nation. It contests these violent epistemologies, something that Hollywood largely continues. Universal's *Dracula* and *Drácula* were adapted from staged versions of Stoker's novel—Hamilton Deane's in London in 1924 and John L. Balderston's in New York in 1927—rather than the novel directly. By maintaining the narrative's location in England, the immigrant-vampire negotiates contradictions within US representational democracy without directly implicating nativism and colonialism. The year 1924 marks significant changes in policy: indigenous nations and their territories were involuntarily absorbed into the republic under the Indian Citizenship Act, European immigration was regulated according to national quotas under the Johnson-Reed Act, and border crossings from Canada and México were regulated by the Border Patrol. Like vampires, immigrants were suspected of multiple allegiances and diminished patriotism.[13] Fears of submersion ignited xenophobia and racism, evident in Henry James's description of Jewish ghettos as evidence of the "Hebrew conquest of New York" ([1907] 1968: 132). Power largely was concentrated in the universalized particular of so-called natural persons, specifically "free white persons," from the Naturalization Act of 1795 until 1952.[14]

The moment of Count Dracula coincides with the apex of US imperialism, when blood served as pseudoscientific yet legally binding confirmation of race/ethnicity, determining degrees of personhood and entitlement to land allotments.[15] Abridged or deferred citizenship becomes waiting forever at the threshold of political representation. The notorious one-drop rules did not involve analysis of blood samples but relied upon appearance, color, and association. Legal definitions of race were sometimes determined by imagined blood quantum to distinguish persons (citizens and free noncitizens) from property (slaves). The United States systematically dismantled indigenous nations through the Dawes Commission's policies of forced assimilation, tribal enrollment, and land allotment beginning in 1893. It overthrew the Hawai'ian monarchy during the same year—and later annexed Guam and Puerto Rico and invaded the Philippines in 1899. To assassinate Count Dracula, English vampire hunters rely upon the brute force of Texan adventurer Quincey P. Morris, who embodies the spirit of the Republic of Texas, which occupied Mexican lands, dispossessed populations, and annexed territory before dissolving into the United States.[16] An ever-shifting nexus of definitions of blood, bodies, and borders determined what territories could be incorporated into the republic and who could own property and therefore count as a full citizen.[17]

The moment of Count Dracula announces the postcolonial condition in the heart of empire, affecting both colonizer and colonized with an impurity and instability brought by empire (cf. Said 1993). The supernatural qualities of Stoker's vampire allow for multiple readings, including contradictory ones. Since sweeping social changes continue to affect our lives, vampire stories often demand inconclusive and speculative models for analysis and interpretation. The figure of the vampire's meaning is highly unstable. Some are associated with exploitation, corruption, and theft, evident in Karl Marx's characterization of capitalism as "vampire-like" and "werewolf-like," which David McNally describes as not "mere rhetorical flourishes" but "means of depicting the actual horrors of capitalism" from child-labor and factory systems to genocides and slavery (2012: 13). Such associations travel widely and sometimes return in critiques of colonialism and capitalism, imperialism and neoliberalism. In her study of rumor and history in colonial Africa, Luise White examines a transnational genre of African stories about people hired by Europeans to capture East Africans and take their blood, calling them "vampire stories" since "no other term conveys the racial difference encoded in one group's need for another's blood" (2000: 9). Updated for a neoliberal moment, such associations reappear in *Laal Rang* (India 2016; dir. Syed Ahmad Afzal), based on events about human blood mafias in the northern Indian state of Haryana and featuring a top blood thief who uses the nickname "Dracula." Other vampires are figures of resistance, empowerment, and generosity, evident in the multitude of responses to vampire film and television, including anticolonial, feminist, postcolonial, queer, and posthumanist appropriations of their stories to challenge power to reclaim both history and dignity. Minoritized writers from Octavia Butler (1976) to Jewel Gomez (1991) employ vampires to critique US colonialism from indigenous, black, and queer perspectives—and speculate fictions about other scenarios for America. Comparably, Amirpour's appropriation of the figure of the vampire speculates about transnational histories and feminisms in ways anticipated by Stoker in the moment of Count Dracula.

Count Dracula Refashioned as "Vampire Ayatollah"

Produced and directed by Francis Ford Coppola, Columbia Pictures' *Bram Stoker's Dracula* features a vampire so outrageously costumed and performed that one critic described it as a "vampire ayatollah," referencing not what the Islamic Revolution meant to Iranians, whether supporting or opposing it, but what it meant to certain Americans. Coppola simultaneously ignites and parodies reactionary politics. Count Dracula is refashioned as a thinly veiled throwback to US foreign policy during the 1970s, which saw challenges to its ability to influence domestic policy in foreign states. The film conjures Christian anxieties over Islam as a supernatural conquest over western ascendancy. It seems to illustrate ways that nationalism and national exceptionalism mask relationships between immigration and globalization through contrivances of Hollywood genre and cinematic citation. Vampires evoke unspeakable frights over erosions to the American Dream by the founding of the Organization of the Petroleum Exporting Countries (OPEC) in 1960, US military defeat in Southeast Asia in 1975, and deposition of the US-backed Iranian monarchy of Reza Shah Pahlavi in 1979. At the same time, the film's outlandish costumes and performances, like Stoker's novel, offer space to critique imperialism.

Bram Stoker's Dracula reflects its moment of production, as Cold War geopolitics crumbled. Count Dracula is orientalized almost as a textbook illustration of Edward Said's landmark study *Orientalism* (1978) on how Europe invented itself as a civilization by inventing an Orient that conflated different historical and cultural aspects of the Middle East, North Africa, South Asia, East Asia, Southeast Asia, Central Asia, and the Balkans into a monolithic and unchanging Other. In Coppola's film, Count Dracula looks Turkish, Japanese, Chinese, Hungarian, and Russian, yet none of these identities entirely. His appearance and performance are explicitly heterogeneous, so as to be anti-mimetic, yet gain power through reality effects of their irreconcilable details more than special effects of supernatural flight and physical transmogrifications. The film's satire buries reactionary politics beneath lavish sets and costumes. Its elaborate and bejeweled costumes even helped hoist orientalist design back onto fashion runways. For audiences inclined towards xenophobia, Count Dracula becomes a new post-Cold War threat that migrated from geopolitics to religion, evoking

Figure 1.1 Gary Oldman as an orientalized Count Dracula welcomes Keanu Reeves as Jonathan Harker at the start of another excellent adventure. *Bram Stoker's* Dracula (USA 1992; dir. Francis Ford Coppola).

the vitriol and furor of the Christian Crusades against the Ottomans during the Middle Ages. Vampire hunters appear heroic, like cowboys in classical Hollywood Westerns. For other audiences, the vampire hunters become emotionally insecure and violence-prone patriarchs—and Count Dracula, an object of desire or identification.

The film also demonstrates Hollywood's vampire-like qualities by revealing its dependency on drawing talent and labor from across the globe before sending products and images into the world. Hollywood acts like a vampire. "Can a vampire resist fresh blood?" asked a journalist about how "Hollywood was destined to discover Hong Kong" in "the rapidly shrinking world of global entertainment" (Ansen 1996: 66). Rather than a vampire unable to resist the *new* (for Hollywood at the time) blood of Hong Kong martial arts and pyrotechnics, the film casts Hollywood as a vampire unable to resist the *vintage* blood of classical and avant-garde European and East Asian filmmaking through copious and conspicuous references to Jean Cocteau, Sergei Eisenstein, and Kurosawa Akira that often overwhelm pretentions of literary faithfulness and historical verisimilitude—and aestheticize its politics. Count Dracula triggers anxieties of Coppola's generation over the US colonial defeat in Southeast Asia, lamented in his *Apocalypse Now* (1979), and the so-called oil crisis, also during the 1970s, that announced the twilight of an American Century. Critics were quick to notice the film's Islamophobia during US military invasions in the MENASA regions (Sinclair 1993: 15; Sharrett 1996: 265–6). The film seemed to restage Stoker's novel as the 1991 invasion of Iraq like the "scripts replayed unrevised" that Pratt observed about the 2003 invasion in relation to European imperialism (2008: xiii). For younger audiences, the vampire hunters' earnestness could only be social satire.

The film's refashioning of Count Dracula allows audiences to speculate about alternatives meanings. Its sympathetic vampire might encourage us to temper patriotic impulses to invade foreign states in search of weapons of mass destruction and cheap oil. Count Dracula (Gary Oldman) is in many ways a better partner for Mina Murray (Winona Ryder) than her fiancé Jonathan Harker (Keanu Reeves), whose occasional ineptitude is annoying. Coppola allows Mina to take command and drive a stake through Count Dracula's heart, releasing him from vampirism. She does not sacrifice her own life, as the female protagonist does in Murnau's *Nosferatu*. Coppola's vampire hunters seek to destroy Count Dracula and a sense of deep historical, transnational connection that he resurrects through love, visualized as Vlad Țepeș and wife Elisabeta in an eastern orthodox mosaic.

Coppola mobilizes *affect* and *spectacle*, more than *ideology* and *narrative*, to structure meaning, suggesting why audiences interpret the film differently. Coppola's Count Dracula becomes a "vampire ayatollah," evoking the terror of the hostage crisis, and conflating the Iranian ayatollah Khomeini with

Iraqi president Saddam Hussein, thereby naturalizing the US invasion of Iraq in a continuum from Christian Crusades to Manifest Destiny. At the same time, Count Dracula becomes a satire of nationalist xenophobia. Coppola emphasizes what he calls the "John Ford Western finale" (Schumacher 1999: 449) by which a transnational brigade of vampire hunters travels from England to Transylvania, where they assassinate the local ruler, much like the so-called Coalition of the Willing assassinated Hussein. Count Dracula does not need to signify Hussein through direct correspondence or resemblance; instead, the figure of the vampire evokes affective responses to universalized villains identified along a so-called axis of evil. Count Dracula is less a signifier of Hussein and Khomeini than the vampire hunters are one of US military intervention in the MENASA regions framed as universalized good (e.g., saving women, promoting democracy) along the emotional register of the white-savior myth that emerged earlier in Westerns. Schatz describes the Western as "America's foundational ritual," suggesting the symbolic rather than the historical accuracy of the genre's "values, attitudes, and ideals associated with westward expansion and the taming and civilizing of the West" in films that "do not celebrate the past itself, but rather our contemporary idealized version of the past" (1981: 46, 63).[18] *Bram Stoker's Dracula* could be said to present an idealized version of the present as the past for some audiences—and an imaginative critique of such certainty for others. It also raises questions about the effects of history on the present. Genre conventions cannot fully erase or silence the presence of transnational history. The film conveys a story of two-way migrations: a vampire migrates to England, and vampire hunters migrate to Transylvania; moreover, some hunters migrated to England from Holland and Texas. *Bram Stoker's Dracula*'s meanings exceed conventional frameworks for Hollywood, US history, and horror. It is not a film that evokes primal or archetypal fears and desires. It is one that is very much about a particular experience of America.

An Iranian American Feminist Screens a Vampire Film at Sundance

Screened at the Sundance Film Festival in 2014, *A Girl Walks Home Alone at Night* examines effects of geopolitical relationships on Iranians and Iranian Americans. She recovers feminist potential in LeFanu's *Carmilla* and abandons masculine insecurities in Stoker's *Dracula*. Her central characters are types. She provides no backstory for their circumstances. They simply exist in Bad City.[19] The film opens with Arash (Arash Marandi), costumed in white T-shirt and blue jeans, stealing a cat (Masuka), who becomes his primary companion in an isolating town. He lives with his father, Hossein "The Junkie" (Marshall Manesh), who pays for the company of Atti "The Prostitute" (Mozhan Marnò) and goes into debt buying heroin from Saeed "The Pimp" (Dominic Rains).

Arash loses his prized possession, a 1957 convertible Ford Thunderbird, to pay his father's debts, then steals excess jewelry from Shaydah "The Princess" (Rome Shadanloo), who has recently had her nose reshaped and still wears the trendy bandage of plastic surgery.

Known only as the Girl (Sheila Vand), the vampire's solitary strolls do not make her vulnerable. Her chador is open, flapping like a cape. Whereas male vampires lure and attack women beneath the street lamps, she protects herself in dimly lit desolate streets to evaluate men by their behavior. She asks "The Street Urchin" (Milad Eghbali) whether he is good and tells him that she is watching him. He runs away, and she takes his skateboard, enhancing her mobility. Her constrained appetite for blood erupts into violence only against men who enact physical or psychological violence against others. After witnessing Saeed's humiliation of Atti, she seduces him by sucking his finger suggestively—mimicking fellatio, as she has previously seen Atti do; then, she severs his finger with her teeth—evoking castration, as she knows Atti is not free to do. She removes Saeed's severed finger from her mouth and traces the contours of his lips with it, parodying conventions from pornography. She bites his neck, drinks his blood, steals his jewelry, and explores his CD collection. By killing him, she enables Arash to recover the car for which he has worked years as a gardener for Shaydah's family.

Arash is different from the other men who the Girl meets as she walks alone at night. In their initial encounter, he is shot to emphasize physical beauty without the violent exhibitionism of Saeed, who had unzipped his tracksuit to showcase his taunt abdominal muscles and elaborate tattoos. The English word "SEX" appears on his chest; the Farsi expression "کس کش" (*koskesh*, vulgar slang for pimp), on his head.[20] His body is ornamented with gold chains, Mohawk haircut, and Fu Manchu mustache. Arash wears a vampire costume that he sewed himself. After failing to seduce Shaydah at a costume party, he wanders alone into a neighborhood that he does not recognize. Transfixed in a cloud of ecstasy and too tired to stand, he is harmless as a male predator. The Girl pushes him home on a skateboard. There, he moves slowly across the frame towards her. His high-collared cape follows behind him in a long take. The scene undercuts conventions of male vampires rapidly attacking female victims. The Girl does not bite Arash. Instead, the scene enfolds as one of intimacy between two lonely characters as the chorus to the song "Death" conveys mixed feelings of attraction and fear.

The film mobilizes music affectively to convey emotional registers of belonging to two places with strained political relations—and also belonging to neither place. Music reveals mutations and migration impelled by political events. Tracks by underground Iranian rock bands Radio Tehran and Kiosk, Armenian-Lebanese-US fusion Bei Ru from Los Angeles's Little Armenia, post-punk White Lies from London, the Spaghetti Western-inspired music

Figure 1.2 The Girl (Sheila Vand) encounters Arash (Arash Marandi), lost under a streetlamp and dressed like a classical Hollywood vampire. *A Girl Walks Home Alone at Night* (USA 2014; dir. Ana Lily Amirpour).

of Federale from Portland (United States), and a ballad by Iranian singer and songwriter Daruish (aka Daruish Eghbali), whose career began in the 1970s, play over carefully choreographed scenes with little or no dialogue. Unlike classical Hollywood's vococentrism, as Michel Chion calls dialogue's prioritization (1994: 5, 1996), the film allows auditory and visual images to produce equivocal meanings. They evoke moods, rejecting explicit causality that typically structures Hollywood films. The love scene is followed by one in which drag queen Rockabilly (Reza Sixo Safai) dances with a child's balloon. The fringe of her cowboy-style shirt sways like the balloon's string. The figure of the vampire becomes a means to understand loneliness, isolation, and forgetting what one wants from life within exploitative social conditions. Characters turn to drugs like heroin, cocaine, and ecstasy for refuge.

Amirpour's film explores how emotions develop within broader political and economic conditions informed by international relations. The film was largely shot in Taft (California), a small town that existed exclusively for petroleum and natural gas production. In a vampire film, shots of oil pumps, moving mechanically to extract petroleum from below the earth's surface, evoke the parasitic relationship of humans to planet. Oil becomes earth's blood and sustenance for materialistic human desires, such as Arash's fancy sports car. Oil also powers escape from exploitative conditions. Bad City defines a bleak world, structured by vampire-like social relations. Saeed exploits Hossein's addiction, which in turn exploits Arash's ability to earn money. Informal economies supplement state failures to provide for citizens. Whether cisgender or transgender, women are particularly vulnerable. There appears little work apart from prostitution, which, like drug addiction, is not uncommon in modern Iran, as documented in Mahnaz Afzali's *Zananeh/The Ladies' Room* (2003). Saeed and Hossein exploit Atti's vulnerable circumstances; a nameless man physically abuses Rockabilly in a scene deleted from the final cut. It is a world where humans have forgotten why they are living and how to dream of something better. It is a also dystopic take on the American Dream—and not only for Iranian Americans, who escaped or whose parents escaped the 1979 revolution, but for Americans who dream of cheap products and lifestyles made from petroleum.

Bad City mixes feelings of estrangement and dislocation along with ones of community and relocation. The film's black-and-white cinematography and uncluttered visual style evoke the look of classical Hollywood's vampire films and the social content of the Iranian new wave, including Farrokh Ghaffari's *Jonoub-e Shahr/South of the City* (1958) and Forough Farrokhzad's *Khanen siah ast/The House Is Black* (1962), whose images of modern Iran contradicted state discourses of modernization in "the American way" by showing evidence that industrialization and oil did not benefit everyone (Sadr 2006: 90–129). Amirpour evokes Dariush Merhju'i's *Gaav/The Cow* (1969), a critique of single-commodity national economies under Mohammad Reza Pahlavi (aka Shah of Iran) that was praised by ayatollah Khomeini (Naficy 2011: 160) for its implicit critique of the Pahlavi monarchy. Amirpour's film acts like its transnational sequel: both are set in remote villages where the precarity of life within petroleum-based economies is palpable. Shots of oil wells also visually evoke David Lynch's experimentation with digital cameras and photo-manipulation software in *Industrial Soundscape* (2002), which animates still photographs into disquieting figures of nightmares. Oil pumps feel like giant creatures from another realm that drain the planet of its vitality and announce the ascension of humans as top predators during the Anthropocene. We might learn something from other species.

Amirpour's film does not minimize difference but points to unequal ways that globalizing forces affect people, particularly Muslim women. She recontextualizes conventions from classical Hollywood vampire films for post-revolutionary Iran and its diaspora. Rather than a horse-drawn carriage, the Girl rides a skateboard. Rather than a black cape, she wears a black chador. The significance of such props is multilayered. While images of girls in hijab on skateboards are hardly unusual—girls participate in the Skateistan NGO's events in Afghanistan to bypass the ban on girls riding bicycles—they might seem unexpected to Hollywood audiences, much like images of Palestinians practicing *parkour* in the ruins of abandoned Israeli settlements in Gaza or videos of Saudis practicing joyriding and drifting in Riyadh. Skate parks are common meeting places for female and male Iranian street artists, such as Icy and Sot, and underground bands such as The Yellow Dogs, featured in

Bahman Ghobadi's *Kasi az gorbehaye irani khabar nadareh/No One Knows about Persian Cats* (2009), about Tehran's skater-artist-musician scene. Modernity remains "at large," as Arjun Appadurai (1995) argues. Modernity is not unified or singular but dis-unified and multiple. It can startle and frighten. If "one of the few privileges that accrue the latecomer [to modernity]" is the "license to play with form and refigure function according to the exigencies of the situation" (Gaonkar 2001: 21), then one of the many obligations of early adopters is understanding the effects of modernity and accepting internal and external critique. Amirpour's film evokes the playfulness of vampire media in unsettling assumptions.

Iran remains ominous for many US audiences. Hollywood profited from Iran's uneasy relationships with the United States in reactionary melodrama *Not Without My Daughter* (1991), Ben Affleck's *Argo* (2012), set during the Islamic Revolution of 1979, and Jon Stewart's *Rosewater* (2014), set during the Green Movement of 2009. Perhaps more than during the hostage crisis, US audiences are habituated by post-9/11 Islamophobia and anti-terrorist/anti-immigrant discourses to see hijab exclusively as women's oppression or menace. Indeed, Said's title *Covering Islam* (1981) evokes "covering" as simultaneously *revealing* through making visible and *concealing* through translating into foreign terms of understanding (Said 1997). Lila Abu-Lughod (2013) argues that US obsessions with "veiling" enable popular support for US military invasions in the name of rescuing women *from* Islam. Amirpour's vampire suggests that things are more complex.

For Iranian exiles, chadors evoke compulsory hijab, visualized in Marjan Satrapi's graphic novel *Persepolis* (2000) and its film adaptation (2007), but chadors do not foreclose feminist agency. Veiling's history in Iran includes Reza Shah's banning of chadors and headscarves on 7 January 1936, resulting in the forceful unveiling of women in public. Veiling in prerevolutionary Iran came to signify political resistance to programs of accelerated modernization, urbanization, and industrialization based on Turkish president Mustafa Kemal Atatürk's western-modeled programs (both of which had disastrous effects on the lives of rural and minoritized populations), along with religious identity and modesty. The Girl's chador asks audiences to reflect upon their assumptions about people based on their appearance, particularly Muslim women's clothing. For many Muslim women, hijab and modest dressing offer protections from unsolicited attention, including the sadistic and fetishistic male gaze around which most Hollywood films continue to be structured.

The chador serves as an occasion to think about history, identity, and geography. Çagla Hadimioglu argues that the term chador's Persian etymology can be traced to the Turkish *chadir*, translating as *tent*. The chador becomes "an extended boundary that assures that she always occupies a private space"

(2011: 216). She explains that a "chador is another skin, a place of inhabitation such as a home," so that the garment literally "alters geography" (2011: 134). Noting the accumulations of meanings imposed upon the chador by Muslims and non-Muslims—feminist or otherwise, Hadimioglu suggests that black chadors differ from the veils-as-screens in the orientalist imagination of subjugated women; however, it is not a garment altogether without meaning. "Perhaps," she suggests, "the black of the chador should be considered not as a void but as the result of an accumulation of inscriptions or projections so dense that they become solid—and an ostensible black 'hole' that is in fact saturated with intention, memory, and meaning" (2011: 130). Amirpour's relationship to chadors is simultaneously involuntary and liberating.

Chadors evoke experiences by Iranian emigrants when they return to Iran as Iranian Americans. Iran is a place where they may have never lived or even been born. In interviews, Amirpour describes her idea for a vampire in a chador as inspired by a visit to Iran with her family. Intrigued by the garment, its weight and fabric, she noticed that she did not disappear into the so-called faceless crowds of women wearing obligatory hijab. She felt self-conscious of her difference but also a sense of familiarity with hearing Farsi spoken everywhere, as at home with her family. Drawing on her own experience as part of a 1.5 generation, who feels out of place in both places, she reworks the vampire as a misunderstood figure like the physically disfigured Joseph Carey Merrick in Lynch's *The Elephant Man* (1980), a film she claims among her favorites. While Sundance journalists found a hijabi vampire on a skateboard to be a "quirky twist" to the longsuffering of "teen vampires" in *Twilight* and *The Vampire Diaries*, the film concerns different configurations of experience that often get erased, silenced, marginalized.

Amirpour establishes relationships of kinship and intimacy, something Auerbach defined as significant to vampires before Stoker's novel shifted meaning to foreignness and violence (1995: 113). The film encourages relationships between the isolated, dispossessed, and marginalized, much like the figure of the vampire. It does not celebrate heroism of colonial and imperial military interventions as a means of saving women and children, typically from the very tyrants installed in power by the United States. Nor does it hide the alienating effects of a global petroleum economy, which Timothy Mitchell (2011) links to possibilities and limitations of democracy. It creates a cinematic space for Iranians and Iranian Americans that is not made exotic but fairly mundane. As a Hollywood film for the current moment, it provides a model for de-exoticizing veiling by considering chadors as clothing whose meaning is as unstable and subject to migration and mutation as Stoker's figure of Count Dracula. The film asks us to look again or look closely, to listen again or listen more closely, to what we might have missed, rather than looking and listening only to what confirms what we think we already know.

THE FIGURE OF THE VAMPIRE AS OBJECT AND METHOD

Comparing *A Girl Walks Home Alone at Night* with *Bram Stoker's Dracula* establishes a range of difference in stories about the United States told as vampire stories. Some convey an emotional sense of debates over political representation for minoritized and often criminalized groups; others critique minoritizing and criminalizing discourses and policies that limit political representation. Most concern shifting relationships between history, identity, and geography—visualized in blood, bodies, and borders. Part of the context of thinking about vampires as both object and method responds to enduring blind spots in universalizing approaches. This book draws upon interventions and interruptions in film, television, and media studies that unsettle the field's critical concepts, historiographical methodologies, and theoretical concerns, based exclusively on Hollywood and European films. It engages comparative, often transnational or transcultural, approaches (Gopalan 2002; de la Mora 2006; Gerow 2010; Ganti 2013) that draw extended critiques (Bogle 1973; García Espinosa [1969] 1983; Rocha [1965] 1983; Solanas and Getino [1968] 1983; Diawara 1993) of nationalist frameworks for conceptualizing film (Bazin [1958–62] 1971; Sarris [1968] 1996; Kracauer [1960] 1997). As both object and method, vampires render Hollywood unbound, though not severed, from its heroic self-invention as privately funded dream factories that thrive within free-market economies. Hollywood produces vampire media outside the territorial United States in the mythical homeland in Europe and the largely unacknowledged former US colony of the Philippines—the imaginary origins and lost frontiers of empire. At the same time, Hollywood vampire films and television series complicate assumptions about the promise of America to provide equitable political representation of all citizens and fair treatment of all noncitizens with the nation-state's territories.

Vampires challenge us to think beyond an uncritical and ostensibly secular faith in realism by displacing the representational with the affective (cf. Majithia 2015). They help us to understand relationships between race/ethnicity and political representation, within relationships between political economy and cinematic representation. The preponderance of Hollywood films that receive theatrical release in parts of Africa, Europe, Latin America, and Southeast Asia during much of the twentieth century cannot be detached from US state support for Hollywood. Like emigration, film distribution is not always entirely voluntary. Critical conventions reproduce what Shohini Chaudhuri calls the "inequities of global film distribution" (2005: 4). Box-office power is maintained indirectly through military power or directly through international policy like the Bretton Woods Agreement (1944) and the General Agreement on Trade and Tariffs (1947).[21] Audiences sometimes love

Hollywood films because there are no alternatives due to conditions of trade, recovery, and even independence agreements.

For this reason, it is unsurprising that anticolonial and postcolonial critics (Memmi 1957; Fanon 1961; Mbembe 2003), along with critics of capitalism (Deleuze and Gattari 1987; Marx [1867] 1990; Hardt and Negri 2004), frequently evoke supernatural figures like vampires to describe experiences of dislocation, self-estrangement, and reinvention.[22] Vampires appear and reappear in writing by intellectuals to recover forms of knowledge that have historically been marginalized and delegitimized. Much as the transnational does not elide the continuing relevance of the national, the postcolonial does not elide the continuing relevance of the colonial and the imperial, which are articulated in terms of structural adjustments and proxy wars. Since colonialism and imperialism involve "the subjection of one people by another," Robert Young argues: "so long as oppressive power of that kind continues, then analysis of the forms and practices of colonialism and imperialism remains relevant to the problems we face today" (2015: 2). Vampire film and television becomes a location where amnesia over US colonialism and imperialism—and, moreover, repression of US postcolonial condition—finds expression in supernatural form.

Vampires emerge where inequalities abound. The myths of America and the realities of the United States function as a *contact zone* between indigenous, colonial, immigrant, imperial, and national histories. Pratt defines contact zones as "social spaces where disparate cultures meet, clash, and grapple with each other, often in highly asymmetrical relations of domination and subordination" (2008: 7), that is, "where peoples geographically and historically separated come into contact with each other and establish ongoing relations" (8). The *postcolonial condition* informs our transnational moment. Her analysis provides a model whose relevance has only amplified in the twenty first century since postcolonial studies, in Gauri Viswanathan's words, examines "cultural interaction between colonizing powers and the societies they colonized, and the traces that interaction left on literature, arts, and human sciences in both societies" (cited in Bahri and Vasudeva 1996: 54). These interactions continue to affect different people in different ways. Amirpour's family did not just happen to immigrate from Iran to the United States any more than Coppola's family immigrated from Italy to the United States. Hollywood's vampire films carry the mark of immigration, past and present.

Contact zones are also useful when thinking about films and series in which humans come into contact with supernatural species. To grapple with contact zones when species meet, Donna Haraway uses the term *figure* because "figures are not representations or didactic illustrations, but rather material-semiotic nodes or knots in which diverse bodies and meanings coshape one another" (2008: 4). Vampires can seem like intruders or emancipators; vampire hunters, like vigilantes or freedom fighters. Globalizing forces, particularly colonialism, imperialism, free trade, and war, figure in ways that are often obscured by extant critical conventions. Early scholarship on vampire films often focused on them as lowbrow entertainment that tapped into so-called archetypal fears and desires, thereby legitimizing them as objects for critical study.[23] Rather than assume a universalized Other met with an equally universalizing response in a dread of difference, this book explores how Hollywood's stories about vampires have been shaped by histories of immigration and globalization that inform films as aesthetically and politically different as Amirpour's *A Girl Walks Home Alone at Night* and Coppola's *Bram Stoker's Dracula*. Like past scholarship that located feminist and queer moments in vampire stories, this book looks for immigrant and indigenous moments—afterlives of race, which have less systematically been explored.

At a point where commerce and migration converge, sometimes around policy, vampire films and series contribute to developments in critical methodologies that do not segregate *textual meaning* of stories, characters, styles, and performance from *political economies* that determine production, distribution, and exhibition. These two axes of analysis comingle and contaminate each another. Although the vampire's migrations and mutations are framed as supernatural, the films and series are remarkably consistent for their explicit or implicit preoccupation with everyday lived experiences of globalization through immigration. Globalization allows some groups to pass as global citizens, others languish as stateless; it also allows films to travel across national borders with some arriving on the other side as art, others as trash. Immigration recruitment and regulation thus share something with film production and distribution in their entanglements with broader shifts within globalization. Everyday market economies of stereotypes of race/ethnicity, sex and gender, class, religion, nationality and nativity, ability, and species reflect the effects of globalization on film production, distribution, and exhibition. Hollywood defends its home and foreign markets by creating illusions of the inferiority of films produced elsewhere, often reinforcing social stereotypes that Mexican films are cheap like Mexican labor. Vampires allow us to see Hollywood—and America—as transnational in ways that other films often obscure.

Hollywood's reliance on professional standards to discredit competition extends discourses of national exceptionalism that diminishes the contributions of, and contestations by, immigrant and indigenous communities to US history. Assumptions that foreclose certain questions about Hollywood can benefit from self-reflection in other fields. "US policymakers depended upon the fantasy of American exceptionalism to authorize their practices of governance," explains Donald Pease, "but historians and literary scholars turned the beliefs imbedded within the fantasy into the principles of selection through which they decided what historical events they would allow representation within the historical record and which literary works they would include within the US canon" (2009: 11). Radway et al. focus on "ways that racialization and gender and sex discrimination have been fundamental to the construction of the American national subject" (2009: 1–6). Whether in textbooks in a university classroom or in clickbait "best films of all time" lists circulated through social media, canonization invariably consolidates historical distortions and misrepresentations. Vampire film and television becomes a site where omissions within national/nationalist discourse resurface within contradictory and inassiminable aspects of a postcolonial United States (cf. Singh and Schmidt 2000), suggesting reasons for the appearance of a vampire riding a skateboard in hijab alongside one refashioned as a poster boy for orientalism.

NOTES

1. Only Native America, configured as a pack of werewolves/shape-shifters, perceives Edward's passing as trespassing. From the perspective of indigenous nations, the very concept of native-born American suggests systemic trespassing-as-passing.
2. First documented use in 1734/1745, the *OED* suggests *vampire* enters from French and Magyar. For etymology, see Wilson [1985] (1998) and Murgoci [1927] (1998). McClelland argues Slavic word *vampir* "was a shorthand (and probably pejorative) label for an individual who either belonged to a specific group or practiced a particular belief or ritual" (2008: 31), organizing around a triad of Jews, Pagans, and heretics (47).
3. On plays, see: Stuart 1994.
4. Theda Bara was Hollywood's transformation of Theodosia Goodman from "nice Jewish girl" into epitome of male anxieties over female agency in *A Fool There Was* (USA 1915; dir. Frank Powell). Her stage name was allegedly an anagram for "Arab Death." As Musidora, Jeanne Roques portrayed Irma Vep in *Les Vampires* (France 1915–1916; dir. Louis Feuillade). Her name an anagram for the word *vampire*, Irma Vep is herself a scrambled character—part victimizer, part victim.
5. For analyses of scholarship, see: Carter 1988: 1–6, Davison 1997, and Gordon and Hollinger 1997.
6. Polidori describes conflicts between Italian nationality and English citizenship: "I, although born in England, am not an Englishman" (cited in MacDonald 1991: 20). Entangled in Anglo-French relations, the Alien Bill (1793) deported foreigners, including Catholics, "on suspicion that they were concerned in practices dangerous to the state" (80).
7. Halberstam questions Stoker's friendship with Burton, author of a "tract reviving the blood libel against Jews in Damascus" and statements against writers for not being "good Christians" (1995: 86).
8. Restrictions were minimal since 1783's repeal of the 1530 anti-Gypsy Act, threatening Roma with execution. Laws preventing immigration begin early twentieth century, targeting Russian and Polish Jews, and expelling Jewish, Chinese, Italian, and German communities.
9. Goldsworthy finds British and US economic interests in the Balkans were minor during the 1920s and 1930s. A nineteenth-century "narrative colonisation," she argues, begins with Lord Byron as "its Columbus" (1998: x).
10. See: Lewis and Wigen 1997 on Europe's continental self-invention.
11. Drawing upon Foucault's arguments that European modernity produces blood

and race as biological entities through clinical descriptions and mappings onto an "anatomical atlas," Linke argues the body is attributed with strategic importance, a "strategy for political power" upon which "a new system of legal justice is imprinted" (1999: 157–159).
12. Southern Democrats coin the term to discredit Lincoln and Republicans; Ku Klux Klan was founded two years later (Gross 2010: 74–75).
13. Theodore Roosevelt demanded "100 percent Americans" over "hyphenated Americans." The 1917 Immigration Act required English-language literacy to discourage immigration from Italy, Poland, and Hungary and bar it from Asia except China, Japan, and Philippines (Hing 2004: 54; Daniels 2002: 278).
14. "Natural person" recognizes corporate personhood as "legal persons." Three-fifths Compromise (1787) determined "all other persons" counted as three-fifths of whole persons.
15. England's *jus soli* came to the United States, yet birthright citizenship excluded racialized nationals (Haney López 1996: 39–40). The first naturalization law (1790) limited eligibility—"fitness for self-government"—to "free white persons" (Jacobson 1998: 7). Only post-Civil War did citizenship became *national*. "Servile blood" of "an ancestor once held in involuntary servitude" was imagined to "contaminate and pollute the Indian blood and render such a person incapable of taking land under a treaty with the United States" (Gross 2010: 163). Mexican American organizations opposed classification as *race* (versus *nationality* or *white ethnicity*) along with prejudices informed by eugenicists like Madison Grant who feared "peon blood" of *mestizaje* (Spanish-Indian-African) produced "race bastards," "amazing racial hybrids," and "ethnic horrors that will be beyond the powers of future anthropologists to unravel" (Foley 2012: 62).
16. Texas was populated with 35,000 whites, who seceded from México to declare Independent Lone Star Republic of Texas in 1836. Annexed in 1845, the United States gained of 55% of Mexican territory with 80,000 inhabitants.
17. Puerto Rico and Philippines were not envisioned for "settler citizens"; New Mexico and Hawai'i were whitened for incorporation as states (Gómez 2007: 7).
18. Turner describes the frontier as a site for productions of Americanness (1920: 1). US national exceptionalism "fails as a useful tool for assessing the current moment because it reads the national past solely from a national perspective" (Rana 2010: 6).
19. Amirpour's graphic novels (2014/2015) tell the Girl's story of wandering through desert in search of death before returning home.
20. I thank Chani Gatto Bradshaw for contacting the film's producer about this term.
21. Criticisms by Hollywood lobbyists overstate subsidies for film industries elsewhere ignore how Hollywood benefits from "a vast array of state, regional and city film commissions," offering "hidden subsidies to the film industry (via reduced local taxes, free provision of police services, and the blocking of public thoroughfares)" (Miller et al. 2005: 96).
22. The Founding Fathers are considered neither immigrant nor indigenous, but somehow naturally—or perhaps supernaturally—"American" (cf. Daniels 2002: 3–4).
23. Early studies include Kracauer 1947, Eisner 1952, Butler 1967, Clarens 1967, Pirie 1972 and 1977, Silver and Ursini 1975, Prawer 1980, Twitchell 1985, Carroll 1990, and Coates 1991.

2. "MAKING" AMERICANS FROM FOREIGNERS

Universal Studio's 1931 release of multiple-language versions of *Dracula* consolidated and popularized Hollywood vampires as aristocratic, cosmopolitan, and humanized. Hungarian-born actor Béla Lugosi's accented performance of Count Dracula in the English-language *Dracula* embodied Hollywood's idea of the vampire for decades. Even Spanish-born actor Carlos Villarías was allegedly directed to model his portrayal of Conde Drácula in the concurrently shot Spanish-language *Drácula* after Lugosi's performance. The iconic image of Lugosi's black cape and tuxedo, pale face, dark hair, and piercing gaze spread globally despite Universal's efforts to control unauthorized use of the costume, makeup, and even the name "Dracula" through international copyright. Hollywood rejected the model of Prana-Films' earlier adaptation of Stoker's novel in *Nosferatu*. Max Schreck was rendered almost unrecognizable as a human actor under prosthetics and makeup that rendered the vampire's features like those of insects, birds, and rats, thus offering little space for projections of desires.

Universal's vampire drew more readily upon conventions from stage and screen melodramas, modeling the vampire looks and acts upon human villains, typically foreigners. The immigrant-vampire's arrival on Hollywood screens actually comes relatively late; other immigrants had already adorned it for decades. Conventions for vampires thus drew upon ones for representing immigrants in other earlier films, including actualities (precursors to newsreels) that belittled immigrants as amusing entertainment and industrial training and state propaganda films that recruited and assimilated select groups of immigrants.

This chapter traces cinematic conventions of narrative, performance, set and costume design in pre- and early Hollywood films that offered models for successful assimilation into the Melting Pot and so-called new race, popularized in Israel Zangwell's 1908 play.[1] The unnatural whiteness of America was key to this social mobility. State and industrial films in particular were employed to americanize immigrants—to whiten them by teaching them what common sense allegedly told (male) citizens to do. Whiteness assimilated certain groups to create a common national identity from selected national identities. Whiteness shifts shape like the figure of the vampire. Vampires contest the racial system that privileged northeastern Europeans over eastern and southern Europeans during the early twentieth century.

Universal's Count Dracula and Conde Drácula might look unquestionably white today, but they did not have the makings of Americans during the 1930s. Most studies of Hollywood vampires films overlook ways that representational and narrative strategies drew upon conventions for depicting "foreign"—whether immigrant or indigenous—bodies on screen. Unlike Graf Orlok in *Nosferatu*, Hollywood's vampires did not exhibit their fangs on screen, nor did they reveal their transformations into bats. Instead, their difference emerged in the vampire's not-quite-white-ness. As a socially constructed category, whiteness passes itself as invisible and unmarked—that is, a "natural" state of appearance that was necessary for political inclusion. By contrast, the vampire's not-quite-whiteness is marked—and leaves a mark, figuratively, the "mark of the vampire," upon his victims/lovers. It functions like an afterlife of race, preventing white-looking (male) eastern Europeans from acquiring the full benefits of US citizenship. As immigration and naturalization policies became more inclusive, so too did Hollywood's representations of vampires. Hollywood's vampire films and series thus serve as indices of how whiteness expands and contracts according to historical circumstances, including immigration recruitment and regulation.

Some audiences found the films *liberating*, since vampires challenged conservative social conventions; others found them *constricting*, since vampire hunters restored the status quo. In part the structure of having two potential protagonists—vampire and vampire hunter—allowed for audiences to project their own fantasies and anxieties into their experience of the films. Depending upon sympathies with vampire or vampire hunter, audiences found pleasure in recognizing national myths of exceptionalism or in questioning them (cf. Pinedo 1997; Williamson 2005; Schott and Moffat 2011). Audiences responded with both panic and yearning to classical Hollywood vampires, who evoked empathy for immigrants from eastern and southern Europe—or feelings of frustration with conservative social codes that limited the rights of citizenship to "free white" men. Understanding the codes and conventions of pre- and early Hollywood segregation comedies, immigration romances, and miscegenation melodramas allows for a more complex understanding of classical Hollywood's first vampires and Hollywood transnational orientations. These films represent directly what Hollywood would later represent indirectly through the supernatural figure of the vampire.

Vampire films negotiate seemingly contradictory impulses that were also at play in Hollywood itself. With Universal's films, the figure of the vampire settled in Hollywood, along with leagues of actual émigrés from Europe, Latin America, and East Asia. Los Angeles became home to privileged classes, who could move freely and exchange national attachments almost at will, to the less privileged classes, who were compelled to emigrate. Although Universal's *Dracula* evokes the predicament of Hungarians, they suggest other groups, including Italians, Russians, Czechs, Poles, Chinese, and Mexicans. They also suggest the condition of gendered and classed groups whose citizenship, once achieved, was often contested or subverted. With significant Mexican and Japanese populations during the 1930s, Los Angeles was not yet a multicultural city. Universal's *Dracula* films evoke contemporary processes that determined which bodies could cross international borders and establish residency in the United States and which bodies could not access the civil, political, or social citizenship, even when born within these borders. Foreigners become citizens, but the afterlives of race often resulted in their being treated as aliens.

Masquerading US Landscapes as Foreign Locales

In *Dracula*, the location of southern California is largely obscured by elaborate sets on Universal's innovative back-lots, yet indigenous flora and fauna—sycamores, spruces, and oaks; armadillos, opossums, and scorpions—appear, despite efforts to conceal them with matte paintings of the Carpathians. Dismissed as continuity errors due to budgetary constraints, the use of North American (i.e., non-European) animals and plants actually has the effect of domesticating the Transylvanian peasants in other scenes as eastern European immigrants.[2] The indigenous flora and fauna suggest a familiar location of southern California more than they exoticize the foreign location of Transylvania. Armadillos would appear unremarkable in B-grade Westerns by Republic and Monograph, yet they seem extraordinary in *Dracula*. Classical Hollywood films demand reading strategies that depart from the conventions of realism. Elizabeth Young finds that Universal's *Frankenstein* films use the monster as a stand-in for racist stereotypes for African American men, thus legitimizing the rescue of white women by the angry mob (Young 2008a). Classical Hollywood's horror cycle conveys complex social negotiations of a nation (of immigrants) in the making. The transnational threads of this history are visualized by making the United States appear foreign, so that foreigners could be made American. This minor shift in the analytic allows us to understand cinematic realism more attentively at the intersections of genre, nation, and race around immigrant experiences.

Even before the opening of the first nickelodeon in 1905, immigrants appeared in Edison actualities. From the perspective of audiences in relatively ethnically homogeneous places such as the Midwest and West, scenes of multiethnic life on New York's Lower East Side appeared like "pictures of exotic foreign lands" (Ross 1998: 44). It is this very quality of producing the *familiar as foreign* that comes to play in Universal's vampire films. David Skal proposes that a Hollywood Gothic develops as a style from the sensationalized narrative of Gothic novels and the stylized performances and visuals of Expressionist art (1990: 7). In *Dracula*, *Drácula*, and *Dracula's Daughter*, the Hollywood Gothic emerges within conflations of Europe and North America that have been ignored by generations of scholars. Hollywood's sound stages might be costumed and accented as London, and its back-lots as Transylvania, but underneath, they are southern California. The films are about coming to America, and part of their allure came from such suggestiveness.

Along with *Dracula* and *Drácula*, other films in Universal's horror cycle, such as *Frankenstein* (USA 1932; dir. James Whale) and *The Mummy* (USA 1932; dir. Karl Freund), were popular successes years before United Artists distributed independent producer Walter Wanger's *Stagecoach* (USA 1939; dir. John Ford), a film credited with elevating the Western from a B-genre of singing-cowboy films to an A-genre of respectable drama. While Westerns have faded as a genre, vampire films have gained in popularity. Vampire films have become an under-acknowledged successor to Westerns in terms of a commercial genre's ability to negotiate transnational history. Critics and academics understand Westerns as the heroic inverse to nightmarish depictions of the postwar United States in detective films or *films noirs*. Westerns share something in common with gangster films; both concern the assimilation of recent immigrants, whether from Ireland and Italy to east-coast and midwestern cities such as New York and Chicago or from the east coast to the so-called western frontier. Cowboys were descendants of English, German, or Swedish immigrants; gangsters, Italian and Irish immigrants. Under the Production Code, gangsters were punished for breaking the law, but cowboys often got away with murder, even when victims were white. Vampires unsettle illusions of national exceptionalism—economic opportunity, social mobility, and political freedom—that buttress Westerns. If Westerns perform the Manifest Destiny and an alleged god-given command to expand westward into México, Hawai'i, and the Philippines, then vampire film perform postcolonial realities of the regulation and control of migration across geopolitical and virtual borders.

Published under the universalizing title of *Qu'est-ce que le cinéma ?* (1958–65), André Bazin's collection of essays argues that the classical Hollywood Western "is the only genre whose origins are almost identical with those of cinema itself and which is alive as ever after almost half a century of uninterrupted success" (140), speculating about the genre's success with "Arabs, Hindus, Latins, Germans, or Anglo-Saxons" (141). Bazin does not consider Hollywood's economic advantages in getting its films to wide audiences. Instead, he postulates that Westerns express something of the "essence of cinema." Laughable today, Bazin was not so naïve as to believe that Westerns—and cinema—represents reality. Westerns, he remarks, often have "only a tenuous relation to historical fact," such that some of the films might be said to represent "the opposite of a historical reconstruction" with "no difference between Hopalong Cassidy and Tarzan except their costume and the arena in which they demonstrate their prowess" (143). Bazin's observation about the interchangeability of costumes and sets in Hollywood adventure films is suggestive of ways to consider the possible interchangeability of locations in Hollywood's earliest vampire films. Classical Hollywood vampire films have as much to say about America as Westerns, which Bazin anointed "le cinéma américain par excellence" (1971: 140).

Rather than anchoring meaning in specific and actual locations through reality effects in set and costume design, classical Hollywood's back-lot sets and contemporary Hollywood's green screens masquerade as foreign places. These imperfect illusions invite us to think in terms more nuanced than one-to-one mimesis. Meaning about place emerges within gaps and fissures within the artifice, much like meaning about gender emerges in drag performances. Vampire films mobilize a cross-dressing of landscapes through interplay of foreign and familiar details. Faraway lands evoke nearby ones that are only recognized when slippages in the artifice of sets, costumes, and performances are interpreted as more than errors and mistakes. Such readings operate according to a strategy comparable to Mary Ann Doane's concept of masquerade (1982), which suggests that female audiences distance themselves from chauvinist and misogynist images, rather than identify with them, through cross-gendered acts to make meaning from films. Reading *Dracula* in such as way also extends some of what film theory has said about sound and image. Rick Altman offered a playful challenge to assumptions that soundtrack is redundant, merely repeating what visual images were already conveying, by suggesting that moving images were ventriloquists for the sound track (1980: 67). He notes that dialogue originates not in actors but in screenwriters, concealed under Hollywood's seamless modes of production. No matter how much the characters' dialogue and the various intertitles try to persuade that story of *Dracula* is located in London or Transylvania, the accents and visual details disrupt this masquerade, thereby opening the films to complex interpretations.

Audiences also looked to other details to support complex reading strategies. In addition to Tom Gunning's concept of a "cinema of attractions" (1986) by which audiences marvel at what cannot exisit in life, vampire films fall within the parameters of his concept of an "aesthetics of astonishment" (1995) through which the aesthetic illusion of *trompe l'œil* triggers disquiet among viewers over conflicting messages as to whether what is seen really exists or existed. With early cinema, "sophisticated urban pleasure seekers" flocked to see projected images, testing the limits of "intellectual disavowal" within a framework of "I know, but yet I see." Gunning opens understanding of complex and contradictory processes of interpreting vampire films, which play upon discrepancies between perceptions and representations. *Dracula* performs a complicated mixing of realist and antirealist codes, so that ruptures to the visual verisimilitude of Universal's sets for Transylvania and London conflate narrative with spectacle in contradictory ways. Locations masquerading as foreign lands are exposed in visual details that relocate the story to southern California, where the film was shot, much like Amirpour's *A Girl Walks Home Alone at Night*. The *Dracula* films tell stories that are less about vampires as foreign immigrants arriving in the United States than they are about immigrants who have already arrived. By looking at representations of immigrants in pre-*Dracula* filmmaking, Universal's vampire films reveal immigrant feelings in supernatural terms.

Unlike the immigrants in films discussed below, Count Dracula does not see the Statue of Liberty, partly because he emigrates to London, but mostly because he is framed as not entitled to the Statue's welcome. Regardless of whether Count Dracula's arrival is located in 1931 when *Dracula* was released or during the 1920s when scholars conventionally establish its narrative, the character is racialized, classed, and sexualized in legal discourse and in everyday social exchanges. Codes and conventions from early (1895–1907) and transitional (1908–17) cinema are particularly relevant. The costumes, beards, and accents of Transylvanians are consistent with the character types and stereotypes for eastern European immigrants established in earlier immigration comedies, including *Making an American Citizen* (1912) by the inventor of narrative cinema, Alice Guy-Blaché, produced in pre-Hollywood New Jersey. Vampires speak in an accented English that is not entirely differentiated from classical Hollywood's immigrant types and stereotypes. The film's representation of England limits local accents to the lower classes, suggesting that maids and butlers might also represent the working-class immigrants from Britain and Ireland that Charlie Chaplin's little tramp pantomimes in *The Immigrant*. As the next chapter discusses, classical Hollywood vampires misunderstand social cues according to conventions established in early cinema. More than foreigners who might be made into Americans, they are aliens— much like Hollywood vampires, particularly before the 1970s.

COMEDIES OF CONTAINED ASSIMILATION AND SEGREGATION

Immigrants shaped film culture—both posh and pedestrian, nickelodeons and picture palaces. Sabine Haenni finds they contributed to an "ethnicization of cinematic cultures," evident in "certain Hollywood visuals and narratives [. . .] shaped by the unprecedented presence of foreign-looking immigrants in US cities" (2008: 20). A Jewish immigrant from Germany, Carl Laemmle opened nickelodeons in Chicago in 1906 and established Universal Pictures in 1912. Nickelodeons ran heterogeneous programs with live music or lecture at low prices for workers and immigrants (Robinson 1996: 91–3). Their attraction to "recent immigrants from eastern and southern Europe," however, ignited fears that cheap amusements might create spaces for "oppositional or alternative" politics (Abel 1999: xi–xii). French company Pathé-Frères dominated the US market in 1905, until cinema was "americanized," leaving Pathé stigmatized as "not white enough" by 1907 (xiii).

Before nickelodeons, immigrants were depicted in Edison actualities, including *Emigrants Landing at Ellis Island* (USA 1903; cin. Alfred C. Abadie), *Arrival of Emigrants, Ellis Island* (USA 1906; cin. G. W. "Billy" Bitzer), *New York City "Ghetto" Fish Market* (USA 1903; cin. James Blair Smith), and *Move On* (USA 1903; cin. Alfred C. Abadie). Months before the Ellis Island film was shot, a bronze plaque with Emma Lazarus's words—"Give me your tired, your poor, / Your huddled masses yearning to breathe free."—was affixed to the Statue of Liberty's base.[3] Edison films record arrivals of steerage-class transatlantic passengers, no longer dominated by German and Irish immigrants, but by Italian and Jewish immigrants, who lived in segregated ghettos on Manhattan's Lower East Side. *New York City "Ghetto" Fish Market* shows a crowded street of fish vendors in a high-angle shot; *Move On,* Jewish and Italian fruit and vegetable vendors ordered to move their pushcarts by a scolding police officer. "It is interesting and amusing to see the expressions of combined fear and anxiety on the faces of the men as they hurry away," explains the description; "the fear of being arrested if they stand, and of losing some of their wares if the carts strike an obstruction in the street."[4] "Jews, Italians, Irish, and various Eastern Europeans all coexisting within the same cramped space" of tenements were "familiar aspects of everyday life to local residents," explains Steven Ross, "but to audiences in small, ethnically homogeneous southern, midwestern, and western towns, they must have seemed like pictures of exotic foreign lands" (1998: 44). Edison highlights the ghetto, home to immigrants from Russia, Austria, Germany, Romania, and Turkey, as a site of incomplete assimilation. Filming the familiar-as-foreign becomes a key strategy in Universal's vampire films with southern California masquerading as both London and Transylvania. Edison Company commemorated nationalist histories and territorial claims in staged enactments of the so-called Indian

Wars. Genocide and dispossession were purportedly legitimized by Christian doctrine of the Manifest Destiny. Vampire films challenge the presentation of colonial crimes as socially acceptable violence. The use of Christian symbols as weapons by intolerant vampire hunters, for example, reveals how faith in religion and faith in nation collapse into one another around questions of race.

As politicians considered restrictions on (eastern and southern) European immigration, filmmakers adopted multi-reel narrative forms. Certain immigrants assimilated, promoting myths of a democratic republic. Despite formal and informal structures to facilitate assimilation, americanization remains incomplete and conditional. Like vampires, immigrants were white-but-not-quite-white. Comedy contained them by maintaining "interesting and amusing" qualities from Edison films. Other stories adopt romance as a mode for assimilation—or melodrama as a mode for differentiation, offering narrative formulas that would be reconfigured into Hollywood's vampire films. The social role of early cinema helps construct an unnatural whiteness of America—one that not only *amalgamated* different European ethnicities but also *appropriated* indigenous nations. White settlers, particularly Southerners and Mormons, claimed native ancestry, often "Cherokee," to legitimize dispossession. Richard Abel argues that early 1910s played a critical role in helping "a creole society like the United States in the early twentieth century" imagine itself as a homogenous "white nation" (2006: 4). He examines "American sensational melodramas—Westerns, civil war films, detective films, and animal pictures —citing Shelley Streeby's analysis of "sensational melodrama" that renders racialized bodies as "alien" (2006: 8). Most early films remain lost, leaving film history invariably distorted. Nonetheless, films such as *A Child of the Ghetto* (USA 1910; dir. D. W. Griffith) suggest fantasies of assimilating (whitening) foreigners into citizens. The Jewish "child" Ruth (Dorothy West) is absorbed into the nation by Irish American police officer Quinn (George Nichols), who represents "an earlier wave of assimilated immigrants" (Simmon 2009: 35). Successful romantic coupling conveys whiteness's ever-expanding inclusiveness, so that race slips from human to nonhuman with Count Dracula and Conde Drácula.

For male immigrants, assimilation becomes a national project, a collective enterprise based on neighborly assistance. In Alice Guy-Blaché's *Making an American Citizen* (1912), a recently arrived eastern European-looking immigrant, Ivan Orloff (Lee Beggs), is made into a productive citizen rather than deported as an unworthy alien. Shot in New Jersey, the film opens with Orloff riding a cart, drawn by his mule and wife (Blanche Cornwell). They encounter other emigrants. Women carry large bundles of belongings; unencumbered men walk freely. Once in "the land of freedom," Orloff receives four "lessons in Americanism" announced by intertitles and performed in vignettes—the first upon arrival, with the Statue of Liberty in the background, the last sending him to court and to work in a chain gang. He beats, whips,

Figure 2.1   Ivan Orloff whips wife and mule in eastern Europe. *Making an American Citizen* (USA 1912; dir. Alice Guy-Blaché).

and verbally abuses his wife, who attempts to "live in the American way" by asking him to help her plow the fields. He abuses her until a valiant "American citizen" intervenes. Orloff's "lessons in Americanism," Gwendolyn Foster argues, are effectively "lessons in whiteness" from earlier generations of European immigrants—"Irish American," "German or Amish, perhaps even Quaker" (2003: 54–6). The film conveys how whiteness becomes white-identified-ness.

Whitening undoes the infantilization and animalization of Orloff as an alien, who arrives wearing a large fur ushanka that matches his unruly hair and beard; his wife, a babushka tied under her chin. Costuming, makeup, and performance style extend familiar conventions for the depiction of "eastern European foreigners with disheveled hair, wild beards, and bulging eyes that shine with madness" (Ross 1998: 65), which reappear decades later in Universal's vampire films to convey the assumed backwardness of eastern Europe and degeneration of miscegenation between whites as Orthodox and Jewish races. Orloff's "Russian friends" are coded as "animal-like," visualized in their "rags [as clothes] and excessive facial hair," producing "the bestial nature of ethnicity" (Foster 2003: 54). Since they do "nothing to intervene" on his wife's behalf, they appear not-quite-white, thus unable or unwilling to perform the duties of citizenship. Once "completely Americanized," Orloff wears a straw hat, combs his hair, trims his beard, and treats his wife with respect. He may not perfectly resemble the native-born citizens with their neatly pressed suits, smart neckties, bowlers, clean shaven faces, light-colored hair, and gentlemanly demeanors, but he has assimilated. As visual confirmation of Orloff's newfound capacity for citizenship, his costume and makeup change. He resembles the male passer-by, whose dark curly hair is neatly kept, his beard trimmed, and his head covered with a straw hat, suggesting that he might be a recently assimilated immigrant. He seems to communicate with Orloff through spoken language rather than nonlinguistic gestures of silent cinema's so-called pantomime. The Orloffs first live in a tenement flat in a neighborhood with Russian- and Yiddish-language signage; later, they move to the country, where they have a field to cultivate and a statue of the Virgin Mary to look over their dining table. The Christian icon appears Catholic or Protestant, not eastern Orthodox. When the Orloffs pray before their meal, they fold their arms across their bodies.

Making an American Citizen maps citizenship on immigrant bodies in cultural and legal terms. The American citizen of the title is clearly Ivan, not his wife, who would have been considered property by gendered standards of the period. The film replicates notions of an "ideal immigrant," mobilized "to shame and discipline the internal minorities, such as African Americans, Native Americans, and Latinos, and in so doing to shift the culpability from the dominant majority to the subjected class" (Behdad 2005: 13). During the 1910s and 1920s eastern Europeans might be "flattered, tutored, or threatened regarding entry into the 'American race' or invited to become naturalized as a white citizen and vote," yet difficulties remained, including the sting of racial slurs like "Hunky" and restrictions on immigration after 1924 and "persistent invective putting their races among those whose unfitness for citizenship threatened the very racial fiber of the nation" (Roediger 2005: 36). These afterlives of race become nodes for contestation in vampire films.

Immigrants from Sicily faced comparable prejudices. Framed as a feature-length visualization of a novel, *The Italian* (USA 1915; dir. Thomas H. Ince and C. Gardner Sullivan) chronicles poor gondolier Beppo Donnetti (George Beban), who emigrates to New York's ghettos in search of fortune, so he can *re-immigrate* and marry his beloved Annette Ancello (Clara Williams). His arrival in "the land of promise" is represented by a shot of the Statue of Liberty, undercut by a woman shouting insults. Beppo works towards his American Dream by setting up a bootblack stand yet quickly learns a more rapid path to economic independence by accepting a bribe from Big Bill Corrigan (Leo Willis) for securing support of his "wop friends" in an election.

Annette emigrates, and they marry, though not without comedy reminiscent of Edison: an ill-prepared immigrant groom, Beppo, forgets the wedding ring. The happy assimilation tale is interrupted when their child, "little Tony," falls ill as "midsummer grips the slums." Beppo searches for pasteurized milk prescribed by a doctor but is robbed. His plaintive pleas for help are rendered in heavily accented and non-fluent English on the intertitles: "I must get-a-de-milk or my baby is die." He is arrested for begging and threatening passers-by. The too-late temporality of melodrama reaches its most poignant when Annette watches Little Tony die. When Beppo returns, a tearful reunion without "poor little Antonio" is rendered in monumentally slow movement towards an empty crib. A month later, Beppo reads that Corrigan's baby is near death and seeks revenge. He stops, however, when he witnesses the baby repeat a gesture that Little Tony once made. Beppo's internalization of the duties of civil citizenship is visually rendered in a dissolve to an earlier scene of Beppo, Annette, and Little Tony: sorrow melts hate and revenge. Although the film draws upon sensational stereotypes, it sustains myths of national exceptionalism: impoverished immigrants arrive from Europe and flourish in the United States. The unnatural whiteness of America expands to include groups once considered Catholic or Orthodox races. Conventions that racialize eastern and southern European male immigrants, nonetheless, fold into ones for vampires. Despite their aristocratic standing, Count Dracula and Conde Drácula revive aspects of ignorant immigrants like Orloff and Beppo, yet they are also romantic figures, thus offering spaces for critiques of national mythologies.

Romance and Literacy as Alternatives to Unionized Labor

The 1910s and 1920s saw films on immigrant experiences that were financed by private and local governmental funding and exhibited outside the studio-controlled theater system. Comedy and melodrama were modes to convey both assimilation of European immigrant couples and romance between foreign-born men with native-born women. Immigrants can be absorbed via romance when they demonstrate skepticism in organized labor movements and faith in national exceptionalism. Romance assimilates immigrants through private relationships rather than government policy. Despite his progressive (pro-union) politics, Charlie Chaplin's *The Immigrant* (1917) facilitates illusions that European immigrants, whether peasants from eastern Europe or the working-class from industrial Britain, could overcome obstacles against immigrants without the aid of organized labor. The film's hopeful intertitle, "The Arrival in the Land of Liberty," is followed by the iconic long shot of the Statue of Liberty before a medium-long shot of the huddled masses. Vignettes show the regulation of immigrant bodies by officials who inspect, not only paperwork, but physical bodies of recently arrived immigrants. Costumed like the Orloffs in *Making an American Citizen*, the immigrants—women in babushkas, men in heavy beards and ushankas—wait behind security ropes until allowed to disembark. Officials verify their identification numbers. This visualization of eastern European peasants becomes a significant detail in Universal's *Dracula* films. Chaplin's own working-class origins contribute to his character of the Tramp, whose social status carries Victorian conceptions of race into the early twentieth-century United States. The Tramp's bowler and suit, however, mark him as white-upon-arrival and as a native-speaker of English. Citizenship was bound with a notion of "providing for the common defense," initially limited to "free white persons" willing and able to suppress slave rebellions and occupy indigenous lands (Jacobson 1998: 25). Citizenship was also linked to productive labor that was obedient and docile. Aristocratic vampires are misfits according to such criteria. Count Dracula and Conde Drácula might be eager to assimilate, but aristocrats were imagined as intractable to processes of making Americans from foreigners.

Sponsored by the US Steel Corp., *An American in the Making* (USA 1913; cin. Carl L. Gregory) presents the immigration story of Hungarian Béla Tokaji (Harry Benham) as a pretext for positive publicity after a 1911 antitrust suit. The company was notorious for replacing unionized workers with unskilled labor, many of whom were injured or killed in work-related accidents: injury and fatality statistics were twice as high for non-English speakers.[5] The Immigration Act of 1917 required English literacy, institutionalizing prejudices against southern and eastern Europeans comparable to ones preventing free black men from voting after 1870 (Hing 2004: 51). Although Béla is identified as Hungarian in the production company notes, he is sometimes Czech or Italian in exhibitor's notes, demonstrating the fluidity of ethnicity as southern and eastern Europeans worked towards uncontested whiteness. Called "the peasant" in the English-language intertitles, Béla receives passage from his brother, along with a letter shown in hand-written Czech script.[6] His brother is assimilated—an "American already made," though not a ready-made American. He avoids presumed dangers of labor unions and alcoholism. He wears a dark suit and tie, dark long overcoat, and bowler like the men in the previous New York scenes. Unfortunately, Béla is determined "unfitted for skilled work" and given employment as a manual laborer. The Illinois Steel Company Employment Office posts safety regulations in English, Hungarian, Polish, Slovakian, and another eastern European language, signaling targeted immigrant audiences.

Much of the film consists of visual displays of safety hooks and goggles, saws and converters, but it narrates Béla's assimilation via romance. "The pretty teacher," the intertitle informs, "is interested in her star pupil," followed by images of Béla, dressed in a dark, well-fitted suit and long overcoat, sitting in a classroom whose chalkboards contain various sentences—"I live here" and "I am here born"—in English, German, and Hungarian. Six years later, Béla is happily married to his teacher (Ethyle Cook). Their child attends a "model school," and Béla ascends the company ranks. He is skilled in factory safety procedures and in citizenship duties. Unlike *Making an American Citizen*, this film structures assimilation via corporate welfare more than good neighbors. Abel characterizes the film's emphasis on "accident prevention and self development" as rendering assimilation as a pretense for displays of technical and mechanical safety instruction.[7] The film, he concludes, promotes an American Dream of a nuclear family whose welfare is secured by a major corporation rather than social programs, along with complete severance of familial ties to Europe. Béla's parents never reappear in the film, even as addressees in letters. Béla's relationship with his brother is dropped. He performs an americanized masculinity whose independence defers only to US Steel Corp.

More didactically, the State of Connecticut's Department of Americanization's *The Making of an American* (USA 1920; dir. Guy Hedlund) points to ideological work in constructing national identity based on English-language acquisition. The film opens with an intertitle's "appeal to all foreigners to learn English," which also appears in Italian and Hungarian, though the word *foreigners* is not included in the non-English versions. The film ends with another intertitle, appealing to English-literate audiences to urge others to attend instructional courses in English at evening school. The film's narrative establishes Peter "Pete" Bruno (Emile De Verny)'s acquisition of fluency as necessary to secure a "position to which his ability entitled him." Entitlement is constructed upon race and gender, qualified by class and "handicapped" by illiteracy in English. Pete is rejected for a position as an elevator operator and begins manual labor with Italian-speaking immigrants and African Americans.[8] Ultimately, he is injured due to illiteracy in English, falling down an elevator shaft. The choice of location for Pete's accident underscores melodramatic devices of coincidence and human bodies as loci for meaning.

After recovering, Pete sees a sign advertising evening school in the three languages of the film's opening intertitles: "Learn English. Imparate la lingua inglese. Vez sie po Angielsku." Through classes at evening school, implicitly held under the auspices of the factory with resources of the public library, Pete gains access to the privileges of whiteness and citizenship. He forgets the "early days of the tenement" to enjoy "happiness of home life," represented in a cutaway shot of his wife, picking grapes near their freestanding home. A long shot of Pete shaking hands with one of his well-dressed "fellow-citizens" in front of the Connecticut capital building in Hartford establishes Pete's new social position on the safety council. "No longer handicapped by ignorance of the language," an intertitle explains in anticipation of a shot of Pete with a well-trimmed mustache, wearing a suit and tie, at a meeting, "Pete was bearing his share of the work—and honors—of the community." Pete's successful absorption into the Melting Pot leaves little trace of ethnic/racial origins. As with other films, these ones emphasize character development as assimilation, racialization through costuming and performances.[9] Universal's Count Dracula and Conde Drácula would continue to be haunted by afterlives of race through accents and mannerisms. Foreign aristocracy is depicted as frightening—potentially socially destabilizing—like unionized labor to the domestic aristocracy of so-called self-made tycoons.

Romantic Assimilation to Productive Citizenship

In classical Hollywood fantasies of ideal assimilation, immigrants might not be eligible for US presidency, but their children might realize this American Dream. The opening credits of RKO's *Romance in Manhattan* (USA 1935; dir. Stephen Roberts) appear over iconic images of the downtown Manhattan skyline, the Statue of Liberty, and Ellis Island. Even before the film's protagonists—Czech male immigrant Karel Novak (Francis Lederer) and female native citizen Sylvia Dennis (Ginger Rogers)—are introduced, these shots establish both location and point of view. They promote psychological investment in national exceptionalism, roughly corresponding to points of view of passengers aboard arriving ships. The editing of shots of New York followed by shots of cheering immigrants on the ship's deck encourage such a reading. However, the film is less concerned with promoting the American Dream to noncitizens as it is with *renewing* it among US citizens during the Great Depression. In fact, many of the film's scenes serve as vignettes wherein Karel helps Sylvia see Depression-era New York from the optimistic perspective of a newly arrived immigrant. Such scenes are romantically and sexually charged. Where Sylvia sees poverty in the tenement building ("cockroaches, isn't that wonderful"), Karel sees luxury ("carpets"). As they see different realities from the building's roof, where Sylvia has arranged a makeshift bed under the stars for Karel, she recognizes their difference. "The way you say 'America'," she suggests, "you'd think it was heaven." Moments later, she internalizes the film's patriotism, asking her brother Frank (Jimmy Butler) whether he ever stops to think "what a great place New York is."

Opening scenes, however, concern physical and financial examinations determining whether aliens are suitable for immigration. They convey information about legal process and establish narrative conflict—and provide occasion to display Lederer's athletic physique. Centered in the frame, a shirtless Karel smiles as the examining doctor tests his reflexes. Later, he ecstatically enjoys a shower. His excitement upon arrival becomes visualized to facilitate erotic investment among audiences in his successful absorption into nation. A low hanging curtain reveals his wet, muscular torso and his bright smile. More than his rustic clothes, Karel's accent and unfamiliarity with colloquial expressions mark him as a recent arrival. Exploratory romantic banter between Karel and Sylvia stages differences between colloquially spoken English and formal English taught in schools in non-anglophone European countries.

Sylvia's decision to marry a foreigner is not without controversy. Native-born female US citizens lost citizenship upon marriage to alien men according to a 1907 law. Campaigns for women's rights to suffrage and citizenship during the 1920s and 1930s initiated debate on revising citizenship status for women in non-derivative terms (Gardner 2005: 14; c.f. Bosniak 2006). The film's narrative is set when alien men did not receive citizenship through marriage, featuring scenes of legal process and exploitative abuses of legal status by corrupt lawyers and quasi-legal regulation of immigration through private steamship companies. Despite Karel's good intentions and positive attitude, he is initially rejected and deported back to Czechoslovakia because he cannot pay an immigration fee. Elsewhere, the film questions New Deal policies through Sylvia's characterization of the Agricultural Adjustment Act (1933–6). "AAA has been paying you fourteen dollars an acre not to grow anything," she cynically inquires to understand why a farmer would be walking the streets of Manhattan. The film frames individual ingenuity, not collective bargaining, as necessary for rebuilding the nation. Karel obeys the taxi drivers' strike, depleting his personal savings by supporting Sylvia and Frank, but later betrays the union. His actions are motivated by need for money to acquire US citizenship and marry Sylvia.

Karel's ingenuity and goodwill are not what enable him to acquire citizenship. Instead, it is help from earlier waves of immigrants, embodied in Irish American police officer Murphy (J. Farrell MacDonald), that facilitates Karel's transformation from alien into citizen. Murphy and fellow police officers deviate from standard practice. Karel's marriage to Sylvia takes place in the middle of the night, comically interrupted by routine protocols of naturalization, including a vaccination. In addition to whitewashing actual conditions of immigration and naturalization under 1930s national quotas, which marked southern and eastern Europeans as undesirable, *Romance in Manhattan* re-establishes nominative gender roles. It lures female audiences with promises of shared power. Karel's naturalization "corrects" gender roles that were being unsettled by movements for women's suffrage and citizenship.[10] It is hardly surprising that the arrival of Count Dracula and Conde Drácula would seduce women with alternative prospects. Born in Prague under Austria-Hungary, Lederer himself would later play Count Dracula, posing as Bellac Gordal, in *The Return of Dracula*.

A decade later, the MGM's *An American Romance* (USA 1944; dir. King Vidor) revisits sexual politics of assimilation after the New Deal (1933–6). The film combines a narrative of romantic assimilation between an eastern European working-class male immigrant and a native-born white female schoolteacher with extended documentary sequences. A voiceover educates audiences about steel production and automated assembly lines for automobiles and airplanes, much like the voiceover and editing patterns in New Deal documentaries, such as *The River* (USA 1937; dir. Pare Lorentz), *The City* (USA 1939; dir. Ralph Steiner and Willard van Dyke), and *The Land* (USA 1941; dir. Robert Flaherty). At times, efforts to integrate this footage with narrative are less than seamless, such as when the voiceover directly addresses the audience, saying: "It might interest you to know that this ladle contains 1040 tons of molten steel." Beyond subordinating women to the domestic space of home and facilitating faith in industrialization, the film emphasizes the possibility for sons of (European) immigrants to become US president. Steve Dango (Brian Donlevy), whose own name was americanized by mining (not immigration) officials, names his sons after US presidents: George Washington, Thomas Jefferson, Abraham Lincoln, and Theodore "Teddy" Roosevelt, who serves as the film's narrator.

Like *Romance in Manhattan*, the film opens with immigrant passengers arriving in New York Harbor. Under the tune of Samuel Francis Smith's "My Country 'tis of Thee" (1832), ships arrive in a heavy fog, followed by shots of immigrants from northern and eastern Europe until a voiceover explains that "to be admitted to this country, you have to be of sound mind, without a criminal record, and not be a polygamist." Count Dracula's three wives would bar his entry. Unlike Karel in RKO's film, Steve is admitted despite having only twenty-one dollars towards a fee of twenty-five, suggesting postwar sensitivity to would-be immigrants who died under German and Italian fascism. Steve appears much like immigrants in Chaplin's *The Immigrant* with his woolen cap and coat, prominently displayed identification tag, and duffle bag of worldly possessions. He demonstrates his exceptional quality as citizen-in-the-making by walking on foot approximately 2,000 kilometers from urban New York to rural Minnesota, where he works in mines. Like later montage sequences of the operation of machinery and assembly lines, Steve's long walk are captured in high- and low-angle shots that emphasize the monumentality of his individual determination as a solitary figure against enormous landscapes in inclement weather.

At a picnic to celebrate the national holiday (Fourth of July) in Minnesota, Steve receives a series of lessons in assimilation, ranging from trivial (peeling a banana) to pedantic (patriotic US history). He is most taken by the lesson that the son of any immigrant can be president. Reference to the highest elected public office becomes a means of distinguishing the United States as more exceptional than Europe. The film functions as propaganda with a narrative that ends in shots of warplanes manufactured in the California assembly lines of Steve and his son Teddy's plant, under music of "My Country 'tis of Thee," just after Japanese attacks on Pearl Harbor (Hawai'i). As with the corporate- and state-sponsored assimilation films, this one emphasizes literacy in English and knowledge acquisition through schools as gateways to citizenship. Steve's assimilation is achieved through marriage to a native-born woman, Anna O'Rourke (Ann Richards). It emphasizes unionization as an obstacle to innovation and good corporate management. Instead of the Statue of Liberty, it features the Hoover Dam, an iconic moment of the New Deal. Performances of good citizenship by Karel and Steve form a striking contrast with the insufficient performance of whiteness by Universal's Count Dracula and Conde Drácula, who may be seductive to women but are not considered by men as docile and flexible for the *work* of assimilation. They are framed by melodrama.

Melodrama and Miscegenation

Peter Brooks's study on the nineteenth-century European melodramatic imagination informs analyses of Hollywood and German melodramatic cinemas, proving useful in thinking about miscegenation melodramas that inform Universal's vampire films.[11] For Brooks, melodrama serves as a point of transition from sacred to post-sacred order, emphasizing internalization of civil law as moral code over religious dogma. Such movement within melodrama from sacred to post-sacred parallels a movement within social definitions of difference from religious to non-religious terms, that is, from binary distinctions of Christians and non-Christians to so-called scientific explanations of race based upon eugenics alongside a shift in faith from god to nation. Melodrama becomes a mode to convey interracial desire before Hollywood's self-censoring ban under the Production Code (1930–68). Hollywood melodrama reframes social problems as individual problems, deflecting accountability from society and state. It was not until 1967 that the US Supreme Court invalidated local laws banning miscegenation, which vampire films sensationalize.

Known in classical Hollywood parlance as "Latin Lovers" due to their association with the Mediterranean (not Latin America), foreign men and their sexual threat to nation were contained through feminized and queered stereotypes. Melodrama shifts focus from immigrant to nativist. Peaceful Arabs and Buddhist Chinese elicit nativist prejudices among male characters but desires among female ones. Melodrama can reinforce populist messages of patriotism through nativism, emphasizing obstacles to assimilation, where afterlives of race return in fears over foreign nativity and anxieties over miscegenation in the *Dracula* films. Exclusion in Hollywood's miscegenation melodramas was often legitimized by racialization and sexualization of immigrant bodies as nonwhite, extending practices of stereotyping Africans and Filipina/os as "primitive" and stereotyping Mexicans and Native Americans as "savage." Nonwhites are presumed to have failed in transforming wilderness into the productive lands demanded by agrarian capitalism.

Susan Courtney finds that "representations of miscegenation have had a far more integral place in the history of American cinema than we have yet to fully recognize," citing what is likely the earliest interracial kiss on film in *What Happened in the Tunnel* (USA 1903; dir. Edwin S. Porter) (2005: xv, 6). She points out that Biograph and Vitagraph produced so-called switch films, including *The Mis-Directed Kiss* (1904), *A Kiss in the Dark* (1904), *Under the Old Apple Tree* (1907), and *Nellie the Beautiful Housemaid* (1908), which invite audiences to identify with the camera and share in a joke whose humor hinges upon "potential breakdowns in the racial order as deriving from the failure of the white male look to *see* racial difference" (2005: 24–5). Comparably, Carlos Cortés notes that early films offered taboos of interracial romance or sexuality as "screen titillation" that codified nonwhites as "sexual threats" (1991: 23). In *Maid in Morocco* (USA 1925; dir. Charles Lamont), a short produced by Jack White, a Caliph (Wallace Lupito) kidnaps a young bride (Helen Foster), inspiring her groom (Lupino Lane) to impersonate one of the Caliph's many wives to penetrate "the harem," which is decorated with blackamoor figures amidst other orientalist ornamentation. Attempting intimacy with her, the Caliph asks to be called "Caly." She is encouraged to join his wives in dance (i.e., a uniquely white form of hopping to music), as her groom races from woman to woman, lifting veils, draped over their faces. He grabs one woman and runs away, lifting her veil to discover a black woman, and faints.

Miscegenation melodramas often concern how citizens protected property, typically land and women, from noncitizens, including noncitizen nationals (so-called blacks, mulattoes, and Indians).[12] How miscegenation melodramas perform US territorial power is perhaps most directly displayed in films about Native America. Biograph's adaptation of Helen Hunt Jackson's 1884 novel into *Ramona* (USA 1910; dir. D.W. Griffith) was the most expensive film made to date. It averts potential scandals of miscegenation through marriage between Spanish (Mexican in the novel) Ramona (Mary Pickford) and "Indian" Allesandro (Henry B. Walthall in redface) by revealing through an intertitle that Ramona has "Indian blood." As "America's sweetheart," Pickford's star persona safely depoliticizes (and whitewashes) history via racial masquerade of costume drama in the realm of stylized romantic tragedy, diffusing the racial reclassification of Ramona as Indian once she marries Allesandro. White inventions of Native American ancestry consolidated occupations of lands and dispossession of actual indigenous peoples.

As Chon Noreiga observes, racial injustice is subsumed into sexual melodrama by professional distribution and exhibition circuits.[13] The film's gentle critique of Native American and Mexican dispossession by "the Whites" after the Mexican American War/La Intervención Norteamericana (1846–8) does not extend to the state's involvement in intra-white conflicts. Noreiga understands the film as narrativizing the "birth" of landlessness for indigenous nations and Mexican Americans.

Films of the period present different outcomes structured according to assumptions about miscegenation that move from human races to supernatural ones in vampire films. The anti-Asian sentiments in *The Cheat* (USA 1915; dir. Cecil B. DeMille) find association with restrictions on Asian immigration, naturalization, and land ownership under social associations of immigrants with degeneracy and immorality, along with national anxieties that Japanese imperialist ambitions might thwart the United States' own imperial ambitions in Hawai'i and the Philippines (Grieveson 2009: 151). Based on Thomas Burke's "The Chink and the Girl," Griffith's *Broken Blossoms* (1919) stars Richard Barthlemass as Cheng Huan—or, as he is called in Griffith's trademark intertitles, "the Yellow Man." The white actor performs yellowface by squinting and walking pigeon-toed, allegedly reproducing the appearance and movements of Chinese and Chinese Americans whom he observed in Los Angeles's Chinatown where Griffith took him to prepare for the role (Henderson 1972: 203). Griffith supplements postures and gestures in Barthlemass's languid performance with soft focus and diffuse lighting, purportedly rendering his features less European. What is striking is the film's ambivalence about interracial romance between Cheng and the "broken blossom" of the film's title, Lily (Lillian Gish). Lucy's stepfather Battling Burrows (Donald Crisp) becomes the locus of reactionary political opinion concerning racialized immigrants, an individualized representation of nativism that deflects attention from social prejudice and institutionalized racism.

In a series of expository intertitles about Burrows, one stands out: "Above all, Battling hates those not born in the same great country as himself." The film does not sanction or provide sanctuary for interracial romance. Instead, it follows melodramatic conventions that culminate in feelings of stagnation and frustration within a world of fated and preordained order. *Broken Blossom*'s purported message of tolerance is undercut when genuine affection between Cheng and Lucy is punished by death: Lucy is beaten to death; Cheng commits suicide in grief. Interracial sexual exchanges for money (prostitution), however, are stigmatized yet *unpunished*. Prostitution is readily available in the "scarlet house of sin" where various Asian actors in turbans and white actors in brownface socialize freely with sexualized white women. Racialization produced illusions of innate predispositions, evident in a racial bar on Asian naturalization due to one court's determination that "the yellow or bronze racial color is the hallmark of Oriental despotisms" (cited in Haney López 1996: 162). Although Cheng travels to London, a stand-in for the United States, to teach a Buddhist message of tolerance and passivity, *Broken Blossoms* is complicit with the Chinese Exclusion Act, which anticipates the national quotas designed to restrict European immigration.

Rudolf Valentino's exotic and erotic looks were exploited by Hollywood in ambivalently suggestive stories of forbidden desires. A contemporary of Lugosi, who was called "Valentino with rigor-mortis," Valentino's iconic role as the Sheik differs from Lugosi's as Count Dracula in one important way: the Sheik is revealed through the contrivances of the film's melodrama as being western, if not entirely northern, European. *The Sheik* (USA 1921; dir. George Melford) opens with a medium shot of a Muslim call to prayer, followed by a long shot of a group of men who prostrate themselves in the direction of the Ka'aba. Described by the intertitles as a "world of peace," they make a distant land seem familiar by reproducing colonial stereotypes that the "children of Araby dwell in happy ignorance that Civilization has passed them by."[14] The film presents the attraction between Sheik Ahmed Ben Hassan (Valentino) and Lady Diana Mayo (Agnes Ayres) as grounded in love rather than colonial desire. Miriam Hansen argues that the film addresses a female audience (1986: 6). Valentino's Sheik Ahmed is feminized; his agency contained by his "to-be-looked-at-ness" of Laura Mulvey's "visual pleasure." He ultimately seduces a New Woman into a consumer culture that leads to "an underpaid job, loneliness, and social insecurity or, in the case of married women, the multiple burdens of wage labor, housework, and childrearing" (23) rather than into a life of agency, adventure, and romance. Diana's fate is like Sylvia's in *Romance in Manhattan*. *The Sheik* is concerned with reinforcing racial hierarchies, not disrupting gendered ones. Valentino's Sheik is feminized as "Theda Bara in trousers" (Boone 2014: 414), a reference to Theodosia Goodman's screen name, rumored to have been an anagram for "Arab death." Whatever queer erotic charge can be found in the sexual attraction between feminized man and masculinized New Women is quickly constrained by hetero-normative and heterosexist assumptions about both gender and sexuality at the service of preventing miscegenation. Lady Diana remarks that Sheik Ahmed's "hand is so large for an Arab." The eroticization of Valentino's hand serves as a clumsy narrative means to reveal that the large hand that Lady Diana desires is appropriately European.[15] A review of the film in the *New York Times* revealed the plot twist to assure audiences that the romantic liaison was not as "offensive" as it might appear.

As Dick Stromgren observes, "screenwriters had learned early in the game that it was possible to have it both ways—that is, providing the titillation of interracial sex while not violating the taboo against it by a simple matter of twisting the plot" with devices such as mistaken identities (1990: 63). Valentino

Figure 2.2   Rudolf Valentino carries away a docile white female body. *The Sheik* (USA 1921; dir. George Melford).

provides a particular type of racially charged titillation, comparable to that of Lugosi. "Like most star vehicles," Hansen argues, "Valentino films have notoriously weak narratives and would probably fail to engage any viewer if it weren't for their hero's charisma" (1986: 17). Valentino's Sheik is like Lugosi's Count Dracula. Hansen describes Valentino's characters as bearing the "stigma of the first-generation, non-Anglo-Saxon immigrant," developing from "seducer/villain of dark complexion, male counterpart of the figure of the vamp" into the "persona of the Latin Lover, marketed as a blend of sexual vitality and romantic courtship" (24). Valentino's leering gaze upon Diana asserts his masculinity, not altogether different from Count Dracula's mesmerizing gaze upon Mina and Lucy—and perhaps even Renfield, though such scenes were not filmed. In *The Sheik*, romantic courtship is ultimately ensured when Sheik Ahmed's *blood* (English father and Spanish mother) is weighed as more truthful than *association* (as a "tribal chieftain," according to the intertitles, to Arab Muslims) with the added proviso that he was "educated in Paris." This narrative device of restored identities anticipates ways that Hollywood's vampires would become gradually more white-upon-arrival and ultimately more American—their blood and accents less alien.

Locating Borders on the Body

It is commonplace to ridicule the geographical, historical, and cultural inaccuracies of Hollywood productions, but they reveal business acumen along with long-end effects of isolationism and budgetary constraints. Recognizing the importance of overseas markets, Hollywood studio heads and producers learned that ambiguous locations and ambiguous national identities reduced the incidence of complaints from foreign governments about negative stereotypes, thus reducing the risk of US government intervention into the industry. Hollywood became transnationally oriented to remain internationally profitable. The swapping of the villain's identity from Japanese to Burmese by replacing intertitles in *The Cheat* suggests Hollywood's disinterest in cultural verisimilitude. "'Foreignness' became less clearly associated with particular ethnic and national groups and became abstracted into an amorphous category of aliens, so that specific interest groups could find fewer grounds for complaint," writes Ruth Vasey about 1930s Hollywood production; "Even geography became less distinct, with 'mythical kingdoms' often standing in for exotic locations in Latin America, Africa, Europe, and the Far East [*sic*], so that the film commerce abroad would not be affected by the casual insult of national stereotyping" (1997: 101). If Hollywood was largely unconcerned with *historical* verisimilitude in its lavish representations and narratives of faraway lands and peoples, then it might have been more concerned with *cultural* verisimilitude in its often self-conscious performances of these people and places. In other words, if the films do not seem to accurately represent or narrate someplace outside the United States, then perhaps the films' representations and narratives might be masquerades, that is, *performances* of America—its *unnatural* whiteness—that adopt sensationalist modes (comedy, romance, melodrama) rather than realist ones.

Unlike the immigrants in these segregation comedies and assimilation romances, neither Count Dracula nor Conde Drácula sees the Statue of Liberty, as subsequent vampires will. At the level of coherent narrative, the vampires immigrate to London, not to New York. At the level of theme and affect, however, they do not see the Statue of Liberty because they are not entitled to the Statue's welcome. Universal's vampire films suggests that aristocratic immigrants from eastern and southern Europe are unfit for the responsibilities of citizenship. They assert the mythical *possibility* for inclusion of immigrants while maintaining the conditionality for americanization and whitening for certain groups. The male immigrant-vampire's desire for, and desirability to, a native-born woman, unfolds according to cinematic codes and conventions for interracial desire, often hinting at homoerotics, within landscapes of assimilation.

Notes

1. The ethnocentric exclusion of Zangwell's melting pot is also associated in his expression "a land without a people for a people without a land," which became a slogan for Zionist movements that denied the existence of Palestinians (Shohat 2010: 47).
2. Sanders (1991)'s title includes armadillos without discussing them.
3. S.S., "Emigrants Landing at Ellis Island (1903)," program notes on *Treasures III: Social Issues in American Film, 1900–1934* (Washington, DC: National Film Preservation Foundation, 2007: 119).
4. Thomas A. Edison, Inc., description for *Move On* (1903), "American Memory Collection" of the Library of Congress' Motion Picture and Television Reading Room.
5. S.S., "An American in the Making (1913)," program notes on *Treasures III*: 123.
6. The intertitle includes: "Ya poslaram peñize dej pozor a prt knet. Tury brater."
7. Richard Abel, audio commentary on *Treasures III*, disc 4.
8. See Roediger (2005) on how European immigrants achieved whiteness at the expense of African Americans.
9. Other films include *The Immigrant* (1915; dir. George Melford), *The Melting Pot* (1915; dir. Oliver D. Bailey and James Vincent), and *The Bravest Way* (1918; dir. George Melford).
10. Despite her chutzpah, Sylvia relinquishes agency. After she loses her job as a chorus dancer, Karel becomes "man of the family."
11. Before Brooks, Elsaesser (1972) examined Hollywood melodrama.
12. Hollywood featured "interracial" desire according to racial hierarchies with "Latinos requiring the most careful international differentiation," since some passed as white ("Spanish") and "Asians, Indians, and Arabs enjoying some flexibility, and African-Americans becoming the least likely to cross the interracial barriers" (Cortés 1991: 25).
13. Chon Noriega, commentary on *Treasures III*, disc 4.
14. Its sequel, *Son of the Sheik* (1924), establishes Arabs as criminals.
15. Large European hands recall racial-sexual panic in Sir Richard Burton's annotations to *The 1001 Nights*.

3. CLASSICAL HOLLYWOOD VAMPIRES: THE UNNATURAL WHITENESS OF AMERICA

Universal Pictures' *All Quiet on the Western Front* (USA 1930; dir. Lewis Milestone) won an Oscar for Best Picture but cost four times as much and required twice as long to produce as *Dracula* (USA 1931; dir. Tod Browning), prompting the studio to redefine itself as a producer of monster movies (Schatz 1996: 82–97). In classical Hollywood, genre conventions were informed by financial and marketing decisions (Altman 1999: 15–16). Studio head Carl Laemmle Jr. envisioned *Dracula* and its Spanish-language counterpart *Drácula* (USA 1931; dir. George Melford) as launching a series of monster movies but was concerned about censorship under the new Production Code. A consequence of primacy of business decisions is our critical habit of thinking about classical Hollywood vampire films primarily according to genre. The English- and Spanish-language versions of *Dracula* establish cinematic conventions and audience expectations for vampires, not as monsters but as immigrants with foreign accents, antiquated customs, and dangerous seductiveness. The films drew upon segregation comedies, assimilation romances, and miscegenation melodramas, discussed in the previous chapter. Genre was actually as fluid as the shape-shifting figure of the vampire. On loan from MGM, director Tod Browning wanted to minimize associations with horror. Billed as "The Strangest Love Story Ever Told," *Dracula*'s scenes of vampires' elongated fangs penetrating male and female necks, of vampire hunters driving wooden stakes through vampires' hearts, and even of the vampire's full body emerging from his coffin in the English-language version were suggested but not visualized. Publicity photos were more suggestive of the vampire's fangs penetrating a female neck than scenes in the films. *Dracula* opened on 12 February 1931 at New York's Roxy Theatre with a pre-screening fanfare that included the high-kicking Roxyettes. The choice to première on a Thursday, rather than a Friday, allegedly avoided inauspicious associations with Friday the 13th. Promoted as *mystery* rather than horror, the film's release close to Valentine's Day invited associations with passion and romance. Count Dracula carried the limp bodies of his female victims into his crypt, reproducing images of Valentino's Sheik Ahmed carrying the limp body of his female conquest into his tent.

This chapter argues that classical Hollywood vampire films served as a means for different audiences to negotiate sweeping social changes that expanded the definition of whiteness—and thus citizenship—while contracting eligibility for immigration and naturalization. Richard Maltby identifies a causal link between the US government's recognition of the role of Hollywood films in attracting immigrants—a legacy of pre-Hollywood immigrant-recruitment films—and the necessity to put limitations on immigration as early as 1926, so that Hollywood films could continue to be exported *safely* (2004: 1). On screen, vampires often elicited violent nativist responses that foreclosed questions about eligibility for naturalization. Hungarian-born Lugosi's performance of Count Dracula departs from early cinema's stereotypes of Hungarians immigrants as Hunkies, a racist equivalent to Greasers for Mexicans. He functions like Latin Lovers in miscegenation melodramas, such as *The Cheat* and *The Sheik*, something more overt in Spanish-born Villarías's performance of Conde Drácula in *Drácula*. Although ethnic-white masculinity becomes less brutish than Orloff in *Making an American Citizen*, the eastern European vampire's white-but-not-quite-white-ness reworks melodrama's tropes of feminization used to represent Arabs, East Asians, South Asians, Southeast Asians, and Native Americans. Although the story of these films is set in London, English is often spoken in US accents and Spanish is almost entirely spoken in a variety of Latin American accents, so that on-screen London functions audibly as a stand-in for Los Angeles, New York, Chicago, or Miami. With the advent of synchronized sound in the late 1920s, difference becomes audible in foreign-accented English.

Classical Hollywood vampire stories convey both pro- and anti-immigration sentiments about groups not considered white-upon-arrival in the 1920s and 1930s, particularly Hungarians, Russians, and Ashkenazi Jews. They avoid representation of racial segregation of nonwhite groups, particularly African Americans, Chinese Americans, and Native Americans. The films served as spaces where audiences witnessed sensationalized stories involving blood, bodies, and borders that were emotionally suggestive of shifting social and legal definitions of whiteness. For socially conservative audiences, the "mark of the vampire" served as uncontestable evidence of betrayal and contamination. Vampirism was equivalent to treason, not only against nation but also against race, so that mixing of blood becomes "a fate worse than death" in the language of Westerns. Hollywood's "strangest love story" negotiates anxieties over race in the US context of the 1930s. Count Dracula elicits panic in white men due to an absence of his clearly defined difference between humans and vampires. He does not have hairy palms or a moustache; his touch does not sting with the chill of a corpse, nor does his breath smell of decomposing flesh, as in Stoker's novel. Anxieties over miscegenation demanded, not only that foreign vampire be "destroyed"—a euphemism for murdered—by native-born men, but also that any woman who had been "bitten" by the vampire—a euphemism for sexual intercourse—also be "destroyed." According to the quotidian racisms and sexisms of the 1920s and 1930s, the vampire's female victim/lover might become pregnant with a so-called mixed-blood child, thereby passing along the stigma of foreignness to future generations.

At the same time, other audiences looked to the films to open thinking about the brutality and violence of nativism, racism, sexism, and homophobia. Vampire films convey the feelings *of* marginalized and stigmatized groups. Citizenship and territory mapped onto bodies when they moved across geopolitical borders or when they were made to feel unwelcome within these borders. Rhonda Berenstein (1996) and Harry Benshoff (1997) argue that classical Hollywood monsters provided spaces where subsequent generations of (white) female and (white) queer audiences could project fantasies of inclusion and agency. As monsters, vampires express social rejection and fears of being seen as abnormal, unattractive—like alien or raced bodies. The films can be understood, as both representations and contestations of xenophobia—both antirealist fantasies about the supernatural or as realist negotiations about social perceptions of immigrants and other marginalized groups—that could not be expressed explicitly under the censorship of the Production Code Administration (PCA). Examined as a group, classical Hollywood's vampire films trace social negotiations over racial tensions and anti-immigrant sentiments that often could not be rendered in realist modes, any more than mixed-race or same-sex relationships, until the Production Code's end in the 1960s.

This chapter considers ways that classical Hollywood vampires emerge within conventions for representations of whiteness that negotiate ever-shifting social tensions. Hollywood's vampire films mark the transition in the United States from the recruitment of immigrants needed to "settle" the frontiers to the regulation of borders formalized in 1924 by three institutions: the Johnson-Reed Act, which established national quotas on immigration based on the 1790 census; the Border Patrol, which inspected documents at entry points along the borders with Canada and México; and the Indian Citizenship Act, which effectively annexed the land where the Five Civilized Tribes (Cherokee, Chickasaw, Choctaw, Creek, Seminole) had been relocated under earlier policy. Classical Hollywood vampire films emerge at the intersections of social and legal assumptions about "making" Americans from foreigners that extends assumptions at work in the films discussed in the preceding chapter. Vampirism becomes both an afterlife of race and a promise of democratization. Historically, political representation is contingent upon definitions of race, even as these definitions themselves shift from appearance to association, from blood quantum to nativity/nationality. Racialization contaminates class, sex and gender, religion, sexuality, and even politics. The "mark of the vampire" interrupts this progressive narrative of emerging diversity, inclusion, and equity. Vampire films also interrupt Hollywood conventions of depicting the unnatural whiteness of America.

Hollywood's Unnaturally White Stars

Audiences flocked to classical Hollywood films to see its stars. Larger-than-life figures, they also appeared whiter-than-life. No stars were whiter than female victims, extending a convention from D. W. Griffith's *The Birth of a Nation* (1915), which positioned the white-female body of Elise Stoneman (Lillian Gish) as a stand-in for the figure of America, allegedly threatened with sexualized occupation by the "mulatto" Silas Lynch (George Siegmann). While African American audiences protested the film's incendiary racism, others understood its representation of white-female discomfort—Elise frets in circles before throwing herself over a cliff—to legitimize violence against black men. Classical Hollywood vampire films unsettle white privilege by making vampires white. Stars of *Dracula* and *Drácula*, Lugosi and Villarías, are unquestionably white today yet were not necessarily read as such at the time. Postwar films erased the afterlives of race for eastern and southern Europeans by featuring actors of northern European ancestry, including Gloria Holden and Lon Chaney Jr. Such conventions extend beyond the classical era. Films featuring A-list stars as vampires typically question whiteness; ones focusing on vampire hunters with non-stars in the role of vampires are more complicit.

In general, Hollywood facilitates the role of whiteness in concealing white privilege. As bell hooks argues, "talk about white supremacy in our society is deemed not only taboo but also irrelevant" (2013: 5). White liberal anti-racism produces what Shannon Sullivan calls "good white people," who use middle-class white privilege to distance themselves from racism by "deflect[ing] responsibility for and complicity with white domination" onto "white trash" and slaveholders; "distancing themselves by race altogether" in color blindness, thus "not seeing race but seeing 'just people' instead"; or "cultivating emotions of white guilt, shame, and betrayal" (2014: 16). Such strategies are counterproductive, along with proposals to "recover ethnic difference within whiteness," which "evade" whiteness rather than *transform* it (2014: 17).[1] Equally destructive are strategies that minimize difference, including the notorious "All Lives Matter" backlash against the Black Lives Matter movement. Academic studies on Hollywood critique whiteness as a structuring principle for Hollywood (Bernardi 1996, 2001, 2007; Benshoff and Griffin 2004). They draw upon work in other fields. Matthew Jacobson points out that "becoming American" has historically been synonymous with "becoming Caucasian" (1998: 13). As embodiments and performances of white privilege, Hollywood stars needed to be produced as white. Vampire films provide a means to take notice of this process.

Murnau's *Nosferatu* serves as a measure by which to gauge the vampire's relationship with whiteness against markers of humanness. Max Schreck's makeup and prosthetics emphasize animalized characteristics—rat-like incisors as fangs, hawk-like talons as fingernails—in his performance of Graf Orlok. Identified with German Expressionism's stylized set and costumes design, graphic editing devices, and performance, the film also draws heavily upon realism via on-location shooting. Murnau incorporates natural explanations—hyenas, Venus flytraps, carnivorous polyps, spiders, plagues—to support the possibility of supernatural phenomenon. In his surrealist-inflected science film *Le Vampire/The Vampire* (1945), Jean Painlevé stages the bloodletting of a guinea pig by an actual vampire bat, intercut with other vampire-like phenomena, including a brief clip from *Nosferatu,* which combines competing ideas about race and science through nonhuman and supernatural devices.

Among the scenes typically discussed for cinematic inventiveness are the fast-motion images of Graf Orlok loading a wagon with fifty "earth-boxes" of his native soil before he immigrates to another land. According to the film's logic, only the self-sacrifice of a "pure heart" can save the village from vampirism, and this pure heart is located inside Mina, renamed Ellen and Nina (Greta Schröder) in different prints. A play of light and shadow visualizes the vampire's presence in animated shadows that creep along the wall up the stairwell to Ellen's room, where they grip her heart. Masking and framing destabilize standard aspect ratio for dramatic effect, such as an elongated rectangle for Hutter (Gustav von Wangenheim)'s leap from the Castle. Shadows abound. Identities cannot be clearly perceived. Like the visual and physical instability of vampires, the film's use of light and shadow seems phantom-like. "To keep German property 'pure'—free of vampires—[Ellen/Nina] must allow her body to become impure," argues Ken Gelder, so that "killing the vampire becomes her responsibility alone—but also, by implication, a civic duty" (1994: 86, 97). If women are conventionally property, then Ellen/Nina protects her own body, though it is symbolically her husband's territory. Critics remark on her masculine-looking appearance and behavior. They also remark upon *Nosferatu*'s stylized representation of the vampire that is a visual culture of anti-Semitic images. Like Roma, Jews were envisioned as itinerant, living from lands that they did not own. Germans sought to differentiate themselves from so-called Asiatic Jewish and Slavic races. Unlike ethnocentric conceptions of German nationality until the late twentieth century, conceptions of US nationality are less clearly defined by purity. Even the Melting Pot acknowledged impurity as inherent to the settler colony's nationality. Universal's humanized vampires draw upon the convention of "making" Americans from foreign immigrants. The vampire's unnaturalized whiteness is both an unstable and destabilizing whiteness and an ungovernable non-whiteness.

Studies on whiteness and racial formation (e.g., Horsman 1981; Crenshaw 1991; McIntosh [1992] 2012; Frankenberg 1993; Harris 1993; Olmi and Winant 1994; Hanley López 1996; Malik 1996; Jacobson 1998; Nobles 2000; Alba and Nee 2003; Allen [1994] 2012a and [1997] 2012b; etc.) provide frameworks on screen constructions of whiteness that produce and reproduce the illusory stability that race is a biological or divine fact and that white privilege is part of the natural order of things and not a form of racism. Richard Dyer suggests that whiteness's power lies in its unacknowledged privilege of speaking for "the commonality of humanity," something that "raced people can't do" since "they [presumably] can only speak for their race" (1997: 2). Daniel Bernardi argues that whiteness "shifts and changes and is replete with contradictions" since "passing as white, at least in the United States, has almost always had something to do with 'acting' or 'looking'—making—white" (2001: xx–xxi). "By studying race as a differentiating mark," argues Eva Cherniavsky, "we learn how this particular difference plays, rather than why the category of difference is the one in play at any given moment" (2006: xiii). Whiteness is not being or becoming white; it is a system of structural advantage. Ruth Frankenberg defines whiteness as "a location of structural privilege" in combination with a "standpoint" of viewing self and other, and "a set of cultural practices that are usually unmarked and unnamed" (1993: 1). Whiteness, as bell hooks argues, is often experienced as "wounds, hurts, tortures" (1992: 169) in the lives of those deemed not possessing it. Whiteness overlaps with being and becoming middle class, heterosexual, capitalist, secular Christian (and/or assimilated Jewish), and able-bodied, so that these vectors of social identity pass themselves as "just American." Films featuring white, middle-class, heterosexual, capitalist, secular Christian (and/or assimilated Jewish), able-bodied protagonists continue to enjoy a privileged status as being "just films"; they are seldom discussed as "white films," "middle-class films," "straight films," "capitalist films," "secular Christian (and/or assimilated Jewish) films," or "able-bodies films." It is perhaps for this reason that countless white actors are able to portray vampires in Hollywood films that do not necessarily foreground the historical instability of the actors' whiteness.

In addition to legal discourses and social conventions, whiteness requires photographic and cinematographic technologies to reproduce itself in actor appearances and performances. Black-and-white film stock facilitates a racial logic predicated on an unnatural combination of chemicals, lighting, and makeup. White actors required special makeup and lighting since they did not appear "white enough," erasing with "gluelike white face paint" and "special lighting" all traces of ethnicity in a practice Gwendolyn Foster calls "whiteface" (2003: 4, 47). Greta Garbo's ethnic features dissolved under this thick substance, low-key lighting, and soft focus. Josef von Sternberg reduced Marlene Dietrich's "broad Slavic nose" with a line of silver makeup and a tiny spotlight, a technique that was used on "other woman stars who had the same 'problem'," including Claudette Colbert, Ginger Rogers, Hedy Lamarr, and Barbara Stanwyck (Dyer 1997: 42–3). Appearing "naturally" white on black-and-white celluloid sometimes also required actors to wear blue makeup under special lighting setups.

Critics often embraced this illusionary whiteness—and, moreover, universalized it. Roland Barthes (1957) celebrates classical Hollywood's creation of "an archetype of the human face," a naked mask, a depersonalized, decontextualized, universalized face. This "face of Garbo" would not exist without the erasure of Garbo's so-called ethnic features under diffuse three-point lighting and a thick layer of white makeup. Barthes's fantasy of a naked mask ignores the "white masks" (Fanon 1952) and "masks of conquest" (Vishwanathan 1990) of colonialism, which have found their way into Hollywood's repertoire of fashioning exceptional nonwhite individuals. Hollywood generally limits the self-destructiveness of internalized racism to the figure of the "tragic mulatta," who dared to pass as white—and was punished by madness or suicide—and rarely considered colonial apologists. Technology itself favored lightness, if not whiteness. Shohat and Stam note that film stocks needed to be "stopped down" or "specially lit" for "darker-complected people" (1994: 186). Since Hollywood looks "to Europe for self-definition and self-understanding," rather than "other multiracial societies in [its] hemisphere" (241), the racial bias is built into technology.

Whiteness has a "special relationship with death," argues Dyer. White people yearn for death according to images of suffering-as-transcendence embodied in a crucified (and invariably whitened) Christ, but white people also bring death to others in acts of colonialism and racism (208). Photography itself has been theorized as an inscription of death upon the subject, so that cinema reanimates the very subject that photography kills (Sontag 1973; Barthes [1980] 1981; Metz 1985). "It is at the heart of the vampire myth," Dyer suggests; "the vampire is dead but also brings death" (210). "Because vampires are dead, they are pale, cadaverous, white," he explains; they evoke "terror of whiteness" as "being without life" and "causing death" (210), not unlike Fanon's description of colonialism as affecting both colonizer and colonized (cf. Kawash 1999). The figure of the vampire reveals ways that whiteness, as a form of death, is simultaneously desired and feared because it reanimates what Hollywood has largely taught us to ignore about whiteness, namely its association with death and bringing about a state of living death for nonwhite and not-yet-white populations.

On classical Hollywood screens, the vampire camouflages itself against the unnatural whiteness of America. European actors Lugosi and Villarías wear heavy makeup to give them a deathly pallor to differentiate them from "natural persons" (i.e., human beings rather than private companies or governmental organizations) who were considered "free white persons of good character" (i.e., eligible for naturalization under the Naturalization Act of 1790). Subsequent Hollywood vampires films, as well as ones produced throughout the world, extend this makeup convention, so that all actors, regardless of race/ethnicity, to some extant display this unnaturalized whiteness. At times, vampire makeup appears more like clownface than whiteface, yet the vampire's unnaturalized whiteness can also become a fetishized whiteness of marble-colored and shimmery vampires in the *Vampire Chronicles* and in *Twilight* novels and films. The films critique racism and nativism even when vampires are expelled or assassinated. The emphasis on Hollywood's human stars who portray most its vampires positions dehumanizing stereotypes as a critique of social codes about entitlements to citizenship.

Accented Arrivals and Deadly Departures

Like other Depression-era films, Universal's *Dracula* distracts audiences from "economic bloodletting of the American public as a result of the breakdown of the economy" and redirecting attention from "concrete social struggle" to "a quasi-mythical battle of good versus evil" (Bronfen 2006: 161). Released in 1931 and 1936, *Dracula* and its sequel *Dracula's Daughter* frame the Great Depression (1932–5) and New Deal (1933–7), when emigration from the United States actually exceeded immigration to it.[2] Nonetheless, public perceptions associated immigrants and organized labor with social and economic problems.[3] Bodies perceived to have crossed international borders seemed alien. The *Dracula* films are theatrical performances of US social assumptions, as much as they are of Stoker's novel. One of the most substantive changes is that Count Dracula is given *direct* dialogue. The vampire speaks, undercutting the nonlinguistic characteristics in *Nosferatu*. Count Dracula's voice is *accented*; his difference and arrival, audible. Hamid Naficy proposes that "if one reads F. W. Murnau's *Nosferatu* (1922) as a tale of exile, with [Count] Dracula as an exilic figure (who carries the earth of his homeland, Transylvania, in his coffin on his mission to England), it becomes more poignant than horrific" since "as an exilic figure, he can rest and find peace only on his home country's soil" (2001: 307 n. 2). His departure is deadly. Vampires speak of poignant immigrant experiences.

Reconfigured from epistolary novel to stage melodrama, *Dracula* and *Drácula* maintain the restructured narrative and character relations of 1920s adaptions of Stoker's novel by Hamilton Deane and John Balderston. "These films are often used to prove the link between horror and the relatively respectable tradition of Gothic literature," writes Mark Jancovich, "but they were, at least initially, produced, mediated, and consumed as the film versions of contemporary theatrical hits" (2002: 3). The plays drew on conventions from legitimate theater, including Aristotelian unities of space, time, and action. They condensed the novel's unruly first-person accounts and third-person newspaper reports, spanning more than seven years and requiring the diligent and painstaking work of Mina to assemble and edit into a comprehensible narrative. They also condense or unify imaginary spaces of Britain and the United States, imaginary times of the 1890s and 1930s, and actions of hunting vampires and regulating immigration.

Adaptation for the screen introduced new meaning. The relative absence of camera movement reflects transition from boxes to blimps around the camera to reduce camera hum on the sound track and experimentation with directional microphones and booms during the 1930s. Although the films accommodated both silent and sound exhibition, dialogue becomes important for content, accent, and intonation. The vampire's physical appearance and age do not alter during the film as in Stoker's novel. Count Dracula appears like a recently arrived immigrant whose fine wrinkles and grey hair do not magically disappear, even under Hollywood's lighting. Adapting the novel involved substituting staged sets and back-lots for actual foreign locations, which is precisely where meaning about everyday social realities is produced. Like costume-dramas whose contemporary hairstyles and expressions disrupt historical verisimilitude, details of set decoration, particularly animals indigenous to southern California but foreign to Europe—armadillos and opossums—disrupt beliefs that the story set in Transylvania and England.

Universal humanizes a literary vampire imbued with powers to transmogrify into vermin, such as rats, bats, and wolves, all of which, like stereotypes for immigrants, carry associations of contamination, degeneration, miscegenation, and, ultimately, unfitness for citizenship. The films avoid direct cuts from actors waving their capes to images of rubber bats. Auerbach describes their vampires as "fangless, solid, and elegantly human," noting that they evoke fear "not of otherness, but eventually, and more subtly, of kinship" (1995: 113). She finds Count Dracula is "overdressed" in "cloak, tuxedo, and medals even indoors," which "whispered of perversity" (77). "Lugosi's Dracula is not only an alien" but "flaunts his alienation as an aesthetic style," she explains; "he owes nothing to his conscientiously conformist Victorian namesake" (113), referring to Stoker's character who carefully studies English customs to assimilate into his adoptive country.

Figure 3.1 Hollywood Gothic's armadillos in the Castle Dracula. *Dracula* (USA 1931; dir. Tod Browning).

Set around the time of national quotas for immigrants from Europe and regulation of borders with Canada and México, Count Dracula's arrival evokes curiosity among women and panic among men. His Star of David-like pendant suggests he might be a Jewish exile or refugee; or a subtle nativist rejection of Ashkenazi Jews into the Melting Pot's new race. Given dramatically reduced national quotas for eastern Europeans, Count Dracula would be one of very few immigrants from Austria-Hungary. The 1929 quota, for example, was less than 2 per cent of prewar immigration (Roediger 2005: 147). Count Dracula is a privileged immigrant. In Cynthia Erb's estimation, he is "a well-dressed count, exhibiting the charm and sex appeal of Erich von Stroheim's decadent aristocrats" (2007: 52–3). She reads the vampire as playing into "lingering anxiety about Eastern Europe as a breeding ground for communism and socialism," citing the speech about the "red mist" of Count Dracula's power by his first victim, Renfield, as evidence for fears of the "red menace" (55). The vampire's uneasy position frames questions about inclusion and exclusion, which, since unstable, raise questions about race and nation.

In Stoker's novel, Count Dracula is chased from London and executed in Transylvania; in the film, he is executed in London itself. The change restricts the vampire's movement and mobility, thus adjusting the narrative's meaning. Despite his financial independence and cosmopolitan savvy, Count Dracula is not free to settle wherever he purchases property. The desacrilized and abandoned Carfax Abbey evokes ethnically segregated neighborhoods, whether Chinatowns or Jewish ghettos. Count Dracula is bound to another country; however, he is bound in a very peculiar way. He must rest in his "earth box," a coffin filled with the blood-soaked soil of his native land, an isomorphic binding of culture and territory, suggesting ties to foreign lands cannot be broken. Vampire hunters suspect that he cannot blend into the Melting Pot's new race. By situating *Dracula* within the context of miscegenation melodramas, particularly ones like *The Cheat* involving interracial desire between feminized Asian men and sexually agentive white women, classical Hollywood's vampires extend Asiatic associations that Stoker gives to Count Dracula, particularly his relationship with Székelys, who descended from that Asiatic invader Attila the Hun (34). Count Dracula himself is the progeny of mixed blood, suggesting afterlives of race resurface when bodies cross borders. Hungarians, particularly Jews, were conflated with the barred Asiatic races in the United States throughout the 1920s.

Dracula is remarkably quiet, with sparse use of ambient sounds and absence of nondiegetic score apart from the opening-credit sequence. Robert Spadoni finds it emphasizes a "voluminous empty soundscape" in which Lugosi's voice performs what critics described as a "mellifluously thick Hungarian accent," a "liquid, if sepulchral, voice," "stately, slightly overripe readings," "succulently foreign intonations," and "bizarre textures and halting rhythms" (2007: 78–9, 63). Count Dracula is distinguished from the only other foreign character, Professor van Helsing (Edward Van Sloan), who is less formal in dress and less assertive in manner. He speaks in what Spadoni describes as "an enunciative richness and a compelling tone that rivals the doom gravity of [Count] Dracula's words" (64–5). Count Dracula's pauses between words—silences in his communication, suspended meaning of his expression—convey fascination and discomfort with a new culture. Details are important because the Immigration Act of 1924 responded, in part, to nativist fears that literacy tests were insufficient for preventing undesirable immigration. The Act returned to data from the Naturalization Act of 1790 for the desirable mix of European nationalities, favoring northern Europeans over eastern and southern ones. To construct an "American" nationality, the Act provided 51,227 slots for Germans and 34,007 for Britons. Professor van Helsing would have competed for one of 1,648 for Dutch; Count Dracula, for one of only 473 slots for Hungarians. If Professor van Helsing were Swedish—his surname is derived from Hällsing, meaning "from the Swedish province of Hälsingland," then he would compete for one of 9,561 slots. More than merely setting into motion a contrast between Professor van Helsing as an embodiment of rational thought against Count Dracula as one of irrational action, accented voices establish racial/ethnic and national hierarchies institutionalized in immigration regulations that are simultaneously naturalized and contested in classical Hollywood. As in vampire plays, the accented characters have a moment of mutual recognition as fellow aliens. Professor van Helsing is an educated Protestant, thus less threatening than Count Dracula, who appears less old and more virile. No one suspects that Professor van Helsing might rape or seduce his daughter or fiancée.

The mythical Melting Pot may have aspired to concoct a new race, but it was not open to all varieties of "old" races. The unnatural whiteness of America is based on selective and incremental inclusion. The unsettling quality of Lugosi's and Villarías's performances gives the figure of the vampire its early cinematic character. Although Lugosi complained about being typecast as Count Dracula, he portrayed a range of other roles in Hollywood, including the Fu Manchu-like Dr. Fu Wong in *The Mysterious Mr. Wong* (USA 1934; dir. William Nigh) and the turbaned Prince Saliano in *You'll Find Out* (USA 1940; dir. David Butler). Charles Musser points out that the star system after 1908 encouraged audiences to appreciate actors capable of playing a wide range of roles, including ethnically diverse ones (1991: 54–5). Nationalities were traded and exchanged as easily as ethnicities in Hollywood.[4] Elsewhere in the United States, patriotism often transitioned into nationalism, xenophobia, and racism with so-called hundred-percenters doubting the patriotism of so-called hyphenated Americans, including German Americans, in Theodore Roosevelt's terms, who were stigmatized with perceptions of committing crimes of treason or miscegenation.

In classical Hollywood, accents define not only immigrants but also classes of immigrants. Geoffrey Nowell-Smith traces a relationship between "national stereotypes and the status of immigrant groups in the United States," whereby "characters in some way coded as 'British' or 'French' are almost always aristocratic or quasi, and often cross-coded to dandyism, effeminacy" (1998: 139). "Since the English and the French are not identified as belonging to the poor, the huddled masses," he explains; "the stereotype of the English or French man follows suit." His analysis does not encompass all racial/ethnic or national stereotypes in supporting cast in Universal's vampire films. The British-accented white servants, for example, fall within the parameters of the "proletariat earthiness" that he observes in national stereotypes for Irish, German, and Italian characters. He defines Hollywood's "strong tendency to relate national stereotypes to the stereotype of the immigrant." As an aristocrat who is neither English nor French, Count Dracula upsets this system. For some audiences, Lugosi's performance carries associations of eastern Europeans with primitivism, feudalism, infantilism, and animalism, like Orloff in *Making an American Citizen*. For other audiences, Count Dracula's illicit foreignness suggested ways to counter the heteronormative, capitalist, patriarchy. Lugosi's performance of Count Dracula embodies social tensions and indecisions about whiteness.

Scarred Bodies, Scared Nations

The "mark of the vampire"—impressions of fangs on the neck—extend earlier scarring marks on female bodies. Much like cowboy vigilantes in Westerns took it upon themselves to murder women allegedly held captive by Native Americans, considering such associations, especially if consensual, as a "fate worse than death," male vampire hunters often seem all too eager to murder women who have been "marked" by vampires. Westerns reinforce prohibitions of interracial/interethnic mixing yet de-emphasize racial/ethnic difference among European immigrants and native-born citizens, contributing to the nation-building project that dissolved intrawhite difference into a single US nationality. Bazin equates Westerns with courtly romances. Cowboys become his noble "white Christians," who are "truly the conqueror of the new world" since the "Indian, who lived in this world, was incapable of imposing man's order" (145). Vampire hunters are fellow "white Christians," who brandish crucifixes and holy water against vampires with the same quest-inspired rage that knights-errant mobilized against infidels and monsters in courtly romances. Vampire films unsettle this project. The mesmerizing power of Count Dracula over Lucy and Mina challenges the logic of captivity narratives in Westerns. Audiences interpret women as giving themselves freely and willingly to the vampire.

Westerns evoke colonial adventure; vampire films, postcolonial realities of when the empire (i.e., former colonial subjects) "returns" to the métropole. Count Dracula's strange and aristocratic passion for ruins and cemeteries suggests aristocratic proclivities deemed unproductive in the Progressive era of industrial capitalism. Most Hollywood vampires are male; their victims, female. Female vampires often function as vamps, whose terror is usually limited to the wellbeing and independence of a specific human rather than the wellbeing and independence of an entire nation. Male vampires compete with cowboys and vampire hunters over the so-called frontier of female bodies. Female bodies also function as a form of property, along with land, livestock, and slaves. In Westerns, the cowboy's anxieties that his cattle might be stolen require him to brand them with the mark of a ranch's ownership. In both Westerns and vampire films, male anxieties that white women might be seduced or raped suggest displaced social anxieties about losing control of land, whether ownership or cultivation. The female body appears as an embodiment of nation, a living extension of sovereign territory (Shohat and Stam 1994).

Mina Steward (Helen Chandler) and Lucy Weston (Frances Dade) are punished for their associations with the wealthy count, who effortlessly lures them away from middle-class feminine domestication. They desire to escape the diminished legal and social status imposed upon them, even at the cost of citizenship. Prior to the film's release in 1931, white women with US citizenship risked losing it by marrying foreigners who were racially ineligible for citizenship. Such marriages were "akin to treason," without the right to a trial, and justified the revocation of birthright citizenship (Haney López 1996: 15, 47; Gardner 2005: 14). Although the law was overturned in 1922, roughly around the time of the film's story, social stigmas lingered. Citizenship was derivative for women. Marriage to male citizens domesticated, civilized, and whitened alien women (Gardner 2005: 15), but the inverse was not true. Women marrying men eligible for US citizenship were legally reclassified from *native* citizen to *naturalized* citizen. If women married men ineligible for US citizenship, they were reclassified as *aliens* until the 1930s. What the vampire drains from female bodies is not blood but access to the rights of citizenship. Nativists accuse Count Dracula of leaving white women, not only drained of blood but, to cite Fanon, "drained of life and of self" (Kawash 1999: 249–50).

Enfranchised political citizens since 1920, white women were hardly equal to white men during the 1930s. Lucy and Mina are economically privileged versions of the unnamed working-class maid (Moon Carroll), who follows orders by male characters and serves as comedic foil to butler Martin (Charles K. Gerrard), who questions whether she is mentally sound.[5] *Dracula* evokes a tradition of sensationalized "white slave traffic" novels and films. The best-selling novel in 1910, Reginald Wright Kauffmann's *The House of Bondage*, involves the seduction of a high-school student from rural Pennsylvania by a Hungarian immigrant, who takes her to a nickelodeon before bringing her to lower Manhattan where she is drugged and awakens naked to an eventual life of prostitution (Simmon 2009: 32). Illicit associations of vampirism with sexual activity and sexually transmitted diseases also carry associations of forced prostitution and dependency. Count Dracula poses a threat to a patriarchal social order that restricts the full rights and duties of citizenship to white men.

As with Latin Lovers, Count Dracula's implicit threat to nation is visualized as scars upon the bodies of New Women who dared to challenge patriarchy. The twin incisions on his victims' necks function much like the marks branded with a hot iron upon the body of Edith Hardy by Haka Arakau/Hishuru Tori in *The Cheat*.[6] If the mark of a branding iron stands in the place of visual representation of rape, then the mark of a vampire might stand for acts

VAMPIRES, RACE, AND TRANSNATIONAL HOLLYWOODS

Figure 3.2   The terrifying mark of interracial romance on the female white body. *The Cheat* (USA 1915; dir. Cecil B. DeMille).

considered more frightening from the standpoint of defining and criminalizing miscegenation, that is, consensual sex. Both the branding of Edith and the puncture marks on the necks of Mina and Lucy are marks of ownership, drawing upon associations of women's legal identities as subsumed under the identities of their husbands upon marriage until the Cable Act of 1922. Feminist scholarship reads the "mark of the vampire" as potentially liberating for women: sexual agency in vampirism transcends repressive domesticity and chastity imposed upon women by the social world of male characters (Auerbach 1995: 143).

Count Dracula's desire for and desirability to white women establishes a structure of relationships like that of Arab and Asian "Latin Lovers," evoking fears of mental and moral degeneration, and potentially compromised legal standing. Not only is Count Dracula perceived to pursue multiple women in London, but he is also believed to have three wives in Transylvania. He violates the monogamy required for assimilation into the Melting Pot. He carries with him the stigma of "the inferiority of the polygamous Islamic world," as Shohat and Stam note in other films, where men have harems of concubines (1994: 156). Although Lugosi's Count Dracula was considered a Latin Lover,

Figure 3.3 Inspecting the stylized mark of the vampire on the female white body. *Dracula* (USA 1931; dir. Tod Browning).

he was not feminized like Barthlemass's Yellow Man, Hayakawa's Hishuru Tori/Haka Arakau, or Valentino's Sheik. Unlike the soft-focus camerawork that desexualizes Barthlemass's limpid performance of Chinese immigrant masculinity, the red tinting of the black-and-white film stock to hypersexualize Hayakawa's sadistic performance of Japanese-and-later-Burmese immigrant masculinity, and the objectifying close-ups on Valentino's face and unclothed body to bisexualize his foreign masculinity, Lugosi's face is captured in medium close-ups shot in deep focus with two lights shining into his eyes to suggest their mesmeric power. Apart from his accent and dress, Count Dracula does not appear substantially different from his hosts.

The overtly sexist and racist trope of "a fate worse than death" in Westerns offers a new way to understand Count Dracula's provocative statement to Lucy and Mina. "To die, to be *really dead*—that must be glorious," he says; "There are far worse things—awaiting man—than death." If death is not the worst fate that awaits men and women, it might be being enslaved like the living dead. White privilege distinguishes "Americans from Indians, who failed to husband resources and subdue nature, and from Europeans, whose advancement was stunted by an unproductive aristocracy" (Glenn 2002: 59).

Count Dracula fails according to standards of white-heterosexual-capitalist patriarchy, thereby opening the system itself to critique. The supernatural denaturalizes hierarchies in social order. Count Dracula's first English victim/lover is actually male. *Dracula* opens with Renfield's traveling to Transylvania. Upon returning, Renfield is diagnosed insane. He is hysterical in gendered and chauvinist senses of the term. He is unfit for participation in civil society and institutionalized in a sanitarium. He becomes entirely dependent upon Dr. Seward. Dependency upon private institutions suggests potential for dependency on public institutions. His body bears psychological scars, if not physical impressions. His whiteness is diminished through encounters with Count Dracula and his wives. His infantilized, animalized, feminized, and queered condition evokes social fears over destabilized white masculinity, lacking self-governing independence, thus almost indistinguishable from women or slaves.[7] Renfield's undead work of catching flies and spiders is hardly the productive free labor demanded by citizenship. It is neither productive of capital, nor is it reproductive of nation building. He operates within a master-servant relationship with Count Dracula that carries associations with chattel slavery of Africans and African Americans and with indentured servitude of previous generations of English and Scottish immigrants.[8] Frye's performance of the character demands as much of an audience's attention due to its to-be-looked-at-ness as Chandler's performance of a post-bitten and sexually agentive Mina. In the Spanish-language version, Pablo Álvarez Rubio's performance of Renfield is even less restrained.

Although Mina loses certain aspects of self-control and enters into a comparable master-servant relationship, she is a woman, not socially considered a "complete" citizen, even after women's enfranchisement. Renfield's loss of rationality and possible awakening to bisexuality, Mina's loss of virginity and awakening to female agency, and her friend Lucy's loss of life, are rendered in melodramatic modes. Angela Smith finds Lucy's death diminishes the "best blood," according to eugenics, whose business was reproducing this blood to build a nation (2011: 47–8). Count Dracula steals it. Vampirism carries with it associations of non-whiteness and un-reproductivity, that is, "ungovernable emotions, a lack of self-control and self-discipline," to borrow Lee Grieveson's terms in his analysis of ways that the nonwhite characters in *The Birth of a Nation* construct the "centrality of whiteness to appropriate governance" (2009: 147). Renfield appears less white as he becomes queer and unproductive, but *Dracula* is less a statement on universalized gender and sexuality than it is a question about particular calibrations of whiteness with citizenship. Despite the horrors of Count Dracula's transgression of social assumptions, differences in his power over white men and white women are significant. Men appear ill equipped to manage vampirism's releases from social conventions. Renfield is rendered dependent. Women, however, become more agentive. They become potentially independent, which is why Count Dracula and Conde Drácula are frightening to vampire hunters.

Hollywood's "Broken Spanish"

Universal shot concurrent English- and Spanish-language versions of *Dracula* for technical and financial reasons related to dubbing and subtitling, yet the studio released the English-language version in non-English-speaking markets, such as France and Japan, with subtitles. *Drácula* allows us to see transnational orientations of Hollywood that extended into Latin America, particularly México, in ways more substantial than overseas sales offices that dotted the globe since the 1910s. *Drácula* was not merely a dubbed or subtitled interpretation of an English-language original. It was a different version, suggesting that the Spanish-language market was actually privileged over the French and Japanese ones. The film premièred between 11 March and 24 April in Havana, Madrid, México D.F., and New York. Shot each night after the crew wrapped the English-language version, *Drácula* was directed by Spanish-illiterate George Melford, who required the assistance of Enrique Tovar Ávalos as an onset "dialogue coach" to translate dialogue and interpret instructions. As Skal notes, Universal's head of foreign-language films, Paul Kohner, hired his future wife Lupita Tovar to star in a number of films, including *Drácula*, though she spoke virtually no English at the time (159). Himself an immigrant from Bohemia (Austria-Hungary), Kohner was initially head of Universal's European division in Berlin. He immigrated to the United States in 1938 and opened a talent agency, representing immigrant talent, including Maurice Chevalier, Marlene Dietrich, Greta Garbo, and Dolores del Río. *Drácula* is thus entangled in transnational Hollywood's connections with both Europe and Latin America.

The film is perhaps even more revealing in terms of national masquerades performed textually on the surface of the film. For audiences of the English-language version, the polyphony of regional, classed, and national accents did not detract from the film's sensational narrative; for audiences of the Spanish-language version, the cacophony of Argentinean, Chilean, Cuban, Mexican, and peninsular Spanish idioms and accents produced a "linguistic hodge-podge that struck Latin America as ludicrous" (Shohat and Stam 1994: 182). Villarías's accented performance of Conde Drácula is difficult to identify as uniquely *foreign* within the film's auditory depiction of a nation splintered by incongruent Iberian and Latin American accents. Characters with Spanish-language names and English-language surnames—Juan Harker, Lucía Weston, Eva Seward—populate London, anticipating the deliberately ambiguous internationalism in the films that Hammer Films would later produce.

Drácula draws parallels with other Hollywood films about Latin Americans in the United States. 20th Century Fox's *Passport Husband* (USA 1938; dir. James Tinling) positions Latin Americans as unacceptable for naturalization—or even employment of Latin American actors. It draws upon associations of its white stars known for their masquerading performance of dangerous foreigners, such as Joan Woodbury in the role of Conchita Montez. After an animated opening-title sequence in which a woman seduces a man, the film opens in Club Havana. The busboy Henry Cabot (Stuart Erwin) watches as the object of his desire, Conchita, dances seductively for wealthy Tiger Martin (Douglas Fowley). Tiger is later deported when his competitor, Blackie Bennet (Harold Huber), informs police of his illegal activities. The film surpasses *Week-end in Havana* (USA 1941; dir. Walter Lang) by having not one but two "Latin American Lothario" characters. After learning that she is herself about to be deported to the South American country where her father betrayed his people, Conchita agrees to marry Henry to acquire US citizenship. A love triangle emerges as the club's "cigarette girl," Mary Jane Clayton (Pauline Moore), herself loves Henry. The film ends with expulsion of the sexualized foreigner Conchita and the reunion of native-born citizens Henry and Mary Jane.[9] While the female Conchita is expelled, the male Conde Drácula is executed.

Ana López analyzes classical Hollywood productions that feature Latin America or Latin Americans during the Good Neighbor era (1931–47), when Hollywood worked closely with the US State Department's Office of the Coordination of Intra-American Affairs. The cooperation provided films for export that the state considered non-offensive to Latin American audiences, a market recognized as strategically important after European ones were closed by fascism (López 1991: 404–6). *Passport Husband* can be grouped with other Hollywood B-productions, making minimal effort to depart from the pre-Good Neighbor era when Hollywood never tired of producing films featuring "lazy peasants and wily señoritas who inhabited an undifferentiated backward land." Latin Americans are criminals and illegal immigrants, associated with illicit sexuality. Fears of Latinization in *Passport Husbands* and among conservative audiences are parodied in *Drácula*. Before the 1960s, Mexican Americans were subjected to *de facto* segregation by custom in the Southwest that had comparable consequences to *de jure* segregation by law in the South, including restricted housing and employment opportunities, that is, "race—specifically, being White—mattered more than US citizenship in the course of everyday life" (Foley 2012: 59–60). *Drácula* raised questions about Latin Americans and whiteness.

The film is praised for technical complexity in editing and camera movements not present in the English-language version. Skal calls it "a shot by shot scathing critique of the Browning version" and a "simultaneous, alternative rendition of a familiar classic, richly illustrating the interpretive possibilities of a single script" (1990: 160). Universal executives ordered that scenes in the English-language version be "reshot and re-edited in accordance with *Drácula*" (Barrenechea 2009: 231). Since *Drácula* was shot for "export," including Spanish-speaking domestic audiences, it was not subject to the Production Code. It includes more violence, sexuality, and interracial romance to evoke social taboos over mixed bloodlines. Conde Drácula rises from his coffin in three separate scenes, and he bites the necks of women on screen. Renfield (Pablo Álvarez Rubio) cuts himself with a knife, rather than a paperclip. Whether human or vampire, women wear revealing lower necklines. Once bitten, Eva gives an on-screen bite to Juan's neck.

Drácula relies less upon visible difference to encode social hierarchies. Villarías's performance of Conde Drácula is remarkably European and perhaps even closer to white-upon-arrival than Lugosi's Count Dracula. The vampire is less accented than some citizens. His pale white skin and dark hair make him resemble the English solicitor Renfield, performed by another Spaniard. Juan Harker (Barry Norton) is fairer than anyone, including the so-called fairer sex. The blondish hair of the Argentinean actor, who anglicized his name from Alfredo Carlos Birabén, appears closer to a mythical Anglo-American ideal than Mexican actors Carmen Guerrero as Lucía Weston and Lupita Tovar as Eva Seward. The film positions Juan as the greatest potential victim since he departs from Hollywood stereotypes of Latin American machismo. Conde Drácula's ease with the decay of Carfax Abbey excites Lucía's passions and frightens Eva, who prefers a man who is "más normal" (*more normal*). Unlike the use of directional lighting to evoke the vampire's mesmerizing gaze in the English-language version, *Drácula* relies on Villarías's performance. His intense stares and expressions suggest wanting to speak but knowing that he will not be understood. He experiences difficulties assimilating to the film's representation of Los Angeles-as-London. Professor van Helsing shows him that he is aware of Conde Drácula's inability to cast a reflection by holding up cigarette case with a mirror. Conde Drácula steps away, then bashes the cigarette case to pieces with his walking stick before apologizing to Doctor Seward for his puzzling behavior. Professor van Helsing frames executing Conde Drácula as liberating him. He seeks to replace "la vida" (*life*) with "la muerte para siempre" (*everlasting death*).

The film's temporal setting is established more exactly. Professor van Helsing interrogates Renfield, who claims that he graduated from University of Oxford in 1927 and passed the bar in 1928. After his encounters with the wives of Conde Drácula in Transylvania—and perhaps even encounters with Conde Drácula himself—Renfield is declared "loco" (*crazy*) in the still image of the newspaper account of the ship's arrival back in England. As in *Dracula*, he lingers in this state of infantilized, animalized, and feminized madness rather than dying, which is the fate of Conde Drácula's first English victim Lucía, perhaps suggesting the women are entirely unsuitable for self-governance since they deteriorate from life into death without stopping at some in-between state of madness. An alternative reading would suggest that men are at a disadvantage in adapting. Renfield is no longer fit for the responsibilities of citizenship.

Drácula also frames vampirism as a supernatural form of social contamination. Mexicans were no longer considered cheap labor that could be americanized as they had been in the 1920s; instead, they are stigmatized "potential carriers of disease" and "hyperfertile," thus overwhelming the white population: a "brown peril" alongside the "yellow" one of East Asians and Southeast Asians (Molina 2006: 128–36). Such threats would later encourage "white flight" that Hollywood would visualize in science fiction films about space invasions (Avila 2006). Natalia Molina examines racial stereotypes that circulate between nativist magazines like *Grizzly Bear*, mainstream ones like *Saturday Evening Post*, and medical journals like the *American Journal of Public Health*, in which medicalized nativism invented evidence that Mexicans were ill-suited for modernity (135). This so-called evidence functions like other nativist discourses invented evidence that Native Americans and African Americans were allegedly unable to adapt from life on the reservation or plantation to life in the modern city. Medical articles proposed that racialized populations suffered high rates of disease due to their "biological inferiority," thereby legitimizing stricter immigration laws. Although the 1924 national quotas were widely criticized after the second World War for complicity with anti-Semitic racism, the quotas outraged nativists due to perceptions of their alleged imbalance in *not barring* Mexicans, who were considered inferior to southern and eastern Europeans (118). With new control over immigration from southern and eastern Europe, brownness presumably became an uncontrollable threat. Nativist rallies to "keep the spirit of '49 alive" repress the transnational history of US annexation of most of México in 1848 before the recruitment of "forty-niners" (gold seekers) to whiten the population (119). Even without consideration for their alleged Indian blood, Mexicans posed a challenge to US claims upon land. Kohner's decision not to hire a Spanish-speaking director for *Drácula* is hardly surprising. In fact, Molina finds that "health officials never questioned whether their own lack of Spanish-language skills might have hampered their understanding of Mexican culture" (99). Kohner's decision was likely supported by the director's experience with miscegenation melodramas and Westerns, as well as earlier Spanish-language films for Universal, such as *Oriente es Occidente/East Is West* (1930), in which Tovar plays Ming Toy. *Drácula*, however, remained largely unknown to non-hispanophone audiences, particularly anglophone ones, who might not understand how the *peninsular* (Iberian) vampire unsettles racial assumptions based on an Anglo American ideal.

Ethnicity after Assimilation

Dracula's Daughter (USA 1936; dir. Lambert Hillyer) and *Son of Dracula* (USA 1943; dir. Robert Siodmak) situate vampires-as-immigrants during a new moment. Ethnicity becomes a "new brand of 'difference' whose basis is cultural" and whose effect deepens the divide between "colored races" and "ethnic whites," serving as a "paradigm for assimilation which erased race as a category of historical experience for European and some Near Eastern immigrants" (Jacobson 1998: 110). With mass migrations of African Americans from rural South to urban North and West, "racial differences *within* the white community lost their salience" (95). Intrawhite race disappears by the third generation (Roediger 2005: 20) since "white folks from all places and classes, speaking all manner of languages" assimilated and "accepted a national identity based on the fiction of race and racism created by white supremacist thought and action" (hooks 2013: 4). Vampirism mutates into family curses rather racial/ethnic difference. Hollywood playfully evoked forced anglicization of names. Vampires change their surnames and flee Europe to invent new identities. Disavowing parts of their identity, vampires offer alternatives to normative gender roles and sexualities for audiences searching for feminist or queer moments in classical Hollywood.

Dracula's Daughter raises questions on subjects previous films ignored, beginning with a rare instance of a vampire hunter's arrest for murdering a vampire, thereby extending to vampires the right not to be murdered—at least on British soil. Scotland Yard arrests and detains Professor van Helsing, whose name is germanicized to Professor von Helsing (Edward Van Sloan). The arrest likely responds to the Production Code, which fined scripts and films with crimes unpunished. Disregarding PCA memos, the film was marketed sensationally: "Save the women of London from Dracula's daughter." The PCA warned producers against heightening lesbian connotations (Berenstein 1996: 26-7). Its narrative fulcrum shifts from tensions between knowledge based on faith (religion, superstition, folklore) and reason (empirical science, historical record, technological reproduction of evidence) to knowledge based on legal and medical (psychological) precedent. Professor von Helsing is not charged with Count Dracula's murder after the corpse disappears. He later travels with Scotland Yard officials to Hungary to assist in the murder of Count Dracula's daughter.

Countess Marya Zaleska (Gloria Holden) steals her murdered father's corpse, intending to cremate it and become cured of her "condition." Her vampirism is often understood as queer sexuality. Classical Hollywood deployed homosexuality—along with bestiality, necrophilia, sadomasochism, and incest—as signifiers of depravity. Countess Zaleska is independent apart from her servant Sandor (Irving Pichel). Despite her financial agency, she wants to live "as a woman," fight her "horrible impulses," and escape the double life that she lives in London's artsy Chelsea district—which, like New York's Greenwich Village, was known for sexual and gendered transgressions (Benshoff 1997: 77–9). English characters disdain Chelsea. Countess Zaleska's heterosexual relationship with Dr. Jeffrey Garth (Otto Kruger) is understood as doomed to failure (Berenstein 1996: 24), when she attacks the young Lili (Nan Grey) and Garth's secretary Janet Blake (Marguerite Churchill). She evokes ambiguous sexuality, gender, and foreignness of European émigrée actors in Hollywood, such as Dietrich and Garbo. Janet refers to her as a "dangerous brunette." Like Orloff's wife in *Making an American Citizen*, Countess Zaleska is positioned to benefit from the purportedly enlightened offerings of the United-States-as-England. Her strange rivalry with Janet, an aristocrat who has entered modernity as a New Woman, over Dr. Garth's professional and personal attention conveys the libidinal structures of americanization.

Whereas servants, police, and minor comedic characters speak with "accented" English (Cockney or Scottish), the upper-class protagonists speak "unaccented" English (Queen's or Hollywood). Use of accents to distinguish protagonists from supporting characters is consistent with practices in *Dracula* with the exception of the female vampire. Countess Zaleska is marked as foreign less by her clothing than by her accessories. She wears a coat, not a cape. Her fashionable dresses facilitate assimilation into London's social scene. She is doubly exotic both as a foreigner and as an artist. When she circulates at night, she veils her hair and sometimes her face, more to conceal her identity than to practice modesty. In addition to her Russian name and Polish surname, the Hungarian countess's ring differentiates her. She mesmerizes and sedates her victims/lovers with the radiance of its large gemstone, as her father did with his radiant eyes. As a family heirloom, her ring conceals its practical functionality while revealing her foreign and aristocratic origin. Jeffrey diagnoses her as "controlled by a dead being," evoking imperatives to disavow ancestry to facilitate assimilation into the Melting Pot's new race.

Countess Zaleska hopes to be freed of ties to her father—"free to live as a woman," "free to take [her] place among the living instead of the shadows of the dead," she explains. When she seduces Lili, the camera tilts upward from a reaction shot of Lili's face to an African mask above her head. The so-called primitivism attributed by European modernity to Africa conveys Countess Zaleska's queer desire. She reconstructs memory and constructs a new identity by playing piano. Notes evoke sounds of bird wings, not bat wings, the barking of dogs, not wolves. Her willful amnesia, however, cannot resist Sandor's pronouncement that she cannot assimilate. At times, her self-alienation resembles internalized racism, sexism, or homophobia. Her ability to pass remains unconvincing, sometimes even to herself, but she does not succumb to the self-destructiveness of the tragic-mulatta stereotype. Ultimately, she dies by an arrow fired by her own servant, suggesting ways that queer sexualities and female agency were repressed.

If *Dracula* and *Drácula* cast suspicion upon the New Woman, upon her unreadiness for self-governance due to her inability to resist Latin Lovers, then *Son of Dracula* casts similar suspicions in less uncertain terms. The dark-haired Katherine "Kate" Caldwell (Louise Allbritton) expresses her desire for lifelong fiancé Frank Stanley (Robert Paige) in ways that her invalid father and blonde sister cannot comprehend. Kate has some of the recklessness of southern belles of classical Hollywood, like Bette Davis's portrayal of Julie Marsden in *Jezebel* (1938) and Vivien Leigh's of Scarlett O'Hara in *Gone with the Wind* (1939). Kate functions like the figure of Dixie more than one of America, embodying a defeated post-Civil War South. She evokes the "Lost Cause ideology of southern nationalism" that turned the figure of the southern lady into "a celebration of the rebirth of a 'nation' defeated" in other films (McPherson 2003: 19). Kate's dangerous desires extend to the occult, fueled by a recent trip to Hungary, where she encountered Count Dracula (Lon Chaney Jr.), posing as Count Alucard, and Queen Zimba (Adeline DeWalt Reynolds). She invites both back to her family plantation, Dark Oaks. She is criticized for being "overboard" in her interest in the occult and superstition and for being "morbid" in her desire to be a vampire. Once transformed, she forbids Frank from calling her a "vampire," saying that her kind prefers to be called "undead."

London is replaced as location by the post-bellum South. Captured in classical Hollywood's three-point lighting, the setting is hardly realist. It depicts a South acoustically devoid of white Southerners. Protagonists do not speak in Southern-accented English. White servants speak with the same accents of working-class characters in Universal's films set in London, and black servants speak imperfect and imperfectly accented US English. Kate and Claire wear dresses with shoulder pads over bullet bras, styles fashionable in the early 1940s, yet there is no diegetic mention of an ongoing world war. Hungary—homeland to Count Dracula and vampire hunter Professor Lazlo (J. Edward Bromberg)—aligned with the Axis powers in 1940. The film combines US isolationism and escapism, retreating into nostalgia for the Old South. Hungarians stand out against the colorful background of African Americans servants and musicians, including a credited role for Etta McDaniel, sister of Hattie McDaniel, the first African American actor to be awarded an Oscar.

Described by other characters as a "Hungarian gypsy," Zimba's costume and hair mark her as even less assimilated than eastern European peasants in the films of Guy-Blaché and Chaplin. Her wildly unkept gray hair, heavy gold earrings, and copious beaded necklaces conflate aspects of Hollywood's iconography of Cajun, Bayou, and Caribbean voodoo. Zimba serves a similar function to superstitious Transylvanian peasants in *Dracula* and *Drácula*.

She lives in a shack in the swamp, an environment bearing less resemblance to Hungary than to Hollywood's Africa in *Condemned to Live* (USA 1935; dir. Frank R. Strayer) about Professor Paul Kristan (Ralph Morgan) bringing vampirism from the "darkest depths of Africa" to Europe. Before Zimba dies from a heart attack after being menaced by a giant bat, she foretells that Kate will marry a corpse. Upon the deaths of Zimba and Colonel Caldwell (George Irving), African American servants flee the plantation. Remarkably—and unlike Scarlett in *Gone with the Wind*—Kate manages fine without them.

Kate's unchecked desire carries dangerous consequences. She plots to gain immortality by marrying Count Alucard only as a means to find everlasting union with Frank. As Dr. Harry Brewster (Frank Craven) and Professor Lazlo discover, Count Alucard is Count Dracula, who reversed the spelling of his surname to conceal his Hungarian origins in a voluntary version of the compulsory anglicization of Jewish and other eastern European names at Ellis Island. Count Dracula speaks fluent English with a US accent. War-torn Hungary is not mentioned, but he leaves a barren Europe for the American Dream. In a discussion with Dr. Berwster, Professor Lazlo recounts his own observations of the Carpathian foothills, once vibrant, now drained. Count Dracula explains to Kate that the "soil is red with the blood of a hundred races" and "there is no life there." "Here," he continues, "you have a young and vital race." The use of the term race is suggestive, not only of racialization on a supernatural scale—human race, vampire race—but also of the promise of the Melting Pot to create a superior new race. Professor Lazlo asks whether Frank used the expression "kill" or "destroy" when declaring his intention to put a stake through Count Dracula's body, perhaps differentiating acceptable and unacceptable murders. The film comes close to questioning distinctions between victims subject to legal protection and ones not afforded such protections. It conveys a moment when assimilation was debated rather than prescribed or denied. Universal's four vampire films opened possibilities for thinking about difference and multidirectional assimilation by which *both* guest and host are *positively* modified through cultural encounters.

Postwar Parodies of Intrawhite Racism

Belated recognition of European fascism's combination of nationalism and racism allowed for reappraisals of universal citizenship that would lead to anti-discrimination policy, such as the Civil Rights Act (1964) and Equal Rights Amendment (1972). It also led to substantial revisions in immigration and naturalization law, most radically the abandonment of national origins quotas with the Hart-Celler Act (the Immigration and Nationality Act of 1965), which shifted criteria for preferential treatment from the country of origin to education and professional training, that is, from race/ethnicity to class. Whereas the unnatural whiteness of Lugosi's Count Dracula is terrifying in *Dracula*, it appears clown-like in his reprisals of the role in postwar films such as *Bud Abbott and Lou Costello Meet Frankenstein* (USA 1949; dir. Charles T. Barton). Lugosi performs fluently in English, yet cel animation allows Count Dracula to transform into a bat on screen. The film emphasizes movie monsters as products of consumerism rather than figures of nightmare and superstition. Count Dracula conceals his identity under a pseudonym, moving freely in his iconic cape at a costume party where other guests appear as stereotypes for Arab Sheiks, American Cowboys, and Indian Chiefs. Classical Hollywood's multispecies horror-comedy focus is less on interspecies relations than on intrawhite difference.

Comedy hinges on Abbott's straight man and Costello's funny man. Costello's Wilbur is funny because his qualities seem diminished in comparison to Abbott's Chick. Wilbur is less thin, intelligent, or capable. He is duped by the émigrée Sandra Mornay (Lenore Aubert), whose seductive eastern European accent evokes Count Dracula's. The film opens with an establishing shot of Trafalgar Square and the title "London," but much of its action is set in locations dominated by tropical foliage and palm trees, evoking the story's thematic location in southern California even more directly than the armadillos in *Dracula* and *Drácula*. The eastern European-accented Lugosi sounds less foreign than Costello, a working-class Italian American from New Jersey. Costello fumbles to confirm stereotypes of Italian Americans as innately inferior to so-called Anglo-Saxons. Since Lon Chaney Jr.'s ancestry was entirely northwestern European (English, French, Irish), his Talbot/Wolf Man is recuperated into white-male-human privilege. As in assimilation romances, the film's humor rests on faith in national exceptionalism through reappraisals of past assumptions concerning race/ethnicity.

Lugosi was reunited with director Browning in MGM's *Mark of the Vampire* (1935), playing a Dracula-like Count Mora. The character is actually one performed by an actor, who assists Professor Zelen (Lionel Barrymore) in trapping Baron Otto von Zinden (Jean Hersholt) for attempted murder of Sir Karrell Borotyn (Holmes Herbert). Once the mystery is solved, Lugosi's character informs his daughter Luna (Carol Borland) that he has an idea for a new stage act, claiming that his portrayal is "greater than any real vampire." Lugosi is wearing a black cape with a high collar, black tuxedo, white ruffled shirt, and black cravat, his face concealed behind heavy white makeup with a dark mark in the shape of a bloody bullet hole near his left temple. Luna wears whiteface, parts her long dark hair in the middle, and walks silently in a long, flowing dressing gown. She lowers herself into the ground by flapping her arms within the gown's cape, so as to suggest bat wings. *Mark of the Vampire* opens with scenes of eastern European gypsy life, with women in headscarves praying as a band plays folk music in front of a Christian church. The women stuff "bat thorn" into bassinettes to keep vampires away from babies. The story's setting in the countryside near Budapest during 1934 is portrayed as a time when people laughed at the notion of "vampires in the twentieth century."

The interior of Count Mora's castle is similar to Count Dracula's in *Dracula*. Although the stairwell is less elaborate, Lugosi and Borland restage a scene from *Dracula* in which the vampire appears to walk through a giant spider web without tearing it to pieces. As in the Universal films, animals and insects native to North America—bats, rats, beetles, and an opossum—suggest that the eastern European location for the story is a masquerade. Accents function similarly. The foreign quality of his Hungarian-like accentuation quickly fades beneath Luna's heavy regional US accent. The film designates US classes by accents. The young protagonists, Borotyn's daughter Irina (Elizabeth Allen) and her fiancé from Prague, Count Fedor Vencenti (Henry Wadsworth), speak with US accents comparable to those of James Stewart and Katherine Hepburn. Scottish-born character actor Donald Meek portrays Doctor Doskil with the accent that he will use for the whiskey Drummer from Kansas City, Samuel Peacock, in *Stagecoach*. Tourists speak in English accents, servants in regional US accents, villagers in Czech accents, the villain in a Danish accent. Vampire comedies allow fantasies that the mark of race is surmountable.

John Carradine's performance as Count Dracula in Universal's monster mashes, *House of Frankenstein* (USA 1944; dir. Earl C. Kenton) and *House of Dracula* (USA 1945; dir. Earl C. Kenton), is less self-reflexive about cinematic genres but no less convinced by postwar US national exceptionalism. Whereas Lugosi *acts* for the camera and, by extension, the audience, Carradine *interacts* with the other characters in the film. Like Meek in *Mark of the Vampire*, Carradine appeared in *Stagecoach* as the villainous and duplicitous Hatfield, who imagines himself to protect his fellow former Confederate Lucy Mallory (Louise Platt) from a "fate worse than death." Carradine extended his performances of villains and vampires in runaway productions shot in the Philippines, discussed in Chapter 4. His Count Dracula differs physically from Lugosi's: he is thin, and his blue eyes appear light in the black-and-white footage. He seems American to characters and audiences alike. He speaks fluent English with a native US accent. His graying hair is combed in a side parting, rather than slicked back. His mustache and sideburns are well trimmed and fashionable for the 1940s. Like Lugosi's Count Dracula, Carradine's wears a black tuxedo with a black cape. Carradine's wears a white tie, rather than Lugosi's ambiguous star pendant. The other characters recognize his name, so he poses as Baron Latos, an anglicized version of the Polish name Latosz. He has no accent or mark of racial difference.

The films mix supernatural and scientific tropes to facilitate assimilation. In *House of Dracula*, Dr. Franz Edlemann (Onslow Stevens) is associated with the University of Bonn. Dramatic and exaggerated shadows in village scenes resemble those in *Cat People* (USA 1942; dir. Jacques Tourneur) about the Serbian-born fashion artist Irena Dubrovna (Simone Simon) in New York. Count Dracula solicits Dr. Edlemann's help in finding a cure, as does Lawrence Talbot aka the Wolf Man. Both Count Dracula and Talbot are unable to assimilate fully with human society. Count Dracula cannot walk freely during the day; Talbot, during nights with full moons. Dr. Edlemann seeks to cure them through the modern science of blood transfusions and mold spores. He cures Talbot, who is immediately rewarded with the affections of the doctor's blonde assistant Miliza (Martha O'Driscoll) after the selfless sacrifice of his brunette assistant Nina (Jane Adams). The hunchbacked Nina painstakingly collected mold spores for her own corrective surgery but selflessly, if amorously, gave them to Talbot for his surgery. Dr. Edlemann fails in curing Count Dracula with transfusions of his own blood, which actually leads to the doctor's own degeneration into a schizophrenic character like Robert Louis Stevenson's character of Dr. Jekyll and Mr. Hyde. He eventually abandons hope of assimilating Count Dracula into society and destroys him with sunlight. The film's narrative of successful normalization of the Wolf Man and failed normalization of Count Dracula point to americanization as a process defined in terms of productiveness: Talbot appears capable, whereas Count Dracula does not.

House of Frankenstein and *House of Dracula* are set in a Hollywood Gothic location that resembles both eastern Europe and southern California. *House of Frankenstein* is set in a rural village at some distance from Budapest. The heavy foliage of southern California and the architectural details of wrought-iron latticework are populated with gypsy dancers. The narrative conflict resolves itself in a marsh with quicksand. Similarly, the post-opening-credit establishing shot of *House of Dracula* comprises a matte painting of Edlemann's castle composited with images of waves crashing against a rocky Californian coast. Elsewhere, the film's setting evokes a similar masquerade—a blending of landscapes to suggests a mixing of races. Architectural elements combine an unembellished, heavy stone masonry, suggestive of European architecture, with vine-covered stairwells and courtyards, accented with ornate iron latticework, that are more suggestive of Californian architecture. The film's opening scene of Count Dracula's arrival at the castle in the form of a bat, lingering outside the window of a sleeping woman, seems a template for the opening scene in Cinematográfico's *El vampiro*, discussed in the next chapter. Like most postwar Hollywood vampire films, neither *House of Frankenstein* nor *House of Dracula* makes any direct reference to the second World War. They affirm US national exceptionalism without acknowledging US complicity with European fascism. They evoke a different moment than *Dracula* and *Drácula*—one when borders had opened to European ethnicities.

In the 1940s, the US Office of War actually mandated that Hollywood film represent the United States as a Melting Pot and "nation of many races." The anti-Semitism of the Nazi Party in Germany was contrasted with the openness of the United States. Set in the outskirts of London during the 1941 blitz, Columbia Picture's *The Return of the Vampire* (USA 1943; dir. Lew Landers) stars Lugosi as Armand Tesla, a vampire since 1744. Tesla comes to London by assuming the identity of Dr. Hugo Bruckner, an escapee from a Nazi concentration camp. Exceptionalist discourses continued into the Cold War (1945–91), though they shifted to emphasize free labor. *The Return of Dracula* (USA 1958; dir. Paul Landres), as Stacey Abbott observes, equates vampires as a "force of evil" with immigrants during the montage of images, such as the Statue of Liberty, to convey Count Dracula's arrival in the United States (2007: 71). Attention to European forms of anti-Semitism prompted reflection upon US immigration policy, resulting in partial acknowledgment of national quotas as a mechanism for racial/ethnic profiling to disfavor Ashkenazi Jews and disqualify Asians and Africans.[10] "There is nothing more un-American," wrote Milton Konvitz, "than the attempt to mold America in conformance with the nationality concept that is at the bottom of our national origins formula" (1953: 61). European quotas were not filled (Daniels 2002: 292).

The Vampire as Frontier Fighter

Classical Hollywood Westerns were oriented towards a fixed past, laden with nostalgia and revisionist fantasy; its vampire films were generally oriented towards the future in an ever-expanding moment of the present. Vampire-Westerns deployed a complicated temporality that is simultaneously oriented towards the past and future. Racism against indigenous nations and Mexicans is often naturalized, yet racism against eastern and southern European immigrants is largely erased. The black-and-white *Curse of the Undead/Mark of the West* (USA 1959; dir. Henry Cass) and the color *Billy the Kid vs. Dracula* (USA 1965; dir. William Beaudine) reveal how vampire films adapt narrative and cinematic conventions from Westerns yet unsettle their assumptions about blood, bodies, and borders. The films reconfigure the vampire, not as "bloodthirsty Indian" or "lawless Mexican bandito" but as an outlaw-hero, who becomes a frontier fighter. Vampires become more like vampire hunters in other films. In a little more than a decade, classical Hollywood's vampires mutate from accented alien figures to unaccented nationalist figures.

The opening-credit sequence of Universal's *Curse of the Undead* culminates with a close-up of a crucifix and a tomb, signaling dangers on the frontier. The tombstone evokes legends of gunfights over stolen livestock and usurped water and mining rights by outlaw cowboys. Buffer (Bruce Gordon) diverts water by damming a river in an effort to force "Doc" Carter (John Hoyt) to sell his ranch. Carter appeals to the law. Sheriff Bill (Edward Binns) claims to have two choices: arrest or kill. Frontier justice frames the exchangeability of these two authorized uses of state violence against a citizen. Carter turns to private means, hiring the mysterious stranger Drake Robey (Michael Pate), who, dressed in a black cowboy hat and costume, rides into town on a black stallion. His onscreen appearances are anticipated by a supernatural-themed musical prompt that unsettles musical conventions in Westerns, which often repurposed Confederate songs (Kalinak 2007). Carter is found dead with a bloody neck wound, leaving his son Tim (Jimmy Murphy) and daughter Dolores (Kathleen Crowley) to keep the ranch from falling under Buffer's control. In a drunken rage, Tim challenges Buffer to a duel and dies. Dolores then decides to have Buffer killed, offering to pay anyone "one hundred dollars for the death of a murderer." The sheriff opposes her vigilantism.

Inspired by the anger of his clients, Drake works as a gun-for-hire. His name is not an anglicized version of Dracula but of Drago. He was Don Drago Robles. Later the very land disputed by Buffer and the Carters is revealed as part of a Spanish land grant sold by the Robles family after a tragedy. A map of Rancho Robles and a portrait labeled "Drago Robles: 1825–1859" situate the narrative within the historical moment of Westerns. A map that shows Buffer's theft of 500 acres resolves the dispute, but Preacher Dan Young (Eric Fleming) shoots and kills Drake with a bullet etched with a cross. The vampire functions like a ghost from the past that haunts the present more than an unwelcome immigrant who determines the future. Drake is dispossessed of his ancestral lands, as were indigenous nations and Mexicans, but he is thoroughly European. Under the colonial Spanish caste system, Don Drago would have been part of the *criollos*, the so-called pureblooded Spanish descending from the *peninsulares*. His social privilege would have been untainted by so-called Indian or African blood as the *mestizos* and *mulatos* were. The film naturalizes a legitimate transfer of rights to territory from Spain-as-México to the United States with the figure of the vampire assisting white colonizers. At the same time, the film naturalizes the vampire as American in values, if not by birth.

Billy the Kid vs. Dracula opens with a stagecoach scene of newly arrived German immigrants. The light blonde Eva Oster (Virginia Christine), her husband Franz (Walter Janowitz), and their daughter Lisa (Hannie Landman) appear sturdy and hardworking. Prior to the Civil War, much of European immigration came from Germany (Hing 2004: 21). As the stagecoach stops to allow the horses to rest, Count Dracula (John Carradine) appears and disparages them as "superstitious immigrants." After the death of their daughter, Eva and Frantz become servants on a ranch. Count Dracula murders a number of characters, but the deaths of all of his victims are not treated equally. The deaths of the white matriarch, Mary Ann Bentley (Marjorie

Bennett), and the German immigrant-youth Lisa are treated as tragedies, that of the unnamed (and uncredited) Native American woman hardly noticed. Count Dracula poses as Betty's uncle James Underhill from Boston. He wears a black top hat, black suit, and red ribbon tie along with a pointy beard and mustache. When he leaves his mark, he leaves four incision marks. Betty (Melinda Plowman) falls in love with the outlaw William "Billy the Kid" Bonney (Chuck Courtney), suggesting a less transgressive possibility for love than in *Dracula* or *Drácula*.

The setting of these Vampire-Westerns in the Southwest demonstrates that the Hollywood Gothic was somewhat always about representing the contemporary United States. On Hollywood's back-lots and sound stages, so-called exotic locations like China, Arabia, and Transylvania, alongside mythical heritage locations, like England, reveal their actual shooting location in southern California through inconsistent accents and costumes. With stars, personas also make reality difficult to differentiate completely from illusion. Lugosi's performance of Count Dracula somewhat overlapped with his performance of "himself" as a political exile. In an interview at the height of his fame, he identifies as a "Hungarian by birth" and "an American now."[11] Few contested his patriotism despite his accent. Vampire hunters may have murdered the accented Count Dracula, but accents faded, particularly among its vampire-cowboys. The deathly departure of Mexican-born Drake renders him as a frontier fighter, a self-sacrificing figure of nation building. If "the saga of European immigration has long been held up as proof of the openness of American society, the benign and absorptive powers of American capitalism, and the robust health of American democracy" (Jacobson 1998: 12), classical Hollywood vampire films offer revisionist and alternative histories, albeit in supernatural terms, to acknowledge the nation's transnational coordinates. Classical Hollywood vampire films address controversial questions. They serve as one means by which fantasies and anxieties about immigration were evoked on screen without representing them directly during moments of radical social transformation and redefinition of legal categories.

Notes

1. Looking at higher education, Sullivan argues "predominantly white universities could place themselves in solidarity with black universities by foregrounding and critically analyzing white racism" instead of assuming that "diversity is a panacea for white privilege" (21).
2. In 1936, migration figures settled to a net gain of 516 persons, yet public perceptions that immigrants were flooding the country continued (Daniels 2002: 287–9).
3. Hoover issues overseas consulates to enforce LPC (likely to become a public charge) clause; Roosevelt's New Deal was "indifferent to the fate of Jewish and other refugees from Hitler's Third Reich" by not distinguishing refugees from immigrants (Daniels 2002: 295–6).

4. The same applies to war-bond campaign films like Famous Players-Lasky Corp.'s *100% American* (1918; dir. Arthur Rosson), starring "America's sweetheart," resident alien from Canada, Mary Pickford, as Mayme. *100% American* was shown in Canada as *100% Canadian*.
5. *Drácula* offers agency to maid Marta (Armelia Senisterra). When Martín (Manuel Arbó) jokes about his employer's mental stability and questions Marta's, she makes a sound of displeasure and briskly walks away.
6. In *Gua Sha/The Treatment* (China 2001; dir. Xiaolong Zheng), *gua sha* is mistaken as child abuse in the United States. Thanks to Qiuxia Shao for this reference.
7. Fears of white slavery date to colonialism (Glenn 2002: 22).
8. Nearly half of immigrants from England and Scotland were indentured servants or redemptioners (worked to repay passage) between 1773 and 1776 and continued to be imported as artisans and skilled craftspeople until the 1830s (Glenn 2002: 61).
9. Other films with immigrants as criminals include First National's *The Match King* (1932; dir. Howard Bretherton and William Keighley) and RKO's *Death of a Scoundrel* (1956, dir. Charles Martin).
10. Wilhelm Marr popularized anti-Semitism against Jews around 1848.
11. Lugosi "used fame generously—and, in retrospect, perhaps imprudently—in aiding the cause to free Hungary from Hitler" (Dello Stritto 1997: 57).

4. INTERNATIONAL HOLLYWOOD VAMPIRES: COSMOPOLITANISMS OF "FOREIGN MOVIES"

During the 1960s and 1970s, Hammer's vampire films redefined not only the transgenre but also British film and Hollywood. Shot on color film stock and accompanied by full orchestral scores, the films rejuvenated vampire stories with new vitality and heightened emotion. Color was employed as an expressive mode. Camera movement was relatively fixed yet punctuated by rapid pans, tilts, and zooms to establish conventions that reappeared for decades. "Hammer vampires and other monsters are not segregated in the black-and-white gloom of 1930s America" (1995: 120), explains Auerbach, but inhabit worlds of "cheerful semi-pornographic opulence" (56). Composer James Bernard's three-note "DRAC-*u-la* motif," balanced by "an emotionally weaker motif representing Van Helsing and the 'good' people on which [Count] Dracula preys" (Larson 1996: 23), staged an acoustic battle alongside the visual one. The figure of the vampire hunter sometimes eclipsed the figure of the vampire, notably in *Captain Kronos, Vampire Hunter* (UK 1972; dir. Brian Clemens), as an object of desire for audiences. Hammer's formula is most associated with Christopher Lee's reinvention of Count Dracula in *Horror of Dracula* (UK 1958; dir. Terence Fisher) and its sequels, along with Peter Cushing's reinvention of Professor van Helsing. The films emerged on US screens as the Production Code, banning unpunished sex, violence, and miscegenation, came to a close. Hollywood partly moved production overseas to make films whose content would have been impossible in the United States.

Shot in British studios by British filmmakers, working for a British company and using predominantly British casts, Hammer's films seemed "to represent something intrinsically and culturally British" (Porter 1983: 179), suggesting why the films have not often featured in analysis of transnational Hollywood.[1] Hammer's dominance of the international horror market was attributed to the studio's creation of an "English Gothic" (Pirie 1977: 77), a style that not only implies comparison with Hollywood but also was sometimes financed by Hollywood. Universal's Hollywood Gothic established conventions for dark, cavernous settings, replete with gigantic spider webs and rubber bats along with live armadillos, opossums, and scorpions, and coy cut-away shots to hide all physical contact between humans and vampires. Hammer's English Gothic established new conventions, evident in the generous depictions of partial nudity and copious amounts of bright red blood that drips and splashes. The films were relatively unconcerned with cinematic realism, a hallmark of British cinema; instead, fantasy, considered a trait of Hollywood cinema, became a preoccupation (Hutchings 1983: 95). Hammer depicted both vampires and vampire hunters as English cosmopolitans. Count Dracula often appears only midway through the films, sometimes with only animalized snarls and no dialogue, but director Terence Fisher and others at Hammer wanted to make "the vampires a bit more human than they usually are" through passions and weaknesses ([1964] 2000: 75). "A bit more human" translated into making vampires a lot more English. Lee's impeccable accent and manners underscore his "sexual attractiveness and ferocity" (Gelder 1994: 92), even as he becomes "increasingly inarticulate," thus "more animal and less chic" (Auerbach 1995: 129).[2] With his foreign looks and familiar accent, Lee's own Italian ancestry combined with his English accent allows him to pass as white-upon-arrival.[3] Hammer also domesticated the Dutch Professor van Helsing.

Exhibited in the United States, the films become "foreign movies" that provided images of modern sexual liberation. For (white) feminist and (white) queer audiences, Hammer's vampires posed a welcome challenge to US patriarchy and homophobia institutionalized under the PCA. The films seemed English, evoked a distant past and noble heritage that somehow also contained aspects of a desired future. For Hollywood's US audiences, the cosmopolitanism of the English vampires and hunters offered a mythical Anglo-Saxon heritage that could be universalized as relevant. Hollywood also financed and produced runaway films that parodied its anglocentrisms. Postwar films featured both vampires and vampire hunters who act cosmopolitan within unmarked frameworks of postwar imperialism. Lee's vampire moves across geopolitical borders as though they were unmarked and unimportant, seducing local women as though their bodies were unclaimed. He seems (and sounds) less threatening—and perhaps even liberating—to women because he appears familiar, not foreign, thus not compromising citizenship like vampires in classical Hollywood. He speaks fluent English with an English accent and appears white-upon-arrival. Hammer's films generate spaces for fantasies of privileged forms of cosmopolitanism based on both *anti-racism* in response to European fascism and *consumerism* in response to postwar European reconstruction, particularly under the European Recovery Program (Marshall Plan), of which the United Kingdom was the largest recipient.

Hollywood's vampire films were thus more *international* than universal, more likely to be distributed by American International Pictures (AIP) than by Universal Pictures. Individual deals with non-US production companies reconfigured Hollywood production from centralized dream factories with in-house labor of assembly lines to fragmented commodity trading and the flexible labor of freelancers. Independent producers reworked Mexican and Philippine vampire films through subtitling, dubbing, and re-editing to make them seem appear less threatening to Hollywood's domestic production. These films circulated according to social hierarchies that diminished the contributions—and sometimes criminalized the presence—of so-called unskilled contract laborers from the Philippines and México (*sakadas* and *braceros*) recruited by the agricultural industry to do the "stoop labor" that white workers were being conditioned to refuse. Dubbed as "cheap foreign movies," Philippine and Mexican films were often altered to appeal to white-male audiences whose egos had been damaged by the US military defeat in Southeast Asia and whose political representation in the United States had been destabilized by antiracism and antisexism during the civil rights and equal rights movements of the 1960s and 1970s. At the same time, the films challenged classical Hollywood's whites-only narratives. They offered nonwhite audiences opportunities to see someone on screen who looked a little more like themselves. They could project themselves into the films, as (white) feminist and (white) queer audiences had done with classical Hollywood films.

This chapter looks at the diversity and heterogeneity of postwar Hollywood vampire films as a way of understanding Hollywood's production of—and presence in—a category of foreign movies that includes Hammer's lavish studio productions shot in Britain, parodies vampire films shot in Europe by rebellious auteurs such as Roman Polański and Paul Morrissey, Mexican vampire and *luche libre* (wrestling) films dubbed for television, and Philippine films re-edited into vampire films for drive-ins. Collectively, the films address controversial topics of racially-striated movements across borders and effects of military interventions. Vampire hunters become central to narratives and audience pleasures, sometimes mutating into luchadores (professional wrestlers) and private detectives. Hammer films revitalized myths of England as a US national homeland, alongside an Anglo-Saxon/Anglo-American "right and duty" to "protect" (by "civilizing") the world; whereas, Mexican and Philippine films were framed to confirm fantasies of racial/ethnic and national inferiority of México and the Philippines.

Feeling American through "Cheap Foreign Movies"

In addition to Hollywood's international sales offices and willingness to remove offensive stereotypes so as not to alienate potential overseas markets, its Motion Pictures Exports Association of America (MPEAA) worked with the US government to reduce restrictions on its films abroad through import tariffs and quotas. When such measures did not succeed, its established overseas production companies. With the advent of synchronized sound in 1929 also came Paramount's Jointville (France) studio to bypass French laws to protect its local film industries. After the 1948 barring of vertical integration of production, distribution, and exhibition under a single company, Hollywood reinvented itself as financer and distributor of films, not only produced by independent producers and companies in the United States, but also by foreign ones abroad. Like a vampire, Hollywood mutated and migrated, financing runaway productions shot in Italy and Austria for one audience and dubbing Mexican and Philippine films for another. Hollywood was less a producer of original content than a trader in acquired and appropriated content. Dubbing and subtitling were also a means of managing difference by producing diversity in essentialized categories. Cultures and cultural productions were regulated according to aesthetic hierarchies that drew on the racial/ethnic hierarchies in immigration and naturalization policies.

Vampire films invite us to see how Hollywood altered foreign productions for domestic audiences as much as it altered its own productions for foreign audiences. Nearly two decades ago, Miriam Hansen suggested we consider classical Hollywood film history, not only as standardization and hegemony of factories and oligopolies, but also as diversity and heterogeneity via "censorship, alternative endings, marketing, and programming practices, not to mention subtitling and dubbing" (2000: 12). A plurality of prints and ways that audiences interpret their stories destabilizes any sense of coherent history, along with theorizations of media based upon retrospective illusions of fixed texts, prints, and histories of unified subjects and sonic spaces. Vampire films push us to rethink film history and theory. Hollywood created "foreign movies" and later "international film" as relational categories to its own productions; typically *art*, if from Europe, and *trash*, if from East Asia, Latin America, or Southeast Asia. Such categories are calibrated according to aesthetic prejudices that followed social cues about race/ethnicity and nationality. Foreign film is conventionally discussed in terms of postwar French and Italian films, which circulated both on upmarket subtitled prints and downmarket dubbed prints. Dubbed films such as . . . *And God Created Woman/Et dieu . . . créa la femme* (France-Italy 1956; dir. Roger Vadim) and *Once Upon a Time in the West/C'era una volta il West* (Italy-USA 1968; dir. Sergio Leone) were understood as sexy and violent alternatives to locally produced Hollywood fare. Considered a mainstream threat after their theatrical success in the 1970s, dubbed prints of Hong Kong films, notably those starring Bruce Lee, such as *Jing wu men/The Chinese Connection* (Hong Kong 1972; dir. Wei Lo) and *Meng long guo jiang/The Way of the Dragon* (Hong Kong 1972; dir. Bruce Lee), were quickly integrated via distribution by the studios. Emphasis on the "lip flapping" of poorly synchronized facial movements and dubbed voices distracted US audiences from Hong Kong's technically more skilled fight choreography and cinematography—and anti-colonial themes.[4]

For certain audiences, Count Dracula was a "citizen of the world" (Gelder 1994: 111). For others, cosmopolitanism was little more than an imperial fantasy of carefree detachment from the pedestrian constraints and civil, political, and social responsibilities of citizenship. Count Dracula's ability to move freely through the postwar world was thwarted by an equally cosmopolitan vampire hunter. Hammer cast Lee as a younger and more athletic Count Dracula than Lugosi's. It also cast Cushing as a younger and more athletic Professor van Helsing than Van Sloan's. Cushing embodied a postwar vampire-hunter ideal, traveling as far as China to hunt vampires. World peace hinged upon England's continued benevolent management of foreign places.

Vampire hunters were not the only ones to travel widely and freely. Businessmen and lawyers now circled the globe as generals and captains had before them, highlighting US national exceptionalism of white men who restore order and propagate the so-called American way in exotic places. Postwar Italy in *It Started in Naples* (USA 1960; dir. Melville Shavelson) looks and sounds like pre-revolutionary Cuba in *Week-end in Havana*. Hollywood equivalencies between Italy and Cuba, however, diminish in terms of the extent to which the female lead's exoticism could be assimilated. Whereas Jay Williams (John Payne) cannot contain and control Rosita Rivas (Carmen Miranda) any more than the United States could colonize Cuba, Michael Hamilton (Clark Gable) domesticates and americanizes Lucia Curcio (Sophia Loren), much like the Marshall Plan enabled certain amounts of US control over western Europe. Lucia's performance of Renato Carosone's song "Tu vuò fà l'americano," typically considered a satire of wanting to feel American, becomes an invitation—not to national belonging of US citizenship but to cosmopolitan complicity with the new US empire, which controlled indirectly. Like a vampire, the businessman Hamilton infects his half-Italian nephew Nando (Marietto) with desire for social mobility, faith in capitalism, and a taste for hamburgers—all as a kind of universalism.

In the postwar period, vampires and vampire hunters served as cosmopolitan agents of imperial desires, some nostalgic for Britain's fallen empire, others excited about the ascension of a US empire. Despite efforts to redeem cosmopolitanism from its antidemocratic origins in ancient Greece, cosmopolitanism often serves to camouflage imperialism. Bruce Robbins associates cosmopolitanism with elite status of aristocrats and merchants, who claim "universality by virtue of its independence, its detachments from the bonds, commitments, and affiliations that constrain ordinary nation-bound lives," but actually works in tandem with nationalism, such that "actually existing cosmopolitanism is a reality of (re)attachment, multiple attachment, or attachment at a distance" (1998: 1–3). Rerouted through postcolonial and multicultural critiques, cosmopolitanism expands to include less privileged statuses of involuntary and coerced forms of transnational movements—slaves, guest workers, refugees, and stateless persons—the "partial equivalences," as James Clifford calls them, of "exile, immigration, migrancy, diaspora, border crossing, pilgrimage, tourism" (1998: 363). Cosmopolitanism becomes an effect of postwar capitalism and imperialism.

International tourism emerged as a leisure activity for privileged classes, blessed by modernity. "Cosmopolitans today," explain Sheldon Pollock et al., "are often the victims of modernity, failed by capitalism's upward mobility, and bereft of the comforts and customs of national belonging" (2000: 582). Non-citizen nationals, such as Filipina/os living in the United States before Philippine statehood and Puerto Ricans living in the commonwealth today, inhabit this liminal space of disempowered containment within the nation-state without access to the rights of full citizenship. Indigenous nations become "stateless entities" (Byrd 2011: xix). They do not enjoy "feeling American" and actively resist it. The "universality plus difference" that writers like Martha Nussbaum and Kwame Anthony Appiah attempt to recover from Kant, suggests Eduardo Mendieta, needs to be reconfigured as a "universality plus difference plus historical consciousness" (2009: 252).[5] Walter Mignolo advocates for history beginning with Spanish and Portuguese colonialism rather than classical Greek philosophy—one from the perspective of *coloniality* rather than *modernity*. He proposes "diversality" instead of universality—not a new form of cultural relativism, but rather "new forms of projecting and imagining, ethically and politically, from subaltern positions" (2000: 743). This historical consciousness can enter through sustained analysis of the political economies of trade, war, immigration, and also Hollywood's cheap foreign movies. Comparably, Chandra Mohanty argues feminism can address difference and equality with "particualized viewing allow[ing] for a more concrete and expansive vision of universal justice" (2003: 231). If Universal's vampire films concerned assimilation into the Melting Pot's new race, then Hammer's concerned interventions into a world whose order had been destabilized by the second World War—and more significantly by decolonization's dismantling of empires abroad and civil rights' more equitable redistribution of power at home.

Hollywood Finances an "English Gothic"

The international success of Hammer's *Dracula*, distributed by Universal as *Horror of Dracula* in the United States, inspired dozens of films by British companies like Amicus, and other companies in Europe, Japan, Pakistan, and elsewhere. Hammer's sequels were often partially financed by Hollywood distributors, directly or through European subsidiaries. Beginning as a production offshoot of Exclusive Films in the 1930s, Hammer was the only British studio to survive the tumultuous 1940s, acquiring licenses from Universal to remake its horror films and earning a Queen's Award for Industry in 1968. Hammer's connections with Hollywood began after the 1951 approval of the X certificate for adult audiences (Gomery 2005: 198–9). Hammer partnered with Robert Lippert Productions in 1951 to get its "first foothold" in the US market (Porter 1983: 195). With 90 per cent of funding from the United States in 1967, "British film companies were beholden to foreign sources of income" (Sanjek 1994: 197), yet Hammer defended against Hollywood's domination of its local market. Peter Hutchings calls Hammer "one of the first British companies to embrace the American film industry rather than viewing it as a threat" (2001: 4). Hammer signed deals with Universal and Columbia after the success of *The Curse of Frankenstein* (UK 1957; dir. Terence Fisher), partly financed by Associated Artists Pictures and distributed by Warner Bros. (Halliwell 1986: 55). "Like many 'independent' film companies,'" Hutchings notes, "Hammer was in fact heavily dependent on American finance and was consequently always attentive to the needs of an American market" (3). Hollywood affected Hammer's rewriting of Count Dracula's story. Christopher Lee claims that he refused to appear in sequels to *Horror of Dracula*, which he found unimaginative, only agreeing when reminded that US distribution rights were pre-sold with his name. Hammer's success hinged on international versions— "one for the United States, a milder one for Great Britain, and one considerably stronger for Japan" (Clarens 1967: 244)—for local censorship.

Pam Cook laments Hammer's "pastiche that is the undoing of authentic identities" after Ealing's "air of authenticity," achieved by using "realism to (finally) confirm a coherent, unified national identity" (1996: 5). Tim Bergfelder, however, argues that understanding European cinemas "to establish a national identity" neglects "features which transcend and contradict these identity formations," notably popular comedy and horror films set "against scenic backdrops of the Middle East, South East Asia and Africa" (2000: 139). By dehistoricizng relations between Europe and these places, he argues, "popular genres of the 1960s suggested to their audiences the possibility of a cosmopolitan and classless identity in a new world, made accessible and commodified by tourism, leisure and lifestyle consumerism" (149–50). In Hammer-like *Incense of the Damned/Bloodsuckers/The Freedom Seekers*

(UK 1972; dir. Michael Burrowes [Robert Hartford-Davis]), Oxford don Richard Fountain (Patrick Mower) travels to Greece to cure sexual impotence. He meets vampire Chriseis (Imogen Hassall) and lifestyles of international jet setters and psychedelic hippies. Films evoke fantasies of pan-European or European-American popular culture—fantasies of the West. Postwar discourses of international tourism and class mobility produce a road to cosmopolitanism paved with imperial privilege.

Horror of Dracula resurrects tropes of British Empire after its collapse by situating evoking postwar realities in conflicts between an anglicized van Helsing and a germanized Count Dracula. *Postwar* occludes *postcolonial*, facilitating flights of fantasy into a prewar moment when imperialism seemed viable and necessary. Orientalism revives centuries-old tropes of eroticism and danger. Hammer produced adventure melodramas, such as *Stranglers of Bombay* (UK 1960; dir. Terence Fisher) set in India, *Terror of the Tongs* (UK 1961; dir. Anthony Bushell) set in Hong Kong, and *Rasputin the Mad Monk* (UK 1966; dir. Don Sharp), set in Russia, revealing, in Carlos Clarens's words, that "the common denominator of [Hammer's] product was not really horror but sadism" (1967: 143). Hammer embraced relaxed censorship, attracting "an increasingly younger audience during a decade when cinema attendance was declining" (Street 1997: 76). Audiences understood films as politically conservative and progressive, yet their erotic connection between sadism and imperialism has not been widely explored.[6] Hammer's imperial fantasies erase histories of actual imperialism and highlight Britain as vigilant against European fascism, resonating with US audiences. Abandoned British aspirations over actual colonies in South Asia and Africa are displaced onto a mythical Middle Europe, severed from history.

Stoker's novel suggests isomorphism between people and place through Count Dracula's "earth-boxes." Hammer destabilizes it. Vampire hunters ignore dirt in the vampire's coffin—and the pillow atop it. Van Helsing explains that many biologists do not believe that vampires must rest in their native soil or in the reanimation of corpses. Postwar anti-racism minimizes isomorphism to emphasize geopolitical borders over racial/ethnic or religious difference. Soil is loosened in association with citizenship via blood and nation. Hammer constructs a cinematically self-referential Transylvania, rejecting Stoker's well-researched representation. In sequels, "pasteboard faceless European villages" hint that audiences "will have no difficulty in recognizing the Bray and Black Park [Hammer studios] familiar from many previous Hammer epics" (Sanjek 1994: 253). Hammer's cities of Klausenberg and Carlstadt are located in a Europe that seems neither western nor eastern (Hutchings 2001: 90). As in *Nosferatu*, locations are accessible within a day by horse-drawn carriage.

Hammer's ambiguous construction of Transylvania collapses upon itself in a surplus of details that signify Englishness despite other information.

Geographic space is condensed, and cultural differences between spaces are ambiguously defined, yet the border that separates Count Dracula's home in Klausenberg from the Holmwoods' home in Carlstadt is clearly demarcated. Border crossing becomes a narrative occasion for slapstick gags, yet political borders announce geopolitics. Borders are *where* law is exercised. A gate serves as a physical marker between spaces governed by separate laws. A customs official (George Benson) controls access and keeps records. During their investigation of Count Dracula's movement, van Helsing and Arthur bribe him. The law that maintains and secures the border is broken during van Helsing and Arthur's near-dawn pursuit of Count Dracula from Carlstadt to Klausenberg. Count Dracula races his carriage through the gate. Emphasis moves from bodies racialized as foreign in classical Hollywood to borders policed against foreigners.

Distance from everyplace else defines Count Dracula's castle, palpable in spatial, temporal, cultural, and secular (Christian) terms with vampires allergic to light, repulsed by garlic, and succumbing to crucifixes. Klausenberg feels like a germanicized outpost of the British Empire. The narrative begins with voice-over reading by Jonathan Harker (John van Eyssen) from his diary entry of 3 May 1885, explaining his intent to assassinate Count Dracula. He kills a female vampire (Valerie Gaunt), but Count Dracula transforms him into a vampire. His undead body is impaled by colleague van Helsing, who returns to Carlstadt, where he tells Arthur Holmwood (Michael Gough), his sister Lucy (Carol Marsh), and his wife Mina (Melissa Stribling) about Harker's death in ambiguous terms. Concealing information is equated with protecting but ultimately endangers by maintaining ignorance in a plot twist that parodies paternalism. Lucy becomes Count Dracula's first victim/lover in Carlstadt. Van Helsing hypothesizes that Count Dracula attacks Lucy in revenge for Harker's murder of the female vampire in Klausenberg.

The vampire hunters find pleasure in "releasing" (euphemism for murdering) Count Dracula's brides, and Count Dracula finds consolation in infecting their sisters and wives. During a final confrontation, van Helsing fights Count Dracula in hand-to-hand combat, breaking a window, so light floods the room, turning Count Dracula into dust and hair, thus leaving no identifiable corpse as evidence of murder. Jimmy Sangster's script emphasizes the vampire hunters' intervention, evoking a covert sense of moral urgency and authority among Britons akin to Rudyard Kipling's "White Man's Burden" (1899). Despite the masquerade of period costumes, vampire hunting functions according to a state of moral exception, wherein international law is ignored allegedly to save a local population from itself. Arriving at Klausenberg, van Helsing points to garlic hung from the inn's ceiling and questions the innkeeper (George Woodbridge) about Count Dracula's "reign of terror." "We haven't asked for any help," the innkeeper says. "You need it all the same," van

Helsing interjects with arrogance. "You're a stranger here in Klausenberg," the innkeeper explains; "some things are better left alone," such as interfering as vigilantes in domestic policies of a foreign state. Van Helsing disagrees, telling the innkeeper, "not only you but the whole world will benefit," should his plot succeed. He justifies vigilante intervention by cloaking it in humanitarian language. The film simultaneously positions van Helsing as hero and questions the logic of heroism. Inverting narrative logic in Stoker's novel, it represents Count Dracula as the vampire hunters' victim. The vampire's fury is motivated by personal revenge, which the vampire hunters find infantile, uncivilized, and animalistic to legitimize their own motivations for murder.[7]

The psychological fright of Count Dracula's penetration of the heart of the British Empire, central to Stoker's novel, is averted by the narrative's relocation, but the terror of the empire collapsing at its edges is heightened. In *Horror of Dracula*, the Holmwoods employ a maid with a non-anglophone name, a narrative choice that signifies their status as colonizers, employing a local underclass to suggest the status of eastern Europe immigrants working as domestic labor in England. The logical disconnect between English-language signage on shops, taverns, and roads and the continental-style of architecture and landscapes point to realism inflected with genre conventions. Along the border, signage is rendered in both French and German. Carlstadt and Klausenberg are German names that were historically used for the Transylvanian city of Cluj-Napoca and the Croatian city of Karlovac, pointing to earlier moments in intra-European colonialism.[8] In his observations about vampirism, van Helsing explains that the hazard for Britons living abroad is that victims' "consciousness detests being dominated by vampirism but are unable to relinquish the practice, similar to addiction to drugs," resonating with fears that adopting local (foreign) ways represents a compromise to remaining English while living in colonies. The Holmwoods are vulnerable to threats of vampirism due to geographical proximity between (colonial English) Carlstadt and (uncolonized Transylvanian) Klausenberg. Imperial cosmopolitanism enables fantasies of remaining English. Count Dracula is no longer an unwanted immigrant; instead, he is a foreign ruler whose very power seems to threaten the British Empire. The resurrection of the convention that vampires burn and disintegrate when exposed to sunlight from *Nosferatu* might even seem an unwitting trope for hope that the eternal sunshine that once bathed and nurtured the empire might return—perhaps via Hollywood financing.

Sequels and Parodies of an Anglo-Saxon Homeland

Hammer's ambiguous representations of national identities and period settings allowed its films to travel largely unencumbered across international borders in search of large audiences. As Hutchings argues, ambiguity "ensured that

Hammer was never as disturbing to audiences, most critics, and the censors, as were most realistic horrors," allowing for "a more fantastic, stylized acting out of event, unencumbered [by] suggestions of realism carried by modern locations" (1993: 65). Except *Dracula A. D. 1972* (UK 1972; dir. Alan Gibson), *The Satanic Rites of Dracula/Count Dracula and His Vampire Bride* (UK 1973; dir. Alan Gibson), and coproduction with Shaw Brothers *The Legend of the Seven Golden Vampires* (UK-Hong Kong 1974; dir. Roy Ward Baker), Hammer's vampires films are generally set outside Britain during the nineteenth century. Hollywood's European partners and subsidiaries like Warner-Pathé and Columbia-Warner often indirectly financed sequels and distributed them in theaters and on television in the United States.

In *Dracula Has Risen from the Grave* (UK 1968; dir. Freddie Francis), Count Dracula resides in London. No longer an invader, he is a resident. The films increasingly rely on partial female and male nudity, recreational drug usage, and hippie culture. Youth like Charles (Francis Matthews) and Diana (Suzan Farmer) in *Dracula, Prince of Darkness* (UK 1966; dir. Terence Fisher) travel as tourists to an unsafe and haunted Middle Europe, requiring rescue by an older, more nationally situated generation. Horror changes from permeable international borders to progeneration of children, whose bodies carry the stigma of being illegitimate according to religious and civic law. Released by Warner Bros., *Dracula Has Risen from the Grave* warns of dangers in multi-religious societies. *Taste the Blood of Dracula* (UK 1970; dir. Peter Sasdy) involves a secret society of old white men, who publically denounce, yet privately practice, social perversions at a smoky brothel whose entertainments include a "Chinese girl" (Lai Ling) and a "snake girl" (Malaika Martin). Corruption is racialized according to orientalist imaginaries in Fu Manchu, Sax Rohmer's personification of the yellow peril, and escalating anxieties over the rise of China, OPEC, and Hong Kong. Old white men of the ruling class become the new helpless maidens who succumb to Count Dracula's charms, thus parodying the established order's nepotism.

Hammer's last *Dracula* film with Lee and Cushing, *The Satanic Rites of Dracula*, examines multinational capitalism. The police solicit advice from Professor Lorrimer van Helsing (Cushing), who interrogates his friend Professor Julian Keeley (Freddie Jones), a Nobel Prize-winning specialist in blood and bacterial warfare and now working for a cult to unleash bubonic plague as a public health crisis. Van Helsing notices Denham Industries' headquarters is constructed on the site of the demolished and desacrilized Christian church in *Dracula A.D. 1972*. He surmises that Count Dracula, disguised as Denham, wants everyone to die. Irrational fears of total annihilation were familiar during the Cold War when nuclear proliferation was rampant. Count Dracula's English was impeccably accented in *Horror of Dracula*, but it is heavily accented as eastern European-sounding in this film. This auditory strategy is also employed in *Vampire Circus* (UK 1972; dir. Robert Young). Anthony Higgins's portrayal of vampire Emil with shoulder-length brown hair, olive complexion, and slight stubble of beard emphasize his role as a circus performer. He represents a younger "bohemian," "gypsy," or "orientalized" version of Lee's Count Dracula. When he transforms into animal form, it is not bat or wolf but black panther.

Coproduced with Shaw Brothers, *The Legend of the Seven Golden Vampires* was marketed as "the first kung fu horror spectacular," which Stephen Teo (2000) interprets as an attempt by both studios to reposition themselves in international film markets.[9] Shot entirely in Hong Kong, the film stars Cushing as Professor van Helsing, who travels to lecture in Chungking (Chongqing), the first Chinese inland port opened to foreigners in 1891, thirteen years before the film's story. He learns of seven golden vampires in a Szechwuan (Sichuan) village. A century earlier, Count Dracula transferred himself into the body of Kah (Chan Shen), high priest of the golden vampires, who traveled to Transylvania to gain Count Dracula's support. While faculty of Chungking University laugh at van Helsing's beliefs, Hsi Sing (David Chiang) confides that his grandfather destroyed one of the golden vampires. With his brothers and Shih Szu (Mai Kwei), he helps Professor van Helsing and his son Leyland (Robin Stewart) defeat the remaining six golden vampires and Count Dracula. Swordplay and martial arts are added to Hammer's battalion of anti-vampire weaponry. Typical of the racial/ethnic economies of Hollywood, only white men and a Chinese woman survive. White people save people of color from themselves and their history. Hammer's later films replace *Horror of Dracula*'s pre-emptive strike with defensive strikes against postcolonial migration. In *The Satanic Rites of Dracula*, a Chinese (or British Chinese) woman, Chin Yang (Barbara Yu Ling), beguiles the ruling class. Imperialist-inflected cosmopolitanism reaches a zenith in *Captain Kronos, Vampire Hunter*, which focuses exclusively on vampire hunters, averting any potential social critique through the figure of the vampire.

Hollywood's runaway films parody Hammer's earnest vampire hunters as guardians of world order. Count Dracula may have given the films box-office appeal, but Professor van Helsing gave them moral certainty. Although gypsies were included in representations of Transylvania, MGM's *The Fearless Vampire Killers, or Pardon Me, Your Teeth Are in My Neck/Dance of the Vampires* (USA 1967; dir. Roman Polański) makes a rare acknowledgment of Jewish communities (cf. Portuges 1997). Professor Abronsius (Jack MacGowran) travels to Transylvania with assistant Alfred (Polański) to pursue research on vampires. Lodging with the Shagal family, they learn that local inhabitants are aware that Count von Krolock (Ferdy Mayne) is a vampire. The film's title questions legitimacy within genre conventions: they are killers *not hunters*, parodying Hammer's gentlemanly duty to invade and intervene. The vampire killers may be fearless, but they are ineffectual. Professor Abronsius is feeble, often freezing into a solid block. Alfred is too timid to impale vampires. They parody the athleticism Cushing brings to his performance of Professor van Helsing. Once Alfred and Abronsius rescue Shegal's daughter Sarah (Sharon Tate) from the vampires' ball, itself a parody of Hammer's *Kiss of the Vampire* (UK 1964; dir. Don Sharp), they flee Transylvania on a sleigh. Sarah bares her fangs to the camera and bites Alfred's neck. Abronsius steers them into a frozen oblivion. The voice-over announces the story's ironic conclusion: "That night, fleeing from Transylvania, Professor Abronsius never guessed that he was carrying away with him the very evil he'd wished to destroy. This evil would at last be able to spread across the world." The film parodies cosmopolitan arrogance.

Shot partly on location in Austria, the film calls attention to classical Hollywood's systematic erasure of Jewish and queer identities, both on and off screen. The patriarch of the Shagal family (Alfie Bass) is costumed as an orthodox Jew. Shagal's name evokes Russian artist Marc Chagall, whose paintings depict Russian Jewish folklore and suffering. Shagal's *bekeshe* (long tailored coat), cap, and *payos* (sidecurls) resemble Chagall's fiddlers, particularly when Rebecca Shagal (Jessie Robins) sees her husband's corpse, frozen in a position resembling *The Green Violinist* (1918/1923–4). Villagers dismiss his death as due to wolf attacks, but Shagal resurrects as a vampire and attacks his maid (Fiona Lewis), who reaches for a crucifix to defend herself. "Oy, have you got the wrong vampire," jokes the Jewish vampire. The film comments on European anti-Semitism that Hammer largely ignored within its air of moral superiority. Von Krolock's hunchback servant, Koukol (Terry Downes), forbids Shagal to place his makeshift wooden coffin near family coffins. Shagal sleeps in the horse stable, restaging segregation based upon race/ethnicity, religion, and class, along with Nazi protocol of evicting Jews from their homes to freeze to death in the streets. Count von Krolock is enchanted with Professor Abronsius's arcane knowledge and thinks that Alfred will make a "nice companion" for his son Herbert (Iain Quarrier). Dressed in a powder-blue suit, the blonde Herbert gazes at Alfred's body, later cruising him as they pass in a corridor. His un-closeted homosexuality parodies the blonde heterosexual vampire, Baron Meinster (David Peel), in Hammer's *The Brides of Dracula* (UK 1960; dir. Terence Fisher) and Nazi notions of an Aryan master race, free of so-called degeneracies such as homosexuality.

Comparably, *Blood for Dracula/Andy Warhol's Dracula* (Italy-USA 1974; dir. Paul Morrissey) points to everyday human interactions as potentially more violent than anything supernatural. At producer Carlo Ponti's suggestion, the film was shot in and around Cinecittà in Rome over a three-week period. Morrissey was a self-proclaimed outsider to Hollywood and New York's anti-Hollywood underground cinema. Preferring nonprofessional actors for the freshness they bring to clichéd roles, Morrissey casts transvestites like Holly Woodlawn and Candy Darling or social castoffs like heroin addicts and welfare recipients. He invites actors to perform fictions of themselves in largely unscripted scenes, undercutting Hollywood's highly controlled conventions for acting and screenwriting. Udo Kier's performance of Count Dracula lampoons Hammer's vampires. He is exceedingly passive, physically weak, and mentally exhausted. His frail body is the inverse to Lee's robustly healthy body. His travels are compelled by discrimination at home, rather than ambition, curiosity, or revenge. At the insistence of his servant Anton (Arno Juerging), he reluctantly lays his sister to rest and leaves for Italy, where they believe they will find virgin blood due to strict Roman Catholicism. They arrive at the villa of the Marchese (Vittorio de Sica) and Marchesa (Maxime McKendry) de Fiore. The film satirizes superficial assumptions. Piety is equated with house size. Eldest daughter Esmeralda (Milena Vukotic) suffers under the social stigma that her broken engagement entails compromised morality. British, French, Italian, US, and Yugoslavian professional and nonprofessional actors portray the family and its one remaining servant, Mario (Joe Dallesandro), who reads the *Communist Manifesto*. In Morrissey's critique of dehumanizing aspects of American-style consumerism and Soviet-style communism, vampirism seems a viable alternative. Count Dracula's close family ties seem antiquated and disconnected from the 1920s, when Morrissey located morality's end and decadence's beginning.

The film opens with a long tracking shot of a pale and grey-haired Count Dracula, sitting forlornly at a vanity as he applies his "Dracula" makeup. He paints his lips red and his hair and eyebrows black, as the camera tracks around him to reveal that he has been working without the guidance of his reflection in the mirror. The film highlights disconnects between conventions and their production of cinematic and social realities. In another scene and another vanity, Mario is only momentarily distracted from attending to his appearance by the reflected image of sisters Saphiria (Dominique Darel) and Rubinia (Stefania Casini) making love behind him, parodying Hammer's so-called lesbian vampire films. Absurdist indifference to conventions unfolds when Count Dracula asks to travel with his collection of books and stuffed birds and when the Marchese leaves for London to have a surreptitiously acquired sample of Count Dracula's urine analyzed. The film lampoons Communist Revolution when Mario rapes fourteen-year-old Perla (Silvia Dionisio) to save her from Count Dracula's seduction. Mario then dismembers the vampire. His ascendancy over Count Dracula and the Marchese conveys a succession of one tyranny over another. Sexual and political revolutions are equally suspicious.

Unlike the resounding tones in *Horror of Dracula*'s musical score to queue suspense or surprise when Count Dracula attacks his victims, *Blood for Dracula* juxtaposes tranquil piano music with scenes of blood drinking.

Since Count Dracula cannot metabolize the blood of non-virgins, he convulses and vomits. The short duration of Hammer's neck-biting scenes are mocked by extended blood drinking and vomiting scenes. When vampires bite virgin women, the women become new vampires; when they bite non-virgin women, the women become slaves. The film establishes exchange economies through which Mario's sexual exploitation of the sisters is set in relation to his economic exploitation by the de Fiores. Like *The Fearless Vampire Killers*, *Blood for Dracula* challenges unquestioned assumptions that England was a homeland for *all* Americans by foregrounding Jewish and Catholic histories. The films destabilize the certainty of vampire hunting and postwar cosmopolitanism.

Silencing through Dubbing, Interpreting through Subtitling

Automated dialogue replacement (ADR) ensures that dialogue is heard clearly. Dialogue is rerecorded and remixed with some precision so that the product appears seamless, unlike dubbing and subtitling, which reveal the seams. The historical consciousness needed to de-imperialize cosmopolitanism thus appears along the seams of Hollywood's production of non-anglophone foreign movies. The seams reveal passages of time, movements across space, and powers of translation, interpretation, and recontextualization—in other words, material history in found footage. In dubbing, one actor's voice is placed sonically over the image of another actor's image, turning actors into ventriloquist's dummies and calling attention to translation, as Mark Nornes phrases it, "in the most troubling of ways" (2007: 208–9). Rather than synchronized and diegetic, voices sound acousmatic (sound without a source image)—"voices that command, invade, and vampirize the image," as Michel Chion describes (1994: 27). Dubbed dialogue often sounds as though actors were reciting text during a read-through or rehearsal rather than performing it before a live theatrical audience or running movie camera. It suggests a rupture in the medium's illusions, an "interruption" in the sense that Lalitha Gopalan (2002) identifies in Indian *masalas* to show the limiting imagination of psychoanalytic and semiotic film theory.

Lee's Count Dracula appears to speak his own mind, whereas Mexican and Filipino vampires appear silenced via dubbing into English. Dubbing interrupts the ever-unfolding present of narrative with historical circumstances of voice replacement. It highlights different moments: when the film was made and when it was dubbed—and for whom. Dubbing also interrupts the cinematic illusion of a coherent space constructed by synchronized auditory and visual images. Dubbed voices reveal differences in physical location of speaker and actor, rather than the causality of plot-driven narrative cinema. Synchronized sound and image stress *temporal* over spatial dimensions, evident in the rarity of close-ups with voices that sound faraway and ubiquity of long shots with character voices that sound nearby (Chion 1994: 129). Trinh T. Minh-ha theorizes subtitles "attempt to protect the unity of the subject" by collapsing the "activities of reading, hearing, and seeing into one single activity, as if they were all the same" (cited in Nornes 2007: 156). Dubbing disrupts the subject's illusory unity. Hearing and seeing are not aligned seamlessly—evident in close-ups to audiences acculturated to synchronized sound, who stare at the speaker's lips, though less evident to audiences acculturated to dubbed sound, who stare at the speaker's eyes, as in face-to-face conversation (Nornes 2007: 221).

Hollywood's foreign vampire movies are exploitation cinema in the double sense that Hollywood *both* exploits generic formulas and cultural stereotypes *and* exploits foreign cinemas as sources of cheap raw material for profit. Hollywood considered Hammer's films ready-upon-arrival for US exhibition, an equivalent to British immigrants who were white-upon-arrival. The Count Draculas in Mexican and Philippine films, portrayed by actors like Germán Robles and Ronald Remy, however, spoke in Spanish and Tagalog, requiring substantive changes before US exhibition. By removing dialogue tracks of potentially unfamiliar languages, images could be freely appropriated and severed from their original meanings. Voices often retained accent when dialogue was translated into US English. British non-working-class accents pass as white-upon-arrival; whereas Mexican and Philippine accents were conceived as foreign for their Hispanic tone and inflections, much like Lugosi's Hungarian accent rendered his English somehow foreign.

Mexican and Philippine vampires were nonetheless modern. The films are part of the alternative modernities that Dilip Gaonkar describes. "Those who submit to the rage of modernity are not naïve; they are not unaware of its Western origins, its colonial designs, its capitalist logic, and its global reach," he explains; "In haphazardly naming everything modern, they are exercising one of the few privileges that accrue the latecomer: license to play with form and refigure function according to the exigencies of the situation" (2001: 21). Mexican and Philippine Count Draculas might resemble Lee's for Hammer, but they cannot command his cosmopolitan power in US prints. They appear as cheap copies—"the same but not the same" in Homi Bhabha's sense of colonial mimicry (1995: 85–92). They appear in films deemed suitable only for marginalized exhibition, such as drive-in theaters and late-night television. The cosmopolitanisms of European, Mexican, and Philippine vampires are relational to social hierarchies in the United States for immigrants from Europe, México, and the Philippines. Certain films are delegitimized, much like certain voices are silenced or excluded from civil, political, and social citizenship.

Dubbed or subtitled films were no longer Mexican, Philippine, or European in the sense that audiences in México, the Philippines, or Europe understood the originals. They were constructed as low-budget cinema, reflecting minimal expense for acquiring US distribution and exhibition rights. Like constructions of race, categories of foreign movies are contextual, contingent, and plural, shifting shape like the figure of the vampire. The foreignness of foreign film—sometimes erotic; other times, horrific—shifts according to racialization. French and German films are produced as artfully transgressive, suitable for educated and professional classes; Mexican and Philippine films are produced as unimaginatively derivative, suitable for working and immigrant classes.[10] Dubbing, subtitling, and re-editing practices along with marginalized exhibition venues *produce* foreign movies—literally, in terms of distribution; figuratively, in terms of contextualization—as a *cheap copies* of "real" Hollywood. Marketing, distribution, and exhibition practices resignify films. Their meaning for most US audiences is primarily *intertextual* in relation to Hollywood vampire films and seldom to other European, Mexican, or Philippine films of any genre. Their meaning is severed from historical consciousness that recognizes hierarchies within the postwar political economies of trade and immigration that affect how foreign movies are produced as a category. Cheap foreign movies also reflect ways that Hollywood differentiated local US productions by making *foreign* an equivalent to *inferior*, thereby facilitating feelings of national superiority even among disempowered white populations, including rural and working classes, war veterans, and children.

Making "Mexicans" in Miami: Mexi-Gothic for US Television

Since the 1920s, Mexican films have had Spanish-speaking US audiences. During the 1960s, Mexican vampire films were dubbed into English. Purchased inexpensively for television as children's entertainment, they circulated within a climate of social stigmas following the Bracero Program (1942–64), which recruited noncitizen labor. Independent producer K. Gordon Murray commissioned dubbed versions with dialogue directed by Manual San Fernando at Soundlab in Coral Gables (Florida), and distributed by AIP-TV. Entirely new films emerged.[11] "Mexicans" were made in Miami for audiences illiterate in Spanish. "Mexi-Gothic" framed Mexican horror and *lucha libre* (professional wrestling) films as cheap imitations of Hollywood according to social hierarchies that criminalize transborder migrations.

Hollywood practices guide assumptions, reducing Mexican films to "the worst of the worst in horror films" (Melton 1997: 212) without reflecting upon how categories like Mexi-Gothic—and "churros" in México—are produced.[12] The films reveal longer histories of dubbed transborder crossings. During the 1940s, Hollywood lured top Mexican actors to dub films into Spanish; México responded by prohibiting dubbed films (Nornes 2007: 232). The films invite re-theorization of sound-image relationships. Rick Altman challenged assumptions that sound merely intensified visual realism. "The sound track is a ventriloquist," he argued; "the dummy/image is actually created in order to disguise the source of the sound" (1980: 67). He describes cinema as an illusory practice, concealing its production—human labor of a screenwriter, who writes lines spoken by actors, *and* technological labor that reroutes sound from apparatus to diegesis—so that separately recorded visual images and sound tracks appear unified. Not only was labor concealed, but race/ethnicity was erased.

Julie Dash's *Illusions* (1982) explores classical Hollywood's history of uncredited African American singers, "lending" their voices to white stars. *Carmen Jones* (USA 1954; dir. Otto Preminger) reveals "a curious spectacle of a black actress voiced by a white singer trying to sound black" (Smith 2003: 39). Dubbing has racial, gendered, and classed dimensions along with temporal and spatial ones. Audiences acculturated to realist conventions demand verisimilitude, an embodiment of voice by image, a *mise en corps* ("putting in the body"), yet dubbing does "not so much guarantee truth" but merely "authorize[s] belief" (Chion 1994: 132, 140, 127). The range of beliefs that dubbing authorizes are under-examined. The dubbing of *El Santo contra las mujeres vampiro* (México 1962; dir. Alfonso Corona Blake) into *Samson versus the Vampire Women* (México-USA 1963; dub dir. Manuel San Fernando) actually stages another wrestling match between audio and visual tracks.

Universal's *Drácula* failed to frighten Mexican audiences, but Cinematográfica's *El vampiro/The Vampire* and *El ataúd del vampiro/The Vampire's Coffin* (México 1957; dir. Fernando Méndez) and *El vampiro sangriento/The Bloody Vampire* (México 1962; dir. Miguel Morayta) succeeded. *Échenme al vampiro/Bring Me the Vampire* (México-Venezuela 1961; dir. Alfredo B. Crevenna) intentionally made them laugh. Recognizing Universal's profits, Cinematográfica's Abel Salazar claims he "basically made *Dracula* set on a Mexican hacienda" (Barrenechea 2009: 233). *El vampiro* indigenizes the Hollywood Gothic of *House of Frankenstein* and *House of Dracula*. Rather than plot and dialogue, meaning is conveyed through "a funeral lyricism with expertly choreographed camerawork and suitably atmospheric sets" (Paranaguá 1995: 243). Large interior spaces contain deep shadows between heavy colonial furnishings, candelabras, gilded crucifixes, and suits of armor.

Banned during the 1917 Revolution, haciendas are haunted by México's colonial past. With the arrival of vampires from Europe, haciendas and woods reanimate relationships between rural poverty and racial/ethnic hierarchies from Spanish colonization. Portrayed by Spanish-born Mexican actor Germán Robles, *El vampiro*'s Conde Duval imports neocolonial exploitation into post-revolutionary México. Under racial and natal hierarchies of Spanish caste systems, Conde Duval is *peninsular*, the highest caste, whose allegedly pure bloodlines are bilateral and include territorial nativity in Spain. Robles

Figure 4.1 The haunted hacienda as adaptation of Hollywood's southern (Alta) California Gothic. *El Vampiro/The Vampire* (México 1957; dir. Fernando Méndez).

adds aggressive sexuality to vampires. He brings boxes of soil from his native Baconia, Hungary, to remote and now cemetery-like mining village Sierra Negra to revive his familiar Conde Karol de Lavud (also played by Robles). They aim to reclaim land and power. Conde Duval imports foreign soil where local soil was unearthed in silver mines by enslaved Africans and indigenous nations. Supernatural terms open questions about *latifundios* (wealthy European merchants and landowners), who profited during colonization and abandoned empty mines and estates in conditions that prevented economic development (Galeano [1971] 1997: 30).

During the 1960s and 1970s, economic and developmental policies encouraged a small urban middle class in México D.F., Guadalajara, Monterrey, and Puebla; however, broader social changes resulted from migration of millions from agricultural to industrial sectors in northern border-towns. Santo (Rodolfo Guzmán Huerta) and luchadores "replaced bullfighters in Mexico as the popular figures of the day" (Clarens 1967: 159). Mexican elites and the Partido Revolucionario Institucional (PRI) detested them; working classes loved them. The silver-masked Santo emerged as a hero in an era of "national deficiency," and the films' success aided the Mexican film industry (Pérez Turrent 1995: 99), though dismissed as evidence of "an industry at the lowest point in its development" (King 1990: 130). Although politics of alternative modernities escape the notice of critics looking only for realist or avant-gardist models (Wood 2008; Barrenechea 2009), Cinematográfica Calderón recast vampires, mummies, zombies, mad scientists, evil brains, and aliens in 200 *lucha libre* films. In *El Santo en El tesoro de Drácula/Santo in "the Treasure of Dracula"* (México 1969; dir. René Cardona), Santo wrestles with Conde Drácula.

Professional wrestling itself crossed from Texas around 1933, quickly becoming an entertainment in the Center and North (Levi 2008: xii–xiii). It developed into a culturally specific practice (sport, performance, ritual) to negotiate social contradictions (modernity, indigenism, machismo, feminism). The PRI banned television broadcast from 1955 until 1991 for allegedly corrupting middle-class audiences with a working-class entertainment that championed the anti-authority figure of the rudo (Greene 2005: 9, 55; Syder and Tierney 2005: 42–4). Film became a medium to transmit the affective power of live matches. Associated with brute force and illegal tactics, rudos provoke hostility among audiences. They show emotions like anger, fear, cowardice, and pride. Técnicos convey athleticism, skill, and strict adherence to rules, thereby supporting PRI-sanctioned modernization. Técnicos like Santo, Blue Demon, and Mil Máscaras wrestle with movie monsters as stand-ins for banned rudos. Masks appropriate pre-Columbian designs from Aztec and Mayan visual culture. Outside the arena, luchadores wear international middle-class fashions like sports coats and turtlenecks. Wrestling requires skills and cooperation among equals, rather than bold gestures and hierarchical control over subordinates, yet rudos create space for contestation. Breaking rules can signify ways that systems work against minoritized populations, who become modernity's victims.

Wrestling and plot/dialogue fulfill different audience expectations. *Lucha libre* films move between *plots* with narrative conflicts and stylized *performances* of historical struggle and class formations. Unlike Hollywood voyeurism, wrestling films invite active participation, bodily and verbally, forging a sense of community at live matches. *El Santo y Blue Demon contra Drácula y el Hombre Lobo* (México 1972; dir. Miguel M. Delgado) opens on a sound stage with painted background and sound effects of a crowded arena where "the multitude's hero" Santo loses to Ángel Blanco (José Ángel Vargas Sánchez). Announcers narrate when luchadores follow or break rules. The film foregrounds wrestling over narrative about Santo and Blue Demon (Alejandro Cruz), foiling a plot engineered by Drácula (Aldo Monti) and wolfman Rufus Rex (Agustín Martínez Solares) aided by hunchback Eric (Wally Barron) to transform everyone into zombies and control the world. Santo and Blue Demon's match against Drácula and Hombre Lobo parallels ones staged on the bodies of Santo's girlfriend, Laura Cristaldi (María Eugenia San Martín), her sister Josefina (Lourdes Bautista), and Laura's niece Rosita (Lissy Fields). Once narrative conflict is resolved, wrestling conflict continues into a final and most spectacular match: tag-team of Santo and Blue Demon defeat Ángel Blanco and unmasked Renato "El Hippie" (Renato Torres) in three rounds.

Since Santo was always dubbed, audiences never heard Guzmán's voice (Levi 2008: 113). Dubbing into English, however, shifts focus from wrestling to narrative, driven by dialogue translated from the context of *lucha libre* to Hollywood horror. Dubbing emphasizes ruptures in narrative causality, coherence, and chronology, so that multilayered complexities of *lucha libre* are flattened. US companies regulated the border, determining which Mexican films entered and how audiences received them (cf. Clarens 1967: 159, Lee 2003: 189). The black-and-white *El Santo contra las mujeres vampiro*, dubbed as *Samson versus the Vampire Women*, conveys how transborder political economies are performed discursively and materially on *lucha libre* films and luchador bodies. The narrative concerns evil men. Only Santo, a "man of steel with a panther's agility and wrestling capacity," can defeat them, as the tagline indicates: "Solo un hombre de acero ... de agilidad de pantera, es capaz de luchar contra las MUJERES VAMPIRO ... y ese hombre es ... SANTO!" Santo is renamed Samson, substituting Samson's hair for the luchador's mask.

The film opens with bats inside a crypt covered with spider webs. The camera stops at a portrait of Rebeca, dated 1761, then pans to a coffin containing a desiccated female corpse. After 200 years, the master beckons vampires to awaken. Queen Zorina (Lorena Velázquez) must relinquish her reign and pass the tiara to her descendant, Diana (María Duval), as prophesied in "Egyptian hieroglyphs" deciphered by Diana's father, Professor Orlaf (Augusto Benedico). The scrolls tell of an "extraordinary young man," believed to be Samson's ancestor. He enlists Samson and Inspector Charlie Andrews (Jaime Fernández). Vampires attack on multiple fronts. One (Fernando Osés) poses as a black-masked wrestler, defeating silver-masked Samson with "karate."[13] Tondra (Ofelia Montesco) asks them to reveal the identity of their "stubborn enemy," but sunlight destroys the vampires. Samson carries Diana to safety.

The denigrated position of dubbed Mexican films becomes clear when compared to Italian *peplum* (sword-and-sandal) films, such as *Goliath and the Vampires/Maciste contro il vampiro* (Italy 1961; dir. Giacomo Gentilomo). The *peplum*'s glorification of masculinity (wisdom, strength, love) is contingent on white-male bodies as spectacle, epitomized by US actor Gordon Scott. His sculpted, tanned, and shaved physique signifies a wealthy body, nourished by quality food, leisure time, and money for bodybuilding and tanning—white-male privilege "put on display in colonialist adventure films" (Dyer 1997:

155). US bodybuilder-stars with contemporary haircuts fashioned after James Dean and Elvis Presley are inserted into historical and mythological settings. Maciste battles opponents in thirteenth-century Asia, seventeenth-century Scotland, and ancient civilizations and underworlds in Europe, Africa, and Central America. Narratives of *Santo* films are set in contemporary México. Santo's body is massive, not one to win international bodybuilding competitions like the youthful body of Reg Park in *Hercules at the Center of the Earth/ Ercole al centro della terra* (Italy 1961; dir. Mario Bava). He lacks muscle definition. Huerta was forty-seven when the film was shot. *Peplum* films are shot and edited for the spectacle of posing in close-ups; *luche libre*, for wrestling in long shots. *Luche libre* films are largely devoid of the homoerotic charge of *peplum* films. *Peplum* films emphasize exceptional white-male bodies; *luche libre*, social interactions.

The film's dubbing is characterized by fluency in standard US-accented English with attention to synchronizing lip movement and psychological motivation. Earnestness in dubbing tone cannot transcend meaning that affects transborder and transgenerational circulation. Accented and performed to sound unaccented, US voices speak through and for Mexican bodies, which perform the acting labor. The films' visual images are retained—raw material to exploit and repurpose—while their auditory tracks (at least, the main dialogues) are silenced and erased. Dubbing practices are structurally comparable to recruitment practices, such as the agricultural industry's Bracero Program or the IT industry's H1-B temporary work visas. Social stigmatization of Mexicans as ineligible for incorporation into citizenry thus appears on the surface of dubbed film.

In one scene, the multitude cheer for their hero "Santo" *in Spanish* as the referee introduces "Samson" *in English*. Two soundtracks, ambient and dialogue, figuratively wrestle. The racial/ethnic and national hierarchies of the border unsettle assumptions in film theory about unified subjects and sonic spaces. It is where Spanish has not been translated during voice replacement that Hollywood's "childlike image of a world" (Rich 2004: 166)—monocultural and monolingual—is interrupted. Cosmopolitanism comes apart at the seams, allowing for re-theorization of sound-image relationships. The film embodies competing impulses within transnational Hollywood. Spanish-language cheers from stadium crowds are part of the sonic environment that establishes primary interest in wresting. Nondubbing and nontranslation of the crowd's voices reorient the film *from* monsters and plot back *to* sport and ritual, from individuals to community.

The scene points to uses of voice that do not merely locate action temporally within a coherent, causal, and chronological plot, but locate it spatially across the discursive border that divides the Mexican American borderlands, calling attention to competing needs and desires. Mary Ann Doane argues that film authorizes a limited number of relationships between voice and body that are "first and foremost unity (through the emphasis on a coherence of the senses) and presence-in-itself" (1980: 30). Voices must be anchored in bodies, and bodies must be anchored in space. This illusion of a unified subject in the dubbed *Santo* film is assaulted. The dubbed English-language track cannot incorporate the original Spanish-language track. As Sergio de la Mora argues, universalizing strategies of cinematic masculinities theorized by Laura Mulvey and Steve Neale are misleading in Mexican cinema, where male actors like Pedro Infante, considered "the maximum embodiment of Mexican masculinity and the archetype of the working-class heterosexual male," can be sexually objectified without unleashing national anxieties since they "talk, sing, and cry excessively about their joys and sadness" (2006: 112, 15), unlike Hollywood's stoic and silent white masculinity.

Aired on 25 March 1995, Mystery Science Theater 3000 (MST3K) lampooned the dubbed film according to post-NAFTA transborder racial politics. MST3K's premise is that two scientists force a temp, Mike (Michael J. Nelson), to watch "cheesy movies, the worst we can find" until he goes insane. MST3K's

Figure 4.2   Parody of dubbing becomes judgment of a "goofy country." Mystery Science Theater 3000 broadcast (USA 1995) of *Samson versus the Vampire Women* (USA 1963; dub dir. Manuel San Fernando).

shadowrama silhouettes and voiceover commentary are imposed over original/dubbed images. Comments exploit US stereotypes. When a giant bat flies over Diane's fiancé Jorge (Javier Loya), the silhouettes joke "if bats get into his hair, they'd drown in Vaseline," evoking the racial panic of the 1855 Greaser Act. A costume ball elicits the response that "Mexico is one goofy country." Two party guests are described as "the entire Mexican middle class," with the inserted extra dialogue of "thank you, we had a really Hispanic time." The commentary conveys angst of increasingly marginalized white-male masculinity. MST3K's broadcast of the dubbed *Santo* film works against transnational working-class solidarity. *Santo* films emphasized contemporary struggles, such as "coyotes" (people smugglers) and nuclear proliferation. For Mexican working-class audiences, the performance, sport, and conventions of wrestling matches gave the films appeal; for non-Mexican American US working- and middle-class audiences, the films were about familiar movie monsters made "goofy" or "cheesy" by presumed incompetence. MST3K reinforces racialized prejudices, rejecting Hollywood films like *Salt of the Earth* (USA 1954; dir. Herbert J. Biberman) that advocate for historical consciousness and gender equality.

Undead, Unidentified, Unacknowledged: "Made for America" in the Philippines

For self-proclaimed aficionados like Quentin Tarantino, Philippine cinema consists low-budget jungle-horror and soft-core *bomba* films (Capino 2010: 3). Like Mexican films, Philippine films circulated in dubbed copies within political economies that extract raw material from colonies and unskilled labor from postcolonies. White US actors dub voices for Philippine actors, giving white perspectives on nonwhite experiences. Runaway Hollywood productions were common. Philippine heroes appear as cheap copies, requiring backup from "real" heroes from the United States. As Bliss Lim observes, villains are "not quite black" (2002: 31–2), bypassing recognizable forms of US racism. As "unincorporated," the Philippines "served to obscure the contradiction between inherent in a democratic republic holding colonial possessions" (Isaac 2006: 3). Unidentifiable threats conceal US presence during the Vietnam War/American War (1955–75). Prehistoric savages are more easily defeated than anti-colonial guerillas. For independent Hollywood producers, the Philippines became a new Poverty Row, free of labor unions. They defined "crass commercialism that characterized the competition among the numerous independent production companies" (del Mundo 1999: 42). Following Kane W. Lynn and Irwin Pizor's Hemisphere Pictures, Roger Corman created New World Pictures, alienating Filipina/o talent with slapdash films (Holcomb 2005). John Ashley, Pam Grier, and stars of 1970s exploitation cinema appeared in films "made to order" for US markets (Lim 2002), which were "not seen by the ex-colonized, who knew the empire's story well, but by the patrons of American drive-in theaters and grindhouses, many of whom were unfamiliar with their country's doings in the former colony" (Capino 2010: 3).

Imperialism functioned like blood contamination. Albert J. Beveridge's "March of the Flag" (1898) revitalized the Manifest Destiny, extolling "statesmen who flung the boundaries of the Republic out into unexplored lands and savage wilderness" of Hawai'i, Puerto Rico, Cuba, and the Philippines, disseminating "the blood of government" (2007: 763). Paul Kramer describes a transnational history of "the racial remaking of empire and the imperial remaking of race" wherein race becomes "most powerful and flexible" in "hierarchies of difference that legitimized varying degrees of disenfranchisement" within a politics of empire that "consisted of the struggle to define the very boundary line between colonizer and colonized, as well as relations across it" (2006: 4, 19, 24). Vampires appear in his analysis of John T. MacLeod's short story "The Sliding Scale," about *mestizos*. "Its narrative of mistaken racial identities, of dangerous male racial hybrids from the periphery who disguise their true identities in the metropole and threaten the racial-sexual purity of white female victims," he notes, "bears a surface resemblance to Bram Stoker's *Dracula*, published thirteen years earlier" (27). The Spanish caste system produced blood (*mestizaje*), bodies (territorial nativity), and borders (Christian/non-Christian) that continue during US occupation. Colonizers "racialize themselves as 'Anglo-Saxon' in order to legitimize the controversial US war as racially and historically inevitable" and simultaneously "racialize Philippine society into a set of fragmented and warring 'tribes' that were incapable of 'nationality'" (89–90). After the Spanish–American War (1898) until independence in 1946, Filipina/os were US subjects, recruited as noncitizen contract laborers (*sakadas*) by Hawai'ian sugarcane, Alaskan canneries, and California agriculture.[14]

The Philippines features in early US cinema, including Edison's battles staged in New Jersey between the US military and "Filipino savages."[15] The first Philippine sound horror film, *Ang aswang* (Philippines 1932; prod. George Musser), based on a folkloric female creature that transforms into a flying fiend at night, was given the English-language title *The Vampire* (Tombs 1998: 49).[16] *Terror is a Man* (Philippines 1959; dir. Eddie Romero and Geraldo de Leon), an adaptation of H. G. Wells's *The Island of Doctor Moreau* (1896), created a market for Philippine horror (Tombs 1996: 245). Amidst gore and female nudity, an Asian personification of Satan (Vic Diaz) enslaves a white US man, Joseph Langdon (John Ashley), in "a small town in Southeast Asia, 1946" in *Beast of the Yellow Night* (Philippines-USA 1971; dir. Eddie Romero). Asian evil is constructed upon racist discourses of yellow peril and Vietcong. The Beast wants to mate with a white woman. A recent DVD re-edition advertises "flesh-eating, devil-worshipping, cannibal monsters on an all-night snacking binge" with reassuring comfort that "thank god this could only happen in the Philippines!"

Philippine vampire films explored colonial history and postcolonial present. Hemisphere Pictures purchased Tagalog-language *Kulay dugo ang gabi* (*Blood is the Color of Night*) and *Ibulong mo sa hangin* (*Whisper to the Wind*), directed by Gerardo de Leon, known for his Filipino Academy of Movie Arts and Sciences (FAMAS) award-winning films. Hemisphere dubbed, re-edited, and renamed them *The Blood Drinkers* and *Creatures of Evil* in 1966, and Independent-International Pictures Corp. distributed re-edited and re-titled them for drive-ins as *The Vampire People* and *Curse of the Vampires* in 1971 (Holcomb 2005). Vampires fear crosses, especially illuminated by sunlight, and bite victims' necks, but make no transnational voyages. They descend from immigrants. Vampirism becomes a family curse among wealthy landowners, lifted by Catholic faith. If racial uncertainty evoked colonial terror, then species uncertainty evokes postcolonial terror. Lim finds the *aswang* has multiple associations in folklore, cinema, and politics, where it was used in "anti-insurgency campaigns launched in the Philippines by American military strategists in the 1950s" and by local officials to quell unrest in poor communities in 1992 (Lim 1997: 81–2). Vampires appear simultaneously modern and archaic, colonizing and colonized, associated with middle-class *mestizos de español* through casting Russian Filipino actor Ronald Remy as vampire Dr. Marco in the first film and through setting the second film during Spanish colonization.[17] Modern hairstyles and colonial costumes suggest contradictory forms of privilege.

A local priest narrates *The Blood Drinkers*, defining vampires as dead bodies whose souls have departed: a colonization of body in political terms, an annihilation of soul in religious terms. Rural setting establishes distance from métropole and colonial administrative capitals. Doña Marisa (Mary Walter) wears her hair and clothes in the style of a nineteenth-century Maria Clara and lives in an estate whose furnishings date to Spanish colonization.[18] She rides in a horse-drawn carriage on roads occupied by modern automobiles. Dr. Marco evokes *ilustrados*, the "enlightened" or "illumined" class, including national hero José Rizal, often educated abroad. He is not a specter of the past like Count Dracula, but a figure of an alternative modernity. His head is shaven. He wears a white shirt, black trousers and cape. His ribbon tie might date to the eighteenth century, but his sunglasses appear from the twentieth century. He appears a contemporary to Victor de la Cruz (Eddie Fernandez), a tourist from the city, who drives a stylish red convertible and wears his hair in a fashionable pompadour like Jorge in *El Santo contra las mujeres vampiros*. The film uses orchestral prompts and insert shots of a bat, Basra, for suspense.

Dr. Marco whips his assistant Tanya (Eva Montes), who sports a modern hairstyle and a giraffe-patterned dress, then licks her bloody wounds off screen. The next shot of a statue of Jesus Christ equates vampirism with perversion.

Shot mostly in black-and-white, later tinted red and blue, the film reserves color stock for scenes of spectacle. Hindi cinema's first color footage appears in song-and-dance sequences in *Mughal-e-Azam* (India 1960; dir. K. Asif), so it is unsurprising that color footage should be reserved for Rubén (Renato Robles)'s musical serenade of Charito, played by Amalia Fuentes, known in hollywoodcentric terms as the "Elizabeth Taylor of the Philippines." The story begins with Dr. Marco's failed attempt to revive his blonde beloved Katrina (also played by Fuentes) with a machine that processes her blood. He needs to replace her heart with her twin sister's. Doña Marisa entrusted Charito to peasants while she raised Katrina herself. Dubbing defines ethnic/racial hierarchies: Victor speaks with a minimal Hispanic accent and Charito speaks in a flawless US accent. Ultimately, prayer frees Dr. Marco and Katrina from vampirism, walking in sunlight shining through a stained-glass representation of the cross. Christianity "reworks death into the ultimate basis for conversion" (1988: xix, 169, 193), as Vincente Rafael argues about the Philippines. Color film depicts their romantic reunion in a lush green valley with bright red orchids and hibiscus.

The all-color sequel, *Curse of the Vampires*, is set during Spanish colonization. Women wear Maria Clara gowns; men, aristocratic and military costumes, cummerbunds, and embroidered shirts. Sets resemble Doña Marisa's home in the previous film and haciendas in Mexican vampire films. Count Dracula's three wives are refigured as Eduardo's three *negritas* in blackface to evoke indigenous Aeta, relocated from Luzon onto *reducciones* (reservations) by the Spanish. Vampirism emerges within the ancestral mansion of a wealthy plantation-owning family. Don Enrique Escudero (Johnny Monteiro) shields his son Eduardo (Eddie Garcia) and daughter Leonore (Amalia Fuentes) from knowing that their deceased mother, Doña Consuelo Escodero de Victoria (Mary Walter), is a vampire. Walter's character looks like her character in the previous film, only she growls like an animal rather than yells like a colonizer.

Vampirism materializes in acts of violence and incest. Doña Consuelo bites her son Edouardo, who bites fiancée Christina (Rosario del Pilar) until she appears "raped and beaten" by a "beast." In succession, Eduardo, Christina, and *negritas* bite Leonore, but the ghost of her beloved, Daniel Castillo (Romeo Vasquez), frees her from the curse of vampirism by impaling her with a large crucifix. Christian priests, nuns, and devotees pray and carry statues of saints outside before setting the mansion on fire. Leonore and Daniel's shadows reunite, embrace, and depart into a pastoral field. Syncretistic temporalities are more normalizing than terrorizing. Modernity does not pass itself as entirely

Figure 4.3   Doña Consuelo Escodero de Victoria (Mary Walter) returns from the grave to visit her daughter Leonore (Amalia Fuentes) on the family estate with *negrita* servants. *Ibulong mo sa hangin/Curse of the Vampires* (Philippines 1966; dir. Gerardo de Leon).

secular. Unlike islands in the South Pacific featured in classical Hollywood romantic musicals, the Philippines remains imperfectly modernized according to US imperial logic.

Runaway US productions convey different perspectives. Produced by Journey Productions "entirely in the Philippines," *Blood Thirst/The Horror from Beyond* (USA-Philippines 1971; dir. Newt Arnold) borrows narrative codes, stylistic conventions, and framing and editing patterns from *films noirs*. Black-and-white stock captures high-contrast images of Manila at night, opening with a close-up of the Barrio Club, followed by Maria Cortes's solitary walk home. Long shots are dominated by light reflected on lush foliage that blows in the wind under starlit skies, producing complex patterns of chiaroscuro imagery that Maria must traverse, occasionally under the black sky that fills nearly two-thirds of the frame. Prompted by nondiegetic orchestral score, Maria screams at the sight of a figure with a disfigured face. A low-angle shot disrupts the montage of eye-level shots. Maria's corpse is found hanging from a tree, her forearms cut and her body drained of blood.

Police captain Miguel (Vic Diaz) suspects a blood cult but calls upon his friend Adam Rourke (Robert Winston), an expert on sex-crime motivation and investigation. A Northwest Airlines jetliner and the modern terminal building establish Manila as a destination for international tourism while reproducing aspects that Allan Isaac attributes to classical Hollywood romantic musicals that "drive away the specter of military violence visited upon Pacific spaces to constitute a newly racially harmonious fantasy" (2006: xxviii). Miguel's adopted sister, Sylvia (Judy Dennis), cautions Adam that he is in a country whose habits and customs are not his own, echoing Count Dracula's caution to Harker in Stoker's novel. Sylvia recently returned from schooling in London, evident in her accent. Amidst the sexual tension between Adam and Sylvia with little danger of miscegenation, he locates the murderer that Miguel cannot. Adam travels with a dummy named Harvey, who absorbs the physical blows of would-be assassins. Displayed in semi-nudity, Adam's muscular white body contrasts with Miguel's (always clothed) soft brown body. The film celebrates international cooperation against threats preceding Spanish colonization in Southeast Asia and Latin America. Murders are a connected to pre-Columbian indigenous cultures, Aztecs or Incas, in "South America" when Serena (Yvonne Nielson), a blonde dancer from Perú, is uncovered as part of an ancient blood-cult. The film ends with Miguel having Harvey repainted and restored, so the Philippines will not appear inhospitable. The film exonerates the United States from any implication in Manila's social problems.

Material traces of historical consciousness emerge along the seams of unseemly films produced by Hollywood independents. Some seams are splice marks from reassembled films. "Exploitation King" Al Adamson's *Horror of the Blood Monsters* (USA-Philippines 1970) intercuts footage from three cave-people films—*One Million B.C.* (USA 1940; dir. Hal Roach), *Unknown Island* (USA 1948; dir. Jack Bernhard), and *Tagani/Flight of the Crab Monsters* (Philippines 1965; dir. Rolf Bayer)—the animated *The Wizard of Mars* (USA 1965; dir. David Hewitt), and original footage shot in California. Black-and-white footage is united with color footage by tinting. Names of the Filipina/o cast and crew were removed from credits, so their images function like *sakadas*, working without political representation. Astronauts land and shoot Tabaton attacking Tagani before they know anything about either group, finding both as evidence that populations "degenerate."[19] One comments that it is like "earth a million years ago—all we need is a Neanderthal man to complete the picture." Tubaton appear less white than Tagani. They have curlier hair, darker skin, and long fangs, yet are less animalized than crab- and bat-people elsewhere in the film. The astronauts kill with careless disregard for (nonwhite) life.

Portrayed by white actor Jennifer Bishop in brownface, Philippine actor Myrna Mirasol's character of Lian is americanized in scenes shot in California.

INTERNATIONAL HOLLYWOOD VAMPIRES

Figure 4.4   Prehistoric cave people from *Tagani* refashioned as vampires. *Horror of the Blood Monsters* (USA-Philippines 1970; dir. Al Adamson).

Lian becomes a human subject for scientific experiments to facilitate communication in (non-fluent) English by changing brain waves. Bishop's performance follows Hollywood convention for white characters allegedly degenerated from being held captive by nonwhites. Lian figures as "projection and displacement of the failure of the colonizer's civilizing project" to whiten the "savage," as Lim describes jungle-horror films, so that there is no fear the savage will turn against his master (2002: 33). Lian is convinced that she should want to be white but cannot understand why she will never achieve whiteness.

Small visual clues reveal different sources of the compiled film. Accented to sound eastern European in phrases such as "many of his wictims," a non-diegetic voiceover establishes background stories of infected blood of vampires carried to earth from distant galaxies. Scientists want to examine Tubaton, but no mission has survived. John Carradine plays senior scientist Dr. Rynning.[20] Willy (Joey Benson) is comedic, possibly Jewish, and falls for Lian, giving her his war medal before abandoning her, much like US soldiers on leave gave trinkets to Filipina lovers before returning to their wives. Bob Scott (Fred Meyers) is impressive in stature, not intelligence, and dies on the planet. With

129

his youth, blondness, physical and mental health, Commander Steven Bryce (Bruce Powers) performs the white man's burden of saving the planet from its own self-destruction, asking Lian with a Boy Scout's caring: "what can we do to help your people?" The film extends what Isaac locates in the inaugural Boy Scout novels (1911), namely "Progressive Era rhetoric imbued with a world mission" which "propels this domestic masculinity to disseminate a universalist 'Americanness' to its brown borders," specifically the "nation's newfound empire along the Mexican border, the Panama Canal Zone, and the Philippine Islands" (2006: xxiv). Like the US military in Southeast Asia from 1965 to 1975, explorers are forced to retreat. If the film is a cautionary tale about space exploration taken "too far," then it is also one of overextended imperialism. The films offer audiences alternative endings to the US defeat in Southeast Asia.

Distributing Childlike Images

Hollywood's production of foreign movies aims to sustain the illusion of the industry's own propaganda that it makes the best films in the world, as MPAA presidents William Hayes and Jack Valenti claimed. Production, however, occurs mostly at the level of *distribution*. Since distribution "organizes information in space and time, accelerating or delaying its delivery in spaces that it differentiates on that basis," Sean Cubitt argues that "distribution is the construction of difference," that is "distinguishing and dividing populations by their temporal and spatial proximity to the economic power and political economy that is increasingly centralized, not at the site of production, but on the terrains of exchange" (2005: 194). Hollywood independent distributors, such as AIP, Independent-International Pictures Corp., Trans-International Film, and UPA Productions of America, contracted English-language dubs and re-edits of films from México, Japan, Hong Kong, and the Philippines. The culturally low status of exhibition circuits for foreign movies reifies assumptions about the countries producing the original films and immigrants from these countries.[21]

If "dead labour which, vampire-like, lives by sucking living labour, and lives more, the more labour it sucks" (1990: 364), according to Marx, then Hollywood partly survived economic and social uncertainties from the 1950s through 1970s by sucking the living labor from films through dubbing, silencing the original dialogue. Visual images become the dead labor of foreign film. The stoop labor of *sakadas* and *braceros* is figuratively reanimated in an undead cinema. Through distribution practices, readymade films from Europe, Latin America, East and Southeast Asia were reduced to found footage for Hollywood's profit. The production of these films as foreign follows Hollywood's informal practices of role segregation and role stratification by race/ethnicity (cf. Wong 1978). It parallels incorporation of immigrants into the United States.

Ignoring or trivializing Mexican and Philippine genre films—and even European ones—as derivative of Hollywood produces no new knowledge; it merely reinforces prejudices and chauvanisms that undergird discourses of bad cinema. The provenance of dubbed films provides insights into ways to infuse film, television, and media studies with transnational awareness and historical consciousness to consider sound-and-image relationships as theoretically sophisticated and politically attune to uneven and unequal distributions of power. Monolingual anglophone audiences are often ill-equipped to evaluate dubbing, explains Mark Betz, due to their "lack of exposure to dubbed films (as they live in an English-language culture and cultural marketplace) and a fetishistic attachment to the idea of the 'authentic' cut of a film, an attachment that dubbing disturbs" (2001: 32). The production of foreign movies through distribution leaves traces in dubbing and subtitling of the historical conditions of political economies rife with uneven and unequal exchange that are based on the legacies of colonial and imperial exchanges.[22] Vampires often point us in the direction of noticing this frequently repressed history.

Cosmopolitanism's conventional ideal of "unity in difference" diverts attention from ways that historical power relations produce *inequalities within unity* and *unevenness within difference*. Independent Hollywood producers contain and control difference by producing different categories of foreign movies, distributed to audiences segregated by market. European vampire films become sexy foreign alternatives to locally produced films censored by the PCA and are exhibited primarily in theaters for middle-class audiences; Mexican and Philippine vampire films are made to seem deficient. Even today, their marketing on DVD invites marginalized (mostly white) audiences to participate in the cosmopolitanism of feeling American. Laughing at "cheap and cheesy foreign movies" served as a means to remind socially alienated soldiers returning from defeat in Southeast Asia during the 1970s of US national exceptionalism. The films contribute to feelings of entitlement to citizenship and territory that distinguish these audiences from *braceros* or "illegals" from México or *sakadas* or "dog-eaters" from the Philippines. Impolite (often racist, sexist, and heterosexist) humor serves as a means of empowering disempowered white audiences, offering reassurances that white appearance equaled whiteness and thus guaranteed nonmaterial privileges in the absence of working wages, social services, economic opportunities, world-class education, and sometimes even political representation. Other audiences looked to these films in other ways. For many, dubbed Mexican and Philippine films were a rare chance to see nonwhite actors in leading roles, as cosmopolitanism was reconfigured into multiculturalism.

NOTES

1. Hammer's repertoire of filmmakers is less unequivocally English. Peter Sasdy was born in Hungary, Roy Ashton in Australia.
2. Lee lost work by looking "too foreign" for Rank Organisation's films. For Hammer, he portrayed Fu Manchu, Grigori Rasputin, Frankenstein's Creature, and Kharis, the Mummy.
3. Robles's vampire in Cinematográfica's *El Vampiro* was "more directly the model for the image that Lee would develop and immortalize than was Lugosi" (Melton 1997: 146).
4. Fans of "bad cinema" recognized themselves outside the films' stories, enjoying fight choreography while laughing at "errors" in sound-image synchronization and "unrealistic" dialogue, often from self-censoring translation practices in Hong Kong. African American audiences recognized themselves within the films' stories as Chinese protagonists defeated European (white) antagonists. See: Prashad (2002).
5. See: Fanon (1952); Memmi (1957); Sartre ([1960] 1985); Glissant (1981); Vishwanathan ([1990] 2015); Young ([1991] 2004); Sunder Rajan (1993); Shohat and Stam (1994); Duara (1995); Mehta (1999); Spivak (1999); Mbembe (2000); Mignolo ([2000] 2012); Eisenstein (2004); Stam and Shohat (2012), among others.
6. Written and produced by middle-aged white men, Hammer films offered a "spectacle of a world in which all the classes knew their place" (Prawer 1980: 263) to audiences as England's significance declined.
7. Count Dracula's revenge resembles the psychological structure of Fanon's patient, who felt both like a vampire and menaced by one. Fanon's patient was a former FLN soldier, who murdered a *pied-noir* woman after French colonial police murdered his mother (Fanon 1961: 261–4).
8. Carlstadt is also a borough of Düsseldorf (Germany). Klausenberg is "a city and department in central Transylvania," "modern Cluj," which "at the turn of the century [. . .] had 34,500 inhabitants" (Wolf 1975: 2, n. 5).
9. Other studios produced *Hand of the Night/Beast of Morocco* (UK 1966; dir. Frederic Goode) and *La Sorella di Satana/The She-beast* (UK-Italy 1966; dir. Michael Reeves).
10. Dubbed prints of *Le Rouge aux lèvres/Daughters of Darkness* (Belgium-Italy-France-West Germany 1971; dir. Harry Kümel) circulated with art value, as did *Nosferatu: The Vampire* (West Germany-France 1979; dir. Werner Herzog). Dubbed prints of *Vampyros Lesbos: Die Erbin des Dracula* (Spain-West Germany 1970; dir. Jess Franco) and *La orgía nocturna de los vampiros* (Spain 1973; dir. León Klimovsky) were framed as artistic.
11. *La maldición de Nostradamus/The Curse of Nostradamus* (1961) and *La sangre de Nostradamus/Blood of Nostadamus* (1961) were assembled from a dozen serial films by Federico Curiel.
12. Named after a type of fried pastry snack, "churros" are considered formulaic, low-budget films.
13. Osés starred as La Sombra Vengadora (Avenging Shadow) in four films shot in 1954, coauthoring *Santo contra los zombies/Invasion of the Zombies* (México 1961; dir. Benito Alazraki) (Tombs 1998: 139).
14. Filipina/os were barred from citizenship in 1910's revision to the Naturalization Act (1879) and repatriated under 1929's Deportation Act. Once a commonwealth, Philippine-born Filipina/os were reclassified from noncitizen national to alien.
15. In 1763, Filipino sailors abandoned Spanish galleons to establish fishing villages in New Orleans, St. Malo, and Manila Village.

16. Philippine films include *Vampira* (1961; dir. Joey Romero) and *Batman Fights Dracula* (1967; dir. Leody M. Diaz), through *Aswan ng QC/Vampire of Quezon City* (2006; dir. Khavn Delacruz), *Patient X* (2009; dir. Yam Laranas), *Ang Darling Kong Aswang* (2009; dir. Tony Y. Reyes), and overseas *Aswang* (USA 1994; dir. Wrye Martin and Barry Poltermann).
17. Other European-looking Filipino actors—Mario Montenegro and Eddie Garcia—portrayed monstrous whiteness (Lim 2002: 34, 36).
18. Named after the idealized protagonist of José Rizal's 1887 novel of national awakening, *Noli me tangere/The Social Cancer* (literally "touch me not"), Maria Clara gowns have a long skirt, blouse with long and wide sleeves, and *panuelo*.
19. Philippine history is sometimes traced to "pre-historic Tabon Caves" (Rafael 2000: 7).
20. Carradine appears in *Vampire Hookers* (USA-Philippines 1978; dir. Cirio H. Santiago) and *Doctor Dracula* (1978; dir. Al Adamson).
21. "Since drive-in theaters did have problems getting quality products, they opened their arms to B movies" (Rhodes 2003: 2).
22. Under the Treaty of General Relations (1946), the United States granted independence to the Philippines bound by conditions of structural dependency, including ninety-nine-year leases of military bases, linked currencies, and the Bell Trade Act (1946), granting US citizens and companies equal access to natural resources and prohibiting Philippine citizens and companies from manufacturing or selling products that compete with US products.

5. VAMPIRES OF COLOR: A CRITIQUE OF MULTICULTURAL WHITENESS

National debates on immigration often replicate Hollywood's childlike vision of the world, ignoring the fact that not all immigration to the United States was voluntary. In AIP's *Blacula* (USA 1972; dir. William Crain), *figurative* slavery of Satanism from Hammer's films is reworked as *actual* slavery of the Middle Passage and *enduring* slavery of institutionalized racism in contemporary Los Angeles. Set in Transylvania during 1780, *Blacula* opens with African prince Mamuwalde (William Marshall), requesting Count Dracula (Charles McCauley) end Europe's slave trade. Count Dracula refuses, enslaves Mamuwalde with an insatiable thirst for human blood, and locks him in a coffin outside of which he leaves Mamuwalde's wife Luva (Vonetta McGee) to die. The sensational story redirects attention from US racism to eastern Europe's so-called backwardness and fall to Communism. The film acknowledges chattel slavery as part of US history. Mamuwalde is renamed Blacula, carrying two markers of racialization: ownership and color. Not inheriting an aristocratic title, he becomes Blacula, and not Count Blacula. He is sold as the property of Count Dracula's estate. His involuntary immigration as cargo evokes the colonial connection between immigration and commerce in the transatlantic slave trade. By contrast, Count Dracula becomes legend—"la crème de la crème of camp," in the words of a queer-identified antiques seller. *Blacula* conveys how afterlives of race encumber Mamuwalde's assimilation in ways about which Count Dracula remains unaware.

In addition to foreign immigrants, Los Angeles is marked by the second Middle Passage, the exportation of millions of African-descended slaves from the Old South to the Deep South and West between 1790 and 1860. As late as the 1950s and 1960s, African Americans were considered "immigrants from the South," requiring assimilation to the North (Omi and Winant 1994: 19). *Blacula* performs a type of historiography. With 10 per cent of the US population descended from African slaves, fictionalized and semi-fictionalized histories satisfy a hunger for black history because substantive primary documents are often nonexistent. *Blacula* recovers a violent and inhumane moment, erased in pre-Civil Rights comedies like *I'm No Angel* (USA 1933; dir. Wesley Ruggles) and *Just Around the Corner* (USA 1938; dir. Irving Cummings), with Gertrude Howard and Bill "Bojangles" Robinson in stereotyped supporting roles. Like Christopher Lee in Hammer's films, Marshall portrays the vampire as soft-spoken, articulate, dignified, and polite. The commanding height of both actors allows them to dominate scenes and shots, control the attention of other characters through sheer physicality, defined in immovable presence and quick purposeful movements. Psychologically, Blacula is not reconciled to murder and torture. His internal conflict suggests W. E. B. DuBois's "double consciousness" through which black subjectivity is divided by "two warring ideals in one dark body, whose dogged strength alone keeps it from being torn asunder" ([1897] 1996: 86). He embodies the existential dilemma of the colonized personality that Fanon (1952) describes. When he recognizes his deceased wife Luva reincarnated in Tina (also played by McGee), he hesitates to take her human life, understanding that his personal happiness condemns her to an eternity of enslavement. In DuBois's terms, he does not wish to "bleach" his "Negro blood" because he knows that his blood has "a message for the world." Blacula inverts the qualities of Count Dracula in Stoker's novel, whose actions are described as the work of "child-thought," demonstrating qualities equated with "man-thought."

Hollywood's blaxploitation films often circulated in the same exhibition venues as its cheap foreign movies. The films mark a post-Civil Rights moment when whiteness was being redefined in anticipation of multiculturalism. Harry Benshoff argues that blaxploitation films "attempt to re-appropriate conventions for racial advancement despite deeply embedded structures that re-inscribe racial tropes" (2000: 42). Blacula's white victims are marginalized after they transform into vampires, residing in abandoned warehouses, moving like zombies, and acting like junkies. One drop of Blacula's blood robs them of their whiteness—just as one drop of Count Dracula's blood robbed Mamuwalde of his Africanness and humanity. *Blacula* displaces ordinary social violence onto extraordinary supernatural violence, while referencing contemporary forms of institutionalized racism. When Blacula cannot repress the animal instincts of vampirism, it is visualized on his face, which looks like a panther, rather than bat or wolf, playing on white fears over black consciousness and nationalist movements such as the Black Panther Party. The white police lieutenant, Jack Peters (Gordon Pinsent), instinctively suspects the murders caused by Blacula are related to reports of "Panther activity." He later is asked why files for black victims so often "go missing," suggesting protection under the law is not distributed equally. *Blacula* evokes the long history of racial profiling masquerading as national security. Under US president Richard Nixon (1969–74), public expenditure shifts from social programs to law enforcement with domestic peace in response to black nationalism prioritized over racial justice (Marx 1998: 240). After the Los Angeles Police Department (LAPD) kills Tina, Blacula commits suicide. The counterpoint to this idealized couple is vampire hunter Dr. Gordon Thomas (Thalmus Rasulala) and his fiancée, Tina's sister Michelle (Denise Nichols), who move seamlessly between professional and personal relationships with African Americans and white people, anticipating multiculturalism's national incorporation of black protest (Marx 1998: 273).

Blacula conveys a preferred path to assimilation for African Americans like the vampire hunter rather than the vampire. It shows how whiteness appropriates non-whiteness. Hollywood plays to audiences both critical of and dependent on white privilege. At the intersection of longstanding faith in whiteness and a newly articulated intervention of multiculturalism, Hollywood mobilizes *multicultural whiteness* as a means to negotiate contradictions between overstated inclusiveness in multiculturalism and understated exclusiveness in whiteness. It emerges as a powerful means to redefine historical difference as an ahistorical diversity and depoliticized inclusion that sustains US national myths of democratic political representation. Hollywood vampires, however, loosen their ties to cosmopolitanism's indifferent detachment from national politics to acknowledge the afterlives of race in *vampires of color*. Reconfigured, the figure of the vampire of color sometimes frightens cosmopolitanism's well-intentioned (and highly privileged) beneficiaries, who championed clichés of tolerance or color blindness, such as "more unites than divides us," that ultimately reject difference. Multicultural whiteness suggests a seemingly benign contour of white power and privilege. It is less about white people than about white-identified people, thus it does not adequately challenge the power to be "just human" in Hollywood's classical era or cosmopolitan in its postwar era. It merely diverts attention from the ongoing processes of its powers and privileges. Vampires of color unsettle them.

Diverse Hollywood, Familiar Habits

Although never adopted as state policy as in Australia and Canada, US multiculturalism responded to legislation such as Executive Order 10925 (1961), advancing Affirmative Action policy through the Civil Rights Act (1964), outlawing discrimination and intimidation based on race/ethnicity and sex in the

Voting Rights Act (1965), outlawing *de facto* disenfranchisement of African Americans that had occurred since Fifteenth Constitutional Amendment in 1870. It also responded to the Immigration Act of 1965, which increased Asian immigration and decreased European and Latin American immigration by replacing quotas based on race/ethnicity-as-nationality to ones based on class and education. Multiculturalism challenged social assumptions that non-European Americans, whether born or naturalized, were foreigners who "carry a figurative border" (Chung 1997: 249) on their bodies and in their blood. Critiques of multiculturalism signal its potential to undermine indigenous rights to both knowledge and land. On Hollywood screens, multiculturalism was reduced to tokenism, which did open some understandings of assimilation as multidirectional.[1] Rather than requiring immigrants to assimilate into a mythical Anglo-American norm by rejecting aspects of identities, multiculturalism allows for guest and host to change one another. Much like a vampire infects its victims/lovers, multiculturalism's unending co-contamination proposes a radical political idea of becoming something else through endless combinations and re-combinations.

During the mid-1970s, financing and marketing strategies for blockbusters enabled Hollywood to take a more direct role in domestic film and television production. Abandoning the Production Code in favor of the more flexible ratings system in 1968, Hollywood studios replicated what Hollywood independents had done by appropriating successful aspects of foreign movies. Films like *Guess Who's Coming to Dinner?* (USA 1967; dir. Stanley Kramer) and *Bonnie and Clyde* (USA 1967; dir. Arthur Penn) represented (unpunished) sexuality, violence, and interracial relations. Like a vampire, whiteness consumes aspects of non-whiteness, severing them from historical context and thereby rendering them incapable of critiquing white privilege. "In an era in which 'white ethnicity emerges as a trope for empowerment'," warns Diane Negra, "[white] ethnic identity is valued for its own sake in opposition to a whiteness deemed sterile" (2001: 4). Without experiencing nonwhite pain or contributing to nonwhite struggles, white ethnic identity benefits from struggles for diversity, inclusion, and equity initiated by people of color.

Multicultural whiteness offered a means to reconceive industrial practices of racial segregation and stratification. Diversity and inclusion did not come with equity. It operates under liberalism's market economics. With suburban multiplexes, producers employed homogenizing strategies in films suitable for so-called undifferentiated audiences while also employing differentiating strategies to represent diversity on screen through token "guest figures," as Sharon Willis (1997) calls them, who reinforced white privilege by serving its institutions. Disproportionate employment of African Americans in government jobs also reflects greater discrimination against them in private industry (Anderson 2016: 122). Multicultural whiteness sustains white privilege without acknowledging it. Racism becomes "post-intentional" (Perry 2011). As a consequence, assumptions that present inequalities as unrelated to historical conditions are naturalized, extending Horatio Alger rags-to-riches myths that success comes from hard work alone, not inherited privileges such as whiteness. At their worst, Hollywood's multiculturalism diverts attention from ethically questionable acts of white-male characters and camouflage nativism as necessary for security.

Hollywood also reconceived Hammer's athletic vampire hunter as a post-feminist white-female slayer, diffusing both multicultural and feminist critiques of dominant power structures to secure white-male privilege in the guise of "girl power." The term is infantilizing, undoing the hard labor of feminism and excusing childish behavior from adult responsibilities, but it recuperates femininity from rampant chauvinism, everyday misogyny, and ever-entrenched patriarchy. White-female slayers were hits with audiences. Vampire films featuring predominantly African American casts, however, were often dismissed for not reproducing faithfully conventions of (white) vampire films. Vampires of color critique multicultural whiteness yet pass largely unnoticed by audiences who prioritize generic conventions along with sexual and gendered transgressions. Even when vampires of color perform multicultural whiteness sufficiently to escape negative stereotypes, racially blind audiences largely read them as ersatz imitations of white vampires. Despite the sexual violence that they initiate, Hollywood frames white men as victims—as "the helpless," to appropriate an expression from Harker's diary in Stoker's novel, and thus expose some of the slippages in signification necessary to maintain white-male privilege.

Such films position white men as potential victims of multiculturalism-as-vampirism. They evoke a white masculinity's appropriation of the representational meaning of *particularity*, which nonwhite groups have secured through political struggles for rights. White-male victimhood recuperates white privilege and its claim to universality, "redefining the normative by citing itself as a marginal identity," often through appeals to "injury" and alleged "losses" (Carroll 2011: 6–7). Racially conscious audiences see through this blatant opportunism and shameless instrumentalization of difference. They align with vampires of color, learning to adopt resistant or oppositional reading strategies like audiences of color. Hollywood's *racial segregation* ("black films"), partly demanded by self-censorship under the Production Code, becomes *racial stratification* (landscape of "bad" people of color against which white people and "good" people of color perform multicultural whiteness). At its most conservative, Hollywood constructs scenarios for victimization of white-male characters by female vampires of color. These stories sublimate violent reactions against programs that address inequalities in political representation. Representations of interracial and interspecies violence displace particular white-male fears of miscegenation and passing onto universalized fears of the supernatural. Multicultural whiteness functions as white-identified-ness.

Despite commitment to profit, Hollywood facilitates production and distribution of films critical of both liberal and reactionary rejections of multiculturalism as "political correctness" during the 1980s and 1990s culture wars.[2] Extending the contradictory stigma/seduction of ethnic whiteness of eastern Europeans in classical and international Hollywood films, vampires appear as African Americans, East Asian Americans, Latina/o Americans, and multiracial Americans, that is, as native-born Americans, not foreign-born immigrants. Vampires of color reveal repressed transnational histories to critique multicultural whiteness and, more broadly, the unnatural whiteness of America. Hollywood begins to depict *"differentiated racialisation"* (Brah 1996: 186) to show ways that racialized groups are positioned socially and politically in relation to one another, rather than solely in relation to the so-called non-race of whiteness. Race's afterlives return through multiculturalism as a disruptive force, signaling that actual diversity, inclusion, and equity are invariably going to make some people feel uncomfortable. White privilege, however, makes everyone without access to it uncomfortable in materially and psychologically significant ways. The key difference is that vampires of color make a group of people feel uncomfortable whose ancestors did not experience the slavery, dispossession, or genocide that solidified white privilege's power.

Vampires of color contest white-identified-ness within multicultural whiteness. They reclaim agency and property, including stolen labor and lands visualized in terms of Count Dracula's "earth-boxes." As Myra Jehlen argues, owning property or acquiring land was a means for whiteness to gain "individualist substance" (cited Bergland in 2000: 4). Annexing territories of indigenous nations not only allowed white men to become substantive, it allowed them to imagine the bodies of indigenous nations as "insubstantial, disembodied, and finally spectral"—in other words, "ghostly Indians," as Renée Bergland (2000: 3) argues. Comparably, Hollywood's multicultural whiteness sometimes exposes its underbelly in nativist fears of foreign contamination, expressed as xenophobia and fears of miscegenation, degeneration, passing, and trespassing. It functions like the "necro citizenship" that Russ Castronovo proposes to describe "how disembodiment empties political identity of specificity even as it hints at the indisputable materiality of bodies that refuse abstraction" into universal citizenship (2001: 5). Vampires of color serve as a means to understand Hollywood's processes of moving from representations of the United States in which racialized groups were *excluded* from national history and relegated to vehicles of capitalism's "dead labour" to representations in which selected "cultural" groups were *incorporated* under an "ideology of dead citizenship" in which cinematic representation is equated with having political representation.

National Passing: Difference Disappearing into Diversity

Vampires of color disrupt whiteness as a so-called natural order for things. They do not mind appearing impolite, aggressive, or uncivilized. Reluctant white vampires refrain from such directness. They simply want to pass as human. In Dan Curtis's daytime soap opera *Dark Shadows* (1966–71), Barnabas Collins (Jonathan Frid) is cursed with vampirism by witch Angelique (Lara Parker) and actively seeks a cure. Reawakened after two centuries, he seems different for more than accent. His dandyish taste in clothing, hairstyle with its Roman bangs, use of heavy eyeliner, ability to transform into a bat, and habit of attacking people mark him as different. He nonetheless passes as human by pretending to return to his family's ancestral home from his native England. *Dark Shadow*'s setting of the Collinwood estate in Collinsport (Maine) signals how past generations of European immigrants renamed territory after themselves. Barnabas upsets things, but *Dark Shadows* is hardly a satire of white privilege.

Curtis directed two spin-off features, *House of Dark Shadows* (1970) and *Night of Dark Shadows* (1971), and a revival series, *Dark Shadows* (1991), starring Ben Cross. The soap opera inspired a remake, *Dark Shadows* (USA 2012; dir. Tim Burton), with Johnny Depp as Barnabas, who assimilates into the all-white, European-named New England town though Elizabeth (Michelle Pfeiffer)'s cover story of a *return* from England. Barnabas passes with agility. As Benshoff explains, the series engaged with themes from Gothic literature, horror films, and "normal" soap operas, seldom touching upon actual political events, in the "resolutely white place" of Collinsport (2011: 82). The film makes copious references to 1970s consumer/hippy culture, ranging from popular fads of lava lamps and macramé to pop music by the Carpenters and Alice Cooper to evoke nostalgia, not for the past, but for its media. Collinsport is economically, politically, and culturally autonomous—utterly unconcerned or unaware of the approaching oil crisis and untouched by civil-rights struggles. The 2012 film conveys how post-multicultural whiteness functions less in direct acts like hate speech and more in self-entitlement to white privilege.

Hollywood's reluctance to unsettle white privilege is hardly surprising. Academia struggles too. Racism emerges in core curricula that segregate non-eurocentric perspectives as electives or frame them in terms of cultural relativism, fearing they might "trigger" discomfort in tuition-paying students. History and theory are conceived in *universal* terms based on the *particular* examples of historically white subjects. Whiteness is a "copy lacking an original," as Gwendolyn Foster points out, "yet it is performed and re-performed in myriad ways, so much that it seems 'natural' to most" (2003: 2). Multicultural whiteness reflects an expanded repertoire of acts within this performance since Americanness itself lacks an original. Indigenous nations signify a destabilizing pre-original. Werner Sollors has argued that indigenous nations became a "substitute ancestor" (1986: 124–5) for generations of European immigrants to solidify their claims to belonging. Americanness needs to be performed and re-performed, so as to pass itself as a legitimate and irrefutable identity. Hollywood is a stage for this unending performance.

Whiteness expanded from Anglo-Saxon to other European races/ethnicities—Irish, Italian, Jewish—in the early twentieth century, so it could also expand to incorporate traditionally nonwhite races/ethnicities in the late twentieth century. No longer confined to classical Hollywood whiteness's so-called invisibility, multicultural whiteness emphasizes so-called national values—individualism, consumerism, patriotism, secularism, and willful amnesia—that sustain foundational myths of a nation of immigrants, land of opportunity, and beacon of democracy. Multicultural whiteness becomes a *passport* to the national rights of citizenship. It is empowered by tokenism, inserting people of color as diversity, as a multicultural landscape of racially blind inclusion. People of color just need to act, speak, and identify in ways are nonthreatening to white people, especially ones without full access to whiteness. Rather than defining whiteness simply in physical (white-looking) characteristics, multicultural whiteness is defined in performative (white-acting, white-thinking, and especially white-identified) characteristics. Performing multicultural whiteness is contingent on acquiring property (fixed residences), reproducing in (heterosexual) nuclear families, consuming material products, assimilating into socio-economic order, and practicing secularized forms of religion (an imagined Judeo-Christianity) that do not interfere with civic law (as *sharia* is imagined). The power of being "normal"—that is, American—emerges in performances of multicultural whiteness by anyone who can pass. Multicultural whiteness is a form of passing, not racial passing, but *national passing*. Racialized identities, including politicized non-hyphenated identities espoused by multiculturalism—African American, Arab American, Asian American, Latina/o American, Hindu American, Jewish American, Muslim American, Native American, et al.—are subsumed by a universalizing US national identity that reduces indigenous *nations* to "cultures."

Multicultural whiteness benefits cisgender white men and women and white LBGTQ groups, diminishing guilt over white privilege without depreciating its benefits. It straddles contradictions of overstated inclusiveness and understated exclusiveness, emerging as an internalization of the unnatural whiteness of America in Hollywood conventions, styles, and production values. Lisa Lowe's notion of "difference incorporated" (1996) conveys how multicultural whiteness functions. It facilitates faith in national exceptionalism by subsuming selected aspects of racialized identity into a universalized national identity, so that once excluded *racial* difference is now included as *cultural* diversity. Hollywood representations of affluent white people, self-authorizing themselves to adopt practices of minoritized cultures appear in films like *Breakin'* (USA 1984; dir. Joel Silberg) in which a white-female jazz dancer finds success in break-dancing with her new African American and Latino American partners. The mythical Anglo-American ideal is decentered but not disempowered. Multicultural whiteness's power primarily benefits white people. "White Americans of mixed European ancestry have been the most uniquely positioned to claim or disclaim aspects of their heritage at will, often electing one ethnicity based on social definitions of what it implies" (2001: 3), notes Negra about opportunism. White people might eat "ethnic food" or speak "foreign languages," but they do so without risking stigmatization or disenfranchisement. Comparably, white vampires benefit from privileges not available to vampires of color.

Multicultural whiteness sustains illusions of US national exceptionalism like the mythical openness of nation to anyone, but it perhaps more purposefully sustains Hollywood's own sense of producing world-class productions with natural or self-evident global appeal. It often reflects bottom-line decisions by producers. Scott Olson suggests that US media "cater[s] to as multicultural an audience as possible," one that "brings with its expectations for movies and television many different ethnic, religious, linguistic, and social backgrounds," so that "the media must pare down narratives to their essentials" (1999: 85). These so-called essentials that make films "relatable"—to borrow an expression of Hollywood accountants—tend to require historical amnesia about a racially/ethnically fraught past of slavery, servitude, dispossession, and colonialism. Multicultural whiteness divorces history and power from political representation, rendering it on screens as though it had not been whitewashed. "Historical amnesia toward immigration," argues Ali Behdad, is inseparable from the founding of the United States as a nation, which required forgetful representations of violent conquests and exploitations of peoples, disavowals of economic need for undocumented labor, and nativism as a crucial component of nationalism (2005: xii–xiii). Hollywood facilitates—and profits from—this amnesia. Multicultural whiteness manages difference, rendering it into consumable styles of "ghetto chic" and "ethno-chic." It ignores historical differences between forced and voluntary immigration, institutionalized racism—practices evident in property laws, public schooling, racial/ethnic profiling, default settings on consumer-grade and professional photographic software and biometric technologies, and the investment of various immigrant groups to assimilate into whiteness. Assimilation varies by region and period. Kehaulani Kauanui explains that whiteness sustains white privilege through inclusion and assimilation to dispossess indigenous nations (2008: 22). The assimilating properties of whiteness camouflage US colonialism in Native America, Mexican America, the Philippines, Puerto Rico, and Hawai'i.

Races/ethnicities function in ever-shifting and ever-unstable relationships to each other. Role stratification and segregation are Hollywood practices that relegate nonwhite actors to supporting roles, based on assumptions that mainstream (white) audiences would not pay to see films featuring so-called minorities in non-stereotyped roles. Role segregation bypassed PCA prohibition of miscegenation, often interpreted as the mere appearance of actors on different races on screen together (Wong 1978; Cortés 1993). The interplay of positive images and negative stereotypes of racial/ethnic groups provides the setting for films in which, as Norman Denzin phrases it, "good and bad dark-skinned others could do battle with one another," positing an "acculturation to white goals (education and hard work) as the preferred path out of the ghetto" (2002: 6). East Asians, particularly Chinese, Japanese, and Koreans, were assimilated from aliens to so-called model minorities. Policy aimed to americanize them, Lowe argues, not segregate them like African Americans and Mexican Americans. "In Hawai'i," which was being whitened for incorporation as a state; however, Kauanui notes, "Asians occupied a racial place comparable to the structural relationship of African Americans to whites during the Reconstruction, where they were considered an economic and political threat" (2008: 19). Capitalist applications of multiculturalism organize and contain difference as diversity without inclusion and equity.

Although Universal's remake of *Dracula* (USA 1979; dir. John Badham) maintains the original film's setting in England, other films and television series represent the United States as the vampire's immigration destination of choice. In most, the United States remains predominantly white identified. Hollywood also produced vampires of color who disrupt the unnatural whiteness of American and unsettle multicultural whiteness, transforming it into a subject for debate and contestation. Certain representations of vampires of color are given greater humanity; others, greater animality. Terminology adapts. Hunters of vampires-as-animals become *slayers* of vampires-as-enemies and *assassins* of vampires-as-humans. Slayers and assassins are even performed by nonwhite actors, yet the figure of the vampire still threatens to disrupt the illusory reality of multicultural whiteness with historical consciousness.

Black Vampires, from Disqualified Immigration to Qualified Citizenship

Historically defined as everything that whiteness is not, blackness is excluded from foundational myths of a land of immigrants, so the slave trade across the North Atlantic and non-slave immigration from the Caribbean received belated recognition as part of US immigration history (Daniels 2002: 53). Black vampires disrupt what multicultural whiteness occludes from this unruly transnational history of US agricultural and industrial power through unpaid slave labor. Hollywood developed "new forms of internal commercial exploitation" in low-budget blaxploitation films between 1969 and 1976 (Miller et al. 2005: 64). After *Cotton Comes to Harlem* (USA 1970; dir. Ossie Davis) and *Sweet Sweetback's Baadasssss Song* (USA 1971; dir. Melvin van Peebles) broke through a presumed color barrier to mainstream (white) success, studios and independents discovered African Americans in supporting roles could become the "central attraction featured in a film's publicity" (Heffernan 2002: 62). Blaxploitation stabilized the financially troubled Hollywood system by representing African America, not as a multidimensional identity with complex histories, but as a unified subculture defined by easy-to-consume fashions, styles, speech, behavior, attitudes, funk, and soul food. They were exhibited in inner-city theaters alongside kung-fu films with Bruce Lee's confrontation of white power in the British colony of Hong Kong, which inspired African American and Latina/o American audiences to confront racial oppression in the United States (Bordwell 2000: 50; Desser 2000: 38; Prashad 2002).

In its appropriation of black cinema, however, Hollywood resisted complex and controversial subjects that did not promise profit. It abandoned the anti-Hollywood style, characters, and narrative of *Sweet Sweetback* while appropriating and depoliticizing what Donald Bogle (1973) and Ed Guerrero (1993) term the "baadasssss nigger," a hero unafraid to challenge institutionalized racism by transgressing its laws. Systemic measures and historical practices that maintained unequal access to citizenship, depicted in Charles Burnett's *Killer of Sheep* (1977), were reconfigured in blaxploitation into assumptions that poverty and violence were evidence of African America's alleged failure to rise, a racist charge challenged in Maya Angelou's "And Still I Rise" (1978). The implicit censorship through non-funding of van Peebles's *La Permission/ The Story of a Three-Day Pass* (1968), examining racism in the racially integrated US military, was uncomfortably like Oscar Micheaux's during the 1910s and 1920s (Siomopoulos 2006) and Spencer Williams's during the 1940s. "Despite the black hipsters and 'foxy' women on screen," Jesse Rhines notes, "much more often than not, whites were in control behind the camera reproducing their own point of view" (1996: 45). Blaxploitation generated short-term profit rather than readdressed long-term inequalities.

Blacula appropriated conventions from Hammer's *Horror of Dracula* to speak about the forced immigration of slavery as a repressed moment in transnational US history. Its sequel *Scream, Blacula, Scream* (USA 1973; dir. Bob Kelljan) appropriated conventions of Hammer's sequels to speak about Caribbean immigration as another forgotten moment. Like black nationalism in *Blacula*, voodoo is criminalized. It is a cult, not a religion. It evokes Haïti, whose 1791 slave rebellion and subsequent civil war became a push factor for refugees, including "free people of color," to Louisiana. The presence of these immigrants gave rise to fears among US slave owners that they "knew about the bloody revolution in the Caribbean" and "would spread sedition among American slaves"; laws were passed to prevent immigrants from the West Indies from landing (Reimers 2005: 18–19). US historians have largely neglected Haïti, "even though the United States gained a large part of its territory thanks to the rippling shock effects of the Haitian Revolution, which triggered French fears and thus the Louisiana Purchase" (Stam and Shohat 2012: 19–20). Jealous of the cult's preference for Lisa (Pam Grier) as his mother's successor, Willis (Richard Lawson) reanimates Blacula to harm Lisa. Blacula, however, asks Lisa to free him from vampirism with voodoo. He opposes intra-racial fighting and exploitation within a system that thrives and profits on such conflict. "You've made a slave out of your sister," he reprimands two pimps, "and you're still slaves imitating your slave master."

The potential critique of multicultural whiteness by black vampires vanishes with AIP's *Old Dracula/Vampira* (UK 1974; dir. Clive Donner). Framed as a comedy in swinging 1970s London, the film centers around accidental blood-mixing via blood samples from fashion models, representing racial/ethnic diversity and inclusiveness: blonde, redhead, and brunette (white) models and token black model. One of the white models has a rare blood type required to revive Count Dracula's wife Vampira (Teresa Graves). When blood samples are confused, Vampira awakens looking black, visualizing irrational and unscientific fears of miscegenation. The film is complicit with archaic blood-quantum theories. Although Count Dracula (David Niven) unenthusiastically rehearses the phrase "black is beautiful," he attempts to whiten Vampira with "white" blood. Meanwhile, Vampira learns to act and talk black after screening blaxploitation's *Black Gunn* (USA-UK 1972; dir. Robert Hartford-Davis), illustrating Stuart Hall's argument (1980) that black people have to learn to perform blackness. The antics continue with Vampira infecting Count Dracula with blackness. The film closes with Count Dracula escaping arrest, claiming that being identified from the back led to mistaken identity, as the camera reveals Niven in blackface in a shot that monumentalizes the racist practice through freeze-frame.

Blaxplotation became a so-called bad cinema. Its popularity with white audiences was often framed as appreciation for "bad acting" and "bad plots." Its crossover success contributed to Hollywood's misunderstanding of radical politics and aesthetics in black independent cinema that developed with the first African American graduates of UCLA. They drew inspiration from New Latin American Cinema, Sembène Ousmane, and African Marxism in Frantz Fanon, Amilcar Cabral, and Ngũgĩ wa Thiong'o. Their films deliberately disregarded key aspects of Hollywood realism, denaturalizing its cinematic strategies for social representation based upon racial/ethnic segregation and stratification embedded in classical continuity style and its progress-driven temporality. *Ganja and Hess* (USA 1973; dir. Bill Gunn) so much rejects Hollywood

Figure 5.1 David Niven in blackface as Count Dracula after "mixing" of blood. *Old Dracula* (UK 1974; dir. Clive Donner).

conventions that it had to be re-edited and re-titled as *Black Vampire*, *Double Possession*, and *Blood Couple* to fulfill expectations of being a "black film."³ The complexities of actual black perspectives on black experiences were not envisioned as entertaining, profitable, or necessary. They might make liberal (white) people feel uncomfortable. Misinterpretations of African American experiences supported abridged citizenship, including pseudo-scientific statistics of insanity in 1830s and 1840s censuses that alleged "freedom drove black people insane" since the "frequency of insanity decreased in nearly exact proportion from north to south" (Nobles 2000: 32). *Ganja and Hess* refuses reductive interpretations. Black independent filmmaking "contested the falsification of African-American history by Hollywood" by searching for "a film form unique to their historical situation and cultural experience, a form that could not be appropriated by Hollywood" (Masilela 1993: 108).

The film depicts middle-class African America as a space of isolation and estrangement. Dr. Hess Green (Duane Jones) lives alone in Westchester County (New York); he is a bilingual (English and French) intellectual, not a member of the slang-speaking underclass of "pimps and hookers," who are suspicious when he comes to feed upon them. These characters contain

Figure 5.2 Beyond blaxploitation: the educated and affluent African American man as the vampire Dr. Hess Green (Duane Jones). *Ganja and Hess* (USA 1973; dir. Bill Gunn).

blaxploitation as a style to be consumed rather than embodied. When the suicidal artist George Meda (Bill Gunn) visits, Hess understands the consequences of police finding a corpse on the only nonwhite homeowner's property. As a location of white flight, affluent suburbs become a site where Hess's alienation draws him towards black Christianity's long history of involvement in Civil Rights. Christianity is not mobilized in terms of protection against an invasion of demons but as salvation from demons already present and embodied. The film opens with a montage of a choir, singing lyrics that convey a history of the cross as an implement of torture and slavery. Counterpoint via intellectual editing places a close-up of Hess licking Meda's blood from floor followed by an extreme close-up of human hands receiving supernatural power in one of Hess's Christian paintings. "The only perversions that can be comfortably condemned are the perversions of others," Hess observes; "I will persist and survive without God's or society's sanction. I will not be tortured. I will not be punished. I will not be guilty."

Representations of death in *Ganja and Hess* are brutal. Wooden stakes, which typically slide almost effortlessly through bodies, are replaced with metal daggers and knives. *Ganja and Hess* resembles *Zinda Laash/The Living Corpse* (Pakistan 1967; dir. Khwaja Sarfraz), a Lahore remake of *Horror of Dracula* in which Dr. Tabani (Rehan) becomes an "evil spirit" (*bad-rooh*). Rather than positing a mythic moment of pre-colonial purity, both films suggest that careful negotiations between colonized and colonizing aspects of daily life are the only viable way to go on living. Hess becomes addicted to blood after being stabbed with a dagger from "the ancient Black civilization of Myrthia," destroyed by blood disease 10,000 years before ancient Egypt. He is drawn by competing forces, visualized in nondiegetic insert shots of a thin, blonde, white man wearing a black tuxedo and silver mask, appearing to invite Hess into a secret society, and shots of a corporeal black woman dressed in African-like ceremonial costume, leading several thin black men through a field. Assimilation and Afrocentrism frame possibilities. Still another appears in the form of Meda's wife, Ganja (Marlene Clark), who inherits Hess's property and condition. Her cunning smile at the film's close is a rejection of both the self-destructive artist Meda and the bourgeois patriarch Hess (Diawara and Klotman 1990: 36). The film's three-part structure suggests options for vampires of color—"Part I: Victim" on Meda's suicide, "Part II: Survival" on Hess's addiction, and "Part III: Letting Go" on Ganja's actualization—without Hollywood's clearly defined heroes and villains. More closely resembling Micheaux's work, the film provides no clearly defined boundaries between normality and monstrosity. Its narrative violates causality, continuity, and coherence; its sounds and images function interdependently and sometime independently.

The legacies of both blaxploitation and black cinema return in the mid-1990s after the so-called crossover success of Eddie Murphy on the comedy series *Saturday Night Live* (1975–present). Distributed by Paramount and coproduced by Murphy, *Vampire in Brooklyn* (USA 1995; dir. Wes Craven) refashions Hollywood's racially unconscious assumptions into critiques of industrial and social structures, inspiring other black filmmakers.[4] Maximillian (Murphy) comes to Brooklyn in search of police detective Rita Veder (Angela Bassett), who does not know she is half-vampire. Her mother conducted research in "the Islands," where she fell in love a vampire. Long shots of dilapidated warehouses and graffiti-covered brownstones show a Brooklyn unlike the middle-class one popularized by *The Cosby Show* (1984–92). The film also inverts Hollywood's racial stratification by inserting white "guest figures" whose psychological complexity is absent. They only appear on screen when at work, not having lives apart from this function. They function as part of the multicultural landscape, which includes white buffoons for comic relief, such as model and celebrity Jerry Hall's satire of everyday prejudices that cloud white liberalism. She performs white privilege by seeing racism only in "individual acts of meanness" rather than "invisible systems conferring unsought racial dominance," as Peggy McIntosh described it ([1992] 2012: 125).

Like *Blacula*, the film's fictionalized account of history suggests an appropriation of the historiographic strategies popularized by Alex Haley's *Roots: The Saga of an American Family* (1976) about descendants of an African Muslim slave. In *The Autobiography of Malcolm X* (1965), Haley shows how Malcolm X learned African American history by chance when incarcerated in a prison whose library happened to have books with content excluded from the textbooks used in the public school system. While scholars debate the *Autobiography*, Haley writes history in its multiplicity, inclusive of stories that not only fall outside the traditional (white) purview because they cannot be documented according to conservative historiographic practices and methodologies. Few formal documents exist, so black histories must be constructed and imagined from informal documents. Fictionalization becomes a historiographic mode. It conveys an embodied and affective history that conventional history's formal documents exclude from representation, much as classifications of African Americans as nonhumans or partial (three-fifths) humans excluded them from political representation. Maximillian tells the story of "nosferatu, the undead, the race of the vampire" being chased away from Egypt to Transylvania, across the Atlantic to an island beneath the Bermuda Triangle. The narrative re-signifies Hebrew biblical stories of exodus from Egypt, European travelogues and novels about Transylvanian vampires, the Middle Passage of enslaved Africans to the Caribbean and Americas, and Cold War-era legend of paranormal activity in the North Atlantic between the British colony of Bermuda, Puerto Rico, and Florida into a critique of multicultural whiteness.

"Getting Civilized"

The afterlives of race for southern and eastern Europeans faded quickly under multiculturalism. In Universal's 1979 remake of *Dracula*, Italian American actor Frank Langella's Count Dracula has none of the brutish stigmas of eastern or southern Europeans. He speaks softly in US-accented English, gives rather than takes blood, and appears civilized—white upon arrival. With shirt unbuttoned, he evokes Valentino's Sheik more than Lugosi's vampire. He shows that whiteness is not "empty" but an "Americanized amalgamation of European ethnic cultures" (Haney López 1996: 169–70). *The Loves of Count Iorga, Vampire* and *The Return of Count Yorga* (USA 1970; dir. Bob Kelljan) feature Robert Quarry as Count Yorga, a blue-eyed vampire from Bulgaria. Upstairs rooms in his house convey assimilation. His basement is filled with giant torches, red carpets and candles, marble sepulchers, and a neatly ordered procession of marble busts leading to a throne, evoking the visual order of Roman imperialism via Italian fascism. Garish colors suggest danger. Vivid green opening credits invert Hammer's red titles. Fashioned after *Playboy*'s Hugh Hefner, Count Yorga wears a red-satin smoking jacket with matching pants; his brides, satin nightgowns in shades of blue, violet, and ivory. There is no narrative explanation for his appearance, suggesting vampires suddenly appear like immigrants in southern California, concealing their subterranean difference.

Afterlives of race do return to frame eastern Europeans as uncivilized according to assumptions that communism is primitive and brutish whereas capitalism is enlightened and refined. In *Love at First Bite* (USA 1979; dir. Stan Dragoti), Count Dracula (George Hamilton) relocates to a world of assimilated Jewish Americans and criminalized African Americans. Evicted by Communists from his castle to use as a training camp for Olympic gymnast Nadia Comaneci, he argues: "My people cleared the land. We tortured innocent peasants for it. We even murdered for it. By Romanian law, that makes it ours." The satire's ideological certainty distracts from comparable US dispossessions and annexations. In television series *Cliffhangers: Curse of Dracula* (USA 1979; dir. Kenneth Johnson), Count Dracula (Michael Nouri) teaches Romanian history in a Californian school. Nouri's partial Iraqi ancestry suggests ambiguous foreignness in a pre-9/11 moment. Count Dracula (Brendan Hughes) leaves Communist Romania for the freedoms of California in *To Die For* (USA 1989; dir. Daren Sarafian).[5]

By the Cold War's end, Hollywood replaces evil spies from Communist Romania with free-market entrepreneurs from post-Communist Romania. *Blood Ties* (USA 1991; dir. Jim M. Bride) opens with the nativist Southern Coalition Against Vampires (SCAV) breaking into a house, murdering a sleeping white couple, and burning the corpses. Shadows of their wooden stakes frame vampire hunters, rather than vampires, as social menaces. Appearing on a local talk show, a SCAV spokesperson (Grace Zabriskie) calls vampires "dirty," saying, "it's disgusting if you have to be in the same room with them or if you have to sit next to one of them on the bus." The scene parodies the climate just before California's controversial Proposition 187 (1994), scapegoating Mexicans and Mexican Americans for failed economic policy. She yells: "what are you waiting for . . . them to take your parking spaces, your jobs . . . they want your jobs!" Although SCAV's proud and defiant racism is attributed to working-class whites with heavy Southern or Midwestern accents—so-called white trash—the film explores other facets of white privilege.

SCAV allows Cody Puckett (Jason London) to "fly back to the nest." Cody seeks refuge with his uncle, Eli Chelarin (Patrick Bauchau), a self-proclaimed free-market economist, who bribes officials in Long Beach (California). Cody meets Harlovan Martinescu (Harley Venton), who self-identifies as a Carpathian American under an anglicized name, Harry Martin, to escape social prejudice. Cody learns that his parents left California, choosing to live "as humans" in Texas. Disputes concern assimilation. For Harry, vampires have worked, paid taxes, and voted for generations. Eli argues that police do not grant equal rights to anyone whose ancestors "dropped from trees to suck the blood from unsuspecting travelers, sleeping afterwards gorged with blood like ticks." Harry counters that ancestors of his girlfriend Amy (Kim Johnston Ulrich) "clubbed one another in the peat bogs of Ireland." "We're all just trying to get civilized," he says; "It's just that some of us have a difficult time getting the hang of it." Amy categorizes Harry's "family's rules about dating people who are not ethnically correct" as "reverse discrimination," parodying fantasies of white victimization from multiculturalism. The film locates SCAV's nativism, Harry's internalized racism, and Amy's inability to empathize on a continuum.

In *Fright Night* (USA 1985; dir. Tom Holland), high-school student Charlie Brewster (William Ragsdale) confronts his new neighbor, vampire Jerry Dandrige (Chris Sarandon), exemplifying what Jules Zanger (1997) calls "the vampire next door." Jerry differs from vampires that Charlie watches on a television show called "Fright Night," hosted by Peter Vincent (Roddy McDowall), who played a vampire hunter on film. Fearing Jerry will seduce his girlfriend Amy Peterson (Amanda Bearse), Charlie enlists Peter to murder Jerry. The film's self-conscious awareness of codes conveys Hollywood's rejuvenation of its generic formulas for audiences with access to film libraries on home video. As with most Hollywood films, people of color appear but seldom speak.[6] With minimal dialogue and no character development, Detective Lennox (Art Evans) is an African American, who enforces a legal system that historically supports white privilege.[7] Set in a planned suburban community in Las Vegas (Nevada), the 3D remake, *Fright Night* (USA 2011; dir. Craig Gillespie), updates the story for an era of reality television's "real housewives." The film satirizes surface appearances. Charley (Anton Yelchin) and his mother (Toni Collette) meet new neighbor Jerry (Colin Farrell). The sanitized neighborhood evokes Showtime's *Weeds* (2005–12) with its widowed single-white mother pushing drugs to sustain a middle-class lifestyle. Jerry wears a sweaty "wife beater" to evoke a stigmatized underclass of "white trash." He holds women captive in his basement, like Hollywood's serial murders. Horror is mediated by cinematic and televisual references.

Other films concern vampires who appear civilized. *The Hunger* (UK-USA 1983; dir. Tony Scott) features ones who mobilize cultural power from northeastern Europe and a whitewashed ancient Egypt. Miriam (Catherine Deneuve) and John (David Bowie) Blaylock stalk victims at clubs, seducing them with promises of unprotected sex and recreational drugs. They remove knives from matching anhk pendants, slicing throats with surgical precision. Immediately afterwards, they shower and cremate the corpses in their private townhouse incinerator. Vampirism grants immortality but not immunity to never-ending aging—the "eternal darkness." Preventing aging becomes Miriam's sole obsession. When John begins to age, she seduces Dr. Sarah Roberts (Susan Sarandon) and stores John in the attic with her other victims/lovers. The film loosens thinking about sexualities with on-screen kisses between two A-list female stars. Thirty years later, its stylish nostalgia returns in *Only Lovers Left Alive* (USA-UK 2013; dir. Jim Jarmusch). Biblically named Adam (Tom Hiddleston) and Eve (Tilda Swinton) hide by "slumming it" in the suburbs of postindustrial Detroit and old medina of postcolonial Tangiers. The great-white navel-gazing reaches its apex when

Marlowe (John Hurt) hints that he is author of Shakespeare's work. White vampires are canonized as civilized.

Transient and Unsettled Whiteness

Jean-Michel Frodon identifies Griffith as the "spiritual father of American cinema" (1998: 85), noting that *The Birth of a Nation* is set during the Civil War (1861–5) rather than the Revolutionary War (1775–83). Griffith depicts African Americans as lazy, deceitful, and opportunistic. The moral demise of the South, however, is blamed on Carpetbaggers, northern whites who migrated south during the Reconstruction (1865–77). Since Carpetbaggers were often middle-class and educated, their arrival terrified southern whites, making them feel closer to "negroes" and "mullatos." They became "white others," people "commonly treated as if they are not fully white" (Foster 2003: 137), distilling anxieties over racial entitlement. In *Near Dark* (USA 1987; dir. Kathryn Bigelow), vampires pose as hitchhikers or cruise roadside bars. They attack people lacking fixed residences and family ties since police will be unlikely to investigate their deaths. Although the film's narrative is set in the Midwest and Southwest, it explicitly evokes (and perhaps blames) the South. The patriarch Jesse Hooker (Lance Henrikson) claims to have "fought for the South," refiguring the Old South as origins for a clan of white-trash vampires who kidnap white adolescents. The film reworks captivity narratives in Westerns (Sharrett 1996) with vampires replacing so-called bloodthirsty Indians. It links racism, sexism, and classism between Old South and Wild West. *The Forsaken* (USA 2001; dir. J. S. Cardone) also features landless and unsettled whiteness with Sean (Kerr Smith) leaving a career as a movie-trailer editor to become a permanently unsettled vampire hunter with fellow hunter Nick (Brendan Fehr). These films extend assumptions in earlier ones with lower budgets that examined transient and unsettled whiteness after multiculturalism.

Vamp (USA 1986; dir. Richard Wenk) situates unsettled whiteness in close proximity to blackness. It opens with an initiation ceremony at a frat house, a temporary lodging for livelong bonds of brotherhood. The main narrative is set at the After Dark Club, a vampire strip-club, located in a desolate inner city at a safe distance from carefree university life. Its main attraction is Katrina (Grace Jones). She is hypersexual, violent, and exploited by her consorts to draw clientele into the club, replicating exploitation in the film's marketing campaign. Jones's star persona signifies exaggerated foreignness—whether Jamaican, British Caribbean, or African. Voluntary immigration from the Caribbean by free black populations also disrupts US binaries of free white and enslaved black. Both Jones-as-celebrity and Jones-as-Katrina are nonetheless situated, as Manthia Diawara observes more generally about black characters in Hollywood films, "primarily for the pleasure of white spectators (male and female)" (1988: 70–1). The film amplifies this structure of spectator pleasure with Jones in the role of a stripper.

Like stereotyped immigrants with little verbal command of English, Katrina communicates through gestures and expressions. She is animalistic, grunting and howling as she licks her victims' bodies. Her transformation is rendered in close-ups of fangs extending from her mouth, her eyes rolling back into her head, and long claws growing from her feet. She is ungovernable and undomesticateable. In strip scenes, Jones's black body is partly concealed beneath white body-makeup, including white makeup, red wig, and blue contact lenses. Her black body is inscribed with commodification by geometric African-like patterns by white artist Keith Haring. Her vocal performance of "Vamp" recalls Shohat and Stam's observation that minoritized groups often appeared only through song on nondiegetic soundtracks, not dialogue. Editing of strip sequence creates eye-line matches between medium shots of white protagonists and close-ups and medium close-ups that fragment Jones's body, often low-angle shots that emphasize her dangerous power. Black female sexuality and agency are riddled with sadism and eroticism. Jones's facial expressions and bodily movements suggest hesitation and uncertainty. The camera never adopts her point of view. Katrina is always under someone else's gaze.

Vampirism is given the ethical purpose of population control through selective "waste disposal," as Vic (Sandy Baron), one of Katrina's old-white-male managers, explains. The strip-club performs an "essential service" by eliminating societal "dregs," who sustain markets for sexual voyeurism and

Figure 5.3 Grace Jones as the voiceless foreign vampire Katrina, trapped under Keith Haring's makeup. *Vamp* (USA 1986; dir. Richard Wenk).

prostitution. The strip club is represented as an unnatural environment for the white protagonists: Keith (Chris Makepeace), A. J. (Robert Rusler), and Alison (Dedee Pfeiffer). Keith and Alison defeat Katrina, demonstrating their exceptionalism. So-called model minorities of East Asian America, however, die. Frat-boy wannabe Duncan (Gedde Watanabe) and vampire/waitress Seko (Leila Lee Olsen) embody two of six orientalist stereotypes that Robert Lee (1999) identifies. *Vamp* suggests that white characters should not fraternize with nonwhite characters—or they might begin to resemble or act like landless and unsettled white populations framed as "exceptions" to national exceptionalism and white privilege.

George A. Romero's *Martin* (1976) situates a transient vampire within uncertainties and instabilities of a postindustrial rust belt. Martin (John Amplas) has blonde hair and blue eyes; he looks forever seventeen. The film shows how whiteness fails certain classes and immigrants and questions behaviors considered socially appropriate or tolerable. *Martin* reveals society as a greater threat to its citizens' wellbeing and health than vampires. It opens with location shots of passengers boarding a passenger train. Martin walks through narrow passageways between sleeping berths, carefully avoiding a white hand that dangles below the privacy curtains in a playful homage to Lugosi's exploratory hand in *Dracula*. Martin locks himself inside a toilet and prepares a syringe. Unclear whether insulin or heroin, he places the syringe in his mouth, exits and heads towards the compartment of a single white woman. As he picks the lock, the ambient noises of the train's creaking disappear behind nondiegetic musical motifs.

Alternating between color and black-and-white footage, this scene establishes the film's primary tensions. Color marks mundane reality; black-and-white, memory, hallucination, or fantasy. The woman transforms from ordinary in color to extraordinary in black-and-white. She wears a white, loosely fitting gown and opens her arms to welcome a lover. In color, Martin forces open the door, revealing an empty interior. After a toilet flush, the woman appears in a bathrobe and facial mask, noticing not fangs in Martin's mouth, but a syringe. He accosts her. Long shot duration and minimal editing emphasize Martin's actions as violent rather than magical. Shots of struggle repeat, rather than develop, action, emphasizing Martin's inability to mesmerize or seduce. The facial mask satirizes the movie magic of sculpted faces produced by classical Hollywood's three-point lighting, which transformed blue makeup into flawless white faces. Once Martin subdues the woman, he removes his shirt, slices her forearm with a razorblade, and drinks her blood before having sex with her lifeless body. Afterwards, he arranges objects to make it appear a suicide. Unmagical scenes frame Martin's actions of murder, rape, and necrophilia.

"There is no magic," Martin tells his cousin Cuda (Lincoln Maazel), noticing crucifixes and garlic bulbs throughout Cuda's house. Martin attempts to disprove Cuda's superstition by exposing secrets to theatrical and cinematic magic. He paints his face white, wears plastic fangs and a black cape to expose Hollywood's artifice. Other scenes critique the American Dream as another kind of magic. Martin stalks a white woman, plotting to attack when her husband is away, but is surprised to discover her in bed with white man. The magical ideal of happily married couple and sexually satisfied housewife is exposed as illusory. Other relationships are equally unmagical. Cuda's niece Christina (Christina Forrest) tolerates the unemployed Arthur (Tom Savini) as a means of leaving her uncle's control and the decaying suburb of Braddock. The new priest, Father Howard (played by Romero) is more invested in tasting wines for mass than indulging the older generation's faith in exorcisms. Magical ideals give way to prosaic realities. Martin believes he can be redeemed, not by Catholicism, but by self-confidence. He thinks shyness and sexual frustrations prompt him to murder. Ironically, the lonely Mrs. Santini (Elayne Nadeau), who makes love to him willingly, commits suicide by slicing her wrists with a razor blade like Martin's staged suicide on the train. The film ends in ironies. Cuda kills Martin for Mrs. Santini's death—the one death in the film, apart from ones suffered in a police raid, for which Martin holds no responsibility. Mrs. Santini commits suicide. Like Romero's zombie films, *Martin* shows whiteness is not always settled or civilized.

MISCEGENATION AND MULTICULTURALISM

"Race and racism are lived by virtue of encounters, real or virtual, with 'raced' bodies," explains Imani Perry, adding parenthetically, "and we all have 'raced' bodies; even those of us who are seen as 'racially ambiguous' are raced by virtue of our culture's fascination with our 'indeterminacy'" (2011: 4). "In the moments of these encounters, individuals read, evaluate, and judge others," she concludes. The possibility of such encounters both increases and decreases for people labeled or self-defining as "mixed-race." Their raced bodies expose how social and legal openness to so-called mixed-blood and mixed-race in individuals and relationships is notoriously uneven and unequal. Some terms are historically pejorative, like mulatto; others have complex histories, such as *mestizo* and *hapa*. In relation to African and Caribbean America, miscegenation and passing disrupt the "collective racist fantasy" of a clearly defined binary of black and white allegedly based on biology (Marx 1998: 75). Potential for social critique develops in films that investigate historical criminalization of miscegenation, stigmatization of passing, and presence of multiracial identities. Mixing between European races was a primary objective of the Melting Pot, but mixing between European and non-European races was prohibited through the notorious one-drop rule and segregation under Jim Crow. Post-Civil War state laws, such as Black Codes in South Carolina and Mississippi, criminalized interracial marriage, or nullified it as in Alabama's constitution, without explicitly prohibiting interracial sex outside of marriage (Nobles 2000: 48). The 1930 census removed the racial category of mulatto. Not until *Loving* v. *Virginia* (1967) did the US Supreme Count overturn laws drawing upon polygenist claims that blacks were inferior that persisted after Charles Darwin's *On the Origin of the Species* (1859). Classical Hollywood films, from *Imitation of Life* (USA 1934; dir. John M. Stahl) through its remake (USA 1959; dir. Douglas Sirk), stigmatized passing and miscegenation through the figure of the tragic mulatta, whose presumed psychological instability was an implied consequence of her mixed blood, not white supremacy. Passing is contingent on misrecognition by the dominant racial group and carries associations with "community abandonment and self-annihilation" within non-dominant racial groups (Gaines 1988: 19). After multiculturalism, however, multiracial identities were freed of historical stigma and valued as legitimate identities (Beltrán and Fojas 2008: 11). Vampires of color interrupt certainties in racial categories that continue to define power relations.

The Old South's rigid social structures become eroticized taboos in films based on Anne Rice's *Vampire Chronicles*. Rice reconfigures literary vampires after cinematic ones in *Dracula's Daughter*—and television monsters in *Frankenstein: The True Story* (USA 1972; dir. Jack Smight)—as reluctant predators. In *Interview with the Vampire: The Vampire Chronicles* (USA 1994; dir. Neil Jordan), French citizen Louis (Brad Pitt) relocates to Louisiana, where his family establishes an indigo plantation on slave labor. Louis becomes American in 1803 when France sells Louisiana to the United States after the 1791 Haitian Revolution. Lestat (Tom Cruise) immigrates as a vampire and transforms Louis into a companion. Unlike Count Dracula, who cannot assimilate with English society, these vampires assimilate into colonialism's creole culture. In the novel, Lestat takes Louis to feed on a "camp of runaway slaves" (1976: 28), emphasizing racial exploitation. The film romanticizes master–slave relations. Louis's slave Yvette (Thandie Newton) asks in the mournful tone of a jilted lover why he no longer visits their quarters.

Lestat tortures a mulatta prostitute (Indra Ové), mocking her Christian beliefs. For audiences, the film marked an important concession in casting two of Hollywood A-list white-male stars in queer, if misogynist, roles. Louis is disturbed by Lestat's sadism but does nothing to intervene. He becomes a silent facilitator. Lestat dislikes "democratic flavor" in the emerging multiracial nation, preferring "pure creole" (European) blood to mixed-race blood. The film shows how colonialism's racial hierarchies determine social relations. The child vampire Claudia (Kirsten Dunst) fetishizes secondary sexual characteristics of a Creole woman (Nicole Dubois) and adopts the French Estelle (Sara Stockbridge) as her surrogate mother. The film distracts from colonialism through a surfeit of cinematic references assembled in a montage allowing Lestat to "see" a sunrise.

Queen of the Damned (USA-Australia 2002; dir. Michael Rymer) extends cinephiliac references into music videos by vampire-turned-rock-star Lestat (Stuart Townsend), borrowing from *Das Kabinett des Dr. Caligari/The Cabinet of Dr. Caligari* (Germany 1919; dir. Robert Weine). Rice's homoeroticism becomes heterosexual love between Lestat and Jesse (Marguerite Moreau), overshadowing possibilities between Marius (Vincent Perez) and David Talbot (Paul McGann). The film plays with race/ethnicity's fluidity. Among the Ancients, the older generations of vampires, Akasha (Aaliyah) is understood as Egyptian. Her skin is whiter-than-white according to Rice's convention of vampire bodies turning to marble-like stone when they enter a deep sleep. Once awoken, Akasha turns black, gaining mobility until the light-skinned Akasha is fully awake to murder every human within reach.

Implicit prohibition against interracial socialization appears in *Vampire's Kiss* (USA 1989; dir. Robert Bierman). Set in the yuppie paradise of 1980s Manhattan, where cell phones are rare but smoking in public spaces is legal, the film situates potential dangers of miscegenation and passing at a distance from middle America's presumed intolerance. The white-male Peter Loew (Nicholas Cage) believes vampire Rachel (Jennifer Beals) infected him. Crosscutting between Rachel's seduction of Peter and Count Orlok's seduction of Ellen in *Nosferatu* places Peter in a feminized position. Elsewhere, white masculinity is equated with financial independence, reinforced visually through plentiful exterior shots of Manhattan's heroic architectural erections to capitalist enterprise. Unable to work, Peter's financial status droops. Suits become dirty; professionally ironed shirts, wrinkled; well-coiffed hair, disheveled. Peter's degraded social standing forces him to purchase inexpensive vampire fangs— the "cheapie" ones, according to the Fang Vendor (Stephen Chen)—a satire of yuppie equations of self-worth with over-inflated price tags and designer labels. The bargain fangs contrast with Peter's expensive sunglasses, which he wears inside, believing that his eyes have become abnormally sensitive to sunlight.[8] Eventually, he wanders outside, asking passers-by to thrust a wooden stake through his heart.

Cage's performance of blatantly sexist and racist behavior becomes satire. Peter's sexual desire for women of color parodies social fears of degeneration through miscegenation (cf. Young 1996), displacing them onto individual fears of impregnating one of these women and endangering a privileged white-male bachelor status.[9] Peter insults his African American girlfriend Jackie (Kasi Lemmons) with racist slurs, murders a white woman (Jill Gatsby) at a disco, and unremorsefully abuses and rapes his Latina American secretary Alva Restrepo (Maria Conchita Alonso). Peter's relationship with Alva parallels Manhattan's relationship to Brooklyn, Queens, Staten Island, and the Bronx with their large populations of people of color, both citizens and immigrants, as cheap labor (cf. Sassen 1991). Terrified by Peter, Alva dreads going to work. Her mother (Sol Echeverría) says she does not have the luxury to work for someone she does not hate. Peter humiliates and abuses women because he feels tortured by Rachel, who asked him to tell her that he loves her. Alva's brother Emilio (Bob Lujan) avenges her rape by murdering Peter. The shot of Peter's impaled corpse in his ransacked apartment is immediately followed by a shot of Rachel speaking directly towards the camera against a solid black background. The extradiegetic shot connotes power relations, actual or imagined. It is information for audiences, not characters, reducing Rachel to the spectacle of cinematic vamp, yet her laughter is ambiguous, perhaps prompted by her destruction of a sexist and racist white man. Although Peter's "Continental bullshit accent," self-indulgences, and other questionable qualities work to demonize him, the film's cinematography and editing work more forcefully to demonize Rachel.[10] Negotiated readings to locate social satire require effort.

White characters appear as multiculturalism's victims. Peter abuses women throughout the film yet murders only an unnamed white woman, reinforcing implicit dangers of white women suffering when white men date "outside" their race. This suffering seems particularly the case when they date light-skinned black women. Peter wanders the streets, searching for a willing assassin. He hallucinates a conversation with his white-female therapist Dr. Glaser (Elizabeth Ashley). She facilitates his psychosis: rape becomes "just a little id release," murder occurs "everyday in New York"—his actions are nothing that should stop his quest for romance. After revealing the cause of his "depression" is a need for genuine love, she offers an amorous fantasy woman, white yuppie Sharon (Jessica Lundy), but Peter violently rejects Sharon. The film again suggests that white women suffer, emotionally and physically, when white men date women of color. Collectively, these films raise questions about whiteness after multiculturalism. Vampires of color unsettle multicultural whiteness to expose how it buttresses white privilege.

Historicizing Multiculturalism

Multicultural whiteness does not represent the diversity of United States, its people, their different desires and fantasies; rather, it represents the structures of power within the United States, the persistence of whiteness as a normative definition of Americanness. It reconfigures white privilege for a postcolonial era of proxy wars and neoliberalism. While vampire hunters distanced themselves from violence by rebranding as slayers, vampires closed the distance between themselves and other species, recovering what Auerbach identifies as a pre-Stoker vampire defined by affinities. Developed while *Låt den rätte komma in/Let the Right One In* (Sweden 2008; dir. Tomas Alfredson), an earlier adaptation of the same novel, was still in theatrical release, Hammer's *Let Me In* (USA 2010; dir. Matt Reeves) transforms the convention of the vampire's need to be invited into a person's home from a trope for deception to one for trust. Set in Los Alamos (New Mexico), where the United States developed nuclear weapons under the Manhattan Project in 1983, the story unfolds at a time when US president Ronald Reagan proclaimed that "evil" existed only "outside America." Los Alamos is one of the least racially/ethnically diverse places in the Southwest. Its location removes the story from the spectacle of so-called illegal immigrations in the borderlands. The southwest becomes a very white place, literally covered in snow. It looks like Sweden. A bond develops between a white boy, Owen (Kodi Smit-McPhee), taunted by his older classmates for seeming like a girl, and a twelve-year-old-looking white vampire, Abby (Chloë Grace Moretz), self-defining as "not a girl" but "nothing." Owen invites Abby into his room and later asks her to invite him into her room. The film transforms vampirism into an empowering trope against gender norms and homophobia. It advocates for interspecies understandings, particularly among neighbors, and hints through Reagan's speech to the Christian undercurrents of militarized secular discourse.

The Addiction (USA 1995; dir. Abel Ferrara) addresses social issues such as urban poverty, drug addiction, and HIV/AIDS by looking to continuities between the second World War and the Cold War. It explores concepts of guilt and accountability by focusing on Kathleen Conklin (Lili Taylor), a doctoral student in philosophy at NYU, who is bitten by a stranger in the East Village. The white-female vampire Casanova (Annabella Sciorra) challenges Kathleen to look her in the eye and tell her to go away. Shot on black-and-white, the mark of the vampire is not the stylized twin prick points of classical Hollywood but a large black circle oozing with viscous blood. Vampirism reveals how people choose their addictions—whether heroin, cocaine, alcohol, tobacco, sex, religion, or patriotism. Kathleen is addicted to European philosophy. She reads Sartre, Heidegger, Kierkegaard, and Nietzsche as a means to understand the so-called evil that humanity carries from generation to generation. The United States, she discovers, is addicted to violence. *The Addiction* is a violent critique of the social violence that reconfigures the stylized violence of vampire films.

The film critiques multicultural whiteness as another form of violence. It maintains Hollywood's racial stratifications with a few token African American characters, including Kathleen's unnamed professor (Paul Calderon) and Black (Fredro Starr), but it normalizes interracial sexual relations in the wake of Spike Lee's *Jungle Fever* (1991), even referencing it in a scene outside a pizza and falafel joint on St. Mark's Place. Most of the cast is recognizably white, from the unnamed anthropology student from Kansas (Kathryn Erbe) to the mysterious vampire Peina (Christopher Walken). The film returns to ways that history has dealt with recent genocides and massacres, outside the United States. It exposes blind-spots in western philosophy to colonialism, including the genocide of indigenous nations and enslavement of Africans.

With her classmate Jean (Edie Falco), Kathleen attends a lecture on the My Lai Massacre and an exhibition on the Holocaust to question how humanity can commit such large-scale atrocities and how responsibility for them is addressed. Kathleen is not satisfied that individual soldiers were held accountable for war crimes when their commanders were not—and, more significantly, when "an entire country" is not. US taxpayers, she reasons, have turned Central America into a "mud muddle." US soldiers were charged with annihilating communism in Southeast Asia, which took the form of beating, raping, torturing, and murdering Vietnamese civilians, including women and children on 16 March 1968. If Hollywood films often reduce multiculturalism to a docile background of diverse faces, then *The Addiction* interrogates the wars, exploitations, and other violent exchanges that precede this ahistorical and depoliticized diversity.

US national myths as a land of equal opportunity and beacon of democracy are complicated by transnational histories that recognize how certain waves of immigration were *driven* to the United States rather than attracted to it. Whether it was the Middle Passage for African Americans, the Holocaust for Jewish Americans, or the war in Southeast Asia for Vietnamese Americans,

Figure 5.4 NYU doctoral student in philosophy, Kathleen Conklin (Lili Taylor), shocked by her own ignorance of US military massacre of women and children in Viet Nam. *The Addiction* (USA 1995; dir. Abel Ferrara).

Cambodian Americans, and Laotian Americans, US multiculturalism follows upon bloody transnational histories. "There is no history," Kathleen postulates; "everything we are is eternally with us." The question, she reasons, is "what can save us from spreading the black and ever widening-circles?" Her choice of words echoes to Harker's characterization of Count Dracula—"a new and ever-widening circle of semi-demons to batten on the helpless"—in Stoker's novel, but her logic is different. History remains eternally with us through historical consciousness, so war crimes are as integral to the United States as heroic myths of refuge to "huddled masses yearning to breathe free." Critiques of the historically—and thus racially—blind national exceptionalism prepare for critiques of neoliberalism, as discussed in the next chapter. Contemplation on complicity open to questions about responsibility and accountability, refusing to allow guilt to end discussion. "We're not sinners because we sin, but we sin because we are sinners," Casanova tells Kathleen in hospital; "we're not evil because of the evil we do, but we do evil because we are evil." Rather than whitewashing US history into multicultural whiteness, *The Addiction*, asks us to live with history, including (overseas) US imperialism.

Notes

1. Cf. Gordon and Newfield (1996).
2. On multiculturalism and liberal pluralism, see: Stam and Shohat (2012: 384–92).
3. *Ganja and Hess* was screened at the Cannes Film Festival, eager to bypass France's own racial violence.
4. Films include *Def by Temptation* (1990; dir. James Bond III), *Vampiraz* (2004; dir. John Bacchus), and *Vampire Assassin* (2005; dir. Ron Hall).
5. This narrative device appears earlier in *Dracula, père et fils* (France 1976; dir. Édouard Molinaro) (Hudson 2011). Other films include *A Polish Vampire in Burbank* (1985; dir. Mark Pirro), *Daughter of Darkness* (1989; dir. Stuart Gordon), *Nadja* (1994; dir. Michael Almereyda), and *Habit* (1997; dir. Larry Fessenden). Ted Nicolaou's *Subspecies* (1991), *Bloodstone: Subspecies II* (1993), *Bloodlust: Subspecies III* (1994); *The Vampire Journals* (USA-Romania 1997), and *Subspecies 4: Bloodstorm* (1998) represent post-Communist Romania. *Dracula: The Prince of Darkness* (2000; dir. Joe Chapelle) conflates Count Dracula and Vlad Țepeș into a democratic and romantic hero.
6. Other predominantly white films, not discussed elsewhere, include: *Dracula (The Dirty Old Man)* (1969; dir. William Edwards), *Guess What Happened to Dracula?* (1970; dir. Laurence Merrcik), *Let's Scare Jessica to Death* (1971; dir. John D. Hancock), *The Velvet Vampire* (1971; dir. Stephanie Rothman), *Grave of the Vampire* (1972; dir. John Hayes), *Nocturna: Granddaughter of Dracula* (1979; dir. Harry Hurwitz), *My Best Friend Is A Vampire* (1988; dir. Jimmy Huston), *Fright Night Part II* (1989; dir. Tommy Lee Wallace), *Innocent Blood* (1992; dir. John Landis), *Midnight Kiss* (1993; Joel Bender), *Once Bitten* (1995; dir. Howard Storm), *Sucker the Vampire* (1998; dir. Hans Radionoff), *Drawing Blood* (1999; dir. Sergio Lapel), *The Little Vampire* (Germany-Netherlands-USA 2000; dir. Uli Edel), *Shadow of the Vampire* (UK-USA-Luxembourg 2000; dir. E. Elias Merhige), *The Room* (2003; dir. Tommy Wiseau), *The Hamiltons* (2006; dir. Butcher Brothers), *An Irish Vampire in Hollywood* (Ireland-USA 2007/2013; dir. Pegarty

Long), *Bloodwine* (2008; dir. Patrick Keith), *Blood on the Highway* (2008; dir. Barak Epstein and Blair Rowan), *Bled* (2009; dir. Christopher Hutson), *Cirque du Freak: The Vampire's Assistant* (2009; dir. Paul Weitz), *Eulogy for a Vampire* (2009; dir. Patrick McGuinn), *Immortally Yours/Kiss of the Vampire* (2009; dir. Kat Hawkes), *Livestock* (2009; dir. Christopher Di Nunzio), *Night Crawlers* (2009; dir. Benjamin Wilibanks), *Jezebeth* (2011; dir. Damien Dante), *Prowl* (USA-UK 2011; dir. Patrik Syversen), *Vamp U* (2011; dir. Matt Jespersen and Maclain Nelson), *Kiss of the Damned* (2012; dir. Xan Cassavetes), *The Thompsons* (USA-UK 2012; dir. Butcher Brothers), *Vamps* (2012; dir. Amy Heckerling), *Vampyre Nation/True Bloodthirst* (2012; dir. Todor Chapkanov), *Fright Night 2: New Blood* (2013; dir. Eduardo Rodriguez), *Dracula Untold* (2014; dir. Gary Shore), and *Vampire Academy* (USA-UK-Romania 2014; dir. Mark Waters). In *Dracula 2000* (2000; dir. Patrick Lussier), by contrast, a multicultural group of vampire hunters emerged around the return of the figure of Count Dracula (Gerard Butler).
7. Such figures also appear in *Children of the Night* (1991; dir. Tony Randel) and *Midnight Son* (2011; dir. Scott Leberecht).
8. The character is parodied in *Geung shut yee sang/Jiang shi yi sheng/Doctor Vampire* (Hong Kong 1991; dir. Jamie Luk) (Hudson 2009).
9. In DVD commentary, Bierman remembers casting Rachel and Jackie with last-minute replacements. Color-blindness is a form of racism.
10. Pauline Kael uses this term for Cage's accent, modeled after the affected speech adopted by his father as a professor of comparative literature, in "*Vampire's Kiss*," *New Yorker* 65:17 (12 June 1989), p. 106.

6. TERRORIST VAMPIRES: RELIGIOUS HERITAGE OR PLANETARY ADVOCACY

If multiculturalism opened understanding to historical consciousness that included slavery, genocide, and dispossession—"everything we are is eternally with us," as Kathleen observes in *The Addiction*, then neoliberalism obscures connections between past and present. Formalized through institutions like NAFTA (1994–present) and WTO (1995–present), neoliberalism rejects the Cold War's other options for capitalism alone. Hollywood was integrated into larger corporations, which contained costs by repurposing content and off-shoring production (Miller et al. 2005). Franchises like *Harry Potter* (2001–11) and *Lord of the Rings* (2001–3) convey how Hollywood financed, produced, distributed, and exhibited fewer films with larger budgets, combining blockbuster's saturated advertising and high concept (Wyatt 1994) with classical Hollywood's economies of scale (Schatz 1996). Hollywood became transnational with its studios owned by corporations based in Australia, Europe, and Japan. Hollywood production of vampire franchises mutates and migrates—*Blade* from Los Angeles to the Czech Republic and British Columbia; *Underworld* from Hungary to Canada to New Zealand—for cheaper labor.

Vampires also migrate and mutate across media platforms, infiltrating film, television, video games, and web series. Teen vampires became ubiquitous. *Twilight* and *The Vampire Diaries* moved from novels to screen. A spinoff of the latter, *The Originals*, moved from television to novels. All experimented to enhance audience engagement with web series. Disparaged by horror fans, teen vampires capture the imagination of a millennial generation. No longer menacing neighbors but instead intimate schoolmates, vampires are normalized as native-born citizens. Within a cultural shift from multiculturalism's mutual contaminations to neoliberalism's hierarchical segregations, vampirism less frequently conveys how difference in race/ethnicity might alter the composition of *an imagined US nation*. Instead, vampirism conveys how difference in species—often as a trope for religion or economics—might save or destroy *the entire world*.

Given neoliberalism's dehumanizing processes, vampires sometimes become advocates for *human* right to rights. Vampire hunters, by contrast, think in anthropocentric terms. Battlegrounds are fragmented and extraterritorial, as during the Cold War, yet they are increasingly privatized in for-profit vigilantism. Neoliberalism masks racial/ethnic profiling as national security and risk assessment. Enemies are considered terrorists to be eradicated, as slayers execute vampires. More than other groups, women—particularly, cisgender counterparts to Lorde's mythical norm (1984: 118)—benefit under post-multicultural neoliberalism. Rather than vampires who unsettle the status quo, white women sometimes become vampire hunters like Buffy in *Buffy the Vampire Slayer* or wannabe vampires like Bella in *Twilight*, whose gender subversions highlight racial hierarchies. Racialization of Arab- and Muslim-looking populations unfolds in "terrorist assemblages" against increased acceptance of LBGTQ citizenry (Puar 2007). Such assemblages also include transborder migrants, criminalized as under-productive ("no" tax revenue) over-reproductive ("too many" babies with birthright citizenship). NAFTA functions through transnational outsourcing and free-trade zones within what David Harvey calls the "financialization of everything" (2005: 33). Based on abstract financial models, economic policies erode political rights for vulnerable groups, notably workers and women, which had been guaranteed under state law. The emergence of outsourced national-security operations, such as private military security companies like Blackwater, is reworked as vampire hunting—patriotic in some media; inhumane and unethical in some films. In others, vampires are aligned politically with anti-globalization movements that advocate for planetary consciousness around issues such as global warming, water scarcity, and species extinction.

Vampires emerge in worlds where multiple supernatural and natural species cohabit. Species difference evokes and avoids racial/ethnic difference in a post-multicultural United States that itself is increasingly integrated into a globalized world. Vampires promote reflection on social tensions after neoliberalism's ascendancy. Scenarios of austerity and scarcity speculated on corporate off-shoring of jobs and safe-harboring of profits, particularly their destabilizing effects on state power to guarantee rights. Vampire media also explore how religious fundamentalisms are disassociated US economic and military policy. Despite discourses of secularism—understood as a separation of church and state—the United States operates within Christian frameworks of understanding. If economic segregation operates according to race and class, then nostalgia for "White Christian America" (Jones 2016) operates according to religion-as-race to mask economic policy. US nationalism follows European models, which mobilized "fanatical religious passion and conflict" by redirecting "rising passion of religion to secular passion for the state, in other words for nationalism itself," as Anthony Marx argues (2003: 193). Moreover, "fanaticized images of clash of civilizations" that "self-righteously condemn" others are constructions that silence and erase "our own earlier discord and exclusion" (201–2). Nationalism's religious underpinning erupts as global capitalism proliferates poverty as a form of exclusion. Christian motifs in Stoker's *Dracula* are reenergized in surprising ways, sometimes through economic integration, such as crucifixes made from toy rifles and condoms filled with holy water. The military term *hostile* becomes a secular version of the religious term *infidel*. Both are located outside human rights.

Christian themes are also linked to national and cinematic heritage. Universal's *Van Helsing* (USA-Czech Republic 2004; dir. Stephen Sommers) updates classical Hollywood's movie monsters while positioning the Vatican as the secret protector of Europe. Transylvania is complicit with its own exploitation by Count Dracula until non-Transylvanian vampire hunter van Helsing (Hugh Jackman) rescues it. His sidekick, Carl (David Wenham), removes the stigma of Roman Catholic prohibitions by announcing he is free to swear and have sex since he is a friar, not a monk. By normalizing Christianity as a trope of inclusion, religion functions as a form of whiteness, as it did during colonialism. Films parody the earnestness with which earlier films mobilized symbols of Christianity like crosses and holy water to kill vampires. Although its symbols might be de-sanctified and discarded to the realm of meaningless cinematic clichés, Christian discourse is hardly disavowed. It appears in less obviously marked ways, such as the cure for vampirism in *Daybreakers* that resembles holy baptism and conflation of Christian sacrilege as Islamic conversion in *Bram Stoker's Dracula*. Interspecies empathy—and thus planetary consciousness—is often thwarted by humanism. Other media explores possibilities for interspecies empathy and legal rights. *True Blood* engages controversial subjects, including the right to rights for LBGTQ communities and nonhuman animals, political corruption, and corporate warfare (Hudson 2013). It also examines the violence of Christian fundamentalism.

With quasi-religious zeal for economic integration and free-market economies—and supernatural speed for outsourcing and offshoring—neoliberalism displaced socially segregating and striating effects of financial policy onto ethnocentrisms and religious fundamentalisms. Box-office battles unfold as actual military battles take place. Religious fundamentalists are imagined as political categories of enemy; undocumented immigrants, as economic and cultural categories. War becomes ubiquitous—in the borderlands, along geopolitical and virtual borders, overseas, at home—shaping social understandings of globalization and immigration. Within the transition from the failed War on Drugs (1971–2011) into the War on Terror (2003–present), Hollywood reconfigures vampire hunters as slayers. Other films reject the "cultural clashes" articulated by Bernard Lewis (1990), Samuel Huntington (1996), and Thomas Friedman (1999) as "a throwback to feverish nineteenth-century imaginings of the Orient as the symbolic obverse to the West" (Ong 1999: 213).

The longer narrative format of film franchises and television series allow for extended cultural and social analysis. They return to repressed traumas, historicizing fear over mixings of bloods and races/ethnicities; they investigate social implications of recognizing mixed-blood populations and mixed-race relationships. Blood appears in synthetic forms like genetically modified and engineered organisms (GMOs and GEOs), sold as food by transnational corporations, threatening with extinction both ecologies (e.g., climate change, threats to biodiversity) and economies (e.g., small farms, businesses, nation-states). Neoliberalism's models for growth and progress are often predicated on fantasies of historical equality that opposes state protectionisms to compensate for centuries of exploitation that naturalize inequalities. Vampires critique unequal exchanges within contemporary globalization, particularly militarization of economies and financialization of wars. The transnational aspects of US national identity are no longer contained to immigrants. Effects of globalization enter most aspects of daily life, as do Hollywood's vampires.

Humanism's Limiting Empathy

Chandra Mohanty extends critiques of "humanism as a Western ideological and political project" that "repeatedly confirms and legitimizes (Western) man's centrality" through its "underlying anthropocentrism and ethnocentrism" (2003: 41). She argues we can decolonize theory by countering and resisting humanism's "totalizing imperative of age-old 'legitimate' and 'scientific' bodies of knowledge" (19). Comparably, by "comparing the working classes and 'stateless people' of the industrial world to the 'savages' of the colonial world," Achille Mbembe develops the concept of *necropolitics* to describe "forms of subjugation of life to the power of death" (2003: 18) that confer the status of "living dead" (40) upon vast populations even after decolonization. "In the eyes of the conqueror," he explains, "*savage life* is just another form of *animal life*, a horrifying experience, something alien beyond imagination or comprehension." Vampire media both contests and reifies this process. Fears of vampires resonate with fears of "illegal immigrants," who allegedly steal jobs, exploit welfare systems, and otherwise destroy nations. Transborder migrants evoke terror when perceived as a pregnant threat, "hopping" borders and "overpopulating" cities under the right of *jus soli*. Transborder migrants become invasive species rather than symptom of transnational political economies. They are associated with illegal narcotics and disassociated from US foreign policy affecting Latin America and the Caribbean. Vampires cannot be reduced to human or nonhuman, offering a means of considering connections between religion and political economy rather than escaping into nostalgia for an earlier moment. They challenge facile assumptions that multiculturalism is a threat. They unmask neoliberalism's role in perpetuating inequalities and segregations that can be stoked by the violence of patriotism and fundamentalism premised on humanist values.

Hollywood combines supernatural species in speculative multispecies worlds, a convention not widely seen since 1970s films by Spanish exiles of Franco's regime. In some, vampires and werewolves battle for supremacy; in others, vampires behave like zombies. Blood and bodies are reconfigured as different races of vampires, half-vampire/half-human or half-vampire/half-werewolf hybrids. Some are defined as predatory species to legitimize extermination and mask racism as security and risk assessment. Nonhumans become terrorists for humans. Hollywood organizes fears of terrorists in spectacular and polarized good-versus-evil battles against vampires who oppose or corrupt Christianity for allegedly irrational reasons or who invade territory for purportedly unknown or unknowable reasons. National security is measured against protection against foreign invasions of undocumented migrants and attacks by terrorist organizations defined by the US State Department, such as al-Qaeda, Hezbollah, Hamas, Boko Haram, and Daesh (ISIS/ISIL). Hiding within the subterranean or nocturnal worlds of nests or sleeper cells, terrorists are imagined as threats to the "American way of life." Threats of foreign invasion are ubiquitous, imagined across the Mexican American borderlands, Alaska, and New York City. Dehumanizing vampires so that they resemble Graf Orlock in *Nosferatu* allows for mass murders that do not contradict humanism because they locate other species outside its rights.

Humanism operates according to Christian ideals. *Twilight* encapsulates depictions of White Christian America as benevolent while simultaneously exposing humanism's limited empathy. The franchise locates interspecies romance against the backdrop of an ongoing war between vampires and werewolves. Humans are unaware of this war, as they are typically unaware of neoliberalism's effects and terrorism's origins. Secular forms of governance, such as police, are ineffectual. Christianity is effective because it is americanized. Based on Stephanie Meyer's novels, the franchise tells the story of Jacob "Jake" Black (Taylor Lautner), a Quileute, who falls in love with his childhood friend, Bella (Kristen Stewart), when she returns to Forks (Washington) to live with her father, police detective Charlie Swan (Billy Burke). Bella falls in love with white vampire Edward Cullen (Robert Pattinson). For many, Bella performs an alternative white-female identity to Buffy. She is brunette and virgin until marriage. *Twilight* describes romantic battles between Jake and Edward for Bella's affection. Conflict is contained by a long-standing treaty between the Volturi, a supranational organization of vampires not recognized (or even known) by the United States, and the Quileute, an indigenous nation recognized (though not as werewolves or shape-shifters) by the United States as a Reservation. Jake and Edward are native-born Americans, as is Bella. Social inequalities between them appear in supernatural terms anchored to Mormon doctrine of quasi-indigenous origins and processes of exaltation by which practitioners become like gods. The franchise is a Mormon retelling of US colonial history that promotes neoliberalism and fantasies of US indigenous origins.[1]

By Hollywood standards, *Twilight* is remarkable for including Native America yet retreats into an anthropocentrism to reveal humanism's reliance on animalizing tropes that limit empathy. Like eco-criticism, critical animal studies proposes a decentering "the human" to expand empathy. It considers animal rights and interrogates speciesism within religion, law, and philosophy that subjugates nonhuman animals and non-animal species and sustains racism, sexism, and other intra-human prejudices.[2] Neither human animals nor nonhuman animals, vampires open thinking about ecological sustainability and political equity. Many avoid killing to escape detection by vampire hunters. They model ways for consuming only what is necessary to survive. They refrain from exhausting planetary resources, evoking alternatives to agribusiness practices that contribute to ecological disasters to public-health crises, often dismissed as "acts of god." Vampire films critique unsustainable practices encouraged by neoliberalism. Human-blood farms visualize indirect and seemingly invisible mechanisms by which some humans are treated according to anthropocentric understanding of animals. Other vampires are more complicit.

Twilight's Edward practices "vegetarianism" by consuming blood of nonhuman animals. His presumed wit rejects scientific research on human diet, environmental health, and animal rights that connect to historical struggles for human rights and democratic political representations. By humanizing vampires, the franchise *animalizes* animals. In *Breaking Dawn, Part 2* (USA 2012; dir. Bill Condon), newbie vampire Bella instinctively craves a mountain climber's human blood but settles for a mountain lion's animal blood—and even saves a deer from becoming the lion's meal in the process. She acts like a human hunter for whom nonhumans are food or sport. Bella appears exceptional; the mountain lion, unexceptional: she overcomes her so-called animal instincts to avoid human prey, whereas the lion is presumably imprisoned by obligate carnivorism to kill deer. The franchise also raises other questions about animalizing humans by depicting indigenous nations, not powerful werewolves but mere shape-shifters, disassociated from indigenous history. Diminished status naturalizes territorial dispossession and abridged citizenship of American Indian Reservations. Nations become tribes under colonialism. Christian colonizers often understood indigenous nations, like nonhuman animals, as not having souls. *Twilight* represents the Quileute as a loving community. When Bella injures Seth (Booboo Stewart), Leah (Julia Jones) runs to comfort him. During the long battle scene against the Volturi, wolves mourn their dead, whereas vampires become enraged. Any suggestion that humans might learn from nonhumans—or from humans who have historically been animalized as savages—is lost beneath humanism.

With stylized use of color filters in *Twilight* (USA 2008; dir. Catherine Hardwicke), vampires are christianized into angels. Much like Anne Rice reworked vampires into dark angels of Catholicism, Meyer reworks vampires into a glittery, Christ-like angels, suggested by one of the earliest images of Edward from Bella's point of view. Sitting in the school's science lab, the stuffed owl's white wings appear attached to Edward's cherubic face. His white skin against a white T-shirt beside white owl and skeleton in center frame contrast with saturated green images of other students' darker skin or clothes. When Edward and Bella marry in *Breaking Dawn, Part 1* (USA 2011; dir. Bill Condon), a Christian priest performs the ceremony. Departing from conventions from *Nosferatu* and *Horror of Dracula*, vampires do not burn, explode, or crumble when exposed to sunlight. They glow all the more brightly, like diamonds, so that their whiteness becomes all the more brilliant—and blinding to white privilege. When vampires are killed, their bodies solidify like cheap plaster replicas of marble statues. Vampires becomes improved human beings—perhaps gods. Anyone can become a vampire *except* a Quileute. Vampire venom kills them, as epidemics brought by European immigrants resulted in genocides of indigenous nations. *Twilight* positions patriotism and religion as humanism, which it understands via neoliberalism.

Within moments of massive change, *Twilight* retreats into a world utterly detached from contemporary realities and even technologies. It authorizes isolationism and exceptionalism. Edward visits Bella's room at night rather than sending an SMS. He broods and behaves like most middle-class white teenagers and even talks like one. He is more mainstreamed "emo" (emotional, confessional) than a sexual predator. The franchise makes no substantial reference to military wars or economic recessions affecting the United States. It glosses a history of civilizing missions and religious conversions. Unlike most Hollywood vampire films, Christian symbols are not mobilized to frighten vampires. There are no Christian crusades again Islamic infidels and captive Janissaries, as in *Bram Stoker's Dracula*; instead, *Twilight*'s Christianity is normalized to the extent that vampire aristocracy lives in a Vatican-like representation of the Italian city of Sienna. *Twilight* points to the underlying role of Christianity and anthropocentrism as foundational elements in US secular democracy, extending from Manifest Destiny to War on Terror.

A Heritage of Christian Crusades

Heritage cinema often adapts literary sources, associated with national patrimony through high production values, attention to historical verisimilitude, and self-awareness of audience expectations for accuracy. Its films cultivate nostalgia for dominant cultures, rather than investigating perceived needs for nationalism in periods of social, economic, and political uncertainty or instability. Post-heritage cinema offers more revisionist depictions of sex, gender, and sexuality further obfuscating operations of power, much like costume dramas. Cross-dressing and homoerotic suggestiveness in David Lean's *Lawrence of Arabia* (1962) and *A Passage to India* (1984), for example, fail to undercut racial/ethnic assumptions within allegedly anti-colonial orientalism.[3] Columbia's *Bram Stoker's Dracula* coincided with other Hollywood heritage productions that purportedly gave audiences historical details excluded in previous adaptations, including *The Last of the Mohicans* (USA 1992; dir. Michael Mann) and *Mary Shelley's Frankenstein* (UK-Japan-USA 1994; dir. Kenneth Branagh) (Dika 1996: 389).

Screenwriter James V. Hart and director Francis Ford Coppola consulted "Dracula expert" Leonard Wolf, supplementing Stoker's novel with Radu R. Florescu and Raymond T. McNally's thesis that Vlad Țepeș (aka Vlad the Impaler) was the model for Stoker's vampire. The film adds a prologue set 400 years earlier than the novel's story and borrows a device from Dan Curtis's *Dracula* and *Blacula,* recasting Count Dracula as a widower in search of his reincarnated beloved. The film is predicated on citations—and citations of citations. It reworks a scene from Universal's 1979 remake of *Dracula* in which Lucy Seward (Kate Nelligan)'s dress shimmers under the light of an extraordinarily large number of candles as she enters Count Dracula (Frank Langella)'s castle. A high-angle shot of her entrance through a spider web serves as a visual metaphor for dangers awaiting her. Visual homage appears in a scene of Count Dracula (Gary Oldman) and Mina Murray (Winona Ryder) dancing in room filled with candles against a blank (literally, black) background with no trace of a spider's web. Veracity is not anchored in history as much as art history.

Kim Newman (1997) satirizes the film's production, so that it appears more like an adaptation of Coppola's *Apocalypse Now* than Stoker's novel. Newman's reference to US war highlights connections between Coppola's film and the first US invasion of Iraq (1990–1). Count Dracula becomes "vampire ayatollah" (1993: 15) for Ian Sinclair. Christopher Sharrett finds the surfeit of allusions to film and art history to frame Islam as a threat after Communism's fall (1996: 265–6). Count Dracula is demonized to evoke Islamophobia.

Aspiring to literary faithfulness, historical accuracy, and cinephiliac citations, Coppola reconfigures Stoker's narrative via enduring orientalist anxieties with references to the Muslim Turks' conquest of Christian Constantinople in 1453, stories of Christian boys taken from Europe to serve as Janissaries to Ottoman Sultans, and eroticized racism in Sir Richard Burton's 1885–8 translation of the *'Alf layla wa-layla/1001 Nights* into the *Arabian Nights*.

Jonathan Harker (Keanu Reeves) records his impressions of entering Transylvania as feeling like "leaving the West and entering the East." His line is cited verbatim from the novel but takes on new meaning after the film's eight-minute prologue. The opening shows the basilica dome of Saint Sofia, religious seat of the eastern Holy Roman Empire, surmounted by a Christian cross that becomes covered by smoke as a voice-over explains the threat of Turkish invaders. The cross falls and breaks into pieces. Another shot follows, showing the dome surmounted by an Islamic crescent. A menacing vampire-like shadow in the shape of the crescent then darkens an antique map of Christian Europe, visualizing a Turkish invasion of Transylvania in 1462. The film's use of expressive shadows carries the so-called threat of Islam into the heart of London. It covers the London pavement as Count Dracula later walks a street, and it reaches out to grab, attack, or embrace characters in homage to shadows in *Nosferatu* and *Dracula: Dead and Loving It* (USA-France 1995; dir. Mel Brooks). Updating Hammer's Satanism, Count Dracula's renunciation of Christianity suggests *implicit complicity* with Islam.

Figure 6.1 Menacing crescent shadow of the Muslim Turks over Christian Europe. *Bram Stoker's Dracula* (USA 1992; dir. Francis Ford Coppola).

Turks in the 1460s and Iraqis in the 1990s are subsumed into a fantasy of irrational Muslims. As Edward Said (1978) argued, European orientalisms have their power precisely because they do not recognize cultural or historical differences. Europe invents itself, not only as *a* continent but also as *the* archetypical continent via orientalism—and defines Asia as lacking a coherent continental identity (Lewis and Wigen 1997: 36–7). By inserting Vlad Țepeș, the film evokes the orientalism that Maria Todorova argues "turned the historical figure of Vlad Țepeș into the immortal figure of Dracula," which "is less an illustration of Balkan violence than an attribute of morose Gothic imagination" (1997: 122).[4] "The gothic imaginary in *Dracula* originates in an anti-Islamic worldview that is deeply rooted in the heritage of Europe," explains Tomislav Longinović; "Europe's young moderns spent the nineteenth century lamenting the destiny of Balkan Christians under the 'Ottoman yoke'" (2002: 50).

Orientalism and eurocentrism conflate China, Japan, Russia, and Turkey. Count Dracula shifts shape, looking like Lon Chaney or Christopher Lee as Fu Manchu in one scene, then like Sergei Eisenstein's Ivan the Terrible or Gustav Klimt's Adele Bloch-Bauerin in another. Count Dracula is also animalized, appearing as a giant bat, an enormous wolf, hundreds of tiny rats, and Jean Cocteau's Beast. Animality is violently sexualized. Count Dracula's forced seduction of Lucy Westenra (Sadie Frost) becomes interspecies rape. Sexuality is also given an imperial flourish. Costumed in revealing orientalist garb akin to that analyzed in Mallek Alloula's *The Colonial Harem* (1986), Count Dracula's wanton brides rape Jonathan. The chaste Mina discusses sexuality with Lucy while paging through Burton's *Arabian Nights*, whose illustrations were considered by the MPAA too sexually explicit for an R-rating (Schumacher 1999: 450).

The film also lampoons imperial logic. Count Dracula's meticulous preparations and eagerness to assimilate contrast with Harker's arrogant underpreparation and lack of interest in any sort of assimilation beyond snatching a few recipes. Count Dracula has economic means, though English characters assume it is ill-gotten. Harker travels to improve his standing back home, implying industrial Britain is unable to provide class mobility to its citizens. Harker seeks financial wealth and social position only possible outside Britain, participating in colonial expansion, according to which "capitalist entrepreneurs undertake the dirty work of conquest and penetration on [the state's] behalf" (Judd 1996: 120). He is not alone. Among Lucy's numerous servants is a Sikh man, situating her family's affluence within empire. Harker is later joined by his fellow countrymen Lord Arthur Holmwood (Cary Elwes) and Dr. Jack Seward (Richard E. Grant), the Dutch Professor Abraham van Helsing (Anthony Hopkins), and the Texan Quincey P. Morris (Billy Campbell), to form a vigilante brigade of vampire hunters that travels to Transylvania to assassinate its ruler. The film's multinational alliance of British, Dutch, and Texan white men anticipates the second US invasion of Iraq in 2003 by a Coalition of the Willing.

Coppola was most excited about filming Count Dracula pursued by the brotherhood of vampire hunters because "nobody's ever shot that John Ford Western finale as Stoker wrote it" (cited in Schumacher 1999: 449). He interprets Stoker from the vampire hunters' perspective. Van Helsing praises Morris as an indication of the bright future of his "new nation," supplementing Stoker's story with US colonial history. Before México's independence from Spain, *empresarios* were recruited from the United States, providing a critical mass needed for Texas to declare itself an independent republic from 1836 to 1846. Van Helsing's praise carries the white man's burden of British colonialism into US colonialism in the Manifest Destiny. Even Hopkins's flippant delivery of lines cannot undercut colonial desire behind the vampire hunter's mission. The film reinterprets the novel as a story about invasions, not by vampires, but by *vampire hunters*. It both sustains imperialist illusion that European civilizations and practices of Christianity are unequivocally good for everyone, yet it also calls attention to them through exaggeration.

Vampires in Post-NAFTA Borderlands

Coppola's "John Ford finale" evokes colonial and religious conquest in the Mexican American borderlands. Charles Ramírez Berg argues Westerns were shaped by the "dogma of America's civil religion" and "civil religion's 'continental crusade'" in the Manifest Destiny (2007: 3). Westerns "rationalize— and sanitize," transforming imperial history into "an entertaining, guilt-free narrative that conformed to core American beliefs (liberty, democracy, freedom, equality) and values (truth honest, fair play)" (3). Vampire films disinter this violent history. In the opening to *The Lost Boys* (USA 1987; dir. Joel Schumacher), the song "People Are Strange" plays over a montage of Chicano American laborers, white punks, and white surfers. Strange people are not equally strange. Surfers signify leisure and recreation. Punks are pale, not tan, loitering rather than patronize businesses. They seem innocent, unlike Chicano Americans, awaiting work as day-laborers. They are stigmatized by California's 1855 Greaser Act, which criminalized loitering by "all persons who are commonly known as 'Greasers' or the issue of Spanish and Indian blood" (Haney López 1996: 145). The film's tagline—"Sleep all day. Party all night. Never grow old. Never die. It's fun to be a vampire."—highlights white privilege that day-laborers will never know. The graffiti tag behind the "Welcome to Santa Clara" billboard, "murder capital of the world," points to social assumptions about ever-present dangers of living near México—of living on stolen lands.

México's criminalization has a long history. Unmarked assumptions yoke social prejudices and scientific racism, often linked to Christianity. Madison Grant's *Passing of the Great Race* (1916) argued "the racial mixture which we call Mexican" demonstrates "incapacity for self-government" (Jacobson 1998: 81). André Bazin described Chaplin's *The Pilgrim* (1923): "We see our hero riding his horse along the borderline between good and evil, which happens to be the Mexican border" (1971: 146). Post-NAFTA migrations are presented as economic and cultural threats. Despite US citizenship, Latina/o Americans are assumed to have crossed borders illegally. White-male-human characters represent formal institutions—Texas Rangers, Border Patrol, and Drug Enforcement Agency (DEA), along with informal institutions of patriotic vigilantes, bounty hunters, and paid mercenaries. Invented threats justify paramilitary border regulations. Described as "our Vietnam [War]," Operation Gatekeeper raised questions about using "police power against human beings seeking productive lives who are involved in a nonviolent activity" (Hing 2004: 201). Vampire films set in the borderlands parody the vativist paranoia that obscures historical perspectives before economic integration. They also reveal Hollywood's offshoring of production to México, New Zealand, South Africa, and Thailand.

In *From Dusk till Dawn* (USA 1995; dir. Robert Rodriguez), Seth and Richard Gecko (George Clooney and Quentin Tarantino) rob, murder, and cross illegally into México, where Carlos (Cheech Marin) promises them new identities. Exaggerated abuses of white privilege and US citizenship heighten satire. The Geckos terrorize US citizens yet are romanticized as outlaws on television news. They cross into México, hidden in the toilet of a camper they have hijacked, holding hostage an ex-minister, Jacob Fuller (Harvey Keitel), his daughter Kate (Juliette Lewis) and adopted Chinese American son Scott (Ernest Liu). Their offshoring of money parodies prejudices against overseas remittances by migrants—and massive offshoring by corporations to bypass US taxes. Like undocumented laborers, Richard and Seth do not fully anticipate what awaits them on the other side of the border.

The central attraction of the Titty Twister, a bar for truckers and bikers, is Santanico Pandemonium (Salma Hayek), who quickly kills Richard. An alliance of amateur vampire hunters fabricate makeshift crosses from toy guns, visually referencing Cushing's use of candlesticks in *Horror of Dracula*. Although the Geckos and Fullers unite with truckers and bikers to form a multicultural alliance, David Sanjek notes that the film's inclusion of African American and Asian American protagonists "pales in comparison with the unexamined valorization of racial stereotypes" (2000: 118). Deaths follow Hollywood's racial logic, but the film complicates the naturalness of such hierarchies and segregations. The vampire hunters make ammunition from condoms filled with holy water, a tongue-in-cheek riff on Eduardo Galeano's observation that "sword and cross marched together in the conquest and plunder of Latin America" ([1971] 1997: 20). Makeshift weapons represent legalized post-NAFTA trafficking. Joseba Gabilondo argues that Seth "smuggles US domestic problems" alongside "interventionist economic policy toward its neighbors—from Mexico to Vietnam—and its consequent inability to continue an imperialist expansion" (2002: 245). México is reduced to cheap intoxications, illicit thrills, and sexualized dangers. The final crane shot of the bar dissolves into a matte painting of a pre-Columbian pyramid. Like consumer goods stored inside its cavernous inner chambers, wreckage of trucks outside is NAFTA's debris. The image exposes an archeology of conquests: Aztecs (1519–21) and Mayans (1551–1697) by Spain; México now by NAFTA.

Shot in South Africa, *From Dusk till Dawn 2: Texas Blood Money* (USA 1999; dir. Scott Spiegel) opens with white lawyers devoured by bats, referencing colonies living between Texas and México, indifferent to geopolitical borders. México attracts US convicts, who congregate at El Coyote motel and solicit women for "el fucko." *From Dusk Till Dawn 3: The Hangman's Daughter* (USA 2000; dir. P. J. Pesce) opens with Ambrose Bierce's disappearance after joining Pancho Villa's revolutionary forces in 1913. US cowboy-outlaw Johnny Madrid (Marco Leonardi) kidnaps the hangman's daughter, Esmeralda (Ria Celi). They meet Bierce and US Christian missionaries, staying at an inn named La Tetilla del Diablo ("The Devil's Nipple"), and encounter vampires ruled by Quixtla (Sonia Braga), mother of half-vampire Esmeralda, who transforms into Santánico. A final shot reveals the inn constructed upon

Figure 6.2 Aztec ruins littered with consumer goods in an archeology of successive conquests. *From Dusk till Dawn* (USA 1995; dir. Robert Rodriguez).

ruins of a pre-Columbian temple, littered with carriages, locating vampirism within ongoing US pillaging.

From Dusk till Dawn: The Series (USA 2014–present; cr. Robert Rodriguez) fuses pre-Columbian past and post-NAFTA present. Vampires become *culebras* ("vipers"). When they bite humans, they can impersonate them. Santánico (Elza González) tells Richie (Zane Holtz) that a snake cult gave offerings to their gods through her. When offerings became human sacrifices, she ran; they caught and cursed her to crave blood. Santánico turns former conquistador Carlos Filipe (Wilmer Valderrama) into her servant. Both as colonizer and vampire, he is driven by money, signaling neoliberalism's underpinning in imperialism. Santánico and Carlos are slaves to the Lords of the Night. They enlist Seth (D. J. Controna) and Richie to help them escape. The series appeals to fans of grindhouse. Evoking the "Royale with Cheese" scene in Tarantino's *Pulp Fiction* (1994), Uncle Eddie (Jeff Fahey) adds scatological trivia about *kopi luwak*, coffee beans collected from feces of wild civets in Indonesia, and toilet design by Thomas Crapper. More significantly, it acknowledges transborder exploitation. The first season addresses the tribute system (*encomienda*) under Spanish rule. The second season foregrounds transborder transactions, including women trafficked as labor in meat-processing plants and strip clubs. Nathan Blanchard (Chris Browning) rents and sells Mexican women at auction. Grindhouse style suggests self-conscious appropriations of codes and conventions from Hollywood's "cheap foreign movies" to produce possibilities for de-imperialized thinking.

Vampires (USA 1998; dir. John Carpenter) relocates John Steakly's novel *Vampire$* (1990) from heartland to borderlands. Vigilante justice becomes a for-profit industry. Vampire hunters are privatized border control. Jack Crow (James Woods), an ex-DEA agent in the novel, loses his entire team except Tony Montoya (Daniel Baldwin) to "the first and most powerful" vampire, Jan Valek (Thomas Ian Griffith), a Catholic priest from twelfth-century Bohemia who lost his faith. The novel's guns and silver bullets are replaced with military-style cross bows. Vampirism is racialized despite so-called unraced white actors portraying vampires. They nest like "illegals." Crow and team infiltrate an abandoned house, impale vampires with arrows, tied by steel cables to their truck, then pull screaming vampires into sunlight where they burst into flames. Smoldering heads are displayed on the truck's hood, evoking warfare in Southeast Asia. *Vampires* parodies sadism, savagery, and "violence deemed acceptable" with "Vietnamization of the Western" (Coyne 1997: 126), following assassinations of John F. Kennedy, Martin Luther King, Robert Kennedy, and Malcolm X; police massacres of students at Kent State; and the military massacre of Vietnamese women and children at My Lai.

Its first sequel, *Vampires: Los Muertos* (USA 2002; dir. Tommy Lee Wallace), positions México as torn between two legacies of European

Figure 6.3 Skulls as trophies within terrorism of privatized border control via vigilante vampire hunters. *Vampires* (USA 1998; dir. John Carpenter).

colonialism—Catholicism and vampirism—opening with a yellow hazard-warning: "Welcome to Mexico—Be Careful—Bienvenidos a México—Tenga Cuidado." Derek Bliss (Jon Bon Jovi) travels undercover as an archeologist since México does not recognize vampire slayers as a profession. His job is to stop migrations: "North Mexico. Suck count's way up. Client wants a preemptive strike, so they don't move to San Diego or Tucson." *Vampires: The Turning* (USA 2005; dir. Marty Weiss) highlights Bangkok's backpacker allies that developed during the US war in Viet Nam, Cambodia, and Laos. Prostitution, drugs, and alcohol sustained military morale but transform into a dangerous landscape where white tourists Conner (Colin Egglesfield) and Amanda (Meredith Monroe) must resist temptation. They fall victim to local traditions—Thai ghost stories and Songkran (new year) festival—until Conner outperforms Thai vampires Niran (Dom Hetrakul) and Sang (Stephanie Chao) and European mercenary vampire-hunter Raines (Patrick Bauchau) at *muay thai* (kickboxing).

Fears of illegal entry also concern northern borders. Set in Barrow (Alaska), *30 Days of Night* (USA 2007; dir. David Slade) reworks encirclement tropes of Westerns. The film opens with the annual migration to avoid thirty sunless days. New Zealand masquerades as Alaska. The remote town becomes disconnected when vampires disable communication and transportation infrastructure, power plant, oil refinery and pipeline. Vampires terrorize as an anonymous horde and uncontainable presence. They speak an indecipherable language of animalized squeals and howls. They use hostages to lure unsuspecting humans from hiding places. Town sheriff Eben Oleson (Josh Hartnett) encourages citizens to protect themselves with guns. "We live here for a reason," observes recluse Beau Brower (Mark Boone Junior); "because no body else can." The town's survival is emotionally elevated to patriotic duty of holding land. Although Inuit inhabit Canada, Russia, and the United States, they are contained to establishing shots and supporting roles. Casting decisions conflate the Pacific Northwest and South Pacific. Billy Kitka (Manu Bennett) appears racially/ethnically ambiguous. Vampire leader Marlow (Jack Huston) proclaims vampires must kill everyone to maintain beliefs that they are not real. They cut oil pipelines and burn the town. Vampires threaten "independence from foreign oil" in rightwing terror scenarios, reinforced in images of a smoldering US flag from Westerns. The sequel, *30 Days of Night: Dark Days* (USA 2010; dir. Ben Ketai), continues with Eben's widow Stella (Kiele Sanchez), relaying the story to audiences as a conspiracy theory and unreported war.

While these films focus on policing borders after economic integration, Guillermo del Toro's *La invención de Cronos/Cronos* (1992) critiques segregations and exploitations from Spanish colonization to NAFTA integration. The film was released on the quincentennial of Columbus's conquest, along with uncritical nostalgia in *1492: Conquest of Paradise* (France-Spain 1992; dir. Ridley Scott) and critical experimentation in *Columbus on Trial* (USA 1992; dir. Lourdes Portillo). Alchemist Umberto Fulcanelli escapes the Spanish Inquisition by fleeing to Vera Cruz in 1536, shortly after Hernán Cortés's conquest. He creates the cronos device to conceal an insect whose secretions enable eternal life. The device is lost until antiques dealer Jesús Gris (Federico Luppi) discovers it inside an archangel sculpture, recovered from a church that crumbled during a 1937 earthquake. Concealing the device inside religious statuary suggests syncretism: Aztec practices of concealing representations of gods within representations of Christian saints during colonization. The device attaches to Gris's body, draws his blood, and leaves a metal barb. He awakens more youthful yet craving blood, nearly attacking granddaughter Aurora (Tamara Shanath) as Greek deity Kronus devoured his own children.

The myth's paternalism and cannibalism suggests US relations with México. Circular temporality conveys histories of successive invasions of territory. Constructed upon the ruins of the Aztec city Tenochtitlan, the Federal District is represented in establishing shots of streets with signs in five languages. Gris's shop is labeled in Spanish and Chinese. With NAFTA and WTO, sixteenth-century Spanish colonialism is replaced by "a new 'non-territorial' colonialism, based primarily on economic changes" (Chorba 2007: 128). The bilingual Dieter de la Guardia (Claudio Brook), a wealthy industrialist with eccentric delusions akin to Howard Hughes, wants the device to recover health. Motivated by an inheritance to finance plastic surgery, his gringo nephew Angel (Ron Perlman) speaks broken Spanish. Dieter's diseased organs are displayed in glass jars after surgical removal and chemical preservation. Plastic bags are draped over archangel statues not containing the device. Jesús's antique shop engages sustainable practices, recycling artifacts from one era for the needs of another. De la Guardia's factory suggests insatiable appetite of flexible accumulation. Dieter hopes to extend his human lifespan, endowing it with immortality and indifference to human suffering akin to transnational corporations.

Warm interior spaces inhabited by the Grises—home, antique shop, dance studio—contrast with the antiseptic and chilly uninhabited spaces of the de la Guardias. Contrasts between sustaining and exploiting relations suggest social values coded as Mexican or American, but *Cronos* evokes more complexity. Before Dieter can kill Gris, Aurora smashes Dieter's head, protecting her grandfather as she did earlier when she smashed cockroaches scurrying from an archangel statue.[5] Gris drinks Dieter's blood, but Angel chases him onto the factory's glass roof, through which they both fall. Only Gris awakens. With a bloodthirsty look in his eyes, he crushes the device and shouts, "Soy, Jesús Gris," sounding like "Soy, Jesús Cristo." The film closes with Gris in a coffin-like bed made by Aurora. She constructs her imaginary home with disposable objects—Russian-language newspapers, boxes labeled in Chinese—pre-NAFTA rubbish. Her rooftop playhouse evokes makeshift houses constructed from shipping crates by the female workers in the maquilladoras in free-trade zones where labor and environmental laws are unenforced. NAFTA registers differently in *Cronos*: foreign infections are not conceived as fatal. NAFTA is one of many conquerors. The film invites us to consider syncretic ways of negotiating neoliberalism's dehumanizing effects in economic integration and militarized borders. *Cronos* reclaims the dismissed and discarded.

The Difference between Slayers and Daywalkers

Casting white women and black men as protagonists offers perspectives often ignored. When slayers are white women, they fight for gender subversion; when African American men, they combat racism. For many audiences, *Buffy the Vampire Slayer* (USA 1997–2003; cr. Joss Whedon) is empowering. Buffy Summers (Sarah Michelle Gellar) subverted expectations for female agency. Buffy "can do anything a man can do—in high heels," to borrow postfeminist cliché. Her best friend, Willow Rosenberg (Alyson Hannigan), is even a lesbian. Moreover, the series has no white-male ideal. Buffy's boyfriends have issues. Her Watcher, Rupert Giles (Anthony Stewart Head), cannot match her skill at killing. Her friend Xander Harris (Nicholas Brendon) functions as "a male version of the 'damsel in distress', the passive and typically female victim needing to be rescued" (Mittell 2010: 339). The series parodies white feminism and postfeminism. In the *Blade* franchise, Blade (Wesley Snipes) is a daywalker, neither vampire nor human. He has two names: birth name Eric Brooks, slayer name Blade. His white-human mentor, Abraham Whistler (Kris Kristofferson), describes a secret war in which humans and vampires form secret treaties, yet vampires "own" the police. Blade is framed and hunted by the FBI. *Blade* is different from *Buffy* in that it has historical consciousness. If vampires contaminate with difference's multiplicities, Blade augments multiplicities whereas Buffy largely combats intersectional identities and transnational histories.

As critics note, celebrating Buffy's girl power requires ignoring how she treats people of color, which is not difficult since there are remarkably few over seven seasons. Non-whiteness is reduced to stylized blackness or inscrutable Chineseness. Buffy might be a stereotype for white-female privilege, but the series' racial stereotypes are often difficult to understand as parody. When the First Evil takes the appearance of dead African American slayer Nikki Wood (K. D. Aubert) as a disguise, she looks like a blaxploitation heroine, suggested a season earlier by Buffy's "sister" Dawn (Michelle Trachtenberg)'s Foxy Brown T-shirt (6.13). When potential slayers arrive in Sunnydale, no one can understand Chao-Ahn (Kristy Wu) from Shanghai. By contrast, Blade first appeared in a 1973 issue of Marvel Comics' *The Tomb of Dracula*, wearing a red jacket and boots, green trousers and goggles, baring his white canine fangs. Performed and produced by Snipes, blaxploitation-like caricatures of Afrocentrism are undone. His birth is updated to 1967. His youth coincides with Civil Rights struggles. He is dark-skinned, soft-spoken, intelligent, ethical, and muscular. He wears a black leather overcoat and trousers—along with a bulletproof vest and large sword. His shoulders, neck, and parts of his head reveal elaborate Balinese tattoos. His room contains a meditation corner and more books than weapons. To curb his appetite for human blood, he injects a garlic compound into his neck. He threatens whiteness precisely because he has risen amidst white domination.

Buffy does gymnastics and impales vampires with wooden stakes. They combust, and leave no evidence. Under the Watchers' Council's protection, she is free to kill with impunity, even slaying former classmates. Killing is normalized when Willow starts to "dust" them. Slippages from human races to supernatural species position Buffy as heroic rather than homicidal. Dracula (Rudolf Martin), however, knows Buffy's reputation as a "renowned killer" who takes pleasure in "hunting" (5.1). He rejects euphemisms of *patrolling* and *slaying* for *hunting* and *killing*. "Dusting" evokes pesticide, framing vampires as unwanted, like stereotyped migrants. Although most vampires are white, slayage resembles racial/ethnic cleansing via vigilante border-patrol. Sunnydale becomes a border town built atop a conquered indigenous city. Vampires cross into Sunnydale from Boca del Infierno, as the Hellmouth was originally known. Sunnydale is evil's epicenter, sitting atop a multidimensional passageway through which vampires and demons tunnel under the border. Vampires crawl out of their graves like newly arrived "illegals." Buffy remarks: "these vamps have been here for a while: they've nested" (5.14). Her expression reproduces anti-immigrant discourse.

Ratified shortly before the series' debut, NAFTA is hardly mentioned. Cordelia Chase (Charisma Carpenter) joins the slayage after seeing knock-off copies of her designer dress. "Exactly what happens with this free trade agreement," she reasons (1.7). NAFTA dissolved borders for goods while militarizing them against people. California acknowledged its inauguration by proposing anti-immigrant Proposition 187 aka Save Our State (SOS) in 1994. Buffy's slayage parodies social misperceptions about economic integration that spur racial segregation and vigilante nativism. Militarization is achieved through a combination of low-tech measures, including walls backed by fences, alongside high-tech measures, including electronic sensors and infrared night vision. Other policies include Spanish-language "Stay Out, Stay Alive" public information campaigns in México (Hing 2004: 193). Buffy's efforts to seal the Hellmouth parallel ones to construct walls into the Pacific Ocean. The series parodies nativist wish fulfillment. Buffy embodies pre-9/11 panic over whites becoming California's majority-minority. Although the series attempts to decenter Buffy as Chosen One through a proliferation of Potentials (potential slayers), this sisterhood is hardly feminist, reminding us that "beyond sisterhood there are still racism, colonialism, and imperialism" (Mohanty 2003: 36).

In *Buffy*, "evil is expressed more deeply through the way that institutions reduce human beings to cogs in the machine, reduce human beings to instruments that further their goals" (2001: 56), explain Brian Wall and Michael Zyrd. They find that the Scooby Gang's actions are "remarkably passive and reactive" since they "patrol for vampires" without a "grand plan to eradicate evil" (59). Efficacy notwithstanding, girl power often lacks feminist empathy. The series subverts slasher conventions: young attractive white women can have sex with men and/or women without being murdered. It nonetheless undercuts intersectional feminism by largely empowering white-female agency through racial insensitivity—sometimes in childishly cruel jokes, other times in self-conscious references to Hollywood. When Buffy and her Scooby Gang travel in a camper, medieval European warriors, rendered multicultural by a token African American, attack them. Although the horde includes no Native Americans, it reactivates stereotypes from Westerns: "bloodthirsty Indians" attacking stagecoaches with allegedly innocent white colonizers. Colonial discourse invented the "vanishing race" to suggest that indigenous nations would naturally become extinct; this episode accepts that Native America has effectively been vanished, surviving only in empty references to irrational villains in Hollywood Westerns. Buffy acts with entitlement to white privilege.

Without reference to 9/11, the series evokes national paranoia via Turok-Hans vampires, who cannot be killed, and Bringers, a class of priests who serve First Evil. Bringers evoke terrorist sleeper cells (7.8) but are linked to the Old South through the First Evil's assistant Caleb (Nathan Fillion), a Southern priest, who destroys the Council. References to the Old South deflect from contemporary forms of racism. Buffy lives at a moment when security is enacted through purportedly racially/ethnically unbiased risk assessments that frequently resemble racial/ethnic profiling. Vampires bear little resemblance to stereotypes of Arab- and Muslim-looking terrorists but elicit comparable emotions—like invasions by "wetbacks" and "border hoppers." Buffy's ex-boyfriend Riley Finn (Marc Blucas) participates in secret military operations against vampires and demons as a "subterranean threat." He later tells her about clandestine missions to prevent demons entering through Central America (6.15), alluding to changes in US policy from *regulating* migration to *preventing* it. Finn calls them "breeders," fearing their reproduction will submerge the (white) human population. His mission in the sixth season (2001–2) is distanced from US warfare in Afghanistan in early October 2001, ratification of counter-terrorism profiling and surveillance under the the USA PATRIOT Act in late October 2001, establishment of an extrajudicial detention center in Guantánamo Bay (Cuba) in January 2002, and the invasion of Iraq in March 2003. Nonetheless, the army refers to demons and vampires as "hostiles" with Spike (James Marsters) renamed Hostile 17. The series' finale determines which characters die and which live. Spike and former vengeance demon Anya (Emma Caulfield) fight alongside Buffy but die. Even white-male-human characters, who betrayed Buffy, live. Andrew Wells (Tom Lenk) is recuperated from domestic terrorist to (queer) patriotic vigilante. Buffy seals the Hellmouth by imploding Sunnydale. The resulting crater is a sensationalized version of ones in Oklahoma City in 1995 and New York City in 2001. The series offers a revisionist fantasy of victory over domestic and foreign terrorists.[6]

The *Blade* franchise more thoughtfully addresses institutional racism by framing human relationships to vampires in non-anthropocentric terms. Vampires maintain humans as "pets," marked with cryptogram tattoos to convey ownership. They see humans as "cattle." The films concern racial purity reconfigured as species purity, locating difference in blood defined as a "vampire virus." In *Blade* (USA 1998; dir. Stephen Norrington), race becomes a category to distinguish "pure blood" vampires, like Gitano Dragonetti (Udo Kier) and the House of Erebus, who were "born" vampires, from ones like Deacon Frost (Stephen Dorff), who were "turned." In *Blade II* (USA 2002; dir. Guillermo del Toro), the vampire overlord Eli Damaskinos (Thomas Kretschmann) invents a new vampire race through genetic manipulation. He creates a son, Jared Nomak (Luke Goss), but abandons him as illegitimate. The new race of Reapers is stronger than vampires. Except for Nomak, they cannot talk. They hop like monkeys and squeal like pigs, have three-way jaws, rather than mandibles, and their tongues are suckers. If starved, they will feed upon vampires, violating prohibitions against cannibalism. Reapers will even eat themselves. In *Blade: Trinity* (USA 2004; dir. David S. Goyer), this feature reappears in the original "patriarch of *homos nocturnos*," Drake (Dominic Purcell), whose self-reinventions include Dracula.

The *Blade* franchise situates African America as *constitutive* rather than supplementary to US national history and identity. It normalizes African American experiences as "just American experiences." When Dr. Karen Jenson (N'Bushe Wright) attempts to cure the vampire virus, she looks at retroviruses used in treatments for sickle-cell anemia, a genetic blood disorder, drastically shortening life expectancy. Culturally coded as African American, it is recoded as "just a virus" that can be used to find a cure for *all* humans. Along with genetic engineering of Reapers at Caliban Industries, Damaskinos oversees blood farming. Promoted as social service, homeless humans are collected and suspended in a near-death state. Their blood is harvested for vampire consumption. The name Caliban signals European colonial exploitation of African and Caribbean slaves.

Blade battles racism disguised as post-race mockery of so-called political correctness. White-male vampires, particularly ones possessing less power than they feel entitled to, insult Blade. "Spare me the Uncle Tom routine," says Frost when Blade refuses to consider humans as "meat." Dieter Reinhardt (Ron Perlman) attempts to intimidate Blade by asking him whether he blushes. Blade reminds him of the joke before killing him, offering redemptive justice to anyone who has suffered or witnessed racism's arrogance. Whether Blade is considered mixed-race or mixed-species, he is a child of violence. Frost bit Blade's mother Vanessa (Sanaa Lathan) before she gave birth, symbolically reproducing familiar narratives of white slave-owners raping black slaves. The violence reappears when white vampire Quinn (Donal Logue) bites/rapes Karen. Close-ups of the traumatized and terrorized faces of Karen and Vanessa are intercut as a visual reminder. They stand in place of millions of unrepresented faces of rape victims that Hollywood could not visualize under the PCA. Blade rejects the notion of passing. He refuses to submit to a social system that produces whiteness as a category of oppression.

Despite its racially conscious reworking of conventions, the franchise reproduces Hollywood's scapegoating of foreigners. Vampires become Russian- and Arab-looking. White-marble-skinned Damaskinos speaks Russian despite a Greek name that literally suggests he is "from Damascus." He embodies stereotypes of ruthless Russian mafia and Arab despots. In contrast to Danica Talos (Parker Posey), Drake's skin appears brown, suggesting Semitic origins. Danica leads expeditions into the Syrian desert of Iraq—the "cradle of civilization" as she calls it, now associated with so-called Iraqi insurgents—to excavate Drake from a ziggurat, evoking the orientalism of mummy films. Unlike *Buffy the Vampire Slayer*, *Blade* highlights ambivalence and undecidability. In *Blade: House of Chthon* (USA 2006; dir. Peter O'Fallon), the pilot for Spike's *Blade: The Series* (USA 2006; cr. David S. Goyer), vampires become "homos nocturni," the same genus as *homo sapiens*.

The "Twilight" of Indigenous Nations and Other Exterminations

The *Underworld* and *Twilight* franchises depict interspecies tensions escalating into policies of extermination. Quests for scientific, philosophical, theological, or legal proof of one supernatural species' superiority reveal conjunctions of human racism, sexism, and speciesism. The franchises investigate concepts of predatory species, allegedly threatening nature's balance. In *Twilight*, a treaty between a supranational entity of vampires and a subnational entity of werewolves/shape-shifters ends fighting, yet both species fear being hunted to extinction by humans. In *Underworld*, humans actively hunt vampires and werewolves, conducting militarized scientific research on them, evoking actual practices on European and US colonial plantations, Nazi death camps, animal testing and meat processing. With different politics, the franchises consider anthropocentrism's linkages to racism and sexism.

Developed from an idea by Kevin Grevioux, who plays werewolf Raze in *Underworld* (UK-Germany-Hungary-USA 2003; dir. Len Wiseman), the *Underworld* franchise depicts two groups of immortal creatures, Vampyres and Lycans (werewolves), battling to control the underworld, a territory whose demarcations are unrecognized by humans yet which occupies the same physical space as their world. Grevioux extends African American science fiction by Octavia Butler and Samuel Delany to imagine black futures in the context of black pasts. Vampyres enslave Lycans as "daylight guardians." The vampire Viktor (Bill Nighy) murders his daughter Sonja (Jázmin Damak) and seeks to exterminate werewolves after learning of her pregnancy by werewolf Lucian (Michael Sheen). He declares hybrids an "abomination," believing mixed bloodlines threaten vampires with extinction. Viktor assembles an army of "death dealers," who function as terrorist cells, inflicting death outside formal structures of war. In *Underworld: Rise of the Lycans* (USA-New Zealand 2009; dir. Patrick Tatopoulos), blood carries personal "blood memories" alongside genetic identity, allowing Viktor to locate the original werewolf William (Brian Steele) by biting his adopted daughter Selene (Kate Beckinsale). Viktor seeks to erase species and history.

Shot in contemporary Budapest, the film suggests Viktor's irrational fears parallel medieval European blood discourses that conceived bodies as volatile, "perpetually threatened by contagion," with race a visualization of bloodline (Linke 1999: viii). Christianity transforms blood into a sacred "symbol of unity" to exclude Jews charged with "violating the integrity of the body of God" (99–100). Supernatural battles also evoke blood wars between Christians and Muslims in medieval and contemporary Europe (Knee 2008), as well as white supremacy within civil war (Magill 2015). By alluding to extermination policies against European Jews and Muslims, enslavement of Africans and African Americans, *Underworld* claims slavery and criminalization of miscegenation in the United States as another history of racially motivated extermination.

Costume and set design reinforce social hierarchies. The Lycans' world is subterranean and homosocial. They are physically grounded and multiracial. Lucian is hirsute and sweats; Raze has massive muscles. They devour humans as food, occasionally "marking" them or transforming them into werewolves. The Vampyres' world is refined and detached, evoking Victorian-Edwardian England. Their violence is covert. The existence of human Michael Corvin (Scott Speedman) exposes distinct bloodlines as Viktor's political manipulation. Michael is a descendent of Alexander Corvinus (Derek Jacobi), a fifth-century Hungarian warlord, whose blood contained an anomaly, allowing him to become immortal. When a wolf bites Corvinus's son William, and a bat bites his twin, Marcus (Tony Curran), they become the first werewolf and vampire, establishing common ancestry for multiple species. A third son remained human, passing a virus through his bloodline to Michael. After Michael is bitten by Lucien and drinks Selene's blood, he morphs into a vampire/werewolf hybrid, stronger than either creature, thereby unsettling assumptions about pure bloodlines.

After Viktor's death, species-based extermination continues. In *Underworld: Awakening* (USA 2012; dir. Måns Mårlin and Björn Stein), humans "purge" supernatural species. Shot in British Columbia, the film opens with an Infected Persons Unit, testing suspects with ultraviolet light and silver nitrate. The Cleansing is a systematic extermination, evoking ethnic cleansing. Vampires blame the werewolf rebellion for bringing human attention to immortals. Selene, Michael, and their unborn child, Eve (India Eisley), are captured and frozen by Antigen, a corporation run by Dr. Jacob Lane (Stephen Rea), researching vaccines to make werewolves stronger and immune to silver. Unfrozen twelve years later, Selene learns from human Detective Sebastian (Michael Ealy) that "the government declared mission accomplished" in exterminating werewolves, prompting "the Feds" to focus on her "kind." Reports of "Lycan captures" suggest someone is replenishing werewolf packs. Species profiling conjures racial profiling by the Department of Homeland Security (DHS) and Transportation Safety Administration (TSA). *Underworld: Blood Wars* (USA 2016; dir. Anna Foerester) reportedly finds interspecies peace.

Werewolves have a history on film that predates classical Hollywood. According to Wheeler Winston Dixon, Henry MacRae's *The Werewolf*

(USA-Canada 1913) is "the first cinematic telling of the werewolf legend," depicting "a young Navajo woman" who "is taught by her vengeful mother to hate all white men and turns into a wolf to attack them when they threaten her hearth or home" (Dixon 2010: 8). *Twilight* maintains such connections but removes anticolonial critique. It appropriates indigenous stories much as whites, particularly Southerners and Mormons whose whiteness was contested at times, invented partial Native American ancestry to legitimize their historical connection to lands.[7] In *Eclipse* (USA 2010; dir. David Slade), Bella hears ancestral stories of Quileute, who transform into wolves to frighten intruders onto their lands. Their warriors defeat the Cold One (Peter Murphy), but the Cold Woman (Monique Ganderton) avenges his death, nearly killing the Quileute Taha Aki (Byron Chief-Moon) until his Third Wife (Mariel Belanger) distracts the Cold Woman by stabbing herself. Later, Bella re-enacts self-mutilation to prevent vampire Victoria (Rachelle Lefevre) from killing Edward. The settled Cullens contrast with Victoria and other American Nomads—James (Cam Gigandet) and Laurent (Edi Gathegi)—who terrorize and torture humans like "bloodthirsty savages" in Westerns. Other vampires are presented as unenlightened, including the ruling Volturi, whose rituals approximate Catholicism rather than the unmarked Mormonism of the Cullens.

Law and territory become central issues. A scene rendered in a sepia-filter shows two Quileute ancestors (William Joseph Elk II and Rick Mora), wearing ceremonial wolf-eared headdresses, discover the colonizer Cullens. Quileute and Cullens claim sovereign territories divided by a stream, reworking historical land disputes between indigenous nations and Mormons. Both groups are barred from acting on the other's land. Quileute can void the treaty should the Cullens create more vampires. Jake lives on the La Push reservation, conveying segregations after dispossession. In *New Moon* (USA 2009; dir. Chris Weitz), he prefers "red" schools to the "pale face" system that allows "red eyes" (vampires), inverting the racist term "red skin." Jake is the last of his cohort to "phase," an expression for sexual maturation and partial degeneration from humanity to animality. Older Quileute like Billy Black (Gil Birmingham) do not phase because no vampires were present at their maturation. Quileute exist as a segregated population whose supernatural qualities are contingent on another supernatural species.

Although *Twilight* includes Native America, it received criticism about casting decisions. In the novels, Quileute are demoted from werewolves to shape-shifters, not true "Children of the Moon," not "*real*" werewolves" (4: 745). The Volturi Caius nearly "hunted them into extinction," evoking colonial policies of dispossession, genocide, and conversion. *Breaking Dawn, Part 2* includes other indigenous nations who became vampires. It opens with a picturesque shots of Giza's pyramids, the Egyptian Museum in Cairo, and camels beside a Tata truck with Hindi-language text in the background. The conflation of Egypt and India introduces an orientalist imaginary that engulfs Latin America. The Amazon becomes the "most remote corner of the world." Living far from the Amazon in the Pantanal wetlands, the Amazon Coven conjures animalizing misunderstandings of indigenous nations by Europeans, parodied in Nelson Pereira dos Santos's anticolonial farce *Como era gostoso o meu Francês/How Tasty Was My Little Frenchman* (1971). Anyone can become vampire, except particular indigenous nations who claim territory presently occupied by the United States.

Natalie Wilson suggests that Mormonism's historical discrimination against Native Americans and African Americans, whom Joseph Smith felt were "cursed," informs Meyer's proselytizing racial/ethnic politics (cf. Jensen 2010: 101). "Once 'cursed' dark-skinned people accepted Mormonism, they would become *white*" (Wilson 2011: 201), she explains. Most Quileute have Hebrew names (Jacob, Sam, Leah, Seth, Paul, Jared) or Scottish or Gaelic ones (Collin, Brady), conveying legacies of civilizing missions, religious conversions, and forced intermarriage. Bella equates beauty with whiteness. Edward's whiteness is angelic and godlike, whereas Jake's russet-colored skin and black hair convey animality. Quileute can be "'exotic rather than traditionally beautiful," Bella records in her diary (61). Edward's nearly albino cousin Irina Denali (Maggie Grace) becomes physically upset when introduced to Bella due to the scent of Quileute Billy Black and Sue Clearwater (Alex Rice). When Jake "imprints on" Bella and Edward's baby, Reneesme, he becomes civilized, domesticated, and otherwise whitened. He controls his so-called animal instincts.

Twilight extends Westerns' disavowal of colonialism through faith in Manifest Destiny. Framing, angle, shot duration, and editing patterns position white colonizers not as invading lands belonging to indigenous nations and México, but as innocent victims of irrational attacks by Native Americans and Mexicans. Shot and edited like encirclement scenes, Quileute surround the Cullen's house. *Twilight* reworks colonial fantasies of virgin lands onto Bella's white body. In the novels, she declares herself "a neutral country," refusing to be "affected by territorial disputes by mythological creatures" (3: 143). On film, she self-defines as "Switzerland," without awareness of what Swiss neutrality actually implies. Bella's pregnancy evokes the virgin (i.e., unmarried) Mary's immaculate conception. The hybrid human/vampire fetus grows at an alarming rate, defying medical knowledge. Although Bella does not openly declare herself "pro-life," she refuses abortion. Reneesme is half-vampire, "born not bitten." Despite its conservative politics, *Twilight* conveys ambivalence about US colonial history by casting white people as invasive. The Cullens may have been born on land claimed by the United States, but their ties are disputable.

Meyer extends strategies from "fic"—fan-authored, self-published fiction that adapts characters and narratives from professionally produced media.[8]

Fic writers insert feminism in "slash fic" by queering heterosexual male characters to offer equity in sexual and romantic relations unavailable in commercial media's gendered hierarchies. "The Storytellers: New Voices of *The Twilight Saga*" encourages fans to submit stories and select winners for adaption as web videos for social media. Released theatrically the same summer as *Eclipse*, 20th Century Fox's *Vampires Suck* (USA 2010; dir. Jason Friedberg and Aaron Seltzer) self-consciously parodies *Twilight*. Bella Swan becomes even less interesting as Becca Crane (Jenn Proske). Brooding vampire Edward Cullen becomes Edward Sullen (Matt Lanter); Jacob Black, Jacob White (Chris Riggi). The film lampoons Bella's white feminism in Becca's comment to Jake that it must be "fun to drink and gamble all day" at reservation schools. When Jake phases, he looks like classical Hollywood's Wolf Man with prosthetic, not CGI, teats. Hollywood's red face is exaggerated. Jake is not feminized but emasculated. His chest and belly hair forms the shape of a vest like ones worn as part of a stylized Indian costume in Westerns. The parody calls attention to *Twilight*'s indifference to white privilege.

Genetically Engineered Species and Neoliberal Wars

Themes of religious fundamentalism in moments of choreographed scarcity and austerity also enter into Hollywood vampire media. Neoliberalism's dehumanization often leaves vampires as advocates for all species, including humans, with imminent economic and environmental crises. Vampires take a planetary perspective that humans miss. The GEO of TruBlood allows for interspecies communities—and potentially planetary consciousness—in *True Blood* yet collapses into dystopic scenarios towards the series' finale. The Sanguinistas support terrorism to undermine mainstreaming by destroying TruBlood plants, forcing vampires to search for alternative sources, including human blood. Sarah Newlin devises a scheme to disseminate the deadly virus Hep-V in contaminated TruBlood. Daughter of Republicans, Sarah is a religious fundamentalist—former wife of Steve (Michael McMillian), who led the anti-vampire Fellowship of the Sun. Her blood is immune to Hep-V. Japanese yakuza hunt her on behalf of TruBlood's developers, seeking to clone and market her blood as New Blood. It will ameliorate but not cure Hep-V, thus creating livelong customers. The plot speculates pharmaceutical companies engaging in business practices akin to planned obsolesce for consumer electronics. *True Blood* ends with economic austerity and public-health crises amidst corporate terrorism and religious fundamentalism by vampires and humans alike.

Other films and series look also to examine shifting configurations of polity via neoliberalism as it affects the right to rights. Their emotional impact frequently hinges on placing white people in precarious positions that people of color have known for generations. Set in a world where humans have poisoned their bloods with "lifestyle excesses" and polluted the air and water, "colonies of vampires" fight amongst themselves for rare supplies of blood in *Live Evil* (USA 2009; dir. Jay Woelfel). African American "blood pusher" Max (Ken Foree) steals clean blood from hospitals, unsettling/re-inscribing social stigmas about African American men. Set in a futuristic world recalling Terry Gilliam's *Brazil* (1985), *The Breed* (USA-Hungary 2001; dir. Michael Oblowitz) imagines humans and vampires negotiating ways to coexist. The vampire–human alliance is complicated by hidden motives and propaganda campaigns. The film recasts characters from Stoker's novel: Chinese vampire Lucy Westenra (Bai Ling) works with African American human Detective Stephen Grant (Bokeem Woodbine) to stop the virus and Chinese American human Jonathan Seward (Ming Lo), who wants war with vampires. Humans develop a virus that kills only vampires, but the vampires have it altered, so that it kills only humans. The film ends with a pledge of cooperation between humans and vampires.

Stake Land (USA 2010; dir. Jim Minle) imagines the United States has toppled following a plague. Often assumed equalizing forces, catastrophes invariably affect different classes (and races) differently. With the "end of America," pockets of human civilization survive, including all-white towns in the Southwest that await a new messiah. A white-male-human loner (Nick Damici), known as Mister, travels to Canada with a young white-male-human orphan, named Martin (Connor Paolo). Mister kills vampires, collecting fangs as trophies like Europeans collected Native American scalps. They encounter a religious fundamentalist/paramilitary group called The Brotherhood, led by Jebedia Loven (Michael Cerveris), who believes a Christian god sent vampires to purify earth and blood. Loven's son attempts to rape Sister (Kelly McGillis), a middle-aged Christian nun. They tie African American ex-US Marine Willie (Sean Nelson) to a tree where he is eaten by vampires. His corpse visually resembles a racially motivated lynching. The Brotherhood drops vampires by helicopter into the refugee camp. Sci Fi's *Slayer/Mexferatu Mexico* (USA 2006; dir. Kevin VanHook) locates vampirism's origins when Queen Isabella sent conquistadors to convert "natives" to Christianity. Vampires inhabit jungles until deforestation by transnational corporations. US troops from Afghanistan are deployed to assassinate them.

Set in 2019, *Daybreakers* (Australia-USA 2009; dir. Spierig Brothers) speculates on the effects of unsustainable policies on the political stability of citizens' rights. Blue filters create the nocturnal world of vampires, who constitute 95 per cent of the earth's population. Its visual style evokes Ridley Scott's *Blade Runner* (1982), but *Daybreakers* avoids techno-orientalism that links Asian bodies, languages, and food to dystopia (Lowe 2002) and camouflages US policy that encourages undocumented Mexican labor (Berg 2002). It points to governmental oversights in not regulating private industry. Neoliberalism's flexible accumulation is more terrifying than Marx's capitalism. The film imagines when capital no longer accumulates. With a "postmodern Sydney" that resembles the United States, the film presents a future of "peak blood," riffing on "peak oil."[9] Human blood is a finite and non-renewable resource, just like petroleum. The "global blood crisis" resonates with the actual global financial crisis in 2008. National laws and state agencies, including the Food and Drug Administration (FDA), are powerless against transnational corporations. Wealthy industrialist Charles Bromley (Sam Neill) oversees a corporation focused on research and development in synthetic blood and blood farming from captured humans.[10] He is not interested in a cure for vampirism since corporate interests demand "repeat business" for both mass-market synthetic blood and premium-price human blood. His practices of profit above lives evoke ones by transnational pharmaceutical corporations.

The film's opening sequence evokes the end of empire. A young female vampire writes a suicide note before watching sunrise. Her body burns to a charred corpse. The opening credits are superimposed atop images of urban structures, such as bus shelters and newsstands, revealing terrifying newspaper headlines like "German Blood Substitute Fails." Civil society deteriorates into a point where human and vampire lives cease to have meaning or value as citizens. Humans are considered "enemies of the state." Vampires stage protests about possible blood rationing in London, the Middle East, and Asia. If vampires do not feed for extended periods, they suffer neurological damage from malnutrition. They mentally and physically degenerate into animalized "subsiders" and are incarcerated. Official regulation of movement and location within territory becomes the primary performance of state power. Disenfranchised citizens occupy the streets at night in search of blood. Where the state fails, private industry profits.

Christianity suggests an alternative faith to neoliberalism. Driving during the day, Lionel "Elvis" Cormac (Willem Dafoe) slams his car into a post and is thrown through black-tinted windows into the sunlight. His burning body is extinguished when he lands in water—and he is again human. His accidental cure suggests Christian tropes of baptism and rebirth. He predicts the "last vestige of humanity will vanish as soon as the blood does." When blood supplies dwindle and the state can no longer afford to feed subsiders and control the "subsider epidemic," public opinion shifts. Mothers support extermination, knowing it is "wrong" but "needing to feed" their children. Soldiers lead chain gangs of Class Four Blood-deprived Citizens to burn under sunlight. Subsiders' emaciated bodies, tattered and filthy clothing, shell-shocked expressions, and mechanical movements evoke images of death camps. While most soldiers cheer successful death operations, Frankie Dalton (Michael Dorman) sees state policies as inhumane and unsustainable. Witnessing the extermination of these impoverished citizens, he questions his loyalty to a state that orders him to hunt his own brother, Edward (Ethan Hawke), who cured himself and aligned with an underground human movement.

The most recent adaptation of Richard Matheson's 1954 novel *I Am Legend* (USA 2007; dir. Francis Lawrence) is set in 2012 after bioengineering a measles virus to cure cancer results in the quarantining of Manhattan as ground zero for a deadly infectious disease. So-called colorblind casting allows Will Smith to portray Robert Neville, an engineer who tests antidotes on rats. His only interspecies socialization is a German Shepherd named Samantha, aka Sam (Abbey and Kona). Neville is immune to the virus and maintains his house on Washington Square, refusing to flee to Vermont. Vampires are animalized, living in "hives." They cannot speak. Their skin burns with exposure to sunlight. They suffer from "social degeneration," whereby "human behaviors become entirely absent." Neville snares a female vampire in a trap, so he can transition his research from animal to vampire-subject trials. Unfortunately, he gets captured in a snare set by vampires. Two humans, nurse Anna Montez (Alice Braga) and boy Ethan (Charlie Tahan), rescue him. The film ends with Neville becoming "legend" by sacrificing his own life, so that Anna and Ethan can escape to Vermont with the antidote contained in his blood. The film imagines a future world of epidemics, wars, scarcity, and austerity that undercut the right to rights for citizens. The film speculates a future of GEOs and neoliberal economics, which threatens to destroy the planet by reifying an abstract financial system as a basis for life and death. Such films and series point to ways that an entire human race can become victimized when ruling elites, whether human or corporate person, exploit systems of structural inequality.

Notes

1. Mormon cosmology suggests four ancient tribes of Israel migrated to the Americas. Darker skinned Lamanites murdered more prosperous Nephites, requiring the Mormons to civilize, whiten, and convert actual indigenous peoples through missionaries. Like other white groups that invent partial indigenous ancestry, some Mormons claim partial Native American ancestry—and even identity. See Gross (2010) on the role of blood quantum, intermarriage, and land annexation.
2. See: Singer (1975); Adams (2010); Huggen and Tiffin (2010); Weil (2012); Wolf (2013).
3. Cf. Rushdie (1984).
4. "The Dracula story, in fact, was a 'bestseller' throughout Europe four hundred years before Stoker wrote his version" (Florescu and McNally 1992: 8).
5. Aurora's rescue of Jésus inverts Santo's rescue of Rosita in *El Santo y Blue Demon contra Drácula y el Hombre Lobo* (1972). Del Toro's *Doña Lupe* (1983) is dedicated "with affection and sadness" to Santo.
6. *Buffy the Vampire Slayer, Season 8 Motion Comic* (2011; dir. Jeff Shuter) adapts comic-book season eight (2007–10).
7. In *Breaking Dawn*, Brazilian "part Ticuna Indian" Kaure was "raised more superstitious—or you could call it more aware—than those who live in the modern

world" (Meyer 2008: 114). Meyer learned about *apotamkin* ("Native American vampire") through a Google search.
8. WB and UPN were receptive to BtVS fic. Anne Rice was antagonistic to VC fic, contributing to apathy among her fans.
9. I thank Sheetal Majithia for her observation about "peak blood."
10. Farming humans appeared in *Thirst* (Australia 1979; dir. Ron Hardy). Vampires in "the brotherhood" manage "the dairy" where "carefully selected blood cows" (humans) become a source of blood.

7. OTHER VAMPIRES, OTHER HOLLYWOODS: SERIALIZED CITIZENSHIP AND NARROWCAST DIFFERENCE

Mythologized as film's competition, television is more accurately the "other Hollywood." With its volume of production, Vancouver is "Hollywood North." Other Hollywoods produce other vampires, offering other perspectives. Production migrates from California to Georgia, Louisiana, Ontario, Texas, and Europe. Off-siting production—and masquerading locations—is nothing new, nor is Hollywood television production. Classical Hollywood film studios partnered with television networks decades before industry deregulation integrated them into media corporations. Big Three broadcasters—CBS, NBC, and ABC—began filming programming in 1949 and rented production facilities from film studios. Disney became the first studio to produce television in 1954. Conceived as a cable network for feature films, HBO re-energized scripted television. Its *True Blood* uses vampires to engage debates on the right to rights with a complexity not possible in feature filmmaking, underscoring how other Hollywoods offer us other perspectives.

Television engages national dialogues and changes thinking across generations. Benedict Anderson argued that citizenship is bound serially to states with each citizen provisionally standing for all others (1983: 184). He looked to newspapers as mechanisms that create imagined communities. Theoretically, each citizen receives the same news, whether living in the capital or provinces, at the same time, thus constructing a national sense of community through simultaneity of knowledge and experience of events. More than film, television fulfills this serializing effect. With live broadcast, audiences received information simultaneously. Film industries invested in hierarchical and segregated models of run-zone-clearance; television industries, in national broadcast. With narrowcasting on cable and satellite, audiences have become fragmented and subnational. Film and television share fixed scheduling; streaming and downloading allow audiences to select content from a library at their convenience.

One conventional distinction is interruptions to content in television—the "flow," according to Raymond Williams (1974). Advertising interrupts broadcasts at predictable intervals, affecting narrative patterns for writers and audiences. Television is conventionally screened at home, among friends and families, interrupted by unrelated conversations about daily events; film is screened among strangers, interrupted by only anonymous sounds of snacking and ringing mobiles. Television narratives are open, allowing for additional seasons. They are multiple and entwined rather than singular and arced. *Buffy the Vampire Slayer* was an early series to adopt seasonal narrative arcs (Mittell 2010: 230). Audiences sometimes shape storylines through engagement. *True Blood* and *The Vampire Diaries* promoted renewed contracts for actors Joe Manganiello and Michael Malarkey as responses to fan popularity of their characters. Television differs from film in its production schedules for weekly episodes on tighter budgets. It relocates quickly to lower costs. Overseas satellite production centers take advantage of favorable currency exchange rates, lower labor costs, and higher tax incentives. Although *The Vampire Diaries* shot its pilot in British Columbia, the series is shot in Georgia. Both shot in Canada, *Valemont* and *Carmilla* engage transmedia storytelling through which "integral elements of a fiction get dispersed systematically across multiple delivery channels for the purpose of creating a unified and coordinated entertainment experience" (Jenkins 2007). More than web series, they can function as alternative-reality games (ARGs) by making users feel like participants.

Television is integral to Hollywood as a transmedia industry, focused on repurposing content for multiple media platforms. Universal reanimated its horror monsters with *Van Helsing*, released simultaneously with a videogame—and followed by a series (USA 2016; cr. Neil LaBute), featuring Abraham's daughter Vanessa "Van" Helsing (Kelly Overton). Shot in London and Hungary, its series for NBC, *Dracula* (USA 2013–14; cr. Cole Haddon), reanimated them again. Like Showtime's *Penny Dreadful*, *Dracula* uses supernatural horror to examine real horrors from imperial and capitalist history. Count Dracula (Jonathan Rhys Meyers) impersonates US industrialist Alexander Grayson, seeking support for wireless geomagnetic energy in London. Battles between competing interests resemble the war of currents between Westinghouse and Edison, during which Edison electrocuted a young elephant. Poisoned milk and explosions sabotage Grayson's demonstrations of alternative energy. *Dracula* speculates on a pre-oil moment when different interests could have furthered a different present in a kind of retro-futurism.

Alternative energy is loosely opposed to colonialism. Count Dracula challenges a British secret society that wants Ottoman lands, believed to be "sitting on petroleum" (1.7).

Comparably, *From Dusk till Dawn: The Series* repurposes the 1995 feature. It tells an alternative version of the story on Rodriguez's television network, which developed as part of cable and internet-service provider Comcast's deal for government approval to acquire NBCUniversal by supporting "minority-owned" networks. While the series offers grindhouse pleasures, it presents Mexican American perspectives on post-NAFTA borderlands. The original film also inspired two direct-to-video sequels, *From Dusk till Dawn 2: Texas Blood Money* (1999) and *From Dusk Till Dawn 3: The Hangman's Daughter* (2000), shot in South Africa, and a first-person shooter (FPS) game for Microsoft Windows in 2001, set on an oil tanker overrun by vampires. While the videogame erases Latina/o American themes, the series politicizes them. It also recognizes Latina/o American audiences as a valuable market for Hollywood—and Latina/o American culture as integral to US culture. Other series are less concerned with transnational US history. ABC's *The Gates* (USA 2010; cr. Grant Scharbo and Richard Hatem) imagined white vampires inside a gated community. MTV's *Death Valley* (USA 2011; cr. Curtis Gwinn and Eric Weinberg) self-consciously parodies reality-television police shows in the San Fernando Valley after vampires, werewolves, and zombies descend.

Hollywood is transnational in the sense of affected by non-US business practices. Even before Sony purchased Columbia in 1989, Japanese consumer markets became a "driver for change" in Hollywood's transition into content personalization when Sony introduced Betamax videocassettes to compete with JVC's VHS (Curtin et al. 2014: 8). Alongside increased personalization of home media, production of direct-to-video features is increasingly offshored. Decisions are often economic—*Lost Boys: The Tribe* (2008), shot mostly in Canada; *Lost Boys: The Thirst* (2010), entirely in South Africa—with both set in California. Economic and cultural considerations overlap with *Vampires: Los Muertos* (2002), shot in México, and *Vampires: The Turning* (2005), shot in Thailand, where stories are set. A theatrical adaptation of the hack-and-slash (H&S) videogame *BloodRayne* (2002), set in 1930s United States, Argentina, and Germany, *BloodRayne* (USA-Germany 2005; dir. Uwe Boll), was shot in Romania; direct-to-video sequels *BloodRayne: Deliverance* (2007) and *BloodRayne: The Third Reich* (2011), in Canada and Croatia.

The significance of nation within transnational convergences persists. Early television developed from the industrial infrastructure of radio, inheriting regulatory systems and concerns for public interests. From Edison's monopoly to the Big Five's oligopoly, cinema self-regulated for private interests. Television is entrusted with national cultural and educational objectives. Unlike state-owned television—Britain's BBC, Canada's CBC, Australia's ABC—most

US television is funded by subscriptions and advertising. Public Broadcasting Service (PBS) competes with the Big Three by sharing programming between affiliates. The Children's Television Workshop's *Sesame Street* (USA 1969–present; cr. Joan Ganz Cooney and Lloyd Morrisett), featuring Jim Henson's Muppets, introduced vampire Count von Count in 1972. Although modeled after Universal's Count Dracula, his pink skin departs from the white makeup worn by Lugosi yet blends into *Sesame Street*'s multicolored and multispecies Muppets—and multiracial and multilingual human cast. The series facilitates learning among underserved and disadvantaged audiences through innovative formats and experimental pedagogies. Count von Count does not seduce and murder. He teaches children how to count, playing upon eastern European folklore of the compulsion of vampires to count spilled seeds. Insulated from pressures of sales and rating but instead evaluated by learning outcomes, *Sesame Street* is localized in 120 versions, becoming "the most widely disseminated American television program in the world" (Mittell 2010: 395, 397–8). It reclaims vampires as figures of empathy and intelligence rather than ethnocentrism and xenophobia. Vampires can also teach us how to live with difference rather than submit to top-down notions of consensus or tolerance.

Television, thus, inhabits both public spaces of free-to-air networks and private spaces of home entertainment. It both interpolates as national citizen and isolates as niche market. *Personalized* entertainment became an alternative to *national* entertainment, which opens Hollywood to stories that it might not otherwise assume financial risk to produce, distribute, or exhibit/transmit. With deregulation and economic integration since the 1990s, narrowcasting on cable and internet, and offshoring to Canada and Europe, facilitate television series, miniseries, and features that address alternatives to the imagined ideal audience of young white men for blockbusters at multiplexes. Other Hollywoods permit other vampires that can activate debates on race and citizenship.

Media Convergence and Conglomerations

Media convergence via digitization is a retrospective myth. Even before television syndication of theatrical films in the 1950s and their subsequent release on home-video formats in the 1970s, different forms of media are historically entwined. Television series extend narrative practices from radio plays and early cinema as stories that develop over time. A century ago, audiences gathered in war-torn Paris for episodes of Louis Feuillade's *Les Vampires* (1915–16), about thieves. Supernatural vampires made guest appearances on television series, including *Alfred Hitchcock Presents* (1955–62), *Tales from the Crypt* (1990–2000), *The X-Files* (1993–2002), *Supernatural* (2005–present), and *American Horror Story* (2011–present). Vampire aesthetics appeared weekly in comedies, *Addams Family* (1964–6) and *The Munsters* (1964–6); vampires, in soap operas, *Dark Shadows* (1966–71) and later *Port Charles* (1997–2003). Hollywood initially turned to television to monetize film libraries in syndicated movie-of-the-week programs. Cassandra Peterson's Elvira hosted *Movie Macabre* (1981–93), updating Maila Nurmi's Vampira from KABC's *The Vampira Show* (1954–5) and evoking Luna in *Mark of the Vampire* (1935). Dick Dyszel portrayed Count Gore de Vol on WDCA's *Creature Feature* (1973–87). Made-for-television features bypassed broadcasting fees, as did offshoring production to Toronto and Montréal since the 1970s.[1] Networks produced miniseries. Stephen King's 1975 novel *Salem's Lot* was twice adapted as a three-hour television miniseries by Warner Bros. for CBS (USA 1979; dir. Tobe Hooper) and TNT (USA 2004; dir. Mikael Salomon), shot in Australia, and inspired a theatrical sequel, *A Return to Salem's Lot* (USA 1987; dir. Larry Cohen). The film opens with an anthropologist filming a human sacrifice by a so-called primitive race of humans in Latin America. When he returns to the United States, he learns that vampires are the "oldest race." Television extends the lives of Hollywood features through broadcast and challenges the marketing logic of multiplex exhibition.

The 1991 deregulation of financial interest and syndication rules ("fin-syn rules") allowed networks to create in-house syndication units (Scott 2004: 187). Film studios established their own television networks, including Paramount's UPN and Warner Bros.' WB, which merged into CW in 2006. "Taken as a whole, then, television-program production looks much like the motion-picture industry in that it is dominated by a limited number of majors embedded in even larger—and expanding—conglomerates complemented by swarms of small independent producers," observes Allen Scott (2004: 189). Deregulation was promoted as increasing diversity. "Instead of needing to design programming likely to be least objectionable to the entire family," notes Amanda Lotz, "broadcast networks—and particularly cable channels—increasingly developed programming that might be most satisfying to specific audience members" (2014: 27). Regulation, however, also ensured content from perspectives that might be omitted under free-market economies, such as stories that convey minoritized experiences. Such changes began in 1987 when the Federal Communications Commission (FCC) eliminated the Fairness Doctrine, which since 1949 compelled broadcasters to include controversial topics from different perspectives. A proliferation of public access, cable, and satellite channels was imagined to fulfill this need. Television transitioned from the New Deal's conviction in universal service and paternalistic care of citizens to neoliberalism's faith in free-market competition (McMurria 2009: 171). Expanding its scope to include internet, the Telecommunications Act of 1996 authorized media cross-ownership. Mergers and acquisitions established horizontal integration (television, internet, mobile phone) and re-established vertical integration (production, distribution, exhibition) banned in 1948. Disney acquired ABC to expand content and delivery platforms. Universal merged with NBC. Comcast bought NBCUniversal, thus "both content and conduits in the new digital ecosystem" (Curtin et al. 2014: 4).

Digitization affects how media produces meaning. Episodes are increasingly screened in solitude on a laptop or mobile device. Interactions might be in person—or via IM apps on the very device used to stream video. Audience choices are often generated algorithmically as recommendations. Television and film are undifferentiated as mediums in recommendations that update broadcast strategies of "hammocking" new or less popular programs between popular ones—or "tent-poling" these hits—to encourage television audiences to "stay tuned." Just as television broadcast of studio film libraries challenged the principle of scarcity behind the run-zone-clearance system, so too are video-on-demand (VOD) services challenging the logic behind DVD and Blu-ray regional codes. Hollywood attempts to sustain "artificial scarcity" in the face of "digital plenitude" of streaming and downloading through geo-blocking online content (Strangelove 2015: 178–87). Entertainment value comes from the sheer quantity of options on subscription services such as Netflix and Hulu, internet services such as Amazon Instant Video and iTunes (which allows file purchase), cloud-based services such as HBO Go, third-party apps for Android and Apple mobile devices, as well as unauthorized P2P file-sharing on video-sharing websites such as YouTube and through BitTorrent on Pirate Bay. Netflix is admired for its original programming today, but its business model is structured around offering subscribers access to the largest array of content ("assets") possible. New metrics have dislodged conventional logic for audience measurements, such as market share, to determine advertising prices and series renewals, so that "audience engagement, rather than size, is the current zeitgeist, but no one knows for sure how to qualify it" (Curtin et al. 2014: 3).

Hollywood's economic power allows it to sell television series around the world. Hollywood's film industry generates more than half its income from overseas markets; Hollywood's television industry, only about a quarter (Scott 2004: 202). More than foreign films on theatrical screens, foreign television series trigger concerns about cultural domination since television's role is conceived as "central to the modernist intent of engineering a national identity" with programming that crossed borders seen as "a 'challenge' to national culture and sovereignty" (Calaby 2005: 1, 3). Series like *Dallas* (1978–91), *Santa Barbara* (1984–93), *The Oprah Winfrey Show* (1986–2011), *The Bold and the Beautiful* (1987–present), and *Baywatch* (1989–2001) found international audiences. They promote US values. WikiLeaks actually revealed a diplomatic cable, suggesting *Late Show with David Letterman* (1993–2015), *Friends* (1994–2004), and *Desperate Housewives* (2004–12) were better US propaganda in Saudi Arabia than the US-supported Alhurra satellite channel.[2] By the 1990s, cable networks localized content for foreign markets rather than simply dubbing it into local languages. "No matter how localized a version of MTV or CNN might be," points out Jason Mittell, "these channels are still understood as American imports, not as television indigenous to other regions" (2009: 440). Foreign producers nonetheless appropriate Hollywood concepts. In 2008, rumors spread that Quezon City-based ABS-CBN Channel 2 had purchased rights for *Takipsilim* ("twilight"), a series based on Hollywood's *Twilight*, with Shaina Magdayao and Rayver Cruz in leading roles. Rumors were false, but television saw *My Darling Aswang* (Philippines 2010–11; dir. Bert de Leon), based on the feature *Ang Darling Kong Aswang* (Philippines 2009; dir. Tony Y. Reyes). Vampires also appear in other series from India, Israel, Malaysia, and South Korea that appropriate or ignore Hollywood models. Hollywood struggles to develop new practices for audiences with access to ever-expanding libraries of content on authorized and unauthorized platforms. Despite its highly publicized objections to piracy, Peter Decherney (2012) argues that classical Hollywood's success was really a "golden age of plagiarism" of plays and novels—and that contemporary Hollywood engages in "guerrilla wars" against fair use and home video while outsourcing production to bypass unions and guilds. The strategy of featuring below-the-line crew in antipiracy campaigns conveys a cynicism in light of the imperative to offshore (Miller et al. 2005: 171). Free-to-air television acculturated US audiences to the illusion that television programming was free, rather than financed through advertising, which now spills over into expectations about cable and internet services and theatrical films. Like a vampire, each medium infects the other in an entertainment industry that itself mutates and migrates like a vampire.

Canada as Hollywood's Home Market

Adapted from the feature *Nick Knight* (USA 1989: dir. Farhad Mann), television series *Forever Knight* (Canada-West Germany 1992–6; cr. Barney Cohen and James D. Parriott) involved being adapted to Canada by relocating its story from Los Angeles to Toronto. *Forever Knight* initially aired in CBS's late-night block, where most content was produced in Canada, fulfilling Canadian Radio-television and Telecommunications Commission (CRTC) requirements for 50–60 per cent of programming with Canadian cultural content, written and produced by Canadians. Nicholas "Nick" Knight (Geraint Wyn Davies) seeks redemption for eight centuries of killing humans by helping police solve homicides. He claims to have a skin disorder that prevents him from working in sunlight but confides in medical examiner Natalie Lambert (Catherine Disher). The series reintroduced vampires to weekly broadcast television and reclaimed them as human allies, imagining multispecies empathy through civic structures. Lower costs for offshored television production allow for storylines not considered lucrative to film producers.

Forever Knight demonstrated Canada's viability as a Hollywood location. Runaway productions of *The X-Files*, *Smallville* (2001–11), and *Battlestar Galactica* (2004–9) transformed Vancouver into "Hollywood North" (Mittell 2010: 445). Although Britain and Australia established quotas on US imports, Canada did not. It was "integrated" into Hollywood's home market during the 1920s when US exhibitors purchased Canadian theaters. Presumed cultural fluidity facilitated Canada serving as a shooting location for features and series set in the United States. Toronto served as an "Anytown, USA." Runaway production was not shared power. "Television-program production represents the 'other Hollywood' in the sense that it runs parallel to but remains in the shadow of a more familiar Hollywood focused on the production of large-scale feature films," argues Allen Scott (2004: 201). Hollywood entices states to compete by offering lower costs and higher tax incentives, typically not benefiting local production. When Canadian productions at Canadian Broadcasting Corporation (CBC)'s British Columbian studios declined in the 1980s, Hollywood productions filled the studios, and the government even built new studios for increased production capacity (Tinic 2006: 159).

Offshored labor is nonunionized, bypassing collective bargaining (Miller et al. 2005: 140). In the 1990s, most runaway production was "movies of the week" for television; by the 2000s, most theatrical features (Scott and Pope 2007: 1371). *Creative* runaway production uses location for story; *economic* runaway production, for lower costs (Scott and Pope 2007: 1365). The latter are termed "service productions" (Miller et al. 2005: 140), offering employment but erasing nation in productions hardly Canadian, much less British Columbian. Mike Gasher argues that it is "first and foremost a commercial endeavour which has everything to do with investment capital and job creation and very little to do with indigenous storytelling" (1995: 233), located in a longer history, including Edison's filming of Niagara Falls in 1899 and Biograph in Vancouver, to maximize profit. Columbia's Central Film of Victoria produced "quota quickies" between 1928 and 1938 to bypass British quotas. Low production values ensured Hollywood production did not face competition (Miller et al. 2005: 160).

Cultural submersion under Hollywood film exhibition and television production affects Canadian state media policies, which affect both the kinds of productions that Hollywood offshores to Canada and Canadian directors and producers pursue. Created in 1936, CBC was entrusted with "fostering a cohesive modern national identity" (Pendakur 1990: 48). National Film Board (NFB) followed in 1939, initially to mobilize Canadians to support the war effort with a mandate to educate, preserve heritage, and conserve images of Canada's national identity. The Canadian Film Development Corporation (CFDC) was formed in 1967 to develop a feature film industry but was ineffective since Hollywood controlled theatrical exhibition, blocking Canadian features from Canadian audiences (Smythe in Pendakur 1990: 22). Canadian anglophone and francophone filmmakers lobbied for national policies to end US monopoly through quotas and taxes. A boom in feature production during the 1970s—in total 708, more than twice the previous half-century—resulted from the Capital Cost Allowance (CCA), begun in 1954 to build infrastructure and produce distinctly Canadian films. The CCA allowed investors to write off 60 per cent of investment against personal income taxes. To be certified as a Canadian film, more than two-thirds of the key creative positions (director, cinematographer, editor, composer, two highest paid actors) needed to be held by Canadians. An elaborate point system was later created to allow more US onscreen talent. By 1976, 100 per cent of talent could be foreign. At the time, the United States abolished its own similar tax shelter, encouraging US investments in Canadian films (Pendakur 1990: 170). Canadian features came to be disparaged as a "national scandal," expressing nothing uniquely Canadian. *Meatballs* (Canada 1979; dir. Ivan Reitman) and *Porky's* (Canada-USA 1982; dir. Bob Clark) were simultaneously "movies from nowhere" and financially successful Canadian films (Melnyk 2004: 113–14, 121).

Before the CCA was terminated in 1981, David Cronenberg produced films that focused on nightmares, science fiction, and pornography while rejecting Hollywood's narrative closure (Melnyk 2004: 148–9). His films exploited "movies from nowhere" conventions, seeming uncanny to US audiences because they "appear like America but not like America," allowing Cronenberg to critique US and Hollywood domination (Morris 1994: 106). Human heads explode in shopping malls in *Scanners* (1981). Other films reinvent vampires. In *Shivers* (1975), a suburban self-contained living complex, Starliners Towers, harbors a sexual (vampiric) parasite shaped like human feces. In *Rapid* (1977), Rose (Marilyn Chambers) undergoes experimental plastic surgery after a motorbike injury, resulting in a vagina-like orifice in her armpit. The orifice contains a phallic stinger, allowing her to drink human blood. Her victims remember nothing and go rabid, biting others and spreading contagion. Cronenberg's visual tropes reappear in Mexican filmmaker Guillermo del Toro's television series *The Strain*.

Canadian filmmakers produced other vampire films.[3] Mary Harron's *The Moth Diaries* (Canada-Ireland-UK 2011) concerns intimate friendship between two young women at a boarding school, evoking LeFanu's novella *Carmilla*. Guy Maddin's *Dracula: Pages from a Virgin's Diary* (2001) adapts a performance by the Royal Winnipeg Ballet, interpreting Stoker's novel as a racialized and sexualized frenzy of nativism. Madden satirizes visual nostalgia for the silent era—tinted black-and-white footage, grainy images, irises, intertitles—with counterpoint that transforms citations of Stoker into critiques of orientalism and xenophobia in state policy. Opening with shots of a map of Europe, phrases "Immigrants!" and "From the east!" are displayed over a trail of blood. Chinese dancer Zhang Wei-qiang performs Count Dracula, thereby satirizing Canada's history of racially determined recruitment and regulation of immigrants through policies to ensure "White Canada Forever."

A decade after *Forever Knight*, vampires return to television with a similar storyline in CBC's *Blood Ties* (Canada 2006; cr. Peter Mohan), broadcast in the United States on Lifetime. Shot and set in Toronto and Vancouver, the series concerns former police detective Vicki Nelson (Christina Cox), who works as a private detective after her vision diminishes. Illegitimate son of Henry VIII of England, Henry Fitzroy (Kyle Schmid) writes and illustrates graphic novels. Vicki and Henry solve supernatural cases, often with the assist of Vicki's former partner (and lover) Mike Celluci (Dylan Neal), and Henry's assistant Coreen Fennel (Gina Holden). The principal cast is Canadian, and the series is based on Canadian novelist Tanya Huff's *Blood Books* (1991–7). Within the highly competitive broadcast market, the series was cancelled after one season. Based on the BBC's *Being Human* (UK 2008–13; cr. Toby Whithouse), Hollywood's *Being Human* (Canada-USA 2011–2014; cr. Jeremy Carver and Anna Fricke) ran for three seasons and included one Canadian actor in one of three lead roles—Meaghan Rath as the ghost Sally Malik—along with a majority of Canadian actors in the recurring roles. The series was shot in Montréal and produced by Muse Entertainment under Québécois and Canadian tax schemes. Despite its epithet as Hollywood North, Canadian film and television does not have access to Hollywood's distribution and broadcast channels.

Asian America, Made for Television

Shot in British Columbia and intended for theatrical release, *Mother, May I Sleep with Danger?* (USA 1996; dir. Jorge Montesi) became a cult television hit for NBC. Two decades later, James Franco remade it as a lesbian-vampire film (USA 2016; dir. Melanie Aitkenhead) for Lifetime. He reworks melodrama into camp. Others draw upon television's role in introducing marginalized perspectives. Elayne Rapping argues that 1950s television assumed a role abandoned by cinema, becoming "the major source for social issue dramas—many of which influenced the direction of public discourse on matters like race, religious prejudice, and war" (1992: 3). By the 1970s, producers realized that television features could fulfill the FCC's desire for content in the public interest while simultaneously generating profits (16). Made-for-television features allow producers to experiment since they "are low-budget, formula narratives with brief lifespans" (23). They contain costs with smaller crews and lower production values. They become adult alternatives to blockbusters.

Since the 1960s, networks commissioned made-for-television features (Gomery 1983: 125). NBC commissioned from Universal; ABC, from MGM. Production costs were reduced by as much as half. Conventions no longer tolerated in theatrical features, such as cross-dissolve flashbacks and montage sequences of repeated footage, generate experiences defined by emotional intensity over narrative continuity. "Men smirk at them, as they do at romance novels and soaps, because they deal emotionally and sometimes melodramatically with the kinds of things women have traditionally concerned themselves with—illness, family tragedy, small-scale injustice," Rapping explains about their marginalization (1992: 31). Recorded television programming ("telefilms") was initially disdained for not realizing broadcast's *raison d'être* of engaging disparate audiences simultaneously in real time (Mittell 2010: 164). Cable television increased production values and social content. Emmy-winning *The Josephine Baker Story* (USA 1991; dir. Brian Gibson) "inspired HBO to develop a series of films that dealt with the history, lives, and problems of marginal and oppressed groups" (Auster 2008: 230). It was released on VHS alongside theatrical films. Asian America also found visibility.

After a theatrical run, *The Jitters* (USA-Japan 1988; dir. John Fasano) reached audiences on VHS. It relocates East Asian Americans from isolated foils, as in *Vamp*, to protagonist community. Opening with images of Chinese shops and music with orientalized instrumentation, it refigures vampire as *goeng si* ("hopping vampire," literally, stiff corpse) from Hong Kong cinema (cf. Hudson 2009). Shot in Toronto-as-New York, Chinatown seems familiar from narratives of white men saving nonwhite women from their own culture. *The Jitters* introduces multidirectional assimilation and comedy. The *goeng si*'s presence is symptomatic of racialized violence against Chinese Americans. Corpses reanimate as a consequence of violent deaths. Attempting to rob shopkeeper Mr. Lee (Handy Atmadja), a multiracial gang harasses his niece, Alice (Marilyn Tokudo), and destroys merchandise. Lee defends himself with martial arts. Joking he does not Chinese traditions because he is a "round eye" and a "capitalist," Alice's white fiancé, Michael (Sal Viviano), urges her to leave. The gang returns and murders Mr. Lee.

Tony Yang Sr. (James Hong) and Tony Yang Jr. (John Quincy Lee) understand Lee will become a *goeng si*. They tame his corpse, costumed in Mandarin robe, blue face, elongated fangs, and pointed ears, popularized in Ricky Lau Koon-wai's *Goeng si sin sang/Mr. Vampire* (Hong Kong 198å5). The narrative rewards or punishes characters for whether they facilitate multicultural harmony. Gang members call Alice a "China doll" and display a Confederate battle flag until chased from Chinatown by *goeng sis*. The Yangs use martial arts and *fashu* (magical incantations and invocations) to defeat the gang, but the film's narrative continues beyond the final fight sequence to the presentation of two mixed-race couples: Alice and Michael, and Tony Jr. and Gina (Lisa

Foster). Michael and Gina, assimilate to Chinatown. East Asian Americans are not model minorities who blend quietly into multicultural whiteness. They fight for rights. Not Michael, but Tony Jr. saves Alice. *The Jitters* anticipates films by Chinese American and Chinese Canadian filmmakers, including Mina Shum's *Double Happiness* (1994) and Quentin Lee and Justin Lin's *Shopping for Fangs* (1997).

Dissatisfied with roles available to women, Shelley Duvall began to produce her own material for Showtime. *Nightmare Classics* adapted stories, including Sheridan LeFanu's, in *Carmilla* (USA 1990; dir. Gabrielle Beaumont), which it relocates from nineteenth-century Styria, an Austrian province on the Hungarian border, to Louisiana. Leo (Roy Dotrice) raises his daughter Marie (Ione Skye) in isolation until she encounters Carmilla (Meg Tilly). The film unwittingly explored racial passing both in contemporary Hollywood and the post-bellum South.[4] Hollywood's use of "Asians, Asian Americans, and Pacific Islanders as signifiers of racial otherness to avoid the more immediate racial tensions between blacks and whites or the ambivalent mixture of guilt and enduring hatred toward Native American[s] and Hispanics" (Marchetti 1993: 6) describes how gender and sexuality camouflage race. African American stereotypes facilitate Tilly-as-Carmilla's ability to pass as both human and white. Close-ups are often shot under bright key lighting, masking Tilly's facial features and giving her an otherworldly aura, underscored by a nondiegetic musical motif. Skye is shot under diffuse, soft lighting, a difference most visible in shot/countershot editing of their intimate conversations.

Carmilla opens like plantation fantasies, with a long shot of black servants outside a white house, surrounded by oak trees, picket fences, and dirt roads, followed by a medium close-up of a young white woman, opening a curtain from inside an upstairs bedroom. It establishes a particular perspective that sees black servants working happily for white masters. Costumed as a stock Mammy figure, Miss Hodgett (Armelia McQueen) sacrifices her own safety to protect her employers without noticing that she has no family of her own. The film continues "mechanisms of cinematic racism," sublimated "under the stronger compulsions of romance, revenge, or sensation" (Snead 1994: 38). "The traditional slave stereotypes are eminently comforting," William Van Deburg notes; "the slavery film is one of Hollywood's most reliable vehicles for the mass sedation of race-based anxiety" (1993: 34–5). Leo fears "outsiders." Carmilla is welcomed into the household, but Leo chides Miss Hodgett for allowing an orphaned African American boy to sleep outside. His xenophobia is psychologized in personal misfortune, minimizing racism as a social institution. He believes his wife ran away with a "Yankee" after "the War." Carmilla actually abducted and integrated her into a vampire "family." Feminist alternatives to colonial patriarchy, however, are crushed. Leo and Marie join hands to drive a stake into his wife and her mother.

Cast as unnamed servants, African Americans are shown but rarely heard. When they speak, they are punished or humiliated. Unpaid black labor becomes Old South nostalgia, visible yet unacknowledged. Carmilla commands bats to murder Miss Hodgett, who suspects Carmilla murdered the young orphan. Miss Hodgett's back is grossly disfigured by bite marks, evoking slaves' bloody and scarred flesh after being flayed by white slave owners and traders. Bats remove her tongue, symbolically silencing her beyond death since dead slaves often appears as ghosts that haunt their masters. Her body is further dehumanized when Inspector Amos (Roddy McDowall) casually holds a cup of tea above it whilst debating cause of death. Carmilla conceals her foreignness by not outwardly opposing, but taking advantage of racial hierarchies. *Carmilla* interprets LeFanu's novella without the frame of homosocial female intimacy primarily for the pleasure of straight-male audiences, as in Hammer's films of the 1970s and their imitators. Although Showtime diminishes allusions to homosexual female desire, it anticipates the Canadian web series *Carmilla*, which opens vampires to new forms of feminist and queer possibilities.

Slaying without a Feminist Role Model, Walking while Black

Within a dearth of feminist television, *Buffy the Vampire Slayer* was praised for its representation of gender and sexuality. First appearing in a theatrical parody of gendered and sexualized conventions in slasher films (USA 1992; dir. Fran Rubel Kazui), Buffy Summers (Kristy Swanson) rejects antiquated norms, transforming from self-absorbed, anti-intellectual cheerleader into vampire slayer. After burning her high school to the ground, Buffy moves from Los Angeles to the nearly all-white fictional town of Sunnydale, for the series. Her old school had a visible, if not audible, East Asian American population, though her friends include only a token African American, Jennifer (Michele Abrams). Her new school is entirely white. The series is a Los Angeles satire of politically conservative San Diego. Set in multiracial Los Angeles, spinoff *Angel* (USA 1999–2004; cr. David Greenwalt and Joss Whedon) engaged racism. 20th Century Fox produced both for Warner Bros.' WB, though *Buffy* moved to Paramount's UPN. Both continue into additional seasons as graphic novels.

Buffy both embodies and parodies reactionary responses to multiculturalism. Camp-inflected slayer "girl power" rejects feminism's demand for a critique of empire and empathy across difference. Vampirism is not a means to investigate racialization or marginalization. Buffy acts like a schoolyard bully, masking insecurities with sarcasm. Kent Ono argues that the series "indirectly and directly shows violence by primarily white vigilante youths against people of color in the name of *civilization*" (2000: 168). Cynthia Fuchs notes that "the series tends to displace raced identity and anxieties about race onto species-related anxieties" via romance (2007: 105). Interspecies relations work best when both species look, act, or identify as white and middle class. The werewolf Oz (Seth Green) is a suitable boyfriend for Buffy's best friend Willow. Buffy calls her church-attending human boyfriend Riley Finn (Marc Blucas) a "bigot" for criticizing Willow's relationship with a nonhuman (4.19). Buffy is hardly a slayer of prejudice. She is afraid of what Riley will think when he learns that she has sex with vampires. When Buffy asks Angel (David Boreanaz) whether the term "undead American" is an appropriate substitute to the "offensive term" of vampire, she becomes a parody of rightwing attacks on so-called political correctness. She avoids self-reflection and allows her emotions to erupt in moments of violent white fragility—unconscious reactions to the discomfort of being confronted by racial difference, commonly tears among liberal-minded white women and rage among conservative-minded white men—or, in this case, Buffy.

When people of color appear, Buffy mocks them. They usually die. Vampires kill nonwhite slayers Kendra (Bianca Lawson) and Nikki Wood (April Weeden-Washington and K. D. Aubert). Buffy, however, is partly controlled by Giles. She is an "instrument of the Council" (5.12). If she refuses to cooperate, the Council will confiscate his green card. Buffy's childish rebellion challenges patriarchal power reconfigured as a docile white masculinity but also points to the series' absence of feminist role models. As the First Slayer, the Primitive (Sharon Ferguson) offers a counter-narrative to fantasies of US national origins in Giles's homeland of England. She conjures scientific theories that all humans developed from AL 288-1 aka Lucy, the oldest identified primate skeleton, found in Ethiopia in 1974. Dark brown skin, heavy dreadlocks, and white face-paint define the Primitive, who never had a Watcher. No man controls her, but Buffy cannot understand her. By highlighting Buffy's inability to listen—and self-authorization to speak on behalf of people of color—the series conveys crucial differences between girl power and feminism. Buffy is a parody of postfeminism.

When Buffy is killed, she becomes neither undead like vampires nor living dead like zombies but *living again*—reborn via a messianic epithet of the Chosen One, evoking the expression Chosen People used by Jewish and Christian groups.[5] Religion is another form of social difference that is minimalized in the series. Buffy sometimes wears a tiny crucifix, and Willow is Jewish. If either practices religion, she does so quietly. Jon Stratton believes that the casting of Gellar frames Buffy as "the apparently all-American, Anglo-American, middle-class girl," who is "non-Jewish-but-Jewish" (2005: 184, 194). He finds that "the lack of anti-Semitism offers American Jews a fantasy image of their acceptance into Anglo-American society" (2005: 187). Within fears of a coming white minority in California, he see the protagonists as "Anglo-American and unified in purpose," so that "there are no minorities here, no need for debates over affirmative action, no racially based demands for multicultural acknowledgement" (182). The series emphasizes US national exceptionalism, hinting at racism without doing the work of scripting discussions about it. Buffy's mother, Joyce (Kristine Sutherland), celebrates the easy assimilation of foreigners, noting Ampata Gutierrez (Ara Celi), a revived Incan mummy/exchange student, "already seems like she belongs here" after only "two days in America" (2.4). If that episode confronts California's Mexican past, another (4.8) confronts its Native American past, requiring Buffy to claim territory on Thanksgiving. National revisionism unfolds in Buffy's "paralysis with regard to dealing decisively with this uncomfortable Chumash situation" contrasted with "apparently unabashed imperialist" positions of the English characters Giles and Spike (Alessio 2001: 734).

Like CBS's *Forever Knight* and *Moonlight* (USA 2007–8; cr. Ron Koslow and Trevor Munson), UPN's *Angel* features a reluctant white-male-vampire who uses his supernatural powers to solve crimes.[6] Angel Investigations is born from the desire of "helping the helpless" and from Angel's belief in the Shanshu Prophecy of a vampire with a soul restored to humanity. *Angel* opens with white-woman-as-potential-victim of multiculturalism, yet the series explores social and political corruption, particularly through clients represented by law firm Wolfram and Hart, founded in 1791. Corporations are more damaging to humans than vampires. Both are immortal. Angel Investigations includes African American vampire hunters Charles Gunn (J. August Richards), half-Ano-Movic demon Allen Doyle (Glenn Quinn), and green-skinned demon Lorne (Andy Hallett), who runs a karaoke bar open to all species. Whites remain a majority with Cordelia Chase (Charisma Carpenter), ex-Watcher Wesley Wyndam-Pryce (Alexis Denisof), physicist Winifred "Fred" Burkle (Amy Acker), Buffy's high-school frenemy-now-vampire Harmony Kendall (Mercedes McNab), and Angel's son Connor (Vincent Kartheiser).

Movement between raced bodies occasionally happens. Fred dies and is reanimated by the spirit of the ancient demon Illyria, who calls Angel and Spike "half breeds" (5.18). *Angel* displaces interracial/interethnic tensions onto interspecies tensions. Demons have unnatural skin color to avoid blackface, yellowface, brownface, and redface. Doyle's human wife Harriet (Kristen Dattilo) arrives, wanting a divorce to marry Ano-Movic demon Richard Straley (Carlos Jacott). Once "nomadic" and now "assimilated," Ano-Movic demons are a "peaceful clan" (1.7). When aroused, they have red faces. Much to Harriet's disgust, Richard's male relatives revive a tradition of eating the bride's first husband's brains, introducing racialized prejudices that determine which foods consumed by immigrants can be assimilated into US cuisines (cf. Mannur 2008). Although she is an ethno-demonologist, Harriet finds the practice "barbaric." One of Richard's relatives calls her a racist.

Systemic identification and extermination of a specific group is examined when Doyle encounters part-human Lister demons, hiding in a basement, after a businessman steals money paid for passage to an island near Ecuador (1.9). They look like emaciated humans with grayish skin, visually reproducing images of Ashkenazi Jews who hid from Nazis in cellars or attics. They fear "The Scourge," a paramilitary group of pureblood supremacists, seeking to exterminate "mixed types." Half-human demons are called "vermin," appropriating the language of Nazi anti-Semitism. Uniforms of pureblood demons evoke Nazi uniforms. Their leader calls vampires "the lowest half-breeds." Demons are held captive to fight unto death as entertainment for rich white people (1.16), recalling the opening of Ralph Ellison's *The Invisible Man* (1952) about the invisible spectacle of African America.

Vampires have no souls, except for the 240-year-old Angel, cursed by gypsies to suffer anguish for his murders. His name is an anglicized version of Angelus, yet his human name was Liam, reflecting his Irish origins in Galway. Angel's arrival is represented in a flashback to Ellis Island in 1902. He sees the Statue of Liberty (4.15). By 1943, Angel supports the Allies against the Nazis by stopping their plan to build an army of vampires (5.13), reinforcing US national exceptionalism as welcoming immigrants and opposing fascism. Angel is more exceptional than English vampire William, who bleaches his hair and changes his name to Spike. Spike mocks Dracula's "showy gypsy stuff" and "special dirt" as a means of defining himself as an assimilated Anglo-American. Spike calls Angel an "Uncle Tom" for refusing to feed upon humans (2.3). The use of a racist expression by a white (English) vampire towards another white (Irish) vampire evokes historical racism while avoiding contemporary forms.

Angel largely places the onus of pointing out racism on token protagonist of color Gunn, who initially dismisses Angel's help: "I don't need advice from a middle-class white dude" (1.20). He points out that "walking while black" (2.13) looks suspicious to the LAPD, suggesting little has changed since *Blacula*'s representation of Los Angeles. Angel Investigations later examines dead white-male officers who return as zombies to racially profile African Americans. Gunn also defends himself against Fred's appropriation of expressions like "bro" and "word" (4.1), critiquing white-female privilege. *Angel* historicizes racism in an episode that establishes Angel's connection to the Hyperion hotel, where Angel Investigations relocates. Angel witnesses an African American family turned away despite vacancies in 1952. The episode's title, "Are You Now or Have You Ever Been" (2.2), reconfigures McCarthyist rhetoric to critique racism against light-skinned African Americans accused of passing. The biracial Judy Kovacs (Melissa Marsala) defines herself as "not one thing or the other" but "nothing." The series includes a place for race in a post-multicultural United States.

Vampires in the New South

Unsettling assumptions about humans basing politics on race/ethnicity, later series show vampires divided by political positions rather than united by species. HBO's *True Blood* (USA 2008–14; cr. Alan Ball), CW's *The Vampire Diaries* (USA 2009–present; crs. Kevin Williamson and Julie Plec), and *The Originals* (USA 2013–present; cr. Julie Plec) engage debates on rights and land through native-born vampires whose historical relationships to the United States unearth historical trauma. In *True Blood*, Confederate soldier Bill Compton (Stephen Moyer) fought during the "War for Southern Independence" (1.5) but was labeled a "Yankee sympathizer" for calling Louisiana's secession a "lost cause" (7.5). In *The Vampire Diaries*, Damon Salvatore (Ian Somerhalder) was a reluctant Confederate soldier. They now exist in a world of destabilized white privilege, witnessing the Emancipation Proclamation (1863) redefine slaves as freedmen and the Thirteenth Amendment (1865) make them citizens. In *The Originals*, Marcel Gerard (Charles Michael Davis) is the "illegitimate" son of a colonial governor and his slave. He rises from slave to New Orleans's ruling vampire, only to be exiled to Algiers, a low-income predominantly African American ward once serving as a port of arrival for slaves. Collectively, the series consider structural inequality as historically rooted. They convey difference as arbitrary and mutable, as characters become hybrid species or move between raced bodies.

Set in predominantly white Mystic Falls (Virginia), *The Vampire Diaries*' early seasons are saturated in Old South nostalgia, with outdoor *Gone with the Wind* screenings and indoor Civil War exhibits. Supernatural species roam freely, but secrets are locked in crypts and caves. Mysterious new student at school Stefan Salvatore (Paul Wesley) rouses Elena Gilbert (Nina Dobrev) from depression over her parents' death. She begins to notice that she inhabits a multispecies world. Stefan and his brother Damon are vampires; Caroline Forbes (Candice Accola) becomes one. Bonnie Bennett (Kat Grahem) is a witch; Tyler Lockwood (Michael Trevino), a werewolf; and her brother Jeremy (Steven R. McQueen), a vampire hunter. Elena herself is doppelgänger for both vampire Katherine Pierce/Katerina Petrova and Amara, immortal beloved of Stefan's own doppelgänger, Silas. Only Matt Donovan (Zach Roerig) is and remains human. Bonnie is the token African American, but no one notices. She is "The Anchor" to the realm of the dead, repeatedly sacrificing her life for her white friends. Elena eventually sacrifices seventy years of her vampire life for Bonnie to have a human life.

Vampires mesmerize humans but cannot enter homes without invitation. Like Count Dracula, they *act* with their eyes, particularly Damon. They have special rings, allowing them to walk in sunlight. They drink alcohol and eat food. Breaking their necks temporarily immobilizes them. They can be killed with wood from the great White Oak tree and weakened by vervaine flowers that grow at its base. Vampires reproduce by infection but were created by witchcraft. The Originals are children of Viking immigrants. According to Rebekah Mikaelson (Claire Holt), her parents, Mikael (Sebastian Roché) and Esther (Alice Evans), left Europe during a tenth-century plague for a land "not yet discovered." She was born in Mystic Falls, along with brothers Elijah (Daniel Gillies), Finn (Casper Zafer), Niklaus "Klaus" (Joseph Morgan), Kol (Nathaniel Buzolic), and Henrik (Devon Allowitz). Esther's sister Dahlia (Claudia Black) raised first-born Fraya (Riley Voelkel). When werewolf "natives" kill Henrik, Mikael asks witch Ayanna (Maria Howell) to transform him into a vampire. She refuses, but Esther concedes. Klaus activates his werewolf gene and becomes hybrid after killing a human. Dying with vampire blood in their bodies, witches become (hybrid) Heretics. The series evokes the inhumanity of animal testing when Damon and Lorenzo "Enzo" St. John (Michael Malarkey) are imprisoned and used in the Augustine Project's experiments (5.10).

The CW series concerns land claims. By representing Originals as Vikings, they reify mythical Anglo-Saxon heritage. Norsemen (Vikings) conquered England in 1066. Leif Ericson arrived in the Americas five centuries before Columbus. Reginald Horsman notes "Anglo-Saxon" never referred to a homogeneous group but comes into usage by nineteenth-century English writers to describe English-speaking people, including Celts and Norsemen (Horsman 1981: 4; Young 2008b; Makdisi 2014). Reinventing Viking history renders Native America as forgotten prehistory. Written in *futhark* (Viking) runes, cave paintings tell stories of (mostly white) werewolves in Mystic Falls before the Mikaelsons. Descendent from actual indigenous nations, vampire hunter Rayna Cruz (Leslie-Anne Huff)'s shaman ancestors sacrificed their lives, so she could incarcerate vampires inside the Phoenix Stone over multiple lifetimes. Her antagonism is supernatural not political. She does not dispute dispossession and genocide. When Lily (Annie Wersching) references "pilgrims and Indians," her son Damon responds: "We call them Native Americans, but we didn't bring you here to correct your outdated racial slurs" (7.7). When he is trapped in the Phoenix Stone, he returns to the Civil War. To leave, he must correct past personal mistakes. The series evokes history without investigating it.

Set in New Orleans, *The Originals* makes scant reference to African Americans displaced by Hurricane Katrina but acknowledges overlapping historical moments. Supernatural species negotiate truces over land and bodies. The series speculates on a world where species is prioritized over race/ethnicity. Inhabiting bodies broaches blackface when Rebekah "possesses"

African American witch Eva Sinclair (Maisie Richardson-Sellers)'s body, offering child-bearing possibilities, and Finn "possesses" African American witch Vincent Griffith (Yusef Gatewood)'s body, offering magical powers. Vampire/werewolf hybrids Klaus and Hayley Marshall (Phoebe Tonkin) are stronger than Originals, rejecting the racist assumption that pure bloodlines are superior. Lucien Castle (Andrew Lees) "upgrades" himself with werewolf blood. He dispossesses werewolves, having them hunted to develop land. Werewolves are organized in multiracial packs; vampires, by blood and sire bonds. The series inserts African American vampires into the US military during the second World War.

True Blood imagines the New South as inhabited by multiple species on multiple planes of reality. It mixes the social realism of everyday experiences of decay, poverty, and violence—hallmarks of Southern Gothic—with supernaturalism. Thwarting expectations for Goth vampires of *Bram Stoker's Dracula* and *Interview with the Vampires*, it introduces vampires with a heavyset white-male vampire in camouflage and a feed cap with a Confederate battle flag, purchasing a six-pack of TruBlood at a convenience store. Although some critics dismissed the series—"*True Blood* is a relic—it airs on television, not the Internet, and it is broadcast rather than streamed" (Peterson et al. 2009)—it included *Babyvamp Jessica's Blog* for Jessica Hamby (Deborah Ann Woll) to communicate with fans, American Vampire League website with messages from Nan Flanagan (Jessica Tuck), and "Reflections of Light" from

Figure 7.1 Buying TruBlood at a convenience store as the first image of "mainstreaming" vampires. *True Blood* (USA 2008–14; cr. Alan Ball).

Sarah Newlin (Anna Camp) on Facebook and Twitter. It engages controversial topics, such as Christian fundamentalism, homophobia, nativism, military invasions, austerity policies, and GEOs.

The series centers on telepathic "half-fae" waitress Sookie Stackhouse (Anna Paquin) and her relationships with vampires Bill Compton and Eric Northman (Alexander Skarsgård), shape-shifter Sam Merlotte (Sam Trammell), and werewolf Alcide Herveaux (Joe Manganiello) in Bon Temps (Louisiana). Since all are white, Sookie risks no social stigmas of mixed-race associations. Vampires cannot fully claim white privilege. "We're white, he's dead," explains Sookie's coworker Arlene Fowler (Carrie Preston) (1.5). Sookie and brother Jason (Ryan Kwanten) trace their ancestry to Descendants of the Glorious Dead, an organization mythologizing white bloodlines, like Daughters of the American Revolution. An underlying obsession with bloodlines emerges in anxieties about miscegenation and incest. Repressed histories of hostilities unfold when vampires advocate for rights and duties of citizenship, raising questions about whether working-class whites, African Americans, and Native/Mexican Americans have access.

Legal and supernatural mechanisms of social power entwine. Blood-quantum laws once defined racial categories; sharing blood now dissolves identity and subjectivity. "We will be one," Eric tells Sookie (4.8). Vampire blood heals human wounds. Just as immigrants require documents to enter countries, vampires require invitations, which can be withdrawn, to enter human homes. Ownership offers conditional sovereignty. Eric informs Sookie that a property deed to her house—"a little piece of paper"—takes away her only power over him (4.2). Mainstreaming by vampires comes after a Japanese company develops synthetic human blood. Whether TruBlood is as good as true (human) blood parodies racist debates on whether one drop of "black blood" contaminated an otherwise white-looking body. As a GEO, TruBlood is an artificial species enabling unnatural interspecies communities in the minds of conservative humans and vampires. The Vampire Authority advocates for a Vampire Rights Amendment. It proposes *multidirectional* interspecies assimilation, requiring the state to change definitions of citizenship to include vampires alongside humans as "natural persons." The amendment satirizes Constitutional fundamentalism that opposes gay marriage and believes citizens can protect themselves with guns.

Vampires from pre-nation-state eras understand interspecies empathy and violence more acutely. The 1,000-year-old Eric sees his Viking parents murdered by werewolves, who give his father's crown to nearly 3,000-year-old Russell Edgington (Denis O'Hare). Eric's maker is 2,000-year-old former Roman slave Godric (Allan Hyde), who hoped vampires would become "less savage" (2.8). The vampire aristocracy believes vampires are superior to humans. The Sanguinistas trace bloodlines to Adam's first wife, Lilith, who

Figure 7.2 Nan Flanagan (Jessica Tuck) advocating for vampire rights on television. *True Blood* (USA 2008–present; cr. Alan Ball).

refused to be dominated. They oppose mainstreaming. When Salomé Agrippa (Valentina Cervi) convinces the Vampire Authority that Lilith (Jessica Clark) has reconstituted from a drop of blood, they embark upon a murderous rampage. Only Eric questions it, placing the onus of interspecies empathy on descendants of vampires who have known slavery's violence.

True Blood speculates about multiple layers of political organization, resembling corporate lobbyists, political action committees, US federal, state, and local law. Russell is Mississippi's king; Eric, Louisiana's sheriff. The Vampire Authority adopts US national-exceptionalist myths of independence from European monarchies. Vampire aristocracy is implicated in transatlantic slave trade and Nazi death camps. Russell manipulates werewolves to serve Nazis in Joseph Goebbels's Operation Werewolf (3.2).[7] Werewolves are marginalized whites, working like "dogs" for drops of Russell's blood. If Nazis are Hollywood's benchmark for evil, *True Blood* realigns evil with enslavement of Africans and African Americans by casting Mississippi aristocrats as slave owners. Colonial plantations model a necropolitics—power to determine who lives and dies (Mbembe 2003)—that anticipates Nazi death camps (Agamben [1995] 1999). Moreover, as Lauren Berlant (2011) argues, dependency on exceptional moments of trauma distracts attention from the everyday and ubiquitous instances of traumatizing systems of power. Some vampires participated in antislavery movements. Fang-banger bar Fangtasia's basement connects to the Underground Railroad (7.4).

Despite speciesism, African Americans suffer most. "People think just cause we got vampires out in the open now race isn't an issue no more," explains Tara Thornton (Rutina Wesley) (1.4). The token African American and woman sheriff's deputy Kenya Jones (Tanya Wright) is passed over for promotion despite her superior qualifications. Racism lingers in everyday interactions. Debating whether to report Sookie's murder of werewolf Debbie Pelt (Brit Morgan), Tara's cousin Lafayette Reynolds (Nelson Ellis) notes self-defense is always believable from white women. The scene evokes requisite whiteness for protection under "stand your ground" laws in places like Arizona, Florida, and Texas, where use of "deadly force" as self-defense is permitted without "duty to retreat." When Tara questions the police shooting of her African American boyfriend, Eggs (Mehcad Brooks), Arlene accuses Tara of manipulating the situation. "I hate it when they make everything about race," she says (3.1). Tara learns from her maker, Pam De Beaufort (Kristin Bauer van Straten), that makers can command their children to do anything. "I'm your slave," she says, as Pam nods; "things fucking stay the same" (5.5). Vampirism appears to equalize but does not undo historical inequalities. Comparably, queerness is "deracialized, normalized, and sanitized" into "homonormative privilege" (Loza 2011: 99, 93). Native America is largely erased. Bartender Longshadow (Raoul Trujillo) is caught embezzling and put to the "true death." Luna Garza (Janina Gavankar) claims Mexican and Navajo ancestry. Jesus Velasquez (Kevin Alejandro)'s family practices *brujería*,

The series introduces new racisms following US military invasions in MENASA regions. Traumatized by war crimes in Iraq, Arlene's husband, Terry (Todd Lowe), fears imaginary "Iraqi insurgents" when not on antipsychotic drugs (4.10). He is tormented by memories of murdering an unarmed Iraqi woman, Zaafira (Anna Khaja), on the orders of his sergeant, Patrick Devins (Scott Foley), who mistook an unarmed Iraqi man as a "hostile" (5.4). The massacre of Iraqi civilians happens as US soldiers celebrate the Fourth of July with drugs and alcohol. The scene foregrounds national exceptionalism as outright hypocrisy: soldiers commemorate US independence while formalizing Iraqi dependence. Terry believes that Zaafira cursed him to suffer the wrath of Ifrit or "the evil" (5.5). When Terry considers suicide, Patrick yells: "Suicide is for Muslims—and you are better than that. You are a goddamned US Marine!" His patriotic racism parodies US military training that sometimes casts the War on Terror as a War on Islam, evidenced in targets at shooting ranges with images of hijabi woman or Qur'anic verses. Parody opens space to consider why US media frame conflicts as ancient and religious—Jew versus Muslim, Shia versus Sunni—rather than political or economic. The series foreshortens critiques of Islamophobia when Zaafira's ghost demands a death match between Terry and Patrick as restitution. Casting Iraqis as vengeful perpetuates associations of Arabs and Muslims as violent in a series that otherwise uses supernatural figures to denaturalize racism, homophobia, and nativism. Like the CW series, *True Blood* is awash in contradictions. Simultaneously radical and reactionary, it suggests possibilities of empathy and respect.

Recognizing Difference: Miami, Toronto, Dublin

Toronto masquerades as New York in *The Strain*; Dublin as London in *Penny Dreadful*; but Miami remains Miami in *Gabriel, amor inmortal*. The political economies of Hollywood's offshoring are as different as the series' vampires, enabling critical aspirations for the future, investigation of the present, and nostalgia of the past. Empathy across difference is key to survival. Offshoring to Canada benefits from US power in NAFTA; offshoring to Europe encounters EU power. As "Hollywood North," Canada signifies differently than Miami does as "Hollywood of Latin America." The United States comprises the world's fifth largest Spanish-language television market. Miami shows geospatial proximities remain significant despite media's deterritorialization (Sinclair 2003: 212). Eleven-episode telenovela *Gabriel, amor inmortal* (USA 2008; cr. Agustin) appeals to Latin Americans due to its foreign setting. It inverts the flow of Latin American telenovelas to the United States, which began in 1959 when Telesistema Mexicano began to videotape them (Havens 2008: 275).

Telenovelas evoke soap operas' "scornful combination of the high-art aspirations and melodramatic excesses of opera with the mundane household products sold by the sponsors that produced the programs" (Mittell 2010: 241). Unlike soap operas, they have limited runs with recognizable beginnings, middles, and endings. ABC's vampire-themed soap opera *Port Charles* adopted a telenovela-like format of thirteen-week "books" (story arcs), sold separately on the overseas market (Bielby and Harrington 2008: 87, 93). Rio de Janeiro-based TV Globo exported its first telenovela to Portugal in 1975, opening an overseas market (75). Broadcast live until the 1960s, soap operas developed distinct visual repertoires of emotional close-ups and musical scores, demonstrative performances, multiple storylines, repetitive cuing, and "two shot west" (Mittell 2010: 241, 191). They prioritize relationships over events, training predominantly female audiences to read emotions through close-ups for unspoken or unspeakable feelings (Modleski 1983: 70). Multiple storylines presume audiences focus attention selectively while fulfilling responsibilities to household and family.

Produced in Brazil, Colombia, México, Venezuela, Portugal, and the Philippines, telenovelas have become hits in post-Soviet Europe, Southeast Asia, and the Middle East. With transnational distribution and production, telenovelas became standardized without being homogenized (Havens 2008:

274). Use of nationally specific accents and locations decline with pan-Latin American casting increasing, but genres (narrative conflicts) assert national particularity: Mexican ones emphasize family; Brazilian, society; Colombian, politics; Venezuelan, "steamy love scenes" (273). Associated with prestige, Miami is a center for independent production, highlighting the city as cultural location and stars from Latin America (282).

Promoted as a departure from Spanish Broadcasting System's telenovelas, *Gabriel* had slower production schedules and higher production values. It borrowed from *True Blood*. Emotion structures meaning via repetition of scenes in flashback, rapid crosscutting between close-ups, and intense musical scores like telenovelas, but vampires sprout enormous wings. Puerto Rican pop star Chayanne portrays Gabriel Márquez, a 300-year-old vampire, unable to bear life. He wants to join his deceased wife Viviana and their unborn son, both brutally murdered by conquistador-vampire Francisco Pizarro, played by Venezuelan actor José Luis Rodríguez aka "el Puma," whom he believes haunts him. Gabriel consults Padre Miguel (Juan David Ferrer) but by chance encounters nurse Eva León (Angélica Celaya). He recognizes her as Viviana's reincarnation. Eva is attracted to Gabriel but cannot understand him. Because he is single, good looking, and lives in Miami Beach, Eva's friend Maribel (Laura Ferretti) suspects he is "gay." Eva's nightmares reveal the truth. She is not only Viviana's reincarnation. She lived before Gabriel's lifetime, fated to be reborn into different bodies, only to be murdered by Pizarro again. Although their love is impossible, Gabriel and Eva enjoy a levitated kiss over Miami's skyline (6), a montage of kisses over the centuries (8), and an extended love scene (11).

Catholicism and Spanish imperial history integrate Latina/o America with Latin America without critiquing US imperial history. Gabriel learns that he can enter a church during a 1991 pilgrimage in Cartagena, Colombia. In Venice in 1797, Gabriel saves a woman from a vampire and returns to her abode, filled with performers, harlequins, and dwarves. He leaves and believes that he sees Pizarro behind a carnevale mask. Finding everyone murdered, he realizes Pizarro is determined to destroy everyone with whom he has contact. An actual historical figure, conquistador Pizarro conquered the Inca Empire in 1533, notoriously taking its last emperor Atahualpa hostage, collecting a ransom in gold, and executing him against orders. Supporters of rival Diego de Almagro later assassinate Pizarro. The telenovela revises history. Pizarro's tomb in Lima Cathedral does not contain his remains because Atahualpa's priestess cursed him to search eternally for blood. Pizarro avenges his curse by murdering people, stopped only when Gabriel wrestles and holds him as the sun rises. The two vampires burn and disintegrate. Eva watches Gabriel's sacrifice. He is reunited with Viviana. The telenovela ends with Eva explaining that she is no longer the Eva León that she once was. Freed from the curse of

Pizarro, she cannot predict the future. She takes over Gabriel's role as narrator, along with his house and special coffin.

Whereas Miami has cachet, US critics sometimes disparage British Columbia as a "Mexico North," extending associations of México with cheapness. A Hollywood production offshored to Toronto with a Mexican creator, FX's *The Strain* (USA 2014–present; cr. Guillermo del Toro and Chuck Hogan) critiques NAFTA's (and, more generally, neoliberalism's) racial/ethnic segregations through economic integration. Contrasting Brooklyn's Red Hook and Manhattan's Upper East Side, it locates segregated first- and third-world conditions in New York. It continues del Toro's preoccupation in *Cronos* and *Blade II* with a self-destructive and terminally ill industrialist and new strains of vampires, facilitated by globalization. The series opens with mysterious deaths of passengers aboard a flight from Berlin that lands, taxis, and goes dark. Two doctors, Ephraim "Eph" Goodweather (Corey Stoll) and Nora Martinez (Mía Maestro), find incisions on victims' necks, leaving no bruise. In the cargo hold, they find black worms. They learn that among the cargo is a last-minute, high-security item: an elaborately carved coffin with an interior latch. They do not learn that vampire Thomas Eichorst (Richard Sammel), who serves the Master, hired Augustin "Gus" Elizalde (Miguel Gomez) to smuggle it and the master vampire into Manhattan.

Contagion functions as public-health and political crisis, alluding to fascism, greed, and rising xenophobia during times of economic recession and political instability. Nora references "the disappeared," forced disappearances of political dissenters in her native Argentina (1.10). Palmer manipulates public opinion through ostensibly charitable and patriotic programs financed by his Stoneheart Corporation. Freedom Centers provide food and water to citizens who enroll for "freedom cards," indicating blood type, allegedly for reference at medical centers. City government's power over state or federal government restages 9/11 panic. Staten Island commissioner Justine Feraldo (Samantha Mathis) secures "the circumference" by instituting checkpoints on the ferry from Manhattan. A widow of a fireman killed when the World Trade Center collapsed, she hangs decapitated vampire bodies in public view at the ferry terminal, suspends constitutional law for martial law, and declares the borough a "plague free zone."

Despite looking inhuman, vampires ask us to consider empathy. The most dangerous enemies might really be human. Echoing *Blood for Dracula*, Thomas performs a morning ritual—"charade," as he calls it—of affixing prosthetics and applying makeup to disguise himself as a human (1.2). He has a wattle but no nasal cartilage. Equally disfigured is terminally ill industrialist Eldritch Palmer (Jonathan Hyde), whose corporation finances the vampire's operations. He hires hacker Dutch Welders (Ruta Gedmintas) for a denial-of-service attack that makes both internet and deep web go dark, preventing people from learning about the virus. Palmer endangers humans for the promise of a few drops of clear or "white" vampire blood, which cures him temporarily. Blood transfusion is administered through the eye.

When vampires bite humans, their bodies are slowly taken over by the virus, eventually killing them. Like vampires in eastern European folklore, they return to kill their kin. They retain aspects of their human memories, including the ability to recognize people. Before transforming, they suffer illness and blood cravings. In early stages, they "nest" by huddling together, physically exhausted by changes to their biology. As goth-rock star Gabriel Bolivar (Jack Kesy) transforms, his genitals drop into the toilet. An autopsy reveals desiccated organs and a new biological system with cloaca (posterior orifice for urine and feces), brille (ocular scale), and projectile tongues with stingers. The Master can see through their eyes, forging a community via surveillance. When Eph and Nora develop a virus for the virus, which they inject into vampires, the Master orders them to commit suicide. Killing the Master kills the spawn, they believe. The Master is "patient zero." When his body is injured, he moves into a new one. Vampires organize according to a "caste system," conveys Holocaust survivor, Abraham Setrakian (David Bradley), who extends his life with vampire blood. His knowledge of "strigoi" dates to his grandmother's stories in Romania in 1932 and his experiences in a Nazi camp in Poland in 1944. Thomas recruits Abraham to carve the elaborate coffin after discovering he carved *khamsa* (protective symbol). In New York, Abraham runs a pawnshop like the antiques shop in *Cronos*. He keeps his wife Mariam's living vampire-heart in a jar, feeding it with his own blood.

New York is multiethnic and multiracial. Characters are predominantly foreign residents or second-generation immigrants. Afterlives of race are ever-present. Thomas taunts Eph: "Goodweather. I'll wager that's not your family's original name. What country did your people immigrate from? Poland? Ukraine? Latvia? What was their original name? Goldstein? Gotlieb? I can smell your sweat. Same stench as the old man's. Bitter. Brackish. Like the Dead Sea" (2.9). His reference to Palestine for Ashkenazi Jews evokes anti-Semitism, not Zionism. Thomas's anti-Semitism explodes when Helga Richtler (Julie Engelbrecht) refuses his romantic advances. Offended by his anti-Semitic comments when he thought she was Christian, Helga later appeals for his help after being arrested by the Nazis. He allows her to be hung publically (2.11). Racism is largely personalized, facilitating US exceptionalist myths. The series evokes dehumanizing state policies, including the Bracero Program, a migrant recruitment scheme from 1942 to 1964 that imported Mexican men to do agricultural labor for minimal wages under segregated conditions after Japanese Americans were sent to so-called detention centers. "You scared to look a Mexican in the eye," Gus confronts Mr. Quinlan (Rupert Penry-Jones), who represents vampires opposing the Master (1.12). Gus later works for Quinlan, building an army with freed prisoners. One questions his motivation: "So we can work for this Quinlan, like *braceros*?" The series also references Mexican *lucha libre* films. Formerly known as "Ángel de plato," Angel Guzman Hurtado (Joaquín Cosio) works as dishwasher. Gus recognizes him from a film (2.4) and recruits him. The second season ends in voiceover, questioning human vanity and naivety in assuming its primacy over the planet. Greed needs to be overcome, or humans will die. Subsequent seasons speculate on this "one last chance." Failed chances include canonical episodes in US history, such as the (belated) US opposition to Nazi Germany, alongside non-canonical ones.

Painful and largely repressed moments in transnational US history also enter into *Penny Dreadful* (USA-Ireland-UK 2014–16; cr. John Logan). Set in nineteenth-century London with reference to canonical literary works—Shelley's *Frankenstein* (1818), Stevenson's *Strange Case of Dr. Jekyll and Mr. Hyde* (1886), Wilde's *The Portrait of Dorian Gray* (1890), Stoker's *Dracula* (1897)—it passed "culture tests" that allowed access EU subsidies to distribute financial risk. Showtime relocated production to Dublin due to Ireland's Section 481 tax incentive. *Penny Dreadful* combines visual style and production values of heritage cinema with the imperial drive of *The League of Extraordinary Gentlemen* (USA-Germany-Czech Republic-UK 2003; dir. Stephen Norrington) more than comedy of monster mashes. Its title refers to inexpensive serial novels like James Malcolm Rymer's *Varney the Vampire, or the Feast of Blood* (1847), published in weekly installments and mentioned when Abraham van Helsing (David Warner) warns Victor Frankenstein (Harry Treadaway) that it contains mistakes but some truth. The series also appropriates classical Hollywood's Ethan Lawrence Talbot aka the Wolf Man, who reinvents himself as Ethan Chandler (Josh Hartnett), escaping his past in the New Mexico Territories to perform at Wild West Shows.

Vampires have exoskeletons over bodies tattooed with hieroglyphs. Sir Malcolm Murray (Timothy Dalton) and Vanessa Ives (Eva Green) solicit antiques broker Ferdinand Lyle (Simon Russell Beale) to interpret them. He finds an unorthodox version of the (ancient) Egyptian funerary text, *Book of the Dead*, in which Amunet and Amun-Ra are conjoined to bring the world's end. When a plague ship arrives from Cairo, Vanessa is possessed to speak in (modern) Arabic. The second season focuses on Night Comers (devil's witches). The final season reinvents Count Dracula as Dr. Alexander Sweet (Christian Camargo), a biologist who bonds with Vanessa over their shared love for taxidermy. Parodying conventions that vampires cast no reflections, the two enjoy a date in a House of Mirrors.

The series situates Gothic nightmares of bodily possession by demons within the context of imperial possession by empires, reworking heritage into *critical nostalgia* by questioning the past while evoking longing for it. Murray defines his African expeditions in tales of "cannibals." Frankenstein believes he "murdered his way down a continent"; Vanessa believes that he "raped women from North Africa to Burundi" (1.7). Returning to Africa in 1892, Murray finds "romance" vanished with Indian Ocean slavery. In Zanzibar, German East Africa, he is nearly robbed. The Apache Kaetenay (Wes Studi) saves him, explaining "old traditions die hard" about scalping a thief (3.1). Murray's home includes art evoking *The Slave Ship* (1840), J. M. W. Turner's contribution towards anti-slavery campaigns. Britain finally abolished slavery thoughout the British Empire only in 1833. Until 1793, it had been "the most successful practitioner of slave-trade in the world," as C. L. R. James noted ([1938/1969] 2012: 38–9). The series' only African character, Murray's butler Sembene (Danny Sapani), is a former slaver. He recuperates lesser-known history and minimizes non-African characters' complicity with slavery. Sembene likely traded in slaves like Zanzibar's sultans, not the West's chattel slavery. He sacrifices his life so Ethan can realize his potential. Kaetenay makes similar sacrifices for Ethan.

Murray's son Peter (Graham Butler) complains of "wogs" in India (1.5). Other characters' lives are affected by racial trauma. With an Indian father and an English mother, Dr. Jekyll (Shazad Latif) is called a "wog." Lyle practices Judaism secretly. Shot on location in Andalucía, Spain, where Spaghetti Westerns were shot, New Mexico Territory is a space organized by racial violence. A white man accosts Kaetenay on a train, insisting that "Indians and niggers" belong in the back car. Bartholomew Rusk (Douglas Hodge), who lost an arm in the Transvaal during the Boer War (1880–1), compares his colonial participation to Ethan's against "redskins" (2.5). He further mentions the US invasion of Haïti, which culminated with occupation in 1915. Frankenstein reminds Ethan of his contribution to genocide. Kaetenay claims Ethan as Apache, becoming his "Apache father" and forcing him to fight alongside remaining Apaches against the United States. Becoming Apache includes becoming a werewolf.

Other politics are interpersonal. Dorian mostly has sex with other characters. He sleeps with Brona Croft (Billie Piper) and Vanessa separately—and with Lily (also played by Piper) and Justine (Jessica Barden) together, bathed in a fat old man's blood. He has onscreen sex with transgendered Angelique and off-screen sex with Ethan. Frankenstein's creature (Rory Kinnear) demands that his creator create a mate for him. A prostitute from Ireland who dies of consumption, Brona is reanimated as Lily Frankenstein, a character borrowed from *Bride of Frankenstein* (USA 1935; dir. James Whale). Witnessing men trample suffragettes, and pimps beating prostitutes, Lily becomes a feminist fighter. Rather than marching with placards, she decides to "go to war" (3.4). With Dorian, she slaughters a group of men who have paid to watch a young woman, Justine, from the Marquis de Sade's novel, humiliated and tortured. She and Dorian aspire to create a "master race, a race of immortals" (2.10).

The final season responds to the first when Vanessa, wreathed in pain, is possessed by demons. She was subjected the cruelty of nineteenth-century practices for treating so-called hysteria and other female psychosexual disorders diagnosed by men. A doctor drills into her head in one procedure. As an alternative to Lily's feminism, the series offers Joan Clayton (Patti LuPone) aka the Cut-wife of Ballentree Moor and later the alienist Dr. Seward (also played by LuPone). The community on the moors scorns Clayton because she performs abortions, branding her with a hot iron and burning her alive. *Penny Dreadful* critiques the hypocrisy and violence of societies that deny women reproductive rights—a perennial debate in the United States—by situating it in a distant past. The series depicts an imperial past, not suffused nationalism, but riddled with sexism, racism, and genocide to engage a critical nostalgia.

Web Series and Queer Feminism

Web series exploit desktop aesthetics of webcams, recombine microcontent into narrative, and move across platforms. An early example, *lonelygirl15* aka *lg15* (USA 2006–8; cr. Miles Beckett and Greg Goodfried), was mistaken for an actual vlog. Developing virally into a multiplatform ARG, including blogs, wikis, parody videos, and response videos, *lg15* illustrates what Lynn Spigel once observed: "Much of the existing literature in television studies now seems as dated as network shows like *Dallas* (and sadly, unlike *Dallas* TV scholarship can't even be repackaged as camp)" (2004: 5). *lg15* reworked strategies of *The Blair Witch Project* (1999), promoted as a student film by Daniel Myrick and Eduardo Sánchez to became a multiplatform collaborative narrative by professionals and nonprofessionals—and experiment in outsourcing publicity to consumers. Fake grassroots websites were "astroturfed" by Hollywood producers and soon imitated by *actual* amateur websites. Web series offer opportunity for creative and financial risk, including fan-driven responses. *The Real Girl's Guide to Everything Else* (USA 2010; cr. Carmen Elena Mitchell) inserted racial and cultural difference into HBO's hyper-consumerist and unrelentingly white *Sex and the City* (1998–2004) to actualize inclusive and equitable potentials in digital distribution.[8] Walt Disney Corporation's Take180 produced *Twilight* parody *I Heart Vampires* (USA 2009–10; cr. Julie Restivo and Kate Feldman).

Web series reconfigure media. *I Kissed a Vampire* (USA 2009–present; cr. Chris Sean Nolan and Laurie Nolan) became one of Apple iTunes' most popular web series before being assembled into a seventeen-song feature film. Among the oldest vampire-themed web series, *The Hunted* (USA 2001–present; cr. Robert Chapin) is a mashup—"part Buffy, part Cops"—that inspired affiliated projects akin to the *CSI* television franchise. Unlike centralized control in television franchises, affiliates imagine competition in *collaborative* terms.

The Hunting's website and YouTube channel hosts the original and affiliated series alongside UGC by fans, sponsoring an annual competition for fans to produce new episodes. A feature adaptation was financed on crowd-sourcing platform Kickstarter. More commonly, web series enhance audience engagement with commercial films.

30 Days of Night was supported retrospectively by two web miniseries—seven-part *30 Days of Night: Blood Trails* (USA 2007; dr. Victor García) and six-part *30 Days of Night: Dust to Dust* (USA 2008; dr. Ben Ketai)—on FEARnet's web network and on-demand platforms. Both were produced by Ghost House Pictures and released in weekly installments on FEARnet. Their narratives and cinematic style closely resembles television production. The story for *30 Days of Night: Blood Trails* was developed from one in a three-volume comic-book miniseries (2002) by Steve Niles and Ben Templesmith upon which the feature was developed. In addition to web series, the comic books were also novelized, allowing fans different points of access into the same fictional universe. *30 Days of Night: Dust to Dust* is set "three weeks after the attacks on Barrow, Alaska," referencing the original theatrical feature; *30 Days of Night: Blood Trails*, two days before this attack. Set in New Orleans (Louisiana), the first web series opens with a recovering drug addict, George Fowler (Andrew Laurich), attempting to warn a police officer (Perry Cornelius) about the vampires' impending attack in Barrow. Covered in blood, shouting aggressively, and running towards the police officer, George is mistaken for a murderer. The remainder of the series is a flashback that returns to this moment, breaking into chapters at moments of suspense. A group of hackers and vampire hunters intercept internet transmissions by vampires about an attack. Judith (Marilyn Johnson) gives Eddie (Trip Hope) a disc that holds ten years of her research. He writes an access code in his own blood on George's forearm just before dying from a vampire bite. George gives the code to Pat (T. J. Zale), who works remotely with Kate (Brittney Kara) in Los Angeles, to "hack into the system." The vampires behead Kate and eviscerate Pat, who transforms into a vampire. George's girlfriend Jenny (Dani Owen) kills Pat, but she is later kidnapped by vampires and herself becomes a vampire. In the final episode, George kills her and runs with a scrap of paper that contains the decoded message about the impending attack on Barrow to alert the police.

30 Days of Night: Dust to Dust extends the story of George in longer episodes with more emphasis on narrative complexity. The series introduces ex-detective Nick Maguire (Christopher Stapleton) and his sister Sara (Mimi Michaels), who works as a nurse at the prison where George has been incarcerated for murder. George has burned the access code onto the skin of his chest. When a vampire attempts to kill George, he slashes Sara's throat. She begins to transform into a vampire. She phones Nick without giving her location.

A passer-by, Tracy (Rainie Davis), rescues Sara and brings her into her home, where Sara's hunger overpowers her. She attacks both Tracy and chihuahua Max. George attempts to explain transformation to Nick, as they drive towards Tracy's home after requesting her phone location be traced. Detective Gina Harcourt (Shawnee Smith) also drives to Tracy's home, where she hopes to arrest George for Tracy's murder. When Tracy transforms, Gina is nearly bitten by her. George saves Gina. At Nick's home, George explains that the number carved into his chest is the combination to a lockbox that contains satellite footage of the attack on Barrow being destroyed by vampires rather than by fire. Sara reappears and attacks Gina in Nick's shower. A vampire arrives and rips the scarred number from George's chest. Sara saves Nick from the vampire before deciding to kill herself by walking into the sunlight. The series ends with Nick drawing a gun on George, who has begun to transform. The two series work to enhance audience engagement with the theatrical feature by providing new stories that function within the same narrative universe of the feature. Storytelling can be pared to moments of intense excitement since viewers are expected to know details from the feature.

A four-episode web miniseries, *The Originals: Awakening* (USA 2014; cr. Julie Plec), was released on CWTV.com to tell a storylines dropped from the broadcast series' second season. Kol manipulates witches Mary-Alice Claire (Keri Lynn Pratt) and Astrid Malchance (Aleeah Rogers) to fight Klaus's witches. Conceived as a teaser for the series' premier, *A Darker Truth* (USA 2009; dir. Christopher Hanada) recounts an untold story in *The Vampire Diaries*. Shot for the web, rather than assembled from outtakes, it exploits DIY aesthetics to match its story of a DIY vampire hunter. Jason Harris (Matt Perello) posts video updates as he hunts Stefan for murdering his sister. The miniseries concluded with revelations that Damon killed her—and kills Jason. It was produced by Retrofit Films, which also developed *The Vampire Diaries: Bloodlines Revealed* (2010), a videogame commissioned by WB to feature AT&T mobile phones. With Facebook Connect, the game integrates pictures and personal information about the user, customizing the experience of tracing ancestry to determine supernatural connections. MTV and Verizon Wireless experimented with ARG *Valemont* (USA-Canada 2009; cr. Brent V. Friedman), which debuted with 2.5-minute "pods" (mini-episodes mixed with advertisements) on the network in conjunction with other content delivered on web and mobile platforms. Registered users received links to engage additional content online.

Much like cable television offered feminist perspectives for earlier generations, web series offer perspectives for a digital generation. Sponsored by U by Kotex (feminine hygiene) in conjunction with its "Save the Undies" campaign, *Carmilla* (Canada 2014–present; cr. Jordan Hall and Ellen Simpson) narrowcasts weekly episodes on KindaTV, the magazine *Vervegirl*'s YouTube

Figure 7.3   Laura Hollis (Elise Bauman) and friends capture her crush, the vampire Carmilla Karnstein (Nathalia Negovanlis), for a university journalism project. *Carmilla* (Canada 2014–present; cr. Jordan Hall and Ellen Simpson).

channel. It reworks single-sponsor format of early television. Kotex is promoted in PSAs, such as "Do Vampires Get Periods?" The series itself embellishes details from LeFanu's novella, such as Styria "embroiled in war with the Ottoman Empire" (1.20), relocating the story to fictional Silas University. Journalism major Laura Hollis (Elise Bauman) narrates the story of her new roommate, Carmilla Karnstein (Nathalia Negovanlis). Carmilla's vampire mother, Lilita Morgan, the Dean of Silas, forces her to seduce five "girls" every twenty years for sacrifice to the Light Demon.

Ranging from three to sixteen minutes, episodes are formatted like vlog posts or reports from Laura's SNN (Silas News Network); between-season stories are formatted as tweets (micro-blogging on Twitter). Scenes are framed by a single fixed camera that approximates laptop-level in Laura and Carmilla's dormitory rooms. The desktop aesthetic includes screen-within-a-screen and text-based interface to communicate with J. P. Armitage, ghost of a nineteenth-century student, sucked into the library's card and computer catalogues, then stored on a flash drive. Laura uses her camera for surveillance, revisiting raw footage to see what happened (1.31). End credits appear only after the season's last episode, so that audiences can watch with only minor interruptions by occasional commercials and popup advisements. Following the end credits, a short scene introduces a cliffhanger for the next season.

Silas University is predominantly white with only two onscreen Asian Canadians. Carmilla has a black older "sister," Matska Belmonde (Sophia Walker), who is killed. The series, however, is a queer-feminist response to straight-male lesbian fantasies in earlier adaptations of LeFanu's novella, notably Hammer's so-called lesbian-vampire films, *Countess Dracula* (UK 1971; dir. Peter Sasdy) and *Twins of Evil* (UK 1971; dir. John Hough), which reduced Carmilla to misogynist, hyper-sexualized fantasies by inflecting LeFanu's story with historical figure Elizabeth Báthory (1560–1614), who allegedly bathed in blood from virgin women to sustain her youthful appearance. Ingrid Pitt's "thick native Polish accent" adds foreignness. *Carmilla* prioritizes female relationships, using vampirism for nonjudgmental intimacy, as slash fic to insert gendered equity. Lola Perry (Annie Briggs) says she is open to listening to Laura's "boy problems, girl problems, or menstrual problems" (1.25).

It also normalizes LBGTQ identities and relationships, incuding LUG (lesbian until graduation). Laura is open about her crushes on Danny Lawrence (Sharon Belle) and Carmilla. Perry secretly loves her childhood friend Susan LaFontaine (Kaitlyn Alexander). Laura and Carmilla fulfill normative expectations of young female beauty, but other characters decenter normativity. Danny and Perry have androgynous names. Danny is tall; Lafontaine wears a fauxhawk. The first season closes with Laura and Carmilla's onscreen kisses. *Carmilla* evokes vampirism-as-intimacy that Auerbach found absent after Stoker. It fulfills needs unmet by Hollywood's indifference to queer-feminist perspectives, conspicuously in *Twilight*, and addresses concerns of female university students. After three students disappear, Laura protests that "girls go missing, and nobody seems to care" (1.6), reverberating with ongoing student protests against institutional apathy and silence regarding sexual assault and rape in campuses. Laura is "busted" for uploading vlog posts on missing peers, which are dismissed as "rumors" by the Dean, who threatens students who continue to make campus events public. *Carmilla* introduces the effects of a pervasive culture of undermining social and political critique on university campuses. If film and television used vampire as empowerment against racism, the web can use them to empower against sexism and homophobia.

Adapting to (and from) Videogames

Adaptations are conventionally conceived as moving from novels to films, as in Coppola's 1992 adaptation of Stoker's 1897 novel as *Bram Stoker's Dracula*, discussed above. With mergers and conglomerations, the concept has expanded to cross-platform adaptations and multi-platform releases. Promoted as an adaptation of both Stoker's novel and Coppola's film, *Bram Stoker's Dracula* (1993) is a multiplatform console game in which players role-play as Harker to escape Count Dracula's castle. Movement from film and television to videogame, however, is not the only direction of movement across horizontally integrated media corporations. *Vampire:*

The Masquerade – Redemption (2000) and *Vampire: The Masquerade – Bloodlines* (2004) for Microsoft Windows were adapted from Fox's television series *Kindred: The Embrace* (1996), which itself adapted White Wolf's tabletop role-playing game *Vampire: The Masquerade* (1991). Like the theatrical adaptation of the action-adventure videogame *Tomb Raider* (1996) into *Laura Croft: Tomb Raider* (UK-Germany-USA-Japan 2001; dir. Simon West), Terminal Reality's H&S videogame *BloodRayne* (2002) was adapted into feature *BloodRayne* (USA-Germany 2005; dir. Uwe Boll) and two direct-to-video sequels in 2007 and 2011. The *BloodRayne* franchise spanned multiple videogames, films, and comics. Console videogames are one of Hollywood's most profitable formats. H&S and FPS games facilitate audience engagement with Hollywood content.

The myth of interactivity in digital media has been challenged by theorists who point to ways that so-called interactive media is typically only reactive to user input, as in videogames. In the realm of Web 2.0 interaction is often a means by which users "gift" their personal data to corporations, as in social networking and e-commerce. The videogame industry, however, is increasingly integrated into Hollywood with A-list stars performing the voices of avatars and *Grand Theft Auto IV* (2008) as the biggest Hollywood release of the year, netting more than US$500 million within its first week. *Call of Duty: Modern Warfare 3* (2011) grossed US$1 billion in sixteen days to become "the fastest-selling cultural product in history," and the video trailer for *Grand Theft Auto V* (2008) functions like a trailer for "a hotly anticipated film" by attracting "millions of views and countless pages of badly spelled fan speculation on the internet."[9] While some journalist and industry insiders imagine videogames as a threat to film and television, others understand difference and potential synergies among the different platforms through audience engagement. Increasingly videogame designers strive for a so-called cinematic experience in terms of graphics and narrative that resembled its blockbusters. Development now focuses on higher quality experiences with 360 degree virtual reality (VR) in videogames, both on console and web platforms, particularly through social media sites such as Facebook and YouTube and in conjunction with e-sports. Much like high-end technical advances in cinema were showcased, if not debuted, in films with racist or colonialist themes—epic narrative scale in *Birth of a Nation*, sound in *The Jazz Singer,* color in *Gone with the Wind*, through the latest 3D technologies in *Avatar*—3D console technologies are narrated as violent colonization of another planet after humans brought environmental devastation to earth in the *Lost Planet* series (2007–13) for Xbox 360.

Among the original vampire-themed videogames released since Adventure Entertainment's text-based adventure game *The Count* (1981), which asked players to collect items to kill Count Dracula, are adaptations of popular films and television series. By and large, such videogames have invited players to role-play as vampire hunters. Although *Buffy the Vampire Slayer* was one of a few with a primary character in a same-sex relationship, the console game removes the storyline and focuses gameplay entirely on killing vampires (Evans 2011: 110), conveying how Hollywood repurposes content for different niche audiences. GameBrains's *Buffy the Vampire Slayer* (2000) offered an alternative experience of the series' fourth season. Between the game play of slaying vampires, animated cut scenes convey a plot and motivation. The game's 2D bitmapped graphics anticipated the series' second videogame adaptation for Xbox, which included 3D vector graphics and the voices of many of the principal actors for the avatars of Angel, Giles, Spike, Willow, and Xander. A subsequent videogame for the Game Boy platform in 2003 includes stills from the series in cut scenes. In 2004, Indiagames produced the first adaptation of the series for mobile phones, *Buffy the Vampire Slayer: The Quest for Oz*, in which the narrative is developed as SMS—Drusilla kidnaps Oz, so Buffy needs to "dust" her—to prompt players to press keys to control the avatar in animated action scenes. The games combine FPS with the hand-to-hand combat of the brawler genre across multiple levels. Videogames have been produced as part of the *Blade* and *From Dusk till Dawn* franchises. *Van Helsing* (2004) presents a FPS version of the feature film. Role-playing extends media engagement as it was theorized for film (e.g., gaze) and television (e.g., flow), but it mostly casts the figure of the vampire as target rather than protagonist. Since game-engine design is more complex than video- and image-editing software, users have tended to respond with content of their own in the form of mashups and memes. Hollywood itself also adapted the fan-based mashup format into films in which US presidents role-play as vampire hunters.

Notes

1. They include *The Night Stalker* (1972; dir. John Llewellyn Moxey), *Desire, The Vampire* (1982; dir. John Llewellyn Moxey), *The Midnight Hour* (1985; dir. Jack Bender), and series pilot *Blood Ties*. *Nightlife* (1989; dir. Daniel Taplitz) and *Slayer/Mexferatu Mexico* are set and produced in México; *Daughter of Darkness* (1990; dir. Stuart Gordon), shot in Hungary; *Dracula 3000* (Germany-South Africa 2004; dir. Darrell Roodt), in South Africa. Offshored to Canada, *Shadow Zone: The Undead Express* (1996; dir. Stephen Williams) was shot in Toronto and *Vampire Wars: Battle for the Universe/Bloodsuckers* (2005; dir. Matthew Hastings) in Vancouver.
2. "Wikileaks: *Desperate Housewives* Does More to Combat Jihad than US Propaganda," *Daily Mail* (8 December 2010): http://www.dailymail.co.uk/news/article-1336778/Wikileaks-Desperate-Housewives-does-combat-jihad-US-propaganda.html.
3. Films include *Graveyard Shift* (1987; dir. Jerry Ciccoritti), *Red Blooded American Girl* (1990; dir. David Blyth), *Blood & Donuts* (1995; dir. Holly Dale), *Karmina* (1996; dir. Gabriel Pelletier), *Jesus Christ Vampire Hunter* (2001; dir. Lee Demarbre), and *The Vampire Conspiracy* (2005; dir. Marc Morgenstern).

4. *Nocturna: Granddaughter of Dracula* (1979; dir. Harry Hurwitz) stars Nai Bonet, whose Vietnamese and French ancestry make her exotic to the Bloodsuckers of America in New York. Lucy Liu escapes stereotyping in *Rise: Blood Hunter* (2007; dir. Sebastian Gutierrez).
5. McClelland argues the being chosen makes Buffy like "vampire slayers of eighteenth-century Bulgaria and Serbia" (2008: 29).
6. In *Moonlight*, Mick St. John (Alex O'Loughlin) befriends reporter Beth Turner (Sophia Myles), whose boyfriend, Josh Lindsay (Jordan Belfi), is assassinated after prosecuting arms dealer Amir Fayed (Navid Negahban), the only Middle Eastern American character. A later episode references a privatized security firm in Afghanistan called Dark Water Associates, evoking Blackwater.
7. In *Modern Vampires* (1998; dir. Richard Elfman). Nazi-vampire Ulrike (Kim Cattrall) tells African Americans: "We should have killed all of you black people when we had the chance." *Blood Creek* (2008; dir. Joel Schumacher) conflates Nazism and fantasies of Nordic race.
8. YouTube is a platform of web series around the world. *An African City* (Ghana 2014–present; cr. Nicole Amarteifio) adapts the HBO series for a new generation of African women, some returned from studies at Harvard and Oxford universities. Likewise, political comedies in Saudi Arabia reflect a generation equally at home in the Kingdom and the West (Hudson and Zimmermann 2015: 156–60).
9. Steven Poole, "Bang, Bang, You're Dead: How Grand Theft Auto Stole Hollywood's Thunder," *The Guardian* (9 March 2012): https://www.theguardian.com/technology/2012/mar/09/grand-theft-auto-bang-bang-youre-dead.

CONCLUSION: HISTORY AND HOLLYWOOD, MASHED-UP

Hollywood vampire films take a digital turn, moving from heritage cinema, like *Bram Stoker's Dracula*, which augmented Stoker's novel with "missing" historical detail, to alternative-reality mashup of *Abraham Lincoln: Vampire Hunter* (USA 2012; dir. Timur Bakmambetov), which imagined a US president as a vampire hunter.[1] Before the latter's release, Google image-searches with keywords "vampire" and "president" returned memes that layer text, such as "I vant to suck your blood," and images, such as fangs, over images of Ronald Reagan, Bill Clinton, George W. Bush, and Barack Obama. Nonprofessional media-makers remix Hollywood conventions to express political views and contest copyright through unauthorized use. Often originating on anonymous imageboards, such as 4chan's /b/ (random content), memes replicate and spread through social networks. They range from apolitical (if anthropocentric) entertainment, such as LOLcats, to incendiary political statements. Comparably, video mashups recombine commercial media, allowing "canons" or "parent products" (i.e., commercial media) to give *birth* to new media. Video mashups transform meaning by speculating alternative scenarios. They extend classical Hollywood's monster mashes, which imagined encounters between Count Dracula, Wolfman, and Frankenstein's Monster, but they use found footage, more in the traditions of compilation films, such as Joseph Cornell's *Rose Hobart* (1936), Bruce Conner's *A Movie* (1958), and Kenneth Anger's *Scorpio Rising* (1964) that foreground creativity through editing, not writing or filming. Originality in recombination overshadows originality of content.

Memes and mashups are part of a broader transformation of media. Do-it-yourself (DIY) aesthetics and peer-to-peer (P2P) file sharing are possible on laptops equipped with preinstalled internet browsers and nonlinear editing and imaging software. Consumer-grade programs allow images to be manipulated. Fans rip files from DVDs or download them via BitTorrents. "Fan culture," explains Henry Jenkins, "stands as an open challenge to the 'naturalness' and desirability of dominant cultural hierarchies, a refusal of authorial authority and a violation of intellectual property" (1992: 18). Memes on /b/ are automatically deleted within weeks, as imageboards accumulate new content, though they often migrate to social-media platforms and blogs, where they remain.[2] They are part of new media ecologies defined by "spreadability" of *potential* dispersal rather than "stickiness" of *centralized* aggregation (Jenkins et al. 2013). Viral distribution is a mode of communication among like-minded "friends" and "followers," which limits exchange of perspectives. Patricia Zimmermann (2000) argues digital technologies and distributed networks *democratize* media by facilitating new generations of progressive leftwing and conservative rightwing media, having *both* positive and negative consequences. Perspectives open with more accessible means of production but narrow via narrowcasting.

Mashups and memes emerge from ways that people communicate through clip culture facilitated by increased access to digitally mediated platforms from narrowcasting on YouTube or Vimeo to social networking on Facebook, Twitter, and Instagram. Amateur music videos (AMVs) populate YouTube, and fans shoot 3D animated video (machinima) in the SIMS's game engine and Second Life's social-networking platform. Nonprofessional media extend practices derived from fic, such as slash-inspired images of romantic or sexual relations between straight-white-male characters Spike and Xander from *Buffy the Vampire Slayer*. A culture of mashups can contest Hollywood control over meaning, argues Barbara Klinger (2006). They renegotiate social contracts with copyright holders. Under transnational media corporations, Hollywood selectively polices copyright and exploits its infringement. More than debates over whether media is racist or sexist, debates focus on *intellectual property* — and the idea of ownership of ideas and their meaning—becomes a site where the meaning is located, much as it did in the 1920s when Stoker's widow sued the producers of *Nosferatu* for unauthorized use of *Dracula*'s story and characters (Skal 1990).

By contrast, Seth Grahame-Smith's illustrated novel *Abraham Lincoln: Vampire Hunter* (2010) was actually commissioned by the publisher with film adaptation in mind. The novel followed his *Pride and Prejudice and Zombies* (2009), mashing Jane Austen's novel and zombie fiction into "search-and-replace historical horror" (Newman 2012: 52). Comparably, *Rosencrantz & Guildenstern Are Undead* (USA 2009; dir. Jordan Galland) mashes vampires into the universe of cult film *Rosencrantz & Guildenstern Are Dead* (UK-USA 1990; dir. Tom Stoppard), itself a speculation about minor Shakespearean characters. Grahame-Smith's novels were adapted into films for theatrical release, but others—*Abraham Lincoln vs. Zombies* (USA 2012; dir. Richard Schenkman), *Cowboys & Vampires* (USA 2010; dir. Douglas Myers), *Cowboys and Aliens* (USA 2011; dir. Jon Farveau)—are released direct-to-video for niche audiences. Commercial filmmaking borrows back from user-generated content (UGC), whether fic or video mashups, in an asymmetrical process that is both radically democratic and predictably exploitative. In trade terminology, nonprofessional audiences become "prosumers," simultaneously producers and consumers. Hollywood entices nonprofessional writers to "gift" ideas by participating in contests, thereby gamifying concept development and acquisition—and outsourcing. Online availability of Hollywood trailers, episodes, and features facilitates video mashups. History is mashed with stories. Mashups and memes mobilize affectionate humor like *Vampires Suck*'s parody of *Twilight* for its antiquated assumptions about race, gender, and species. Mashup films inspire mashup images, such as one of Abraham Lincoln hunting vampire Edward, dressed in his all-American baseball jersey.

President-vampire mashups and memes serve as a platform for DIY political dissent that rejects copyright while revealing perceptions about national

Figure C.1 Internet mashup of Edward Cullen from *Twilight* (USA 2008; dir. Catherine Hardwicke) pursued by Abraham Lincoln from *Abraham Lincoln: Vampire Hunter* (USA 2012; dir. Timur Bakmambetov).

identity. Refashioning presidents as bloodthirsty vampires updates political cartoons of corrupt heads of state in Soviet Europe, such as Nicolae Ceaușescu, in print journalism. The memes are meaningful because the US presidency consolidates aspirations of national exceptionalism. They reify First Amendment rights to express dissent. As a base-image, some use a 2004 *Village Voice* cover with Bush biting the Statue of Liberty's neck, which later made a cameo on *True Blood*. A version that replaces Bush with Obama includes an upside-down US flag to suggest national distress. Mashing vampires and presidents reanimated Auerbach's mid-1990s insight: "Vampires and American presidents began to converge in my imagination, not because all presidents are equally vampiric, but because both are personification of their age" (1995: 3). As discussed earlier, MGM's *An American Romance* shows an eager immigrant naming his sons after US presidents and dreaming one might be elected to the office.

In general, images of white presidents-as-vampires borrow *humanizing* conventions from Béla Lugosi's Count Dracula. Images of the Bushes and Clintons may be layered with sharp fangs, deathly pallor, and eyes agog, but they are recognizably human. Images of Obama more often borrow *animalizing* features and *cadaverizing* behaviors from Max Schreck's Count Orlok: elongated rat teeth, pointy bat ears, reptilian skin color.[3] In addition to anti-Semitic associations, animalized features resurrect a long history of dehumanizing images of African Americans applied to Obama (cf. Apel 2009). Such memes attempt to undermine the legitimacy of his presidency, spreading rumors that Obama was born in Kenya or Indonesia rather than Hawai'i. Other images show Obama recoiling at crosses or displaying a cross-shaped burn mark on his forehead to discredit his Christian faith. Another mashes Obama with *Abraham Lincoln: Vampire Hunter* to create "Ibrahim Obama: Vampire Helper," promoted as the film's sequel.[4] The memes pull into focus how audiences repurpose pre-existing imagery. Some anti-Obama memes use images of a live-sized, green zombie target, whose head and face the National Rifle Association found to resemble Obama as their base-image. As Black Lives Matter campaigns fight institutionalized racism, the design of the target clearly reactivates racial violence, including a national historical trauma of lynching African Americans.

Base-images for most anti-Obama memes are a Halloween mask that mashes Obama and Count Orlok into "Barakula." Although Halloween masks facilitate carnivaleque subversions of power, the Barakula mask *unmasks* white domination and nativism. It gains power by extending familiar forms of anti-black racism from blackface in minstrel shows to orientalist blackamoors, still featured in White House pressrooms, and grotesque "negro" lawn jockeys, mostly removed from public spaces.[5] The Barakula mask facilitates fantasies that Obama is an inhuman and foreign threat to nation. The meme enhances the mask's racism and adds nativist sentiments in layers of text, such as "out to suck your blood taxes dry." Implying that Obama is foreign delegitimizes his presidency by calling into question his allegiance. The meme visualizes Tea Party charges that Obama is a secret Muslim or freedom-hating Socialist. Implying that Obama is a tyrant flames interpretations of the Second Amendment, particularly its legitimization of militia for state security against governmental tyranny, foreign invasions, and slave rebellions. The meme re-engages false rumors to delegitimize Obama's presidency by suggesting that he is not a native-born US citizen. It emerges within the Republican Party's anti-immigration stance, which is less about "saving jobs" for working-class white people than it is about limiting potential new voters, since new immigrants are predominantly people of color (or anti-white-supremacists) who conventionally vote for candidates of the Democratic Party.

Anti-Obama memes yoke fantasies that Obama is a *tyrant*, who acts singularly on executive orders, is a *foreigner* and *Muslim*, who thus cannot act on behalf of US interests, and, perhaps most significantly, is *black*. In particular, white populations, who fail to "rise" socially and financially, interpret Obama's presidency as somehow *shaming* them and triggering feelings of aggrievement. Obama's success is imagined as entitlement under Affirmative Action. As Carol Anderson argues, black advancement is a trigger for white rage, and Obama became the "ultimate affront" (2016: 5). "First known as 'waste people,' and later as 'white trash,' marginalized Americans were stigmatized for their inability to be productive, to own property, or to produce healthy and upwardly mobile children—the sense of uplift on which the American dream is predicated," notes Nancy Isenberg (2016: xv). Emboldened by the Tea Party movements, they disavow the hard work of becoming *successful while black* in America. Studies estimate that African Americans are two centuries behind white populations—a time span that matches the duration of slavery—in accumulating wealth, revealing the structural inequality enabled by law and policy (Asante-Muhammed et al. 2016). Paranoid perceptions of being shamed by an African American president sometimes erupt in unabashed racism and violence.[6] Republicans capitalized on emotions stirred by the Tea Party to block Obama's economic and healthcare policies. Obama's popularity with nonwhite voters was interpreted as a threat to the conservative political platform's future, extending an underlying racism that dates to the infamous Southern Strategy through which anti-Civil Rights Democrats joined the Republican Party. Multiculturalism—or "political correctness," as its detractors call it—destabilizes white entitlement. Racism detracts from solidarity that could challenge a system oppressing *both* nonwhite and white populations.

Obama masks enter into Hollywood's vampire media. In *True Blood*, a group of bigots dress in army camouflage and hide their faces behind rubber Obama masks as they shoot shape-shifters and chant, "yes, we can" (5.5–6).

Appropriating an Obama campaign slogan implies a right to gun violence under the Second Amendment.[7] Civilian use of camouflage visualizes paramilitarization within culture wars. By mocking the slogan, the bigots perform the Barakula meme's DIY politics. They come to be called "the Barack Obamas." They parody vigilante groups and disaffected and downwardly mobile white populations, who express dissent without historical consciousness. They feel that they live in a world where, as one describes it, "it's some sort of crime now being a regular old human!" Their narrow-minded reasoning lampoons the white rage that sees equal treatment under the law as favoritism (cf. Anderson 2016: 35). They parody Tea Party racism in the 2012 presidential election and anticipate the overt racism of the 2016 Republican Party slogan "Make America Great Again." The bigots represent white fragility and rage—defensive responses, ranging from guilty tears over unconscious bias to angry denial of racism and accusations of so-called reverse racism—emerging as racial stress among white people whose lives typically insulate them from thinking about racial difference (DiAngelo 2011) or who see structural racism not working in their favor (Anderson 2016).

Unlike overtly animalized and cadaverized Barakula masks, the Obama mask worn by the bigots is a *human mask*. The Obama mask raises questions about assimilation and tolerance through tokenism. It is not Fanon's "white mask" of internalized racism. It is perhaps more like the light-colored mask in *La Noire de . . ./Black Girl* (France-Sénégal 1965; dir. Sembène Ousmane), which haunts the well-intentioned white man when worn by a young black boy. The mask's meaning becomes indecipherable according to colonial systems of reason. In *True Blood*, the bigots open questions about broader shifts in thinking about race. One African American among the bigots, Tyrese (Johnny Ray Gill), does not transform an entire body of predominantly bigots into an "African American gang," as one drop of "black blood" allegedly revealed "invisible blackness" in white-looking bodies during the early twentieth century. The inclusion of an African American reveals how tokenism can work to discredit critiques of structural inequality and institutional racism—and how racism can be masked as speciesism. *True Blood* raises other questions about conjunction of race, gender, and power through the rubber masks. For a vial of "V" (vampire blood as a drug), gay-black Lafayette gets straight-white Jason to dance provocatively in his underpants and a Laura Bush mask, while he video-records it, parodying rumors of George W. and Laura Bush's youthful cocaine habits (1.3). The fetishistic use of masks appears elsewhere. In *Vampires Suck*, the awkward Becca attempts to seduce Edward by wearing an Obama mask as part of a role-playing sex fantasy.

The mashing of presidents and vampires foregrounds race within transnational US history in a continual processes of revision. With its tagline "Are you a patriot or a vampire?," *Abraham Lincoln: Vampire Hunter* removes the novel's frame device of the narrator's discovery of Lincoln's secret diaries during the Democratic Party primary when Obama was nominated. Lincoln and Obama are linked. Recounting "the hidden history of vampires in America," "their role in the birth, growth, and near death of our great nation," and "the one man who saved that nation from tyranny" (14), the novel envisions Lincoln battling political corruption of Southern congressmen "beholden to vampire interests" (198). In real life, southern Democrats campaigned against Lincoln in 1864, interpreting "the subtext and secret agenda of Lincoln's two principles of amalgamating the North and the South, and emancipating the slaves, was to bring about a racial amalgamation between black and white" (Young 1995: 146). Lincoln, however, did not support "social and political equality between the white and black races" and favored a resettlement plan of freed slaves to the Chíriquí region of present Panamá (Anderson 2016: 14, 9). In the novel, Lincoln is idealized as the Great Emancipator. He learns from Edgar Allan Poe that "America was a paradise where vampires could exist without fierce competition over blood" (203). Practiced from England to Croatia, vampire hunting pushed vampires to emigrate. America's pull develops when vampires discover a seemingly inexhaustible supply of blood, parodying actual colonizers allegedly discovering unclaimed lands. "They loved its lawlessness," Poe explains; "but more than anything, Lincoln, they loved its *slaves*. For here, unlike any other country fit for civilized men—here was a place they could feed on the intoxicating blood of man without fear of reprisal" (203).

The novel mashes history and speculation to convey US ambivalence over slavery. Poe tells Lincoln that "America's vampires took up the fight" against the British during the Revolutionary War. "They are as American as you or I, Lincoln," he concludes; "True patriots—for America's survival is their survival" (203). He describes colonial plantations where Africans are condemned to die under a system of everyday terrorism in rape and separation from family, forced and unpaid labor, and punishments of whipping and hanging. In his diaries, Lincoln records that "killing a slave was not considered murder, no matter the circumstances," because "it was merely considered 'destruction of property'" (22). The novel mashes actual legal definitions of Africans and African Americans as *property* of white men. Owning property enabled legal citizenship, contained by race (Harris 1993). Lincoln recognizes a pattern among victims—"free blacks, vagrants, prostitutes, travelers, and the mentally impaired," that is, "people whose murders were unlikely to incite angry mobs seeking justice." To him, a victim's dead face looks like a "mask of terror" (23). When a vampire murders his father, "red faces" (49) are suspected. The novel frames motivations for ending slavery as fears that it might spread beyond "Negros," "the first of the living to be enslaved" (227). As a vampire hunter, Lincoln defends slaves to protect *whites* from becoming slaves. He is indifferent to genocides of indigenous nations. His regard for life extends to turkeys, not to Shawnee and Sauk. The novel re-centers whiteness as a universal signifier. When the freedom of white people is placed at risk, vampirism becomes tyranny. The logic makes African Americans an afterthought, yet also evokes Martin Niemöller's "first they came" condemnation of Nazism.

In the film, Lincoln (Benjamin Walker) explains, "history will only remember a fraction of the truth," signaling not only its revisions in adding vampires but its elisions in idealizing the historical Lincoln. The film equates vampirism and slavery as tyranny benefiting *foreigners*, thereby minimizing the significance of slavery in US ascendency as a world power. Hunting vampires becomes opposing slavery, as the film erases and silences transnational abolitionist movements, including physical and intellectual labor of African American abolitionists. The Underground Railroad that transported slaves to freedom in the North and Canada becomes a means by which Lincoln's wife, Mary Todd Lincoln (Mary Elizabeth Winstead), and large cast of unnamed freed slaves smuggle silver into the South to support the war against vampires. The film imagines a historically significant role for a white woman, participating in Hollywood's "white savior complex" (Hughey 2014). The actual Mary Todd came from a prominent Kentucky slave-owning family, divided in allegiance to the Union and Confederacy. The film's redemptive whiteness includes heroic white-male vampire Henry Sturgess (Dominic Cooper), who mentors Lincoln in vampire hunting, explaining that vampires came to the so-called New World centuries before European colonizers and slave traders. They fed freely, "slaughtering native tribes and early settlers," he explains. When slave traders arrived, vampires saw a "sinister opportunity." Vampires are complicit with human racism by supporting the Confederacy, but they are not explicitly racist; for them, all races are equal sources of blood. Vampires exploit human racism.

Will Johnson (Anthony Mackie) fights alongside Lincoln and Sturgess, suggesting equity potential among European Americans and African Americans, reinforced by images of Lincoln's (anachronistic) desegregated troops. Sturgess is a psychologically complex character with numerous lines of dialogue and even a bathtub sex scene; Johnson has little dialogue and is never shown outside his interactions with Lincoln. He is brawn and symbol; Lincoln and Sturgess, exceptional individuals, national heroes. The film attempts to unsettle everyday racism of so-called polite society that functions according to Wendy Brown's analysis of "tolerance as a practice is always conferred by the dominant" and "a certain expression of domination even as it offers protection or incorporation to the less powerful" (2008: 84, 178). Efforts to rewrite national history as antiracism are undercut by Hollywood's conventions of racial stratification and segregation, much like the current Republican Party's self-definition as "Party of Lincoln" whitewashes the party's post-Lincoln recruitment of pro-slavery southerners Democrats, now constituting its base.[8]

Even before Lincoln became a vampire hunter, Obama was mashed into *Barakula: The Musical* (USA 2008; dir. Mike Lawson). Described by its creators as "a short political horror rock musical about young Obama having to stave off a secret society of vampires at Harvard when he was inducted into presidency at the Harvard Law Review in 1990," the twelve-minute video parodies secret societies that secure power and wealth for their members at the expense of everybody else, often by coopting the face of diversity to mask power. It critiques political exploitation of black faces. Obama struggles to maintain his convictions amidst political pressures. The video appropriates conventions from Broadway musicals coded as culturally "low" forms, much like *Abraham Lincoln: Vampire Hunter* appropriates the genre of DIY mashup. Its two song-and-dance sequences differentiate Harvard Yard, where four women rush to join Obama (Justin Sherman) in singing and dancing to "Running," and Harvard Law Review, where vampires only belatedly and reluctantly join him for "This Is Our Time."

Obama wears a clichéd *red* tie, *white* shirt, *and blue* blazer over khaki trousers. His unfashionable attire contrasts with fashionable black sweaters and trousers worn by the vampires. The lead vampire, Count Ben (Nathan Bell), pops his collar to look like Count Dracula's cape, mentioning the appeal of something "intangible" about Obama, who seems aware of the value of his skin color to the all-white law review. Invited to joint their "secret society," Obama will become the first of his "kind" to lead the law review, whose former members include fifty-six senators, twenty-two former presidents, and a senator and his wife from Arkansas. The video satirizes secret societies that ensure certain people have greater access to equal opportunity. Obama refuses "conversion," singing and dancing to the refrain "Honolulu, Indonesia, never Transylvania; Chicago, L.A. and Africa, I can never be Barackula," offering to "be" one of them without "being" one of them, so that "mortals and immortals" can live together. The video counters racism in the Barakula meme, evoking the audacity of hope for US-style democracy. Unlike Lincoln, Obama does not become a vampire hunter. He finds a nonviolent way to live alongside vampires, drawing upon the actual Obama's reputation for bipartisanship.

What is at stake in thinking through transnational Hollywood vampires is not working towards a post-race United States, governed by well-intentioned color blindness, but rather dealing with a postcolonial and a post-human one, where questions of white-identified-ness are raised. To think about a postcolonial United States is not to think about independence after the Revolutionary War. It is to think about ongoing imperial relations between the United States and African America, within the Mexican American borderlands, into the Philippines and Southeast Asia, Caribbean, MENASA regions, Africa, and indigenous nations. It is not only to think in terms of minoritized voices "writing back" by appropriating national myths, but instead in terms of *reading back* into these national myths from the vantage point of *desegregated and de-imperialized histories*. Transnational Hollywood's vampires help us to unsettle discourses of blood, bodies, and borders that foment the unnatural whiteness of America. Vampires do not project the myths of America with a blind faith in national exceptionalism; instead, they interrupt nationalist projections that suppress transnational histories. They unsettle settler myths and deprovincialize frontier myths, along with mythologies that democracy and ingenuity are uniquely European—and later quintessentially American— institutions. Since many democratic ideals were actually appropriated from indigenous nations (Stam and Shohat 2012: 13), US forms of democracy are products of two-way assimilation of European and indigenous polities.

Vampires advocate for the right to rights for humans who have historically been denied that status under US law or custom. They prompt us to consider other ways of being, including the right of rights for other species—and acknowledgment that human intelligence is not superior in every way to nonhuman intelligence. Just as vampires ask us to consider indigenous and immigrant histories as part of an unfolding transnational history, they ask us to think about nonhuman histories and what it means to think in terms of planetary awareness that extends to nonhuman animals and nonanimal beings that are significant to our lives. Much as postcolonial scholars have used supernatural creatures as tropes for colonial and postcolonial experiences, scientists and journalists have used the expression "the walking dead" to describe nonhuman animal species on the verge of extinction. By humanizing vampires, Hollywood might be said to contribute towards a more holistic discussion of the right to rights for nonhuman species, as well as the need to understand codependence within cohabitation. The repulsion that audiences might feel when vampires *farm* humans for blood can translate into a repulsion when humans *farm* nonhuman animals for food, extending the repulsion that audiences might have felt when Hollywood's vampire films and series raised questions about not extending the right to rights to people of color, immigrants, and indigenous nations. Learning from vampires and other supernatural creatures requires a rethinking of polity, migrating and mutating away from the anthropocentric and nation-state-centric models that continue to dominate our thinking. Vampires and werewolves and other supernatural creatures figure questions that we need to ask about considering polity in terms that are not limited to human ones.[9]

Notes

1. Christopher Farnsworth's "Nathaniel Cade" novels (2010–14) feature vampire and US president.
2. I thank Isabelle Galet-Lalande for pointing out this feature of 4chan.
3. Obama appears like Baracula in Presidential Monsters' action figures.

4. Red Square, "Movie Sequel — Ibrahim Obama: Vampire Helper," *The People's Cube* (22 June 2012): http://thepeoplescube.com/peoples-blog/movie-sequel-ibrahim-obama-vampire-helper-t9171.html.
5. I thank Awam Amkpa for pointing out blackamoors in press photos of Obama.
6. It avoids a continuum in foreign policy from Bush to Obama, noticed by Lebanese protestors. "Bush Wears Obama Mask," *Al Monitor* (7 September 2013): http://www.al-monitor.com/pulse/ar/galleries/lebanon-photo-of-the-day.html?displayTab=bush-wears-obama-mask&page=4. Conspiracy theorist Alex Jones depicts Obama removing a mask to reveal Bush's face for his *The Obama Deception: The Mask Comes Off* (2009).
7. Black Panther party leader Bobby Seale's expression "right on" was depoliticized into BIC Corporation's "Write on!" campaign for selling ballpoint pens (Ewen 1988: 251).
8. Nixon's Southern Strategy appealed to their racism following the Civil Rights Act and Voting Rights Act, signed by Democratic president Lyndon Johnson in 1964 and 1965 (Anderson 2016: 98–137).
9. India granted rights to cetaceans (bottlenose dolphins, orcas), suggesting a more capacious understanding of "life, liberty, and well-being."

FILMOGRAPHY

30 Days of Night (USA 2007; dir. David Slade)
30 Days of Night: Blood Trails (USA 2007; dir. Victor García) [web series]
30 Days of Night: Dark Days (USA 2010; dir. Ben Ketai)
30 Days of Night: Dust to Dust (USA 2008; dir. Ben Ketai) [web series]
Abraham Lincoln: Vampire Hunter (USA 2012; dir. Timur Bakmambetov)
Addiction, The (USA 1995; dir. Abel Ferrara)
American in the Making, An (USA 1913; cin. Carl L. Gregory)
American Romance, An (USA 1944; dir. King Vidor)
Angel (USA 1999–2004; cr. David Greenwalt and Joss Whedon) [television series]
Arrival of Emigrants, Ellis Island (USA 1906; cin. G. W. "Billy" Bitzer)
Aswang, Ang (Philippines 1932; prod. George Musser)
Ataúd del vampiro, El/The Vampire's Coffin (México 1957; dir. Fernando Méndez)
Barakula: The Musical (USA 2008; dir. Mike Lawson)
Beast of the Yellow Night (Philippines-USA 1971; dir. Eddie Romero)
Being Human (Canada-USA 2011–14; cr. Jeremy Carver and Anna Fricke) [television series]
Being Human (UK 2008–13; cr. Toby Whitehouse) [television series]
Billy the Kid vs. Dracula (USA 1965; dir. William Beaudine)
Birth of a Nation, The (USA 1915; dir. D. W. Griffith)
Black Girl/La Noire de . . . (France-Sénégal 1965; dir. Sembène Ousmane)
Blacula (USA 1972; dir. William Crain)
Blade (USA 1998; dir. Stephen Norrington)
Blade II (USA 2002; dir. Guillermo del Toro)
Blade: House of Chthon (USA 2006; dir. Peter O'Fallon)
Blade: The Series (USA 2006; cr. David S. Goyer) [television series]
Blade: Trinity (USA 2004; dir. David S. Goyer)
Blair Witch Project, The (USA 1999; dir. Daniel Myrick and Eduardo Sánchez)
Blood Creek (USA 2008; dir. Joel Schumacher)

Blood Drinkers, The aka *Kulay dugo ang gabi/Blood is the Color of Night* (Philippines 1966/1971; dir. Gerardo de Leon)
Blood for Dracula/Andy Warhol's Dracula (Italy-USA 1974; dir. Paul Morrissey)
Blood Thirst/The Horror from Beyond (USA-Philippines 1971; dir. Newt Arnold)
Blood Ties (Canada 2006; cr. Peter Mohan) [television series]
Blood Ties (USA 1991; dir. Jim M. Bride)
BloodRayne (USA 2002; dev. Terminal Reality) [videogame]
BloodRayne (USA-Germany 2005; dir. Uwe Boll)
BloodRayne: Deliverance (Canada-Germany 2007; dir. Uwe Boll)
BloodRayne: The Third Reich (USA-Canada-Germany 2011; dir. Uwe Bol)
Bram Stoker's Dracula (USA 1992; dir. Francis Ford Coppola)
Breaking Dawn, Part 1 (USA 2011; dir. Bill Condon)
Breaking Dawn, Part 2 (USA 2012; dir. Bill Condon)
Breed, The (USA-Hungary 2001; dir. Michael Oblowitz)
Bride of Frankenstein (USA 1935; dir. James Whale)
Brides of Dracula, The (UK 1960; dir. Terence Fisher)
Bring Me the Vampire/Échenme al vampiro (México-Venezuela 1961; dir. Alfredo B. Crevenna)
Broken Blossoms (USA 1919; dir. D. W. Griffith)
Bud Abbott and Lou Costello Meet Frankenstein (USA 1949; dir. Charles T. Barton)
Buffy the Vampire Slayer (USA 1992; dir. Fran Rubel Kazui)
Buffy the Vampire Slayer (USA 1997–2003; cr. Joss Whedon) [television series]
Buffy the Vampire Slayer (Malaysia 2000; dev. GameBrains) [videogame]
Buffy the Vampire Slayer: The Quest for Oz (India 2004; dev. Indiagames) [videogame]
Captain Kronos, Vampire Hunter (UK 1972; dir. Brian Clemens)
Carmilla (USA 1990; dir. Gabrielle Beaumont)
Carmilla (Canada 2014–present; cr. Jordan Hall and Ellen Simpson) [web series]
Cat People (USA 1942; dir. Jacques Tourneur)
Cheat, The (USA 1915; dir. Cecil B. DeMille)
Child of the Ghetto, A (USA 1910; dir. D. W. Griffith)
Cliffhangers: Curse of Dracula (USA 1979; dir. Kenneth Johnson)
Condemned to Live (USA 1935; dir. Frank R. Strayer)
Count, The (USA 1981; dev. Adventure International) [videogame]
Countess Dracula (UK 1971; dir. Peter Sasdy)
Cow, The/Gaav (Iran 1969; Dariush Merhju'i)
Cowboys & Vampires (USA 2010; dir. Douglas Myers)
Creatures of Evil Drinkers aka *Ibulong mo sa hangin/Whisper to the Wind* (Philippines 1966/1971; dir. Gerardo de Leon)
Cronos/La invención de Cronos (México-USA 1992; dir. Guillermo del Toro)
Curse of the Undead/Mark of the West (USA 1959; dir. Henry Cass)
Dark Shadows (USA 1966–71; cr. Dan Curtis) [television series]
Dark Shadows (USA 1991; cr. Dan Curtis) [television series]
Dark Shadows (USA 2012; dir. Tim Burton)
Darker Truth, A (USA 2009; dir. Christopher Hanada) [web series]
Darling Kong Aswang, Ang (Philippines 2009; dir. Tony Y. Reyes)
Daybreakers (Australia-USA 2009; dir. Spierig Brothers)
Death Valley (USA 2011; cr. Curtis Gwinn and Eric Weinberg) [television series]
Drácula (USA 1931; dir. George Melford)
Dracula (USA 1931; dir. Tod Browning)
Dracula (USA 1979; dir. John Badham)
Dracula (USA 2013–14; cr. Cole Haddon) [television series]
Dracula A. D. 1972 (UK 1972; dir. Alan Gibson)

Dracula Has Risen from the Grave (UK 1968; dir. Freddie Francis)
Dracula, Prince of Darkness (UK 1966; dir. Terence Fisher)
Dracula: Dead and Loving It (USA-France 1995; dir. Mel Brooks)
Dracula: Pages from a Virgin's Diary (Canada 2001; dir. Guy Maddin)
Dracula's Daughter (USA 1936; dir. Lambert Hillyer)
Emigrants Landing at Ellis Island (USA 1903; cin. Alfred C. Abadie)
Fearless Vampire Killers, or Pardon Me, Your Teeth Are in My Neck, The /Dance of the Vampires (USA 1967; dir. Roman Polański)
Forever Knight (Canada-West Germany 1992–6; cr. Barney Cohen and James D. Parriott) [television series]
Forsaken, The (USA 2001; dir. J. S. Cardone)
Frankenstein: The True Story (USA 1972; dir. Jack Smight)
Fright Night (USA 1985; dir. Tom Holland)
From Dusk till Dawn (USA 1995; dir. Robert Rodriguez)
From Dusk till Dawn 2: Texas Blood Money (USA 1999; dir. Scott Spiegel)
From Dusk Till Dawn 3: The Hangman's Daughter (USA 2000; dir. P. J. Pesce)
From Dusk till Dawn (USA 2001; dev. GameSquad) [videogame]
From Dusk till Dawn: The Series (USA 2014–present; cr. Robert Rodriguez)
Gabriel, amor inmortal (USA 2008; cr. Agustin) [television series]
Ganja and Hess (USA 1973; dir. Bill Gunn)
Gates, The (USA 2010; cr. Grant Scharbo and Richard Hatem) [television series]
Girl Walks Home Alone at Night, A (USA 2014; dir. Ana Lily Amirpour)
Hercules at the Center of the Earth/Ercole al centro della terra (Italy 1961; dir. Mario Bava)
Horror of the Blood Monsters (USA-Philippines 1970; dir. Al Adamson)
Horror of Dracula (UK 1958; dir. Terence Fisher)
House of Dark Shadows (USA 1970; dir. Dan Curtis)
House of Dracula (USA 1945; dir. Earl C. Kenton)
House of Frankenstein (USA 1944; dir. Earl C. Kenton)
Hunger, The (UK-USA 1983; dir. Tony Scott)
Hunted, The (USA 2001–present; cr. Robert Chapin) [web series]
I Am Legend (USA 2007; dir. Francie Lawrence)
I Heart Vampires (USA 2009–10; cr. Julie Restivo and Kate Feldman) [web series]
I Kissed a Vampire (USA 2009–present; cr. Chris Sean Nolan and Laurie Nolan) [web series]
Immigrant, The (USA 1917; dir. Charlie Chaplin)
Incense of the Damned/Bloodsuckers/The Freedom Seekers (UK 1972; dir. Michael Burrowes [Robert Hartford-Davis])
Interview with the Vampire: The Vampire Chronicles (USA 1994; dir. Neil Jordan)
Italian, The (USA 1915; dir. Thomas H. Ince and C. Gardner Sullivan)
Jitters, The (USA-Japan 1988; dir. John Fasano)
Kindred: The Embrace (USA 1996; cr. John Leekley and Mark Rein-Hagen) [television series]
Kiss of the Vampire (UK 1964; dir. Don Sharp)
Legend of the Seven Golden Vampires, The (UK-Hong Kong 1974; dir. Roy Ward Baker)
Let Me In (USA 2010; dir. Matt Reeves)
Let the Right One In/Låt den rätte komma in (Sweden 2008; dir. Tomas Alfredson)
Live Evil (USA 2009; dir. Jay Woelfel)
Living Corpse, The/Zinda Laash (Pakistan 1967; dir. Khwaja Sarfraz)
lonelygirl15 (USA 2006–8; cr. Miles Beckett and Greg Goodfried) [web series]
Lost Boys, The (USA 1987; dir. Joel Schumacher)

Lost Boys: The Thirst (South Africa-USA-Germany 2010; dir. Dario Piana)
Lost Boys: The Tribe (USA-Canada 2008; dir. P. J. Pesce)
Love at First Bite (USA 1979; dir. Stan Dragoti)
Loves of Count Iorga, Vampire, The (USA 1970; dir. Bob Kelljan)
Maid in Morocco (USA 1925; dir. Charles Lamont)
Making an American Citizen (USA 1912; dir. Alice Guy-Blaché)
Making of an American, The (USA 1920; dir. Guy Hedlund)
Mark of the Vampire (USA 1935; dir. Tod Browning)
Martin (USA 1976; dir. George A. Romero)
Modern Vampires (USA 1998; dir. Richard Elfman)
Moonlight (USA 2007–8; cr. Ron Koslow and Trevor Munson) [television series]
Moth Diaries, The (Canada-Ireland-UK 2011; dir. Mary Harron)
Mother, May I Sleep with Danger? (USA 2016; dir. Melanie Aitkenhead)
Move On (USA 1903; cin. Alfred C. Abadie)
Mr. Vampire/Goeng si sin sang (Hong Kong 1985; dir. Ricky Lau Koon-wai)
My Darling Aswang (Philippines 2010–11; dir. Bert de Leon) [television series]
Nadja (USA 1994; dir. Michael Almereyda)
Near Dark (USA 1987; dir. Kathryn Bigelow)
New Moon (USA 2009; dir. Chris Weitz)
New York City "Ghetto" Fish Market (USA 1903; cin. James Blair Smith)
Nick Knight (USA 1989: dir. Farhad Mann) [television series]
Night of Dark Shadows (USA 1971; dir. Dan Curtis)
Nocturna: Granddaughter of Dracula (USA 1979; dir. Harry Hurwitz)
Nosferatu: A Symphony of Horror/ Nosferatu, eine Symphonie des Grauens (Germany 1922; dir. F. W. Murnau)
Old Dracula/Vampira (UK 1974; dir. Clive Donner)
Only Lovers Left Alive (USA-UK 2013; dir. Jim Jarmusch)
Originals, The (USA 2013–present; cr. Julie Plec) [television series]
Originals: Awakening, The (USA 2014; cr. Julie Plec) [web series]
Passport Husband (USA 1938; dir. James Tinling)
Penny Dreadful (USA-Ireland-UK 2014–16; cr. John Logan) [television series]
Port Charles (USA 1997–2003; cr. Carolyn Culliton, Richard Culliton, and Wendy Riche) [television series]
Queen of the Damned (USA-Australia 2002; dir. Michael Rymer)
Ramona (USA 1910; dir. D. W. Griffith)
Rapid (Canada 1977; dir. David Cronenberg)
Return of Count Yorga, The (USA 1970; dir. Bob Kelljan)
Return to Salem's Lot, A (USA 1987; dir. Larry Cohen)
Rise: Blood Hunter (USA 2007; dir. Sebastian Gutierrez)
Romance in Manhattan (USA 1935; dir. Stephen Roberts)
Salem's Lot (USA 1979; dir. Tobe Hooper) [miniseries]
Salem's Lot (USA 2004; dir. Mikael Salomon) [miniseries]
Samson versus the Vampire Women (México-USA 1963; dub dir. Manuel San Fernando)/*El Santo contra las mujeres vampiro* (México 1962; dir. Alfonso Corona Blake)
Santo en El tesoro de Drácula, El/Santo in "the Treasure of Dracula" (México 1969; dir. René Cardona)
Santo y Blue Demon contra Drácula y el Hombre Lobo, El (México 1972; dir. Miguel M. Delgado)
Satanic Rites of Dracula, The/Count Dracula and His Vampire Bride (UK 1973; dir. Alan Gibson)
Scanners (Canada 1981; dir. David Cronenberg)

Scream, Blacula, Scream (USA 1973; dir. Bob Kelljan)
Sesame Street (USA 1969–present; cr. Joan Ganz Cooney and Lloyd Morrisett) [television series]
Sheik, The (USA 1921; dir. George Melford)
Shivers (Canada 1975; dir. David Cronenberg)
Slayer/Mexferatu Mexico (USA 2006; dir. Kevin VanHook)
Son of Dracula (USA 1943; dir. Robert Siodmak)
Stake Land (USA 2010; dir. Jim Minle)
Strain, The (USA 2014–present; cr. Guillermo del Toro and Chuck Hogan) [television series]
Tagani/Flight of the Crab Monsters (Philippines 1965; dir. Rolf Bayer)
Taste the Blood of Dracula (UK 1970; dir. Peter Sasdy)
To Die For (USA 1989; dir. Daren Sarafian)
True Blood (USA 2008–14; cr. Alan Ball) [television series]
Twilight (USA 2008; dir. Catherine Hardwicke)
Twins of Evil (UK 1971; dir. John Hough)
Underworld (UK-Germany-Hungary-USA 2003; dir. Len Wiseman)
Underworld: Awakening (USA 2012; dir. Måns Mårlin and Björn Stein)
Underworld: Blood Wars (USA 2016; dir. Anna Foerester)
Underworld: Rise of the Lycans (USA-New Zealand 2009; dir. Patrick Tatopoulos)
Valemont (USA-Canada 2009; cr. Brent V. Friedman) [television series]
Vamp (USA 1986; dir. Richard Wenk)
Vampire Circus (UK 1972; dir. Robert Young)
Vampire Diaries, The (USA 2009–present; cr. Kevin Williamson and Julie Plec) [television series]
Vampire Diaries: Bloodlines Revealed, The (USA 2010; dev. Retrofit Films) [videogame]
Vampire in Brooklyn (USA 1995; dir. Wes Craven)
Vampire's Kiss (USA 1989; dir. Robert Bierman)
Vampires (USA 1998; dir. John Carpenter)
Vampires, Les (France 1915–16; dir. Louis Feuillade)
Vampires Suck (USA 2010; dir. Jason Friedberg and Aaron Seltzer)
Vampires: Los Muertos (USA 2002; dir. Tommy Lee Wallace)
Vampires: The Turning (USA 2005; dir. Marty Weiss)
Vampiro sangriento, El/The Bloody Vampire (México 1962; dir. Miguel Morayta)
Vampiro, El/The Vampire (México 1957; dir. Fernando Méndez)
Van Helsing (USA-Czech Republic 2004; dir. Stephen Sommers)
Werewolf, The (USA-Canada 1913; dir. Henry MacRae)

BIBLIOGRAPHY

Abbott, Stacey (2007), *Celluloid Vampires: Life after Death in the Modern World*, Austin: University of Texas.
Abel, Richard (1999), *The Red Rooster Scare: Making Cinema American, 1900–1910*, Berkeley: University of California.
Abel, Richard (2006), *Americanizing the Movies and "Movie-Mad" Audiences*, Berkeley: University of California.
Abu-Lughod, Lila (2013), *Do Muslim Women Need Saving?*, Cambridge, MA: Harvard University.
Adams, Carol J. [1990] (2010), *The Sexual Politics of Meat: A Feminist-Vegetarian Critical Theory*, 20th-anniversary edn, New York: Continuum.
Agamben, Giorgio [1995] (1999), *Homo Sacer: Sovereign Power and Bare Life*, trans. Daniel Heller-Roazen, Stanford: Stanford University.
Alba, Richard and Victor Nee (2003), *Remaking the American Mainstream: Assimilation and Contemporary Immigration*, Cambridge, MA: Harvard University.
Alessio, Dominic (2001), "'Things are different now'?: A postcolonial analysis of *Buffy the Vampire Slayer*," *The European Legacy* 6:6, pp. 731–40.
Allen, Theodore W. [1994] (2012a), *The Invention of the White Race, Volume 1: Racial Oppression and Social Control*, 2nd edn, London: Verso.
Allen, Theodore W. [1997] (2012b), *The Invention of the White Race, Volume 2: The Origin of Racial Oppression in Anglo-America*, 2nd edn, London: Verso.
Alloula, Mallek (1986), *The Colonial Harem*, Minneapolis: University of Minnesota.
Altman, Rick (1980), "Moving lips: Cinema as ventriloquism," *Yale French Studies* 60, pp. 67–79.
Altman, Rick (1999), *Film/Genre*, London: British Film Institute.
Anderson, Benedict (1983), *Imagined Communities: Reflections on the Origins and Spread of Nationalism*, London: Verso.
Anderson, Carol (2016), *White Rage: The Unspoken Truth of Our Racial Divide*, New York: Bloomsbury.

Ansen, David (1996), "Movies: Chinese takeout," *Newsweek* (19 February), p. 66.
Anyiwo, U. Melissa (2015), "Introduction," in U. Melissa Anyiwo (ed.), *Race in the Vampire Narrative*, Rotterdam: Sense Publishing, pp. 1–6.
Anzaldúa, Gloria (1987), *Borderlands: The New Mestiza: La Frontera*, San Francisco: Aunt Lute.
Apel, Dora (2009), "Just joking? Chimps, Obama and racial stereotype," *Journal of Visual Culture* 8, pp.134–42.
Appadurai, Arjun (1995), *Modernity at Large: Cultural Dimensions of Globalization*, Minneapolis: University of Minnesota.
Arata, Stephen D. [1990] (1997), "The Occidental tourist: Dracula and the anxiety of reverse colonization", in Bram Stoker, *Dracula: A Norton Critical Edition*, ed. Nina Auerbach and David J. Skal, New York: W. W. Norton, pp. 462–70.
Asante-Muhammed, Dedrick, Chuck Collins, Josh Hoxie and Emanuel Nieves (2016), *The Ever-growing Gap: Without Change African-American and Latino Families Won't Match White Wealth for Centuries*, Washington, DC: Institute for Policy Studies and the Corporation For Economic Development.
Auerbach, Nina (1995), *Our Vampires, Ourselves*, Chicago: University of Chicago.
Auster, Al (2008), "HBO's approach to generic transformation," in Gary R. Edgerton and Brian G. Rose (eds), *Thinking Outside the Box: A Contemporary Television Genre Reader*, Lexington: University of Kentucky, pp. 226–46.
Avila, Eric (2006), *Popular Culture in the Age of White Flight: Fear and Fantasy in Suburban Los Angeles*, Berkeley: University of California.
Bahri, Deepika and Mary Vasudeva (1996), "Pedagogical alternatives: Issues in postcolonial studies: Interview with Gauri Viswanathan," in Deepika Bahri and Mary Vasudeva (eds), *Between the Lines: South Asians and Postcoloniality*, Philadelphia: Temple University, pp. 54–63.
Barrenechea, Antonio (2009), "Hemispheric horrors: Celluloid vampires from the 'good neighbor' era," *Comparative American Studies* 7:3, pp. 225–37.
Barthes, Roland (1957), *Mythologies*, Paris: Éditions du Seuil.
Barthes, Roland [1980] (1981), *Camera Lucida: Reflections on Photography*, trans. Richard Howard, New York: Hill and Wang.
Bazin, André [1958–62] (1971), *What is Cinema?*, trans. Hugh Gray, Berkeley: University of California.
Behdad, Ali (2005), *A Forgetful Nation: On Immigration and Cultural Identity in the United States*, Durham: Duke University.
Beltrán, Mary and Camilla Fojas (2008), "Mixed race in Hollywood film and media culture," in Mary Beltrán and Camilla Fojas (eds), *Mixed Race Hollywood*, New York: NYU, pp. 1–20.
Benshoff, Harry M. (1997), *Monster in the Closet: Homosexuality and the Horror Film*, Manchester: Manchester University.
Benshoff, Harry M. (2000), "Blaxploitation horror films: Generic reappropriation or reinscription?" *Cinema Journal* 39:2, pp. 31–50.
Benshoff, Harry M. (2011), *Dark Shadows*, Detroit: Wayne State University.
Benshoff, Harry M. and Sean Griffin (2004), *America on Film: Representing Race, Class, Gender, and Sexuality at the Movies*, Malden: Blackwell.
Berenstein, Rhonda J. (1996), *Attack of the Leading Ladies: Gender, Sexuality, and Spectatorship in Classic Horror Cinema*, New York: Columbia University.
Berg, Charles Ramírez (2002), *Latino Images in Film: Stereotypes, Subversion, Resistance,* Austin: University of Texas.
Berg, Charles Ramírez (2007), "Manifest myth making: Texas history in the movies," in Daniel Bernardi (ed.), *Classic Whiteness, Classic Hollywood*, Minneapolis: University of Minnesota, pp. 3–27.

Bergfelder, Tim (2000), "The nation vanishes: European co-productions and popular genre formula in the 1950s and 1960s," in Mette Hjort and Scott MacKenzie (eds), *Cinema and Nation*, New York: Routledge, pp. 139–52.
Bergland, Renée L. (2000), *The National Uncanny: Indian Ghosts and American Subjects*, Hannover: University Press of New England.
Berlant, Lauren (2011), *Cruel Optimism*, Durham: Duke University.
Bernardi, Daniel (ed.) (1996), *The Birth of Whiteness: Race and the Emergence of U.S. Cinema*, New Brunswick, NJ: Rutgers University.
Bernardi, Daniel (2001), "Introduction: Race and the Hollywood style," in Daniel Bernardi (ed.), *Classic Whiteness, Classic Hollywood*, Minneapolis: University of Minnesota, pp. xiii–xxvi.
Bernardi, Daniel (ed.) (2007), *The Persistence of Whiteness: Race and Contemporary Hollywood Cinema*, New York: Routledge.
Betz, Mark (2001), "The name above the (sub)title: Internationalism, coproduction, and polyglot European art cinema," *Camera Obscura* 46:16:1, pp. 1–45.
Beveridge, Albert J. [1898] (2007), "March of the flag," in Gary Colombo, Robert Cullen, and Bonnie Lisle (eds), *Rereading America: Cultural Contexts for Critical Thinking and Writing*, 7th edn, Boston: Belford/St. Martin's, pp. 762–7.
Bhabha, Homi K. (1995), *Location of Culture*, New York: Routledge.
Bielby, Denise D. and C. Lee Harrington (2008), *Global TV: Exporting Television and Culture in the World Market*, New York: NYU.
Bogle, Donald (1973), *Toms, Coons, Mulattos, Mammies, and Bucks: An Interpretive History of Blacks in American Films*, New York: Viking.
Boone, Joseph Allen (2014), *The Homoerotics of Orientalism*, New York: Columbia University.
Bordwell, David (2000), *Planet Hong Kong: Popular Cinema and the Art of Entertainment*, Cambridge, MA: Harvard University.
Bosniak, Linda (2006), *The Citizen and the Alien: Dilemmas of Contemporary Membership*, Princeton: Princeton University.
Brah, Avtar (1996), *Cartographies of Diaspora: Contesting Identities*, New York: Routledge.
Bronfen, Elisabeth (2006), "Speaking with the eyes: Tod Browning's *Dracula* and its phantom camera," in Bernd Herzogenrath (ed.), *The Films of Tod Browning*, London: Black Dog Publishing, pp. 151–72.
Brooks, Peter (1976), *The Melodramatic Imagination: Balzac, Henry James, Melodrama, and the Mode of Excess*, New Haven: Yale University.
Brown, Wendy (2008), *Regulating Aversion: Tolerance in the Age of Identity and Empire*, Princeton: Princeton University.
Butler, Ivan (1967), *Horror in the Cinema: From Goulies and Ghosties; and Long-Legitty Beasties; and Things that Go Bump in the Night—Good Lord Deliver Us, from an Old Cornish Litany*, London: A. Zwemmer.
Butler, Octavia E. (1976), *Fledgling*, New York: Grand Central.
Butler, Judith (1986), "Sex and gender in Simone de Beauvoir's *Second Sex*," *Yale French Studies* 72, pp. 35–49.
Byrd, Jody A. (2011), *The Transit of Empire: Indigenous Critiques of Colonialism*, Minneapolis: University of Minnesota.
Calaby, Jean K. (2005), "Towards an understanding of media transnationalism," in Jean K. Calaby (ed.), *Transnational Television Worldwide: Towards a New Media Order*, London: I. B. Tauris, pp. 1–13.
Capino, José B. (2010), *Dream Factories of a Former Colony: American Fantasies, Philippine Cinema*, Minneapolis: University of Minnesota.
Carroll, Noël E. (1990), *The Philosophy of Horror, or Paradoxes of the Heart*, New York: Routledge.

Carroll, Hamilton (2011), *Affirmative Reaction: New Formations of White Masculinity*, Durham: Duke University.
Carter, Margaret L. (1988), *Dracula: The Vampire and the Critics*, Ann Arbor: UMI Research.
Castronovo, Russ (2001), *Necro Citizenship: Death, Eroticism, and the Public Sphere in the Nineteenth-century United States*, Durham: Duke University.
Chanan, Michael (ed.) (1983), *25 Years of the New Latin American Cinema*, London: British Film Institute.
Chatterjee, Partha (1993), *The Nation and Its Fragments: Colonial and Postcolonial Histories*, Princeton: Princeton University.
Chaudhuri, Shohini (2005), *Contemporary World Cinema: Europe, Middle East, East Asia, South Asia*, Edinburgh: Edinburgh University.
Cheah, Pheng and Bruce Robbins (eds) (1998), *Cosmopolitics: Thinking and Feeling beyond the Nation*, Minneapolis: University of Minnesota.
Cherniavsky, Eva (2006), *Incorporations: Race, Nation, and the Body of Capital*, Minneapolis: University of Minnesota.
Chion, Michel [1990] (1994), *Audio-vision: Sound on Screen*, trans. Claudia Gorbman, New York: Columbia University.
Chion, Michel [1982] (1999), *The Voice in Cinema*, trans. Claudia Gorbman, New York: Columbia University.
Chorba, Carrie C. (2007), *Mexico, from Mestizo to Multicultural: National Identity and Recent Representations of the Conquest,* Nashville: Vanderbilt University.
Chung, Robert S. (1997), "A meditation on borders," in Juan F. Perea (ed.), *Immigrants Out!: The New Nativism and the Anti-Immigrant Impulse in the United States*, New York: NYU, pp. 244–53.
Clarens, Carlos (1967), *An Illustrated History of the Horror Film*, New York: Capricorn.
Clifford, James (1998), "Mixed feelings," in Pheng Cheah and Bruce Robbins (eds), *Cosmopolitics: Thinking and Feeling beyond the Nation*, Minneapolis: University of Minnesota, pp. 362–70.
Clover, David (1996), *Vampires, Mummies, and Liberals: Bram Stoker and the Politics of Popular Fictions*, Durham: Duke University.
Coates, Paul (1991), *The Gorgon's Gaze: German Cinema, Expressionism, and the Image of Horror*, Cambridge: Cambridge University.
Connor, Walker (1994), "Man is a rational animal," in *Ethnonationalism: The Quest for Understanding*, Princeton: University of Princeton, pp. 195–209.
Cook, Pam (1996), *Fashioning the Nation: Costume and Identity in British Cinema*, London: British Film Institute.
Cortés, Carlos E. (1991), "Hollywood interracial love: Social taboo as screen titillation," in Paul Loukides and Linda K. Fuller (eds), *Beyond the Stars: Stock Characters in American Popular Film*, Bowling Green: Bowling Green State University, pp. 21–35.
Cortés, Carlos E. (1993), "Them and us: Immigration as societal barometer and social education in American film," in Robert Brent Toplin (ed.), *Hollywood as Mirror: Changing Views of Outsiders as Enemies in American Movies*, Westport: Greenwood, pp. 53–74.
Courtney, Susan (2005), *Hollywood Fantasies of Miscegenation: Spectacular Narratives of Gender and Race, 1903–1967*, Princeton: Princeton University.
Coyne, Michael (1997), *The Crowded Prairie: American National Identity in the Hollywood Western*, London: I. B. Tauris.
Craft, Christopher [1984] (1997), "'Kiss me with those red lips': Gender and inversion in Bram Stoker's *Dracula*," in Bram Stoker, *Dracula: A Norton Critical Edition*, ed. Nina Auerbach and David J. Skal, New York: W. W. Norton, pp. 444–66.

Crenshaw, Kimberlé (1991), "Mapping the margins: Intersectionality, identity politics, and violence against women of color," *Stanford Law Review* 43:6, pp. 1241–99.
Cubitt, Sean (2005), "Distribution and media flows," *Cultural Politics* 1:2, pp. 193–214.
Curtin, Michael, Jennifer Holt, and Kevin Sanson (2014), "Introduction: Making of a revolution," in Michael Curtin, Jennifer Holt and Kevin Sanson(eds), *Distribution Revolution: Conversations about the Digital Future of Film and Television*, Oakland: University of California, pp. 1–17.
Daniels, Roger [1990] (2002), *Coming to America: A History of Immigration and Ethnicity in American Life*, 2nd edn, New York: Perennial/HarperCollins.
Davison, Carol Margaret (ed.) (1997), *Bram Stoker's Dracula: Sucking Through the Century, 1897–1997*, Toronto: Dundurn.
de la Mora, Sergio (2006), *Cinemachismo: Masculinities and Sexuality in Mexican Film*, Austin: University of Texas.
Deane, Hamilton and John L. Balderston (1993), *Dracula: The Vampire Play* [1927], in David J. Skal (ed.), *Dracula: The Ultimate, Illustrated Edition of the World-famous Vampire Play*, New York: St. Martin's.
Decherney, Peter (2012), *Hollywood's Copyright Wars from Edison to the Internet*, New York: Columbia University.
Deleuze, Gilles and Félix Guattari [1980] (1987), *A Thousand Plateaus: Capitalism and Schizophrenia*, trans. Brian Massumi, Minneapolis: University of Minnesota.
del Mundo, Clodualdo A. (1998), *Native Resistance: Philippine Cinema and Colonialism, 1898–1941*, Maynila: De la Salle University.
del Mundo, Clodualdo A. (1999), "Philippine cinema: An historical overview," *Asian Cinema* 10:2, pp. 29–66.
Dello Stritto, Frank J. (1997), "Lugosi in politics," in Gary Don Rhodes (ed.), *Lugosi: His Life in Films, on Stage, and in the Hearts of Horror Lovers*, Jefferson: McFarland, pp. 57–64.
Dennison, Stephanie and Song Hwee Lim (2006), *Remapping World Cinema: Identity, Culture and Politics in Film*, London: Wallflower.
Denzin, Norman K. (2002), *Reading Race: Hollywood and the Cinema of Racial Violence*, London: Sage.
Desser, David (2000), "The Kung Fu craze: Hong Kong cinema's first American reception," in Poshek Fu and David Desser (eds), *The Cinema of Hong Kong: History, Art, Identity*, Cambridge: Cambridge University, pp. 19–43.
DiAngelo, Robin (2011), "White fragility," *International Journal of Critical Pedagogy* 3:3, pp. 54–70.
Diawara, Manthia (1988), "Black spectatorship: Problems of identification and resistance," *Screen* 29:4, pp. 66–76.
Diawara, Manthia (1993), "Black American cinema: The new realism," in Manthia Diawara (ed.), *Black American Cinema*, New York: Routledge, pp. 3–25.
Diawara, Manthia and Phyllis Klotman (1990), "*Ganja and Hess*: Vampires, sex, and addictions," *Jump Cut* 35, pp. 30–6.
Dika, Vera (1996), "From Dracula—with love," in Barry Keith Grant (ed.) (1996), *The Dread of Difference: Gender and the Horror Film*, Austin: University of Texas, pp. 388–400.
Dixon, Wheeler Winston (2010), *A History of Horror*, New Brunswick, NJ: Rutgers University.
Doane, Mary Ann (1980), "The voice in the cinema: The articulation of body and space," *Yale French Studies* 60, pp. 35–50.
Doane, Mary Ann (1982), "Film and the masquerade: Theorising the female spectator," *Screen* 23:3–4, pp. 74–87.

Dresser, Nadine (1989), *American Vampires: Fans, Victims, and Practitioners*, New York: Vintage.
Duara, Prasenjit (1995), *Rescuing History from the Nation: Questioning Narratives of Modern China*, Chicago: University of Chicago.
DuBois, W. E. B. [1897] (1996), "Strivings of the Negro people," in Cary D. Wintz (ed.), *African American Political Thought, 1890–1930: Washington, DuBois, Garvey, and Randolf*, Armonk: M. E. Sharpe, pp. 85–90.
Dunbar-Ortiz, Roxanne (2015), *An Indigenous Peoples' History of the United States*, Boston: Beacon.
Dundes, Alan (ed.) (1998), *The Vampire: A Casebook*, Madison: University of Wisconsin.
Dyer, Richard (1997), *White*, New York: Routledge.
Eisenstein, Zillah (2004), *Against Empire: Feminisms, Racism, and the West*, London: Zed.
Eisner, Lotte H. (1952), *L'Ecran démoniaque: les influences de Max Reinhardt et de l'expressionnisme*, Paris: E. Losfeld.
Elsaesser, Thomas (1972), "Tales of fury: Observations on the family melodrama," *Monogram* 4, pp. 2–15.
Erb, Cynthia (2007), "Movies and the voice," in Ina Rae Hark (ed.), *American Cinema of the 1930s: Themes and Variations*, New Brunswick, NJ: Rutgers University, pp. 48–68.
Evans, Elizabeth (2011), *Transmedia Television: Audiences, New Media, and Daily Life*, New York: Routledge.
Ewen, Stuart (1988), *All-consuming Images: The Politics of Style in Contemporary Culture*, New York: Basic.
Ezra, Elizabeth and Terry Rowden (eds) (2006), *Transnational Cinema: A Film Reader*, New York: Routledge.
Fanon, Frantz (1952), *Peau noire, masques blanches*, Paris: Éditions du Seuil.
Fanon, Frantz (1961), *Les Damnés de la terre*, Paris: François Maspero.
Fisher, Terence [1964] (2000), "Horror is my business," in Alain Silver and James Ursini (eds), *Horror Film Reader*, New York: Limelight, pp. 67–75.
Florescu, Radu R. and Raymond T. McNally [1972] (1992), *In Search of Dracula: A True History of Dracula and Vampire Legends*, revised edn, New York: Houghton Mifflin.
Fluck, Winfried, Donald E. Pease, and John Carlos Rowe (eds) (2011), *Re-Framing the Transnational Turn in American Studies*, Hanover: Dartmouth College.
Foley, Neil (2012), "Becoming Hispanic: Mexican Americans and whiteness," in Paula S. Rothenberg (ed.) (2012), *White Privilege: Essential Readings on the Other Side of Racism*, 4th edn, New York: Worth, pp. 55–65.
Foster, Gwendolyn Audrey (2003), *Performing Whiteness: Postmodern Re/Constructions*, Albany: SUNY.
Frankenberg, Ruth (1993), *White Women, Race Matters: The Social Construction of Whiteness*, Minneapolis: University of Minnesota.
Frayling, Christopher (1991), *Vampyres: Lord Byron to Count Dracula*, London: Faber and Faber.
Friedman, Lester D. (ed.) (1991), *Unspeakable Images: Ethnicity and the American Cinema*, Chicago: University of Illinois.
Friedman, Thomas L. (1999), *The Lexus and the Olive Tree*, New York: Farrar, Straus and Giroux.
Frodon, Jean-Michel (1998), *La Projection nationale: cinéma et nation*, Paris: Éditions Odile Jacob.
Fuchs, Cynthia (2007), "'Did anyone ever explain to you what "secret identity" means?': Race and displacement in *Buffy* and *Dark Angel*," in Lisa Parks and Elana Levine (eds), *Undead TV: Essays on Buffy the Vampire Slayer*, Durham: Duke University, pp. 96–116.

Gabilondo, Joseba (2002), "Like blood for chocolate, like queers for vampires: Border and global consumption in Rodríguez, Tarantino, Arau, Esquival, and Troyana (notes on baroque, camp, kitsch, and hybridization," in Arnaldo Cruz-Malavé and Martin F. Manalansan IV (eds), *Queer Globalizations: Citizenship and the Afterlife of Colonialism*, New York: NYU, pp. 236–63.
Gaines, Jane (1988), "White privilege and looking relations: Race and gender in feminist theory," *Screen* 29:4, pp. 12–27.
Galeano, Eduardo [1971] (1997), *Open veins of Latin America: Five centuries or the pillage of a continent*, trans. Cedric Belfrage, New York: Monthly Review.
Ganti, Tejaswini (2013), *Bollywood: A Guidebook to Popular Hindi Cinema*, 2nd edn, London: Routledge.
Gaonkar, Dilip Parameshwar (2001), "On alternative modernities," in Dilip Parameshwar Gaonkar (ed.), *Alternative Modernities*, Durham: Duke University, pp. 1–23.
García Espinosa, Julio [1969] (1983), "For an imperfect cinema," trans. Julianne Burton, in Michael Chanan (ed.), *25 Years of the New Latin American Cinema*, London: British Film Institute, pp. 28–33.
García Riera, Emilio (1985), *Historia del cine mexicano*, México D.F.: Secretaría de Educación Publica.
Gardner, Martha (2005), *The Qualities of a Citizen: Women, Immigration, and Citizenship, 1870–1965*, Princeton: Princeton University.
Gasher, Mike (1995), "The audiovisual locations industry in Canada: Considering British Columbia as Hollywood North," *Canadian Journal of Communication* 20:2, pp. 231–54.
Gelder, Ken (1994), *Reading the Vampire*, London: Routledge.
Gelder, Ken (2012), *New Vampire Cinema*, London: British Film Institute.
Gerow, Aaron (2010), *Visions of Japanese Modernity: Articulations of Cinema, Nation, and Spectatorship, 1895–1925*, Berkeley: University of California.
Gibson, Matthew (2006), *Dracula and the Eastern Question: British and French Vampire Narratives of the Nineteenth-Century Near East*, New York: Palgrave Macmillan.
Glenn, Evelyn Nakano (2002), *Unequal Freedom: How Race and Gender Shaped American Citizenship and Labor*, Cambridge, MA: Harvard University.
Glissant, Édouard (1981), *Le Discours antillais*, Paris: Gallimard.
Glover, David (2012), *Vampires, Mummies and Liberals: Bram Stoker and the Politics of Popular Fiction*, Durham: Duke University.
Goldsworthy, Vesna (1998), *Inventing Ruritania: The Imperialism of the Imagination*, New Haven: Yale University.
Gomery, Douglas (1983), "Television, Hollywood, and the development of movies made-for-television," in E. Ann Kaplan (ed.), *Regarding Television: Critical Approaches–An Anthology*, Los Angeles: American Film Institute, pp. 120–29.
Gomery, Douglas (2005), *The Hollywood Studio System: A History*, London: British Film Institute.
Gomez, Jewel (1991), *The Gilda Stories*, Ann Arbor: Firebrand.
Gómez, Laura (2007), *Manifest Destinies: The Making of the Mexican American Race*, New York: NYU.
Gopalan, Lalitha (2002), *Cinema of Interruptions: Action Genres in Contemporary Indian Cinema*, London: British Film Institute.
Gordon, Joan and Veronica Hollinger (eds) (1997), *Blood Read: The Vampire as Metaphor in Contemporary Culture*, Philadelphia: University of Pennsylvania.
Gordon, Avery F. and Christopher Newfield (1996), "Introduction," in Avery F. Gordon and Christopher Newfield (eds), *Mapping Multiculturalism*, Minneapolis: University of Minnesota, pp. 1–18.

Grahame-Smith, Seth (2010), *Abraham Lincoln: Vampire Hunter*, New York: Grand Central.
Grant, Barry Keith (ed.) (1996), *The Dread of Difference: Gender and the Horror Film*, Austin: University of Texas.
Greene, Doyle (2005), *Mexploitation Cinema: A Critical History of Mexican Vampire, Wrestler, Ape-Man and Similar Films, 1957–1977*, Jefferson: McFarland.
Grewal, Inderpal (2005), *Transnational America: Feminisms, Diasporas, Neoliberalisms*, Durham: Duke University.
Grieveson, Lee (2009), "Movies and the State of the Union," in Charlie Keil and Ben Singer (eds), *American Cinema of the 1910s: Themes and Variations*, New Brunswick, NJ: Rutgers University, pp. 139–59.
Gross, Ariela (2010), *What Blood Won't Tell: A History of Race on Trial in America*, Cambridge, MA: Harvard University.
Guerrero, Ed (1993), *Framing Blackness*, Philadelphia: Temple University.
Gunning, Tom (1986), "The cinema of attraction: Early film, its spectators, and the avant-garde," *Wide Angle* 8:3–4, pp. 63–70.
Gunning, Tom (1995), "An aesthetic of astonishment," in Linda Williams (ed.), *Viewing Positions: Ways of Seeing Film*, New Brunswick, NJ: Rutgers University, pp. 114–33.
Hadimioglu, Çagla (2011), "Black tents" in Zoya Kocur (ed.), *Global Visual Cultures: An Anthology*, Chichester: Wiley-Blackwell, pp. 126–35.
Haenni, Sabine (2008), *The Immigrant Scene: Ethnic Amusements in New York, 1880–1920*, Minneapolis: University of Minnesota.
Halberstam, Judith (1995), *Skin Shows: Gothic Horror and the Technology of Monsters*, Durham: Duke University.
Hall, Stuart (1980), "Encoding/decoding" in Stuart Hall, Dorothy Hobson, Andrew Lowe, and Paul Willis (eds), *Culture, Media, Language*, London: Hutchinson, pp. 128–38.
Halliwell, Leslie (1986), *The Dead that Walk*, London: Grafton/Collins.
Haney López, Ian F. (1996), *White by Law: The Legal Construction of Race*, New York: NYU.
Hansen, Miriam Bratu (1986), "Pleasure, ambivalence, identification: Valentino and female spectatorship," *Cinema Journal* 25:4, pp. 6–32.
Hansen, Miriam Bratu (2000), "Fallen women, rising stars, new horizons: Shanghai silent films as vernacular modernism," *Film Quarterly* 54:1, pp. 10–22.
Haraway, Donna J. (1996), "Universal donors in a vampire culture: It's all in the family: Biological kinship categories in the twentieth-century United States," in William Cronon (ed.), *Uncommon Ground: Rethinking the Human Place in Nature*, New York: W. W. Norton, pp. 321–66.
Haraway, Donna J. (2008), *When Species Meet*, Minneapolis: University of Minnesota.
Hardt, Michael and Antonio Negri (2004), *Multitude: War and Democracy in the Age of Empire*, New York: Penguin.
Harris, Cheryl I. (1993), "Whiteness as property," *Harvard Law Review* 106:8, pp. 1707–91.
Harvey, David (2005), *A Brief History of Neoliberalism*, Oxford: Oxford University.
Havens, Timothy (2008), "Globalization and the generic transformation of telenovelas," in Gary R. Edgerton and Brian G. Rose (eds), *Thinking Outside the Box: A Contemporary Television Genre Reader*, Lexington: University of Kentucky, pp. 271–92.
Hebel, Udo J. (ed.) (2012), *Transnational American Studies*, Heidelberg: Universitätsverlag Winter.
Heffernan, Kevin (2002), "Inner-city exhibition and the genre film: Distributing *Night of the Living Dead* (1968)," *Cinema Journal* 41:3, pp. 59–77.

Heiss, Lokke (2009), "Discovery of a Hungarian *Drakula*," in Elizabeth Miller (ed.), *Bram Stoker's Dracula: A Documentary Jounrey into Vampire Country and the Dracula Phenomenon*, New York: Pegasus, pp. 296–300.
Henderson, Robert M. (1972), *D. W. Griffith: His Life and Work*, Oxford: Oxford University.
Higbee, Will (2014), *Post-beur Cinema: North African Émigré and Maghrebi-French Filmmaking in France since 2000*, Edinburgh: Edinburgh University.
Hing, Bill Ong (2004), *Defining America through Immigration Policy*, Philadelphia: Temple University.
Holcomb, Mark (2005), "Gerardo de Leon Ilagan," *Senses of Cinema*, <http://sensesofcinema.com/2005/great-directors/de_leon/>.
Holte, James Craig (2001), "*Blade*: A return of revulsion," *Journal of Dracula Studies* 3, pp. 27–32.
hooks, bell (1992), *Black Looks: Race and Representation*, Boston: South End.
hooks, bell (2013), *Writing beyond Race: Living Theory and Practice*, New York: Routledge.
Horsman, Reginald (1981), *Race and Manifest Destiny: The Origins of American Racial Anglo-Saxonism*, Cambridge, MA: Harvard University.
Hudson, Dale (2006), "'Just play yourself, "Maggie Cheung"': *Irma Vep*, unthinking national cinemas, and rethinking transnational stardom," *Screen* 47:2, pp. 213–32.
Hudson, Dale (2007), "Vampires of color and the performance of multicultural whiteness," in Daniel Bernardi (ed.), *The Persistence of Whiteness: Race and Contemporary Hollywood Cinema*, New York: Routledge, pp. 127–56.
Hudson, Dale (2009), "Modernity as crisis: *Goeng si* and vampires in Hong Kong cinema," in Caroline Joan (Kay) Picart and John Edgar Browning (eds), *Draculas, Vampires, and Other Undead Forms: Essays on Gender, Race, and Culture*, Lanham: Scarecrow, pp. 203–33.
Hudson, Dale (2011), "Transpolitical Spaces within Transnational French Cinemas: Vampires and the Illusions of National Borders and Universal Citizenship," *French Cultural Studies* 22:2, pp. 111–26.
Hudson, Dale (2013), "'Of course there are werewolves and vampires': *True Blood* and the right to rights for other species," *American Quarterly* 65:3, pp. 661–83.
Hudson, Dale (2014), "Vampires and transnational horror," in Harry M. Benshoff (ed.), *A Companion to the Horror Film*, Chichester: Wiley-Blackwell, pp. 463–82.
Hudson, Dale and Patricia R. Zimmermann (2015), *Thinking through Digital Media: Transnational Environments and Locative Places*, New York: Palgrave Macmillan.
Huggen, Graham and Helen Tiffin (2010), *Postcolonial Ecocriticism: Literature, Animals, Environment*, London: Routledge.
Hughey, Matthew W. (2014), *The White Savior Film: Content, Critics, and Consumption*, Philadelphia: Temple University.
Huntington, Samuel P. (1996), *The Clash of Civilizations and the Remaking of World Order*, New York: Simon and Schuster.
Hutchings, Peter (1983), "Critical theory and 'British cinema'," *Screen* 24:4–5, pp. 80–95.
Hutchings, Peter (1993), *Hammer and Beyond: The British Horror Film*, Manchester: Manchester University.
Hutchings, Peter (2001), *Terence Fisher*, Manchester: Manchester University.
Isaac, Allan Punzalan (2006), *American Tropics: Articulating Filipino America*, Minneapolis: University of Minnesota.
Isenberg, Nancy (2016), *White Trash: The 400-Year Untold History of Class in America*, New York: Viking.

Jacobson, Matthew Frye (1998), *Whiteness of a Different Color: European Immigrants and the Alchemy of Race*, Cambridge, MA: Harvard University.

James, Henry [1907] (1968), *The American Scene*, Bloomington: Indiana University.

James, C. L. R. [1938/1969] (2012), *A History of Pan-African Revolt*, Oakland: PM Press.

Jancovich, Mark (2002), "General introduction," in Mark Jancovich (ed.), *Horror, the Film Reader*, New York: Routledge, pp. 1–20.

Jenkins, Henry (1992), *Textual Poachers: Television Fans and Participation Culture*, New York: Routledge.

Jenkins, Henry (2007), "Transmedia storytelling 101," *Confessions of an Aca-fan: The Official Weblog of Henry Jenkins*, <http://henryjenkins.org/2007/03/transmedia_storytelling_101.html>.

Jenkins, Henry, Sam Ford, and Joshua Green (2013), *Spreadable Media: Creating Value and Meaning in a Networked Culture*, New York: NYU.

Jensen, Kristian (2010), "Noble werewolves or native shape-shifters," in Amy M. Clarke and Marijane Osborn (eds), *The Twilight Mystique: Critical Essays on the Novels and Films*, New York: Peter Lang, pp. 92–106.

Jones, Maldwyn Allen (1960), *American Immigration*, Chicago: University of Chicago.

Jones, Robert P. (2016), *The End of White Christian America*, New York: Simon and Schuster.

Judd, Dennis (1996), *Empire: The British Imperial Experience from 1765 to the Present*, New York: BasicBooks.

Kalinak, Kathryn (2007), *How the West Was Sung: Music in the Films of John Ford*, Berkeley: University of California.

Kaplan, E. Ann (ed.) (1983), *Regarding Television: Critical Approaches–An Anthology*, Los Angeles: American Film Institute.

Kauanui, J. Kehaulani (2008), *Hawaiian Blood: Colonialism and the Politics of Sovereignty and Indigeneity*, Durham: Duke University.

Kawash, Samira (1999), "Terrorists and vampires: Fanon's spectral violence of decolonization," in Anthony C. Alessandrini (ed.), *Frantz Fanon: Critical Perspectives*, New York: Routledge, pp. 235–57.

Khair, Tabish and Johan Höglund (eds) (2013), *Transnational and Postcolonial Vampires: Dark Blood*, New York: Palgrave Macmillan.

King, John (1990), *Magical Reels: A History of Cinema in Latin America*, New York: Verso.

King, C. Richard (ed.) (2000), *Postcolonial America*, Bloomington: University of Illinois.

Kirihara, Donald (1996), "The accepted idea displaced: Stereotype and Sessue Hayakawa," in Daniel Bernardi (ed.), *The Birth of Whiteness: Race and the Emergence of US Cinema*, New Brunswick, NJ: Rutgers University, pp. 81–99.

Klinger, Barbara (2006), *Beyond the Multiplex: Cinema, New Technologies, and the Home*, Berkeley: University of California.

Knee, Adam (2008), "Race mixing and the fantastic: Lineages of identity and genre in contemporary Hollywood," in Mary Beltrán and Camilla Fojas (eds), *Mixed Race Hollywood*, New York: NYU, pp. 157–81.

Konvitz, Milton R. (1953), *Civil Rights in Immigration*, Ithaca: Cornell University.

Kracauer, Siegfried (1947), *From Caligari to Hitler: A Psychological History of the German Film*, Princeton: Princeton University.

Kracauer, Siegfried [1960] (1997), *Theory of Film: The Redemption of Physical Reality*, Princeton: Princeton University.

Kramer, Paul A. (2006), *The Blood of Government: Race, Empire, the United States, and the Philippines*, Chapel Hill: University of North Carolina.

Larson, Randall D. (1996), *Music from the House of Hammer: Music in the Hammer Horror Films, 1950–1980*, Lanham: Scarecrow.
Latham, Rob (2002), *Consuming Youth: Vampires, Cyborgs, and the Culture of Consumption*, Chicago: University of Chicago.
Lee, Robert G. (1999), *Orientals: Asian Americans in Popular Culture*, Philadelphia: Temple University.
Lee, Michael (2003), "Unmasking patriarchy's savior: Gender politics in *Samson versus the Vampire Women*," in Gary D. Rhodes (ed.), *Horror at the Drive-in*, Jefferson: McFarland, pp. 187–97.
LeFanu, Joseph Sheridan [1872] (1993), "Carmilla," in *In a Glass Darkly*, Oxford: Oxford University, pp. 243–319.
Levi, Heather (2008), *The World of Lucha Libre: Secrets, Revelations, and Mexican National Identity*, Durham: Duke University.
Lewis, Bernard (1990), "The roots of Muslim rage," *The Atlantic Monthly*, pp. 47–60.
Lewis, Martin W. and Kären E. Wigen (1997), *The Myth of Continents: A Critique of Metageography*, Berkeley: University of California.
Lim, Bliss Cua (1997), "The politics of horror: The *Aswang* in film," *Asian Cinema* 9:1, pp. 81–98.
Lim, Bliss Cua (2002), "'American pictures made by Filipinos': Eddie Romero's jungle-horror exploitation films," *Spectator* 22:1, pp. 23–45.
Lim, Bliss Cua (2009), *Translating Time: Cinema, the Fantastic, and Temporal Critique*, Durham: Duke University.
Linke, Uli (1999), *Blood and Nation: The European Aesthetics of Race*, Philadelphia: University of Pennsylvania.
Longinović, Tomislav Z. (2002), "Vampires like us: Gothic imaginary and 'the Serbs'," in Dušan I. Bjelić and Obrad Savić (eds), *Balkan as Metaphor Between Globalization and Fragmentation*, Cambridge, MA: MIT, pp. 39–60.
López, Ana M. (1991), "'Are all Latins from Manhattan': Hollywood, ethnography, and cultural colonialism," in Lester D. Friedman (ed.), *Unspeakable Images: Ethnicity and the American Cinema*, Chicago: University of Illinois, pp. 404–24.
Lorde, Audre (1984), *Sister Outsider: Essays and Speeches*, Freedom: Crossing.
Lotz, Amanda D. (2014), *The Television Will Be Revolutionized*, 2nd edn, New York: NYU.
Loukides, Paul and Linda K. Fuller (eds) (1991), *Beyond the Stars: Stock Characters in American Popular Film*, Bowling Green: Bowling Green State University.
Lowe, Lisa (1996), *Immigrant Acts: On Asian American Cultural Politics*, Durham: Duke University.
Lowe, Lisa (2015), *The Intimacies of Four Continents*, Durham: Duke University.
Loza, Susana (2011), "Vampires, queers, and other monsters: Against the homonormativity of *True Blood*," in Gareth Schott and Kirstine Moffat (eds), *Fanpires: Audience Consumption of the Modern Vampire*, Washington, DC: New Academia, pp. 91–118.
Lu, Sheldon Hsia-Peng (1997), *Transnational Chinese Cinemas: Identity, Nationhood, Gender*, Honolulu: University of Hawai'i.
McClelland, Bruce (2008), *Slayers and Their Vampires: A Cultural History of Killing the Dead*, Ann Arbor: University of Michigan.
MacDonald, D. L. (1991), *Poor Polidori: A Critical Biography of the Author of The Vampyre*, Toronto: University of Toronto.
McIntosh, Peggy [1992] (2012), "White privilege: Unpacking the invisible knapsack," in Paula S. Rothenberg (ed.), *White Privilege: Essential Readings on the Other Side of Racism*, 4th edn, New York: Worth, pp. 97–101.
McMurria, John (2009), "Regulation and the law: A critical cultural citizenship

approach," in Jennifer Holt and Alisa Perren (eds), *Media Industries: History, Theory and Methods*, Oxford: Blackwell, pp. 171–83.

McNally, David (2012), *Monsters of the Market: Zombies, Vampires and Global Capitalism*, London: Haymarket.

McPherson, Tara (2003), *Reconstructing Dixie: Race, Gender, and Nostalgia in the Imagined South*, Durham: Duke University.

Magill, David (2015), "Racial hybridity and the reconstruction of white masculinity in *Underworld*," in U. Melissa Anyiwo (ed.), *Race in the Vampire Narrative*, Rotterdam: Sense, pp. 81–90.

Majithia, Sheetal (2015), "Rethinking postcolonial melodrama and affect with Deepa Mehta's *Earth*," *Modern Drama* 58:1, pp. 1–23.

Makdisi, Saree (2014), *Making England Western: Occidentalism, Race, and Imperial Culture*, Chicago: University of Chicago.

Malik, Kenan (1996), *The Meaning of Race: Race, History, and Culture in Western Society*, New York: NYU.

Maltby, Richard (2004), "Introduction: 'The Americanization of the world'," in Melvin Stokes and Richard Maltby (eds), *Hollywood Abroad: Audiences and Cultural Exchanges*, London: British Film Institute, pp. 1–20.

Mannur, Anita (2008), *Culinary Fictions: Food in South Asian Diasporic Culture*, Philadelphia: Temple University.

Marchetti, Gina (1993), *Romance and the "Yellow Peril": Race, Sex, and Discursive Strategies in Hollywood Fiction*, Berkeley: University of California.

Marciniak, Katarzyna, Anikó Imre, and Áine O'Healy (2007), *Transnational Feminism in Film and Media*, New York: Palgrave.

Marciniak, Kataryna and Bruce Bennett (eds) (2016), *Teaching Transnational Cinema: Politics and Pedagogy*, New York: Routledge.

Marcus, Jana (1997), *In the Shadow of the Vampire: Reflections from the World of Anne Rice*, New York: Thunder's Mouth.

Marx, Karl [1867] (1990), *Capital: A Critique of Political Economy*, trans. Ben Fowkes, Harmondsworth: Penguin.

Marx, Anthony W. (1998), *Making Race and Nation: A Comparison of the United States, South Africa, and Brazil*, Cambridge: Cambridge University.

Marx, Anthony W. (2003), *Faith in Nation: Exclusionary Origins of Nationalism*, Oxford: Oxford University.

Masilela, Ntongela (1993), "The Los Angeles school of black filmmakers," in Manthia Diawara (ed.), *Black American Cinema*, New York: Routledge, pp. 107–17.

Mayall, David (1992), "British Gypsies and the state," *History Today* 42:6, p. 6.

Mbembe, Achille (2000), *De la Postcolonie, essai sur l'imagination politique dans l'Afrique contemporaine*, Paris: Karthala.

Mbembe, Achille (2003), "Necropolitics," trans. Libby Meintjes, *Public Culture* 15:1, pp. 11–40.

Medovoi, Leerom (1998), "Theorizing historicity, or the many meanings of *Blacula*," *Screen* 39:1, pp. 1–21.

Mehta, Uday Singh (1999), *Liberalism and Empire: A Study of Nineteenth-century British Liberal Thought*, Chicago: University of Chicago.

Melton, J. Gordon (1997), *Videohound's Vampire on Video*, Detroit: Visible Ink.

Melnyk, George (2004), *One Hundred Years of Canadian Cinema*, Toronto: University of Toronto.

Memmi, Albert (1957), *Portrait du colonisé, précédé par Portrait du colonisateur*, Paris: Buchet/Chastel.

Mendieta, Eduardo (2009), "From imperial to dialogical cosmopolitanism," *Ethics and Global Politics* 2:3, pp. 241–58.

Metz, Christian (1985), "Photography as fetish," *October* 34, pp. 81–90.
Meyer, Stephanie (2008), *Breaking Dawn*, New York: Little, Brown and Company.
Mignolo, Walter (2000), "The many faces of Cosmo-polis: Border thinking and critical cosmopolitanism," *Public Culture* 12:3, pp. 721–48.
Mignolo, Walter [2000] (2012), *Local Histories/Global Designs: Coloniality, Subaltern Knowledge, and Border Thinking*, new edn, Princeton: Princeton University.
Miller, Toby, Nitin Govil, John McMurria, and Richard Maxwell (2005), *Global Hollywood 2*, London: British Film Institute.
Mitchell, Timothy (2011), *Carbon Democracy: Political Power in the Age of Oil*, London: Verso.
Mittell, Jason (2010), *Television and American Culture*, Oxford: Oxford University.
Modleski, Tania (1983), "The rhythms of reception: Daytime television and women's work," in E. Ann Kaplan (ed.), *Regarding Television: Critical Approaches–An Anthology*, Los Angeles: American Film Institute, pp. 67–75.
Mohanty, Chandra Talpade (2003), *Feminism without Borders: Decolonizing Theory, Practicing Solidarity*, Durham: Duke University.
Molina, Natalia (2006), *Fit To Be Citizens?: Public Health and Race in Los Angeles, 1879–1939*, Berkeley: University of California.
Morris, Peter (1994), *David Cronenberg: A Delicate Balance*, Toronto: ECW.
Mulvey, Laura (1989), *Visual and Other Pleasures*, Bloomington: Indiana University.
Murgoci, Agnes [1927] (1998), "The vampire in Roumania," in Alan Dundes (ed.), *The Vampire: A Casebook*, Madison: University of Wisconsin, pp. 47–56.
Musser, Charles (1991), "Ethnicity, role-playing, and American film comedy: From *Chinese Laundry Scene* to *Whoopee* (1894–1930)," in Lester D. Friedman (ed.), *Unspeakable Images: Ethnicity and the American Cinema*, Chicago: University of Illinois, pp. 39–81.
Mutch, Deborah (ed.) (2012), *The Modern Vampire and Human Identity*, New York: Palgrave Macmillan.
Naficy, Hamid (2001), *An Accented Cinema: Exilic and Diasporic Filmmaking*, Princeton: Princeton University.
Naficy, Hamid (2011), *A Social History of Iranian Cinema, Volume 2: The Industrializing Years, 1941–1978*, Durham: Duke University.
Negra, Diane (2001), *Off-white Hollywood: American Culture and Ethnic Female Stardom*, New York: Routledge.
Newman, Kim (1997), "Coppola's Dracula," in Stephen Jones (ed.), *The Mammoth Book of Dracula*, New York: Carroll and Graf.
Newman, Kim (2012), "Abraham Lincoln: Vampire Hunter," *Sight and Sound* 22:8, p. 52.
Nobles, Melissa (2000), *Shades of Citizenship: Race and the Census in Modern Politics*, Stanford: Stanford University.
Nornes, Abé Mark (2007), *Cinema Babel: Translating Global Cinema*, Minneapolis: University of Minnesota.
Nowell-Smith, Geoffrey (1998), "The beautiful and the bad: Notes on some actorial stereotypes," in Geoffrey Nowell-Smith and Steven Ricci (eds), *Hollywood and Europe: Economics, Culture, National Identity, 1945–1995*, London: British Film Institute, pp. 135–41.
Olson, Scott Robert (1999), *Hollywood Planet: Global Media and the Competitive Advantage of Narrative Transparency*, Mahwah: Lawrence Erlbaum.
Omi, Michael and Howard Winant (1994), *Racial Formation in the United States from the 1960s to the 1990s*, 2nd edn, New York: Routledge.
Ong, Aihwa (1999), *Flexible Citizenship: The Cultural Logics of Transnationality*, Durham: Duke University.

Ono, Kent A. (2000), "To be a vampire on *Buffy the Vampire Slayer*: Race and ('other') socially marginalizing positions on horror TV," in Elyce Rae Helford (ed.), *Fantasy Girls: Gender in the New Universe of Science Fiction and Fantasy Television*, Lanham: Rowman and Littlefield, pp. 163–86.

Paranaguá, Paul Antonio (ed.) (1995), *Mexican Cinema*, trans. Ana M. López, London: British Film Institute and Consejo Nacional Para la Cultura y las Artes de México.

Pease, Donald E. (2009), *The New American Exceptionalism*, Minneapolis: University of Minnesota.

Pendakur, Manjunath (1990), *Canadian Dreams and American Control: The Political Economy of the Canadian Film Industry*, Detroit: Wayne State University, pp. 58–9.

Pérez Turrent, Tomás (1995), "Crises and revolutions (1965–91)," trans. Ana M. López, in Paulo Antonio Paranaguá (ed.), *Mexican Cinema*, London: British Film Institute and Consejo Nacional Para la Cultura y las Artes de México, pp. 94–115.

Perry, Imani (2011), *More Beautiful and More Terrible: The Embrace and Transcendence of Racial Inequality in the United States*, New York: NYU.

Peterson, Michael, Laurie Beth Clark, and Lisa Nakamura (2009), "Vampire politics," *FlowTV* 11:03, <http://flowtv.org/2009/12/vampire-politicslisa-nakamura-laurie-beth-clark-michael-peterson/>.

Picart, Caroline Joan (Kay) and John Edgar Browning (eds) (2009), *Draculas, Vampires, and Other Undead Forms: Essays on Gender, Race, and Culture*, Lanham: Scarecrow.

Pinedo, Isabel Cristina (1997), *Recreational Terror: Women and the Pleasures of Horror Film Viewing*, Albany: SUNY.

Pirie, David (1972), *A Heritage of Horror: The English Gothic Cinema, 1946–1972*, London: Paul Hamlyn.

Pirie, David (1977), *The Vampire Cinema*. London: Paul Hamlyn.

Pollock, Sheldon, Homi K. Bhabha, Carol A. Breckenridge, and Dipesh Chakrabarty (2000), "Cosmopolitanisms," *Public Culture* 12:3, pp. 1–14.

Porter, Vincent (1983), "The context of creativity: Ealing and Hammer Films," in James Curran and Vincent Porter (eds), *British Cinema History*, London: Weidenfeld and Nicolson, pp. 179–207.

Portuges, Catherine (1997), "Hidden subjects, secret identities: Figuring Jews, Gypsies, and gender in 1990s cinema of eastern Europe," in Gisela Brinker-Gabler (ed.), *Writing New Identities: Gender, Nation, and Immigration in Contemporary Europe*, Minneapolis: University of Minnesota, pp. 196–215.

Prashad, Vijay (2002), *Everybody Was Kung Fu Fighting: Afro-Asian Connections and the Myth of Cultural Purity*, Boston: Beacon.

Pratt, Mary Louise (2008), *Imperial Eyes: Travel Writing and Transculturation*, 2nd edn, New York: Routledge.

Prawer, S. S. (1980), *Caligari's Children: The Film as Tale of Terror*, Oxford: Oxford University.

Puar, Jasbir K. (2007), *Terrorist Assemblages: Homonationalism in Queer Times*, Durham: Duke University.

Radway, Janice A., Kevin K. Gaines, Barry Shank, and Penny von Eschen (2009), "Introduction," in Janice A. Radway et al., *American Studies: An Anthology*, Malden: Wiley-Blackwell, pp. 1–6.

Rafael, Vicente L. (1988), *Contracting Colonialism: Translation and Christian Conversion in Tagalog Society under Early Spanish Rule*, Durham: Duke University.

Rafael, Vicente L. (2000), *White Love and Other Events in Filipino History*, Durham: Duke University.

Rana, Aziz (2010), *The Two Faces of American Freedom*, Cambridge, MA: Harvard University.
Rapping, Elayne (1992), *The Movie of the Week: Private Stories Public Events*, Minneapolis: University of Minnesota.
Reimers, David M. (2005), *Other Immigrants: The Global Origins of the American People*, New York: NYU.
Rhines, Jesse Algeron (1996), *Black Film/White Money*, New Brunswick, NJ: Rutgers University.
Rhodes, Gary D. (2003), "Introduction," in Gary D. Rhodes (ed.), *Horror at the Drive-in*, Jefferson: McFarland, pp. 1–6.
Rice, Anne (1976), *Interview with the Vampire*, New York: Alfred A. Knopf.
Rich, B. Ruby (2004), "To read or not to read: Subtitles, trailers, and monolingualism," in Atom Egoyan and Ian Balfour (eds), *Subtitles: On the Foreignness of Film*, Cambridge, MA: MIT/Alphabet City, pp. 153–69.
Rickels, Laurence A. (1995), *The Vampire Lectures*, Minneapolis: University of Minnesota.
Robbins, Bruce (1998), "Introduction Part I: Actually existing cosmopolitanism," in Pheng Cheah and Bruce Robbins (eds), *Cosmopolitics: Thinking and Feeling beyond the Nation*, Minneapolis: University of Minnesota, pp. 1–19.
Robinson, David (1996), *From Peep Show to Palace: The Birth of American Film*, New York: Columbia University.
Rocha, Glauber [1965] (1983), "An aesthetics of hunger," trans. Burnes Hollyman and Randal Johnson, in Michael Chanan (ed.), *25 Years of the New Latin American Cinema*, London: British Film Institute, pp. 13–14.
Roediger, David R. (2005), *Working Toward Whiteness: How America's Immigrants Became White*, New York: Basic.
Ross, Steven J. (1998), *Working-class Hollywood: Silent Film and the Shaping of Class in America*, Princeton: Princeton University.
Rothenberg, Paula S. (ed.) (2012), *White Privilege: Essential Readings on the Other Side of Racism*, 4th edn, New York: Worth.
Rushdie, Salman (1984), *Imaginary Homelands*, New York: Granta.
Sadr, Hamid Reza (2006), *Iranian Cinema: A Political History*, London: I. B. Tauris.
Said, Edward W. (1978), *Orientalism*, New York: Vintage.
Said, Edward W. (1993), *Culture and Imperialism*, New York: Vintage.
Said, Edward W. [1981] (1997), *Covering Islam: How the Media and the Experts Determine How We See the Rest of the World*, new edn, New York: Vintage.
Salyer, Monte (1993), "Educators and cultural diversity: A six-stage model of cultural versatility," *Education* 113:3, pp. 503–08.
Sanders, Clinton R. (1991), "The armadillos in Dracula's foyer," in Paul Loukides and Linda K. Fuller (eds), *Beyond the Stars: Stock Characters in American Popular Film*, Bowling Green: Bowling Green State University, pp. 143–69.
Sanjek, David (1994), "Twilight of the monsters: The English horror film 1968–1975," in Wheeler Winston Dixon (ed.), *Re-viewing British Cinema, 1900–1972: Essays and Interviews*, Albany: SUNY, pp. 195–209.
Sanjek, David (2000), "Same as it ever was: Innovation and exhaustion in the horror and science fiction films of the 1990s," in Wheeler Wilson Dixon (ed.), *Film Genre 2000: New Critical Essays*, Albany: SUNY, pp. 111–23.
Sarris, Andrew [1968] (1996), *The American Cinema: Directors and Directions 1929–1968*, New York: De Capo.
Sartre, Jean-Paul [1960] (1985), *Critique de la raison dialectique*, Paris: Librairie Gallimard.
Sassen, Saskia (1991), *The Global City: New York, London, Tokyo*, Princeton: Princeton University.

Schatz, Thomas (1981), *Hollywood Genres: Formulas, Filmmaking, and the Studio System*, New York: McGraw-Hill.
Schatz, Thomas [1988] (1996), *The Genius of the System: Hollywood Filmmaking in the Studio Era*, Minneapolis: University of Minnesota.
Schott, Gareth and Kristine Moffat (eds) (2011), *Fanpires: Audience Consumption of the Modern Vampire*, Washington, DC: New Academia.
Schumacher, Michael (1999), *Francis Ford Coppola: A Filmmaker's Life*, New York: Crown.
Scott, Allen J. (2004), "The other Hollywood: The organizational and geographic bases of television-program production," *Media, Culture and Society* 26:2, pp. 183–205.
Scott, Allen J. and Naomi E. Pope (2007), "Hollywood, Vancouver, and the world: Employment relocation and the emergence of satellite production centers in the motion-picture industry," *Environment and Planning A* 39, pp. 1364–81.
Senf, Carol A. (1982), "*Dracula*: Stoker's response to the new woman," *Victorian Studies* 26, pp. 33–49.
Sharrett, Christopher (1996), "The horror film in neoconservative culture," in Barry Keith Grant (ed.), *The Dread of Difference: Gender and the Horror Film*, Austin: University of Texas, pp. 253–76.
Shohat, Ella (2001), "Area studies, transnationalism, and the feminist production of knowledge," *Signs* 26:4, pp. 1269–72.
Shohat, Ella (2010), *Israeli Cinema: East/West and the Politics of Representation*, revised edn, London: I. B. Tauris.
Shohat, Ella and Robert Stam (1994), *Unthinking Eurocentrism: Multiculturalism and the Media*, New York: Routledge.
Silver, Alain and James Ursini (1975), *The Vampire Film*, South Brunswick: A. S. Barnes and Company.
Simmon, Scott (2009), "Movies, reform, and new women," in Charlie Keil and Ben Singer (eds), *American Cinema of the 1910s: Themes and Variations*, New Brunswick, NJ: Rutgers University, pp. 26–47.
Sinclair, Ian (1993), "Invasion of the blood," *Sight and Sound* 3:1, p. 15.
Sinclair, John (2003), "'The Hollywood of Latin America': Miami as regional center in television trade," *Television and New Media* 4:3, pp. 211–29.
Singer, Peter (1975), *Animal Liberation*, New York: HarperCollins.
Singh, Amritjit and Peter Schmidt (2000), "On the borders between US studies and postcolonial theory," in Amritjit Singh and Peter Schmidt (eds), *Postcolonial Theory and the United States: Race, Ethnicity, and Literature*, Jackson: University of Mississippi, pp. 3–71.
Siomopoulos, Anna M. (2006), "The birth of a black cinema: Race, reception, and Oscar Micheaux's *Within Our Gates*," *The Moving Image* 6:2, pp. 111–18.
Skal, David J. (1990), *Hollywood Gothic: The Tangled Web of* Dracula *from Novel to Stage to Screen*, New York: W. W. Norton.
Skal, David J. (1993), *The Monster Show: A Cultural History of Horror*, New York: Faber and Faber.
Smith, Jeff (2003), "Black faces, white voices: The politics of dubbing in *Carmen Jones*," *The Velvet Light Trap* 51, pp. 29–42.
Smith, Angela (2011), *Hideous Progeny: Disability, Eugenics, and Classic Horror Cinema*, New York: Columbia University.
Snead, James (1994), "Birth of a nation," in Colin MacCabe and Cornel West (eds), *White Screens, Black Images: Hollywood from the Dark Side*, New York: Routledge, pp. 37–46.
Solanas, Fernando and Octavio Getino [1968] (1983), "Towards a third cinema: Notes and experiences from the development of a cinema of liberation in the third world,"

trans. Julianne Burton and Michael Chanan, in Michael Chanan (ed.), *25 Years of the New Latin American Cinema*, London: British Film Institute, pp. 17–28.
Sollors, Werner (1986), *Beyond Ethnicity: Consent and Descent in American Literature and Culture*, Oxford: Oxford University.
Sontag, Susan (1973), *On Photography*, New York: Anchor/Doubleday.
Spadoni, Robert (2007), *Uncanny Bodies: The Coming of Sound Film and the Origins of the Horror Genre*, Berkeley: University of California.
Spigel, Lynn (2004), "Introduction," in Lynn Spigel and Jan Olsson (eds), *Television after TV: Essays on a Medium in Transition*, Durham: Duke University, pp. 1–40.
Spivak, Gatatri Chakravorty (1999), *A Critique of Postcolonial Reason: Toward a History of the Vanishing Point*, Cambridge, MA: Harvard University.
Stafford, Roy (2014), *The Global Film Book*, New York: Routledge.
Stam, Robert (2000), *Film Theory: An Introduction*, Malden: Blackwell.
Stam, Robert and Ella Shohat (2012), *Race in Translation: Culture Wars around the Postcolonial Atlantic*, New York: NYU.
Stephanou, Aspasia (2014), *Reading Vampire Gothic through Blood: Bloodlines*, New York: Palgrave Macmillan.
Strangelove, Michael (2015), *Post-TV: Piracy, Cord-Cutting, and the Future of Television*, Toronto: University of Toronto.
Stratton, Jon (2005), "Buffy the Vampire Slayer: What being Jewish has to do with it," *Television and New Media* 6:2, pp. 176–99.
Street, Sarah (1997), *British National Cinema*, New York: Routledge.
Stoker, Bram [1987] (1997), *Dracula: A Norton Critical Edition*, ed. Nina Auerbach and David J. Skal, New York: W. W. Norton.
Stromgren, Dick (1990), "The Chinese syndrome: The evolving image of Chinese and Chinese-Americans in Hollywood films," in Paul Loukides and Linda K. Fuller (eds), *Beyond the Stars: Stock Characters in American Popular Film*, Bowling Green: Bowling Green State University, pp. 61–77.
Stuart, Roxana (1994), *Stage Blood: Vampires of the Nineteenth-century Stage*, Bowling Green: Bowling Green State University.
Sullivan, Shannon (2014), *Good White People: The Problem with Middle-class White Anti-racism*, Albany: SUNY.
Sunder Rajan, Rajeswari (1993), *Real and Imagined Women: Gender, Culture and Postcolonialism*, London: Routledge.
Syder, Andrew and Dolores Tierney (2005), "Importation/Mexploitation, or, How a crime-fighting, vampire-slaying Mexican wrestler almost found himself in an Italian sword-and-sandals epic," in Steven Jay Schneider and Tony Williams (eds), *Horror International*, Detroit: Wayne State University, pp. 33–55.
Teo, Stephen (2000), "Local and global identity: Whither Hong Kong cinema?," *Senses of Cinema*, <www.senseofcinema.com/contents/00/7/hongkong.html>.
Teo, Stephen (2015), *Chinese Martial Arts Cinema: The Wuxia Tradition*, Edinburgh: Edinburgh University.
Tinic, Serra (2006), "Global vistas and local reflections: Negotiating place and identity in Vancouver television," *Television and New Media* 7:2, pp. 154–83.
Todorova, Maria (1997), *Imagining the Balkans*, Oxford: Oxford University.
Tombs, Pete (1996), "The Philippines," in Kim Newman (ed.), *The BFI Companion to Horror*, London: Cassell, p. 245.
Tombs, Pete (1998), *Mondo Macabro: Weird and Wonderful Cinema from Around the World*, New York: St. Martin's/Griffin.
Toplin, Robert Brent (ed.) (1993), *Hollywood as Mirror: Changing Views of Outsiders as Enemies in American Movies*, Westport: Greenwood.

Trinh, T. Minh-ha (1992), *Framer Framed*, New York: Routledge.
Turner, Frederick Jackson (1920), *The Frontier in American History*, New York: Henry Holt.
Twitchell, James B. (1985), *Dreadful Pleasures: An Anatomy of Modern Horror*, Oxford: Oxford University.
Valente, Joseph (2002), *Dracula's Crypt: Bram Stoker, Irishness, and the Question of Blood*, Urbana: University of Illinois.
Van Deburg, William L. (1993), "A popular culture prophecy: Black American slavery in film," in Robert Brent Toplin (ed.), *Hollywood as Mirror: Changing Views of Outsiders as Enemies in American Movies*, Westport: Greenwood, pp. 19–40.
Vasey, Ruth (1997), *The World According to Hollywood, 1918–1939*, Madison: University of Wisconsin.
Vishwanathan, Gauri [1990] (2015), *Masks of Conquest: Literary Study and British Rule in India*, New York: Columbia University.
Wall, Brian and Michael Zyrd (2001), "Vampire dialectics: Knowledge, institutions and labour," in Roz Kaveney (ed.), *Reading the Vampire Slayer: An Unofficial Critical Companion to Buffy and Angel*, London: Tauris Parke, pp. 53–77.
Weil, Kari (2012), *Thinking Animals: Why Animal Studies Now?*, New York: Columbia University.
Weinstock, Jeffrey (2012), *The Vampire Film*, London: Wallflower.
White, Luise (2000), *Speaking with Vampires: Rumor and History in Colonial Africa*, Berkeley: University of California.
Williams, Raymond (2003), *Television: Technology and Cultural Form (1974)*, 3rd edn, New York: Routledge.
Williamson, Milly (2005), *The Lure of the Vampire: Gender, Fiction and Fandom from Bram Stoker to Buffy*, London: Wallflower.
Willis, Sharon (1997), *High Contrast: Race and Gender in Contemporary Hollywood Film*, Durham: Duke University.
Wilson, Katharina [1985] (1998), "The history of the word vampire," in Alan Dundes (ed.), *The Vampire: A Casebook*, Madison: University of Wisconsin, pp. 3–34.
Wilson, Natalie (2011), "It's a wolf thing: The Quileute werewolf/shape-shifter hybrid as noble savage," in Maggie Parke and Natalie Wilson (eds), *Theorizing Twilight: Critical Essays on What's at Stake in a Post-vampire World*, Jefferson: McFarland, pp. 194–208.
Wolf, Leonard (1975), *The Annotated Dracula*, New York: Clarkson N. Potter.
Wolf, Cary (2013), *Before the Law: Humans and Other Animals in a Biopolitical Frame*, Chicago: University of Chicago.
Wong, Eugene Franklin (1978), *On Visual Media Racism: Asians in American Motion Pictures*, New York: Arno.
Wood, David (2008), "With foreign eyes: English-language criticism on Latin American film," *Journal of Latin American Cultural Studies* 17:2, pp. 245–59.
Wyatt, Justin (1994), *High Concept: Movies and Marketing in Hollywood*, Austin: University of Texas.
Young, Robert J. C. (1995), *Colonial Desire: Hybridity in Theory, Culture, and Race*, London: Taylor and Francis.
Young, Lola (1996), *Fear of the Dark: "Race", Gender and Sexuality in the Cinema*, New York: Routledge.
Young, Robert J. C. [1991] (2004), *White Mythologies: Writing History and the West*, New York: Routledge.
Young, Elizabeth (2008a), *Black Frankenstein: The Making of an American Metaphor*, New York: NYU.

Young, Robert J. C. (2008b), *The Idea of English Ethnicity*, Chichester: Wiley-Blackwell.
Young, Robert J. C. (2015), *Empire, Colony, Postcolony*, Chichester: Wiley-Blackwell.
Zanger, Jules (1997), "Metaphor to metonymy: The vampire next door," in Joan Gordon and Veronica Hollinger (eds), *Blood Read: The Vampire as Metaphor in Contemporary Culture*, Philadelphia: University of Pennsylvania, pp. 17–26.
Zimmermann, Patricia R. (2000), *States of Emergency: Documentaries, Wars, Democracies*, Minneapolis: University of Minnesota.
Zinn, Howard (2005), *A People's History of the United States: 1942–Present* [1980], 20th-anniversary edn, New York: HarperCollins.

INDEX

Note: *italic* signifies figures

"100 percent Americans," 44n13
1001 Nights/'Alf layla wa-layla aka *Arabian Nights* (stories), 67n15, 171
1492: Conquest of Paradise (film, 1992), 178
20th Century Fox (studio), 3, 86, 188, 205
30 Days of Night (film, 2007), 177–8, 222
30 Days of Night: Blood Trails (comic-book miniseries, 2002), 222
30 Days of Night: Blood Trails (series, 2007), 222
30 Days of Night: Dark Days (film, 2010), 178
30 Days of Night: Dust to Dust (series, 2008), 222–3
4chan, 229
9/11, 1, 38, 182, 217

Abbott, Bud, 93
Abbott, Stacey, 96
ABC (network), 3, 193, 195, 198, 203, 215
Abel, Richard, 52, 57
Abraham Lincoln: Vampire Hunter (film, 2012), 19, 229, 230, *231*, 232, 234–7
Abraham Lincoln: Vampire Hunter (novel, 2010), 230, 234–7
Abu-Lughod, Lila, 38
Adamson, Al, *129*
Addams Family (series, 1964–6), 2, 197
Addiction, The (film, 1995), 18, 21, 159–61, 163
Adventure Entertainment (videogame developer), 226
advertising, 163, 196, 198–9, 223

affect, 2, 33, 66
Affirmative Action, 136, 207, 233; see also Executive Order 10925
Africa or African, 26, 31, 40, 44n15, 62, 66, 84, 90, 92, 96, 97, 106, 107, 118, 121, 134–5, 148, 149, 153, 160, 183, 185, 213, 220, 228n8, 235, 237
African City, An (series, 2014–present), 228n8
Agricultural Adjustment Act (1933–6), 59
Ahmadinejad, Mahmoud, 21
AL 288–1 (Lucy), 206
"All Lives Matter" (racist backlash to "Black Lives Matter"), 71
Alfred Hitchcock Presents (series, 1955–62), 196
Alger, Horatio, 138
Alhurra (satellite channel), 199
aliens, 47, 50, 52–3, 58–9, 66, 70, 75–6, 79, 81, 119, 143, 166
All Quiet on the Western Front (film, 1930), 68
Alloula, Mallek, 172
alternative modernities, 115, 119, 125
alternative-reality games (ARGs), 2, 194, 221, 223
Altman, Rick, 49, 116–17
Álvarez Rubio, Pablo, 84, 87
Amazon Instant Video, 198
America Broadcasting Corporation *see* ABC
American Dream, 32, 37, 54, 57, 58, 92, 155, 233
American Horror Story (series, 2011–present), 196
American in the Making, An (film, 1913), 56

INDEX

American International Pictures (AIP), 102, 130, 134, 145
American Romance, An (film, 1944), 60, 232
American Studies, 11
American War *see* Vietnam War
Amicus (production company), 106
Amirpour, Ana Lily, 1, 6, 17, 21–4, 31, 36–9, 41–2, 44n19, 50
amnesia
 historical, 8, 41, 142
 willful, 18, 90, 141
 see also memory
And God Created Woman/Et dieu . . . créa la femme (film, 1956), 103
"And Still I Rise" (poem, 1978), 144
Anderson, Benedict, 193
Anderson, Carol, 233
Andy Warhol's Dracula see *Blood for Dracula/Andy Warhol's Dracula*
Angel (series, 1999–2004), 205, 207–9
Angelou, Maya, 144
Anger, Kenneth, 229
Animal Studies, 168
animal testing, 210
animalization, 22, 26, 28–9, 53, 72, 84, 87, 101, 109, 128, 153, 168–9, 172, 177, 187, 232, 234
Anthropocene, 37
anthropocentrism, 7, 16, 164, 166, 168, 170, 182, 184, 229, 238
Anti-Gypsy Act (1530), 43n8
anti-Semitism, 18, 72, 88, 96, 99n10, 112, 206, 208, 218, 232
anticolonialism, 20n8, 27, 31, 41, 104, 186, 187; *see also* colonialism and colonization
Anyiwo, U. Melissa, 20n2
Anzaldúa, Gloria, 12
Apache (indigenous nation), 220
Apocalypse Now (film, 1979), 33, 170
Appadurai, Arjun, 38
Appiah, Kwame Anthony, 105
Arata, Stephen, 25
Argo (film, 2012), 38
armadillos, 18, 47, 76, 77, 93, 101
Arrival of Emigrants, Ellis Island (film, 1906), 51
"Aryan race," 14, 112
Ashley, Elizabeth, 158
Ashley, John, 123, 124
Ashkenazim or Ashkenazi, 69, 77, 96, 208
Aswang, Ang (film, 1932), 124
Atatürk, Mustafa Kemal, 38
audiences, 60, 68, 94, 102, 103, 107, 114, 142, 196–8
 engagement, 163, 198, 222–3, 226
 expectations, 68, 119, 170
Auerbach, Nina, 6, 39, 76, 100, 158, 225, 232
Australia or Australian, 9, 13, 132n1, 136, 157, 163, 189, 192n10, 195, 197, 200
Australian Broadcast Corporation (ABC), 195
Austria-Hungary Empire (1867–1914), 59, 77, 85
authorized streaming services, 10
automated dialogue replacement (ADR), 114–16

Ávalos, Enrique Tovar, 85
Aztecs (1519–21), 119, 128, 175, *175*, 178

/b/ (image board), 229–30
Badham, John, 143
Balderston, John L., 30, 76
Balkans, 27, 28, 32, 43n9, 172
Bara, Theda (Theodosia Goodman), 24, 43n4, 64
Barakula (meme), 232–4, 237
Barakula: The Musical (film, 2008), 237
Barthes, Roland, 74
Barthlemass, Richard, 63, 83
Bassett, Angela, 148
Báthory, Elizabeth, 14, 225
Batman Fights Dracula (film, 1967), 133n16
bats, 46, 72, 76, 90, 92–5, 120, 123, 125, 140, 172, 175, 185, 205, 232
Battlestar Galactica (series, 2004–9), 200
Baudelaire, Charles, 24
Bava, Mario, 121
Bazin, André, 49, 80, 174
Beast of the Yellow Night (film, 1971), 124
Behdad, Ali, 142
Bei Ru (band), 35
Being Human (series, 2008–13), 202
Being Human (series, 2011–14), 202
Bell Trade Act (1946), 133n22
Benshoff, Harry, 70, 135, 140
Berenstein, Rhonda, 70
Berg, Charles Ramírez, 173
Bergfelder, Tim, 106
Bergland, Renée, 139
Berlant, Lauren, 213
Berlin Conference (1884–5), 26
Bernard, James, 100
Bernardi, Daniel, 73
Betz, Mark, 131
Beveridge, Albert J., 124
Bhabha, Homi K., 115
BIC Corporation, 239n7
Billy the Kid vs. Dracula (film, 1965), 96, 97–8
Biograph (studio), 62, 200
Birth of a Nation, The (film, 1915), 71, 84, 152, 226
BitTorrent, 198, 230
Black Codes, 156
Black Girl/La Noire de . . . (film, 1965), 234
Black Lives Matter (movement), 71, 232
Black Panther Party, 135, 239n7
blackface, 126, 145, *146*, 207, 210
Blacula (film, 1972), 2, 18, 134–6, 145–8, 170, 208
Blade franchise, 19, 163, 179–80, 182–4, 227
 Blade (film, 1998), 182
 Blade II (film, 2002), 182–3, 217
 Blade: House of Chthon (film, 2006), 184
 Blade: The Series (series, 2006), 184
 Blade: Trinity (film, 2004), 183
Blade Runner (film, 1982), 189
Blair Witch Project, The (film, 1999), 221
blaxploitation, 2, 135, 144–8, 180
blood
 blood and soil (*Blut und Boden*), 29
 blood cult, 128

blood (*cont.*)
  blood drinking, 3, 23, 29, 113–14, 154, 168, 179, 185, 201
  blood farming, 168, 183, 190, 238
  blood libel, 43n7
  blood-quantum theory, 23, 30, 71, 145, 212
  blood transfusion, 95, 218
  bloodletting, 72, 75
  "bloodthirsty Indian" or "bloodthirsty savage," 96, 152, 181, 186
  and Christianity, 26
  discourses of blood, bodies, and borders, 17, 21–30, 40, 69, 96, 238
  and exterminations, 184–6
  and genetic engineering, 186–91
  and imperialism, 30, 124
  "Indian blood," 44n15, 62, 88, 97, 173
  jus sanguinas (right of blood), 26
  mixed blood, 19, 23, 28–9, 69, 78, 87, 97, 145, *146*, 155–8, 166, 183–4
  mixed-blood children, 29, 70, 78
  and modernity, 43–4n11
  and nationalism/citizenship, 14, 23, 28, 44n15, 65, 71, 81, 84, 107
  "Negro blood" or "black blood," 97, 135–7, 145, *146*, 212, 234
  one-drop rule, 30, 155
  "pure bloodlines," 97, 117, 182, 185, 208, 211–13
  and race/racism, 31, 92, 236
  and sexuality, 29
  synthetic blood, 166, 190, 212
  vampire blood, 129, 210, 212, 218, 234
  virgin blood, 14, 113–14, 225
Blood Creek (film, 2008), 228n7
Blood Drinkers, The aka *Kulay dugo ang gabi/Blood is the Color of Night* (film, 1966/1971), 125–6
Blood for Dracula/Andy Warhol's Dracula (film, 1974), 18, 112–14, 217
Blood Thirst/The Horror from Beyond (film, 1971), 127
Blood Ties (film, 1991), 150
Blood Ties (series, 2006), 2002
BloodRayne franchise, 195, 226
  BloodRayne (film, 2005), 195, 226
  BloodRayne (videogame, 2002), 195, 226
  BloodRayne: Deliverance (film, 2007), 195
  BloodRayne: The Third Reich (film, 2011), 195
Bloody Vampire, The/Vampiro sangriento, El (film, 1962), 117
bodies
  borders on the body, 66, 70, 137
  and citizenship/territory, 10, 23, 26, 28, 70, 72, 80–1, 124, 139
  and colonialism/empire, 120–2, 125, 127–8, 135, 187, 190
  discourses of blood, bodies, and borders, 17, 21–30, 40, 69, 96, 238
  female bodies, 6, 10, 26, 65, 69, 71–2, 80–1, 82, *83*, 101, 127, 153, 187, 190, 205
  and immigration, 23, 28–9, 47, 54–6, 62, 75, 78, 137
  national body, 28
  and political power, 43–4n11
  and possession, 210–11
  and race, 52, 108, 152, 155, 184, 207, 209
  and reincarnation, 135, 170, 216
  scarred bodies, 80–5, 205, 223
  and sexuality, 83, 101, 112–13, 120–2, 205
  taxonomies of, 25
  of vampires, 28–9, 68, 92, 108, 125, 157, 169, 190, 217–19
  and voice, 122
Boer War (1880–1), 220
Bogle, Donald, 144
Bohemia or Bohemian, 85, 111, 176
Bold and the Beautiful, The (series, 1987–present), 198
Boll, Uwe, 195, 226
Bollywood, 2, 20n1
bomba films (Philippine export genre), 123
Bonnie and Clyde (film, 1967), 137
Book of the Dead, 219
borders
  border crossing, 25, 28, 30, 42, 47–8, 75, 78, 102, 105, 108, 116, 198
  "border hoppers" (racist term), 12, 19, 182
  Border Patrol, 30, 70, 174, 180
  border regulation, 15, 22, 70, 77, 120, 174, 182, 190
  borderlands/la frontera, 12, 27, 121, 159, 166–7, 173–9, 237
  borders on the body, 66, 70, 137
  discourses of blood, bodies, and borders, 17, 21–30, 40, 69, 96, 238
  and empire, 107–9, 130
  post-NAFTA borderlands, 122, 173–9, 181, 195
  and race, 52, 95, 102, 107–8, 121, 152, 155, 184, 207, 209
  transborder migration, 116, 120–2, 159, 164, 166–7, 176
  see also immigration
Boreanaz, David, 206
Bracero Program (1942–64), 116, 121, 218
braceros (contract laborers from México), 102, 130, 131, 219
Bram Stoker's Dracula (film, 1992), 2, 17, 19, 31–4, 40, 42, 165, 169, 170–3, 211, 225, 229
Bram Stoker's Dracula (game, 1993), 225
Brazil or Brazilian, 22, 191n7, 215, 216
Brazil (film, 1985), 189
Breakin' (film, 1984), 142
Breaking Dawn (novel, 2008), 191–2n7
Breaking Dawn, Part 1 (film, 2011), 169
Breaking Dawn, Part 2 (film, 2012), 168, 186
Breed, The (film, 2001), 189
Bretton Woods Agreement (1944), 40
Bride of Frankenstein (film, 1935), 220
Brides of Dracula, The (film, 1960), 112
Bring Me the Vampire/Échenme al vampiro (film, 1961), 117
British Broadcasting Corporation (BBC), 195, 202
Broken Blossoms (film, 1919), 17, 63–4
Brooklyn, 148, 157, 217
Brooks, Mehcad, 214

Brooks, Mel, 171
Brooks, Peter, 61
Brown, Chris, 176
"brown peril" (racist term), 88
Brown, Wendy, 236
brownface, 63, 128, 207
Browning, Tod, 4, 68, 77, 83, 86, 93
Bud Abbott and Lou Costello Meet Frankenstein (film, 1949), 2, 93
Buffy the Vampire Slayer (film, 1992), 7, 15
Buffy the Vampire Slayer (series, 1997–2003), 2, 7, 15, 19, 164, 179–84, 195, 205–7, 228n5, 230
Buffy the Vampire Slayer (videogame, 1992), 227
Buffy the Vampire Slayer (videogame, 2000), 227
Buffy the Vampire Slayer, Season 8 Motion Comic (film, 2011), 191n6
Buffy the Vampire Slayer: The Quest for Oz, (videogame, 2004), 227
bullying, 205
Burke, Billy, 167
Burke, Thomas, 63
Burnett, Charles, 144
Burton, Sir Richard, 43n7, 67n15, 171, 172
Burton, Tim, 140
Bush, George H. W., 6
Bush, George W., 14, 21, 229, 232, 239n6
Bush, Laura, 232, 234
Bushell, Anthony, 107
Butler, David, 79
Butler, Gerard 162n6
Butler, Graham, 220
Butler, Jimmy, 58
Butler, Judith, 23
Butler, Octavia, 31, 184

Cabinet of Dr. Caligari, The/Das Kabinett des Dr. Caligari (film, 1919), 157
Cable Act of 1922, 82
Cabral, Amilcar, 145
Cage, Nicholas, 157, 162n10
Call to Duty: Modern Warfare 3 (videogame, 2011), 226
Cambodia and Cambodian, 161, 177
camp, 11, 134, 202, 205, 221
Camp, Anna, 212
Campbell, Billy, 172
Canada or Canadian, 3, 9, 10, 18, 30, 70, 77, 99n4, 136, 163, 178, 186, 189, 194–6, 199–202, 215, 223–4, 227n1, 236
Canadian Broadcasting Corporation (CBC), 195, 200, 202
Cannes Film Festival, 161n3
Canadian Film Development Corporation (CFDC), 201
Canadian Radio-television and Telecommunications Commission (CRTC), 199
Capital Cost Allowance (CCA), 201
Captain Kronos, Vampire Hunter (film, 1972)
Carmen Jones (film, 1954), 117
Carmilla (film, 1990), 194, 201, 204–5
Carmilla (novella, 1871–2), 24, 34, 201

Carmilla (series, 2014–present), 19, 223–5
Carpenter, Charisma, 181, 207
Carpenter, John, 176, *177*
Carpenters, The (band), 140
Carpetbaggers, 152
Carradine, John, 94, 97, 129, 133n20
caste systems, 12, 97, 117, 124, 218
 criollo (colonial Spanish caste), 97
 mestizo (colonial Spanish caste), 44n15, 97, 124, 125, 155
 mulato (colonial Spanish caste), 62, 71, 74, 90, 97, 155–6
 peninsular (colonial Spanish caste), 88, 97, 117
Castronovo, Russ, 139
Cat People (film, 1942), 95
Catholicism, 12, 25, 43n6, 54–5, 113, 114, 125, 155, 165, 169, 176, 186, 216
CBC *see* Canadian Broadcasting Corporation (CBC)
CBS (network), 3, 193, 197, 199, 207
Ceaușescu, Nicolae, 232
cetaceans (bottlenose dolphins, orcas), 239n9
CFDC *see* Canadian Film Development Corporation (CFDC)
Chagall, Marc, 112
Chaney, Lon, Jr., 71, 91, 93, 172
Chaplin, Charlie, 50, 55, 56, 60, 91, 174
Chatterjee, Partha, 27
Chaudhuri, Shohini, 40
Cheat, The (film, 1915), 17, 63, 66, 69, 78, 81–2, *82*
checkpoint, 217
Cheney, Dick, 14
Cherniavsky, Eva, 73
Cherokee (indigenous nation), 52, 70
Chevalier, Maurice, 85
Child of the Ghetto, A (film, 1910)
Children of the Night (film, 1991), 162n7
China or Chinese, 43n8, 44n13, 47, 61, 63, 83, 98, 104, 110–11, 132n4, 143, 172, 189, 202, 203–4
"China doll" (racist term), 203
"Chink and the Girl, The" (story, 1917), 63
Chinatown, 63, 78, 203–4
Chinese Connection, The/Jing wu men (film, 1972), 104
Chinese Exclusion Act, (1882), 64
Chion, Michel, 36, 114
Christianity, 25–8, 31, 43n7, 73, 110, 124, 126, 156, 165–70, 184–5, 189–91
 black, 147
 Catholicism, 12, 25, 43n6, 54–5, 113, 114, 125, 155, 169, 176, 186, 216
 Crusades, 33, 34, 169, 170–3
 and Manifest destiny, 52
 missionaries, 191n1
 Mormonism, 52, 168, 186–7, 191n1
 Orthodox, 53–5
 Protestantism, 25, 54, 79
 and race, 61
 saints, 126, 171, 178
 secular, 73, 108, 159
 "white Christians," 80, 165, 167
Cinecittà (studio), 112

Cinematográfico (studio), 95, 117, 119, 132n3
cisgender, 7, 36, 141, 164
citizenship
   abridged or deferred, 28, 30, 146, 169
   birthright, 44n15, 81, 164
   and blackness, 143–9
   and blood, 14, 23, 28, 44n15, 65, 71, 81, 84, 107
   and bodies, 10, 23, 26, 28, 70, 72, 80–1, 124, 139
   and gender, 47, 54, 57, 59
   native or native-born, 22, 29, 43n1, 54, 55, 58, 60, 61, 80, 81, 86, 139, 164, 168, 233
   naturalized, 54, 81
City, The (film, 1939), 60
Civil Rights Act (1964), 92, 136–7, 239n8
Civil War (1861–5), 4, 12, 97, 209, 210
civilization, 15, 27, 32, 121, 148, 165, 173, 183, 189, 205
Clarens, Carlos, 107
class
   and assimilation, 90, 91
   and audiences, 119, 123, 131
   and citizenship, 10, 23
   and colonialism, 122–3, 125
   and immigration, 50, 54–7, 60, 90–1, 93, 137, 233
   and language/accents, 90, 91, 115
   and market stereotypes, 42
   middle class, 7, 73, 81, 119, 123, 125, 131, 146, 148, 151, 152, 169, 206, 208
   mobility, 107, 110, 172
   and politics, 6, 233
   and race, 12, 71, 92–3, 146, 148, 150
   ruling class, 110, 111
   and segregation, 112, 165
   and sexuality, 122–3
   and whiteness, 73, 81, 151, 152
   working class, 50, 55–6, 60, 81, 91, 93, 115, 119, 122–3, 150, 212, 233
Cliffhangers: Curse of Dracula (film, 1979), 150
Clifford, James, 105
Clinton, Bill, 229, 232
Clinton, Hillary, 14, 232
Clooney, George, 174
Coalition of the Willing, 34, 173
Cocteau, Jean, 33, 172
coffins, 23–4, 27, 29, 68, 75, 78, 87, 107, 112, 120, 134, 217–18
Colbert, Claudette, 74
Coleridge, Samuel Taylor, 24
Colombia, 215, 216
Colonial Harem, The (book, 1986), 172
colonial plantations, 88, 91, 92, 126, 156, 184, 204, 213, 235
colonialism and colonization
   anticolonialism, 20n8, 27, 31, 41, 104, 186, 187
   blind spots to, 160
   and bodies, 120–2, 125, 127–8, 135, 187, 190
   decolonization, 105, 166
   European colonization, 25–6, 176, 236
   and immigration, 41, 109, 134

   and indigenous populations, 166, 168–9, 181, 187, 220
   and interactive media, 226
   mimicry, 115
   and myth of US independence, 20n8
   and neoliberalism, 176, 178
   and Philippine vampire films, 123, 125, 131
   and race, 14, 28, 31, 124–6, 128–9, 135, 147, 181, 234
   reverse colonialism, 25
   and slavery, 12, 99n7, 183–4, 213, 235
   Spanish colonization, 97, 105, 117–18, 126, 128, 178
   stereotypes of, 64
   US colonization, 12, 26, 31, 33, 104, 142, 156, 173, 184, 187, 213, 235
   and violence, 52
   and Westerns, 80, 187
   and whiteness, 74, 120, 129, 165
   see also empire and imperialism; postcolonialism
color-blindness (racism), 71, 136, 138, 141, 162n9, 191, 237
Columbia Broadcasting System *see* CBS
Columbia-Warner (Hollywood subsidiary), 110
Columbus on Trial (film, 1992), 178
Columbus, Christopher, 19, 178, 210
Comaneci, Nadia, 150
Comcast (cable provider), 195, 198
comics, 10, 180, 191n6, 222, 226
communism, 77, 113, 134, 149–50, 160, 170
Communist Manifesto (1848), 113
Communist Revolution, 113
Condemned to Live (film, 1935), 92
Confederacy and Confederates, 94, 97, 203, 209, 211, 236
Conner, Bruce, 229
consensus, 8, 16, 196
consumerism, 6, 18, 64, 93, 102, 106, 113, 140–2, 175, *175*, 195, 221
contamination, 5, 23, 42, 44n15, 69, 76, 88, 124, 137, 139, 164, 180, 188, 212
continuity errors, 11, 47
Cook, Ethyle, 57
Cook, Pam, 106
Cooper, Alice, 140
Cooper, Dominic, 236
Coppola, Francis Ford, 17, 31–4, 41–2, 170–1, 173, 225
copyright, 10, 45, 229–31
Corman, Roger, 123
Cornell, Joseph, 229
corporate conglomerations, 9
corporate mergers, 10
corporate personhood, 44n14, 191
corporate terrorism, 188
corporate welfare, 57
Cortés, Carlos, 62, 67n12
Cortés, Hernán, 178
Cosby Show, The (series, 1984–92), 148
cosmopolitanism, 18, 25, 28, 45, 101–2, 104–15, 121, 131, 136

INDEX

Costello, Lou, 2, 93
Cotton Comes to Harlem (film, 1970), 144
Count, The (videogame, 1981), 226
Count Chocula (breakfast cereal), 6
Count Dracula and His Vampire Bride see Satanic Rites of Dracula, The/Count Dracula and His Vampire Bride (film, 1973)
Countess Dracula (film, 1971), 225
Courtney, Chuck, 98
Courtney, Susan, 62
Cow, The/Gaav (film, 1969), 37
cowboys, 33, 48, 80, 93, 96, 98; see also Westerns (genre)
Cowboys and Aliens (film, 2011), 231
Cowboys & Vampires (film, 2010), 231
Craft, Christopher, 24–5
Craven, Frank, 92
Craven, Wes, 148
Creature Feature (series, 1973–87), 197
Creatures of Evil Drinkers aka *Ibulong mo sa hangin/Whisper to the Wind* (film, 1966/1971), 125, *127*
Crenshaw, Kimberlé, 12
criminalization, 23–4, 28, 40, 82, 102, 116, 144, 150, 155–6, 164, 173–4, 185
criollo (colonial Spanish caste), 97
Cronenberg, David, 201
Cronos/La invención de Cronos (film, 1992), 19, 178, 179, 217, 218
CRTC see Canadian Radio-television and Telecommunications Commission (CRTC)
crucifixes, 24, 27, 80, 96, 108, 112, 117, 126, 154, 165, 206
Cruise, Tom, 156
Cuba or Cuban, 85, 104, 124, 182
Cubitt, Sean, 130
Curse of Frankenstein, The (film, 1957), 106
Curse of the Undead/Mark of the West (film, 1959), 96
Curtis, Dan, 140, 170
Cushing, Peter, 7, 100, 104, 110–12, 174
CW (cable network), 3, 197, 209, 210, 215
CWTV.com, 223
Czech Republic, 9, 163, 165, 219
Czechoslovakia, 59

Daesh (aka ISIS or ISIL), 167
Dafoe, Willem, 190
Dallas (series, 1978–91), 198, 221
Dallesandro, Joe, 113
Dance of the Vampires see Fearless Vampire Killers, or Pardon Me, Your Teeth Are in My Neck, The /Dance of the Vampires (film, 1967)
Dark Shadows (film, 2012), 140
Dark Shadows (series, 1966–71), 2, 140, 197
Dark Shadows (series, 1991), 140
Darker Truth, A (series, 2009), 223
Darling Kong Aswang, Ang (film, 2009), 199
Darwin, Charles, 25, 29, 156
Dash, Julie, 117
Davis, Bette, 91

Davis, Charles Michael, 209
Davis, Ossie, 144
Davis, Rainie, 223
Dawes Commission (1893), 30
Daybreakers (film, 2009), 165, 189–90
daywalkers, 179–80
de la Mora, Sergio, 122
de Leon, Bert, 199
de Leon, Gerardo, 124–5, *127*
de Sica, Vittorio, 113
Dean, James, 121
Deane, Hamilton, 30, 76
Death Valley (series, 2011), 195
Decherney, Peter, 199
defense of territory, 10
degeneration, 29–30, 53, 76, 82, 95, 139, 157, 186, 191
del Río, Dolores, 85
del Toro, Guillermo, 178, 182, 201, 217
Delany, Samuel, 184
DeMille, Cecil B., 17, 63, 82
democracy, 14, 17–19, 30, 34, 39, 98, 141, 160, 170, 173, 237–8
Democratic Party, 233, 235, 236, 239n8
Denzin, Norman, 143
Department of Homeland Security (DHS), 186
Deportation Act (1929), 132n14
deregulation, 10, 19, 193, 196, 197
Desperate Housewives (series, 2004–12), 198
detention center, 8, 182, 218
Diawara, Manthia, 152
Diaz, Vic, 124, 128
Dietrich, Marlene, 74, 85, 90
difference, minimizing, 8, 37, 71
digitization, 196
direct-to-video features, 11, 195
Disney, 193, 198, 221
dispossession, 12, 62–3, 139, 142, 150, 163, 169, 210
and appropriation of indigenous-nation identities, 52, 62, 186, 191n1
diversity, 15, 19, 71, 98n1, 102, 103, 136–45, 158, 160, 197, 237
Dixon, Wheeler Winston, 185–6
do-it-yourself (DIY), 223, 230, 231, 234, 237
Doane, Mary Ann, 49, 121–2
Doctor Dracula (film, 1978), 133n20
Dobrev, Nina, 209
"dog-eaters" (racist term for Filipina/os), 131
Doña Lupe (film, 1983), 191n5
Double Happiness (film, 1994), 204
Dracula (film, 1931), 1, 2, 3–4, 12, 13, 22, 45–52, 55–6, 58–9, 61, 64, 65, 66, 68–70, 71, 75–98
Drácula (film, 1931), 1, 2, 12, 13, 45–52, 55–6, 58–9, 61, 66–70, 71, 76–98
Dracula (film, 1979), 143, 149, 170
Dracula (novel, 1897), 14, 17, 20n2, 22–34, 39, 45, 70, 75–9, 107, 109, 124, 128, 135, 138, 161, 165, 170–3, 189, 201–2, 219, 225, 229
Dracula (series, 2013–14), 194
Dracula, Prince of Darkness (film, 1966), 110

269

Dracula: Dead and Loving It (film, 1995), 171
Dracula: Pages from a Virgin's Diary (film, 2001), 201
Dracula, père et fils/Dracula, Father and Son (film, 1976), 161n5
Dracula 2000 (film, 2000), 161–2n6
Dracula 3000 (film, 2004), 227n1
Dracula A. D. 1972 (film, 1972), 110
Dracula Has Risen from the Grave (film, 1968), 110
Dracula's Daughter (film, 1936), 2, 17, 21, 48, 75, 89, 156
Drakula halála/The Death of Dracula (film, 1921), 20n11
Dresser, Nadine, 6
Drug Enforcement Agency (DEA), 174, 176
dubbing, 9, 18, 85, 102–4, 114–17, 120–3, 125, 126, 130–1, 199
Dublin, 215, 219
Dubois, Nicole, 156
DuBois, W. E. B., 135
Duvall, Shelley, 204
Dyer, Richard, 73, 74
Dyszel, Dick, 197

"earth-boxes" or "earth-homes," 27, 29, 72, 107, 139
Eclipse (film, 2010), 186, 189
Edison Company, 3, 17, 48, 51–2, 55, 124, 194, 195, 200
Eghbali, Daruish, 36
Eghbali, Milad, 35
Egypt or Egyptian, 27, 120, 148–9, 151, 157, 186–7, 219
Eisenstein, Sergei, 33, 172
Elephant Man, The (film, 1980), 39
Ellis Island, 51, 58, 92, 208
Ellison, Ralph, 208
Elsaesser, Thomas, 67n11
Emancipation Proclamation (1863), 209
Emigrants Landing at Ellis Island (film, 1903), 51
émigrés, 9, 47, 90, 93
empathy
    feminist, 181, 205
    intercultural and interspecies, 8, 165, 166–70, 200, 212–13, 215
    vampires as figures of, 2, 5, 11, 15, 46, 196, 215, 217
empire and imperialism, 14, 17, 24, 28, 30–3, 80, 101, 105, 111, 130, 149, 172–3, 175–6, 181, 190, 207, 219
    Austria-Hungary, 59, 77, 85
    British Empire, 104, 107–9, 220
    Holy Roman Empire, 171
    Inca Empire, 216
    Japanese imperialism, 63
    Ottoman Empire, 27, 28, 33, 171–2, 195, 224
    US imperialism, 30, 40–1, 104, 124, 161
    see also colonialism and colonization
enfranchisement, 15, 84
English, non-US-accented (language), 13
English, US-accented (language), 121, 149
Enlightenment, European, 27

Equal Rights Amendment (ERA) (1972), 92
equity, 5, 15, 71, 137, 139, 143, 168, 188, 225, 236
Ericson, Leif, 210
Ethiopia, 206
European Recovery Program (Marshall Plan) (1948–52), 102, 104
Exclusive Films (production company), 106
Executive Order 10925 (1961, advancing Affirmative Action policy), 1
Expressionism, German, 48, 72

Facebook, 212, 226, 230
Facebook Connect, 223
Fairness Doctrine (1949–87), 197
faith, 12, 27, 40, 52, 61, 89, 176, 187
Fanon, Frantz, 74, 81, 132n7, 135, 145, 234
fans or fandom, 132n4, 163, 176, 188, 192n8, 194, 221–2, 226, 227
    fan culture, 230
    fan fiction (fic), 7, 187–8, 192n8, 225, 230, 231
"fanboys," 13
Farnsworth, Christopher, 238n1
Farrokhzad, Forough, 37
Farsi, 5, 35, 39
fascism, 9, 18, 60, 86, 92, 95, 102, 107, 149, 208, 217
"fate worse than death," 69, 80, 83, 94
Fearless Vampire Killers, or Pardon Me, Your Teeth Are in My Neck, The/Dance of the Vampires (film, 1967), 18, 111, 114
FEARnet (web network), 222
Federal Communications Commission (FCC), 197, 202
Federale (band), 36
feminism, 31, 82, 89, 105, 181, 205–6, 220–1
    hijabi, 16–17, 21
    Muslim, 1, 6, 34–9, 42
    postfeminism, 7, 138, 179, 206
    queer, 221, 223–5
    white (non-intersectional), 7, 101, 102, 138, 179, 188
Ferrara, Abel, 21, 159, *160*
feudalism, 80
Feuillade, Louis, 43n4, 196
Fifteenth Amendment *see* US Constitution
file sharing, peer-to-peer (P2P) or unauthorized, 198, 230
Filipino Academy of Movie Arts and Sciences (FAMAS), 125
films noirs (detective films), 48, 127
Film, Television, and Media Studies, 11, 40, 131
financial interest and syndication rules ("fin-syn rules") (1991), 197
First Amendment *see* US Constitution
First National (studio), 99n9
Fisher, Terence, 100, 101, 106, 107, 110, 112
Five Civilized Tribes (Cherokee, Chickasaw, Choctaw, Creek, Seminole), 70
Flaherty, Robert, 60
Flight of the Crab Monsters/Tagani (film, 1965), 128
Florescu, Radu R., 170

INDEX

flow, 194, 227
folklore, 1, 3, 6–7, 16, 22, 24, 29, 89, 112, 124–5, 196, 218
Food and Drug Administration (FDA), 190
Fool There Was, A (film, 1915), 43n4
Foucault, Michel, 43–4n11
Founding Fathers (nationalist myth), 44n22
Ford, John, 34, 48, 173
Forever Knight (series, 1992–6), 199–200, 202, 207
Forsaken, The (film, 2001), 152
Foster, Gwendolyn Audrey, 53–4, 74, 140
Foster, Helen, 62
Foster, Lisa, 203–4
foundational myths, 18, 140, 143, 160
   beacon of democracy, 18, 141, 160
   nation of immigrants, 18, 141, 143
   land of opportunity, 18, 141, 160
franchises, 2, 3, 18–19, 163, 166–9, 179–84, 221, 226–7
Franco, Francisco, 167
Franco, James, 202
Frankenberg, Ruth, 73
Frankenstein (film, 1932), 47–8
Frankenstein (novel, 1818), 219–20
Frankenstein: The True Story (film, 1972), 156
free market or free trade, 40, 42, 150, 164, 179, 181, 197
free white persons, 30, 44n15, 46, 56, 75, 152
free-to-air networks, 3, 196, 199; see also ABC (network); CBS (network); NBC (network)
freed slaves, 4, 146, 209, 235
freedom, 15, 48, 52, 146, 150, 173, 217, 236
Freedom Seekers, The see Incense of the Damned/Bloodsuckers/The Freedom Seekers (film, 1972)
freelancing, 3, 16, 102
Freud, Sigmund, 25
Friedman, Brent V., 223
Friedman, Thomas, 166
Friends (series, 1994–2004), 198
Fright Night (film, 1985), 18, 151
Frodon, Jean-Michel, 152
From Dusk till Dawn (franchise), 227
   From Dusk till Dawn (film, 1995), 19, 174–5, *175*
   From Dusk till Dawn (videogame, 2001), 195
   From Dusk till Dawn: The Series (series, 2014–present), 19, 176, 195
   From Dusk till Dawn 2: Texas Blood Money (film, 1999), 175, 195
   From Dusk Till Dawn 3: The Hangman's Daughter (film, 2000), 175, 195
Frye, Dwight, 84
Fu Manchu (character), 35, 79, 110, 132n2, 172
Fuentes, Amalia, 126, *127*
FX (network), 3, 217

Gabilondo, Joseba, 175
Gable, Clark, 104
Gabriel, amor inmortal (series, 2008), 19, 215
Game Boy (videogame platform), 227
GameBrains (videogame developer), 227
Ganja and Hess (film, 1973), 18, 145–7, *147*, 161n3
Gaonkar, Dilip, 115
Garbo, Greta, 74, 85, 90
Gates, The (series, 2010), 195
Gelder, Ken, 72
gender, 42–3, 47, 84, 123, 204–5, 225
   cisgender, 7, 36, 141, 164
   and citizenship, 47, 54, 57, 59
   cross-gendered acts, 49
   feminization, 61, 64, 69, 78, 83, 84, 87, 157, 188
   masculinity, 57, 65, 69, 83–4, 120, 122–3, 130, 138, 157, 206
   masculinization, 64
   normative, 54, 59, 64, 89, 159, 205
   queered, 61, 84
   subversion, 47, 164, 179, 181
   transgender, 36, 220
   transgressions, 84, 90, 138
General Agreement on Trade and Tariffs (GATT) (1947), 40
Genetically Modified Organism (GMO) or Genetically Engineered Organism (GEO), 166
genocide, 14, 31, 52, 139, 160, 163, 169, 186, 210, 220, 221, 235
Germany or German, 3, 22, 29, 43n8, 48, 49, 51, 53, 57, 60, 61, 72, 78, 79, 96–9, 109, 116, 132n8, 132n10, 157, 116n6, 184, 190, 195, 199, 219, 220, 226, 227n1
Geung shut yee sang/Jiang shi yi sheng/Doctor Vampire (film, 1991), 162n7
Ghana, 228n8
ghetto, 30, 51, 54, 78, 142, 143
Ghobadi, Bahman, 38
Ghost House Pictures (Hollywood production company), 222
Gillies, Daniel, 210
"girl power," 13, 19, 138, 180–1, 205–6; see also postfeminism
Girl Walks Home Alone at Night, A (film, 2014), 1, 5–6, 17, 21, 34–40, 42, 50
Gish, Lillian, 63, 71
global warming, 164
globalization, 164, 217
   and immigration, 32, 41–2, 166
Glover, David, 25
Goebbels, Joseph, 213
goeng si ("hopping vampire," literally, stiff corpse), 203
Goeng si sin sang/Mr. Vampire (film, 1985), 203
Goldsworthy, Vesna, 28, 43n9
Goliath and the Vampires/Maciste contro il vampiro (film, 1961), 120
Gomez, Jewel, 31
Gomez, Miguel, 217
Gone with the Wind (film, 1939), 91, 92, 209, 226
"good white people," 71
Goodman, Theodosia *see* Theda Bara
Gopalan, Lalitha, 114
Gothic (genre), 10, 11, 48, 76, 77, 95, 98, 101, 106–9, 116–17, *118*, 140, 172, 211

271

Goyer, David, 183, 184
Grahame-Smith, Seth, 230–1
Grahem, Kat, 209
Grand Theft Auto IV (videogame, 2008), 226
Grant, Madison, 44n15, 174
Grant, Richard E., 172
Greaser Act, California (1855), 123, 173
"greasers" (racist term), 69, 173
Great Depression (1932–5), 58, 75
Green Movement (2009), 38
Green Violinist, The (painting, 1918/1923–4), 112
Grevioux, Kevin, 184
Griffith, D. W., 17, 52, 62, 63, 71, 152
Griffith, Thomas Ian, 176
Gua Sha/The Treatment (film, 2001), 99n6
Guerrero, Carmen, 87
Guerrero, Ed, 144
Guess Who's Coming to Dinner? (film, 1967), 137
Gunn, Bill, 145, 147
Gunning, Tom, 50
Guzmán Huerta, Rodolfo, 118–20

haciendas, 117, *118*, 126
Hadimioglu, Çagla, 38–9
Haenni, Sabine, 51
Haitian Revolution (1791–1804), 145, 156
Haley, Alex, 148–9
Hall, Jerry, 148
Hall, Jordan, 223, *224*
Hall, Stuart, 145
Hallet, Andy, 207
Halloween, 232
Hallyuwood, 2, 20n1
Hamas, 167
Hammer Films (studio), 2, 7, 85, 100–15, 132nn1–2, 132n6, 134–5, 138, 144, 149, 159, 171, 205, 225
hammocking, 198
Hansen, Miriam, 64–5, 103
hapa, 155
Haraway, Donna, 29, 41
harems, 26, 62, 82
Haring, Keith, 153, *153*
Harry Potter (film franchise, 2001–11), 163
Harvey, David, 164
Hawai'i or Hawai'ian, 30, 44n17, 48, 61, 63, 124, 142, 143, 232
Hawke, Ethan, 191
Hayakawa, Sessue, 83
Hayek, Salma, 174
Hays, Will, 9
HBO (cable network), 3, 193, 203, 209, 221, 228n8
HBO Go, 198
Hefner, Hugh, 149
Heidegger, Martin, 159
Hemisphere Pictures (Hollywood production company), 123, 125
Henson, Jim, 196
Hercules at the Center of the Earth/Ercole al centro della terra (film, 1961), 121
heritage cinema, 170–3, 219, 229
Hezbollah, 167

Hindu, 49, 141
historiography, 5, 9, 135
Hogan, Chuck, 217
Holden, Gina, 202
Holden, Gloria, 71, 89
Holland, Tom, 151
Holocaust, 9, 160, 218
Holt, Claire, 210
Holt, Zane, 176
Holy Roman Empire (962–1806), 171
home entertainment, 196
homeland, 23, 29, 40, 75, 91, 102, 114
homelessness, 183
homoeroticism, 66, 121, 157, 170
homophobia, 70, 90, 101, 159, 212, 215, 225
Hong Kong, 3, 9, 33, 14, 107, 110–11, 130, 132n4, 144, 203
hooks, bell, 4, 12, 71, 73
Hooper, Tobe, 197
Hopkins, Anthony, 172–3
Horror from Beyond, The see *Blood Thirst/The Horror from Beyond* (film, 1971)
Horror of Dracula (film, 1958), 2, 18, 100, 106–11, 113, 144, 147, 169, 174
Horror of the Blood Monsters (film, 1970), 18, 128, *129*
Horsman, Reginald, 210
House Is Black, The/Khanen siah ast (film, 1962), 37
House of Bondage, The (novel, 1910), 81
House of Dark Shadows (film, 1970), 140
House of Dracula (film, 1945), 17, 94–5, 117
House of Frankenstein (film, 1944), 17, 94, 95, 117
How Tasty Was My Little Frenchman/Como era gostoso o meu Francês (film, 1971)
Howard, Gertrude, 135
Hulu, 3, 198
humanism, 24–5, 31, 165, 166–70
Hungary or Hungarian, 3–4, 13, 20, 32, 44n13, 45, 47, 56–7, 69, 78, 81, 89–92, 94, 98, 99n11, 115, 118, 132n1, 163, 184, 185, 189, 194, 204, 227n1
Hunger, The (film, 1983), 151
"hunky" (racist term), 54
Hunted, The (series, 2001–present), 19, 221
Huntington, Samuel, 166
Hussein, Saddam, 34
Hutchings, Peter, 106, 109–10
hyphenated Americans, 8, 44n13, 79, 141

I Am Legend (film, 2007), 191
I Am Legend (novel, 1954), 191
I Heart Vampires (series, 2009–10), 221
I Kissed a Vampire (series, 2009–present), 221
I'm No Angel (film, 1933), 135
Icy and Sot (artists), 37
ideology, 33
Illusions (film, 1982), 117
Imitation of Life (film, 1934), 156
Imitation of Life (film, 1959), 156
Immigrant, The (film, 1917), 50, 55, 60
Immigration Act of 1917, 44n13, 56
Immigration Act of 1924, 76

Immigration Act of 1965, 18, 137
imperialism *see* empire and imperialism
Inca Empire (1438–1532), 128, 207, 216
Incense of the Damned/Bloodsuckers/The Freedom Seekers (film, 1972), 106–7
inclusion, 14–15, 18, 46, 66, 70–1, 77, 79, 136–7, 139, 141–3, 165
Independent-International Pictures Corp. (Hollywood production company), 125, 130
India (South Asia) or Indian, 27, 31, 67n12, 107, 114, 126, 170, 187, 199, 220, 239n9
Indiagames (videogame developer), 227
Indian Citizenship Act (1924), 30, 70
"Indians" (as racist term), 96, 152, 181, 210, 220
Indonesia or Indonesian, 176, 232, 237
individualism, 6, 18, 63, 139, 141
Industrial Soundscape (film, 2002), 37
infantilization, 13, 53, 80, 84, 87, 109, 138
integration
  economic, 22, 165, 174, 178–9, 181, 196, 217
  horizontal, 197, 225–6
  racial, 144
  social, 11
  vertical, 103, 198
intellectual property, 230
internationalism, 5, 85
internet memes, 14, 19, 227, 229–34, 237
intersectionality and intersectional identities or feminisms, 8, 11–12, 180, 181
Interview with the Vampire: The Vampire Chronicles (film, 1994), 2, 18, 28, 156, 211
Inuit (indigenous nation), 178
invasion, 11, 13, 17, 27, 30, 33–4, 48, 88, 147, 167, 170–1, 173, 178, 182, 212, 214, 220, 233
Invisible Man, The (novel, 1952), 208
Iran or Iranian, 5, 17, 21, 31–3, 34–9, 41
Iranian Revolution and hostage crisis (1979–81), 21, 33, 38
Iraq or Iraqi, 17, 33–4, 150, 170, 172, 173, 182, 183, 214
Isaac, Allan, 128, 130
Isenberg, Nancy, 233
ISIS or ISIL ("Islamic State") *see* Daesh
Islam, 1, 6, 19, 26–7, 31–3, 37–9, 64–5, 82, 164–5, 169–72, 182, 185, 214–15, 233
"Islamic fundamentalists," 19, 165
Islamophobia, 33, 38, 170–1, 214
Island of Doctor Moreau, The (novel, 1896), 124
It Started in Naples (film, 1960), 104
Italian, The (film, 1915), 54–5
Italy or Italian, 41, 44n13, 48, 103, 104, 112–13, 120–1, 132n9, 132n10
iTunes, 198, 221

Jackman, Hugh, 165
Jackson, Helen Hunt, 62
Jacobson, Matthew, 72
James, C. L. R., 220
James, Henry, 30
Janissaries, 28, 169, 171

Japan or Japanese, 31, 44n13, 47, 61, 63, 66, 83, 85, 106, 130, 143, 163, 170, 172, 188, 195, 203, 212, 218, 226
Jazz Singer, The (film, 1927), 226
Jenkins, Henry, 230
Jew or Jewish *see also* Ashkenazim or Ashkenazi, 7, 12, 27, 30, 43n2, 43n4, 43n7, 43n8, 51–3, 69, 72, 73, 77, 78, 92, 96, 98n3, 111–14, 129, 141, 150, 160, 185, 206, 208, 214, 218
Jezebel (film, 1938), 91
Jitters, The (film, 1988), 203–4
Johnson, Lyndon B., 239n8
Johnson-Reed Act (1924), 30, 70
Jointville (Hollywood studio in France), 103
Jones, Duane, 146, *147*
Jones, Freddie, 110
Jones, Grace, 152–3, *153*
Jones, Julia, 169
Jordan, Neil, 156
Judaism, 7, 12, 27, 30, 31, 43n4, 43nn7–8, 51–3, 69, 72–3, 77–8, 92, 96, 98n3, 99n10, 111–12, 114, 150, 185, 220; *see also* Jew or Jewish
  anti-Semitism, 18, 72, 88, 96, 99n10, 112, 206, 208, 218, 232
Jungle Fever (film, 1991), 159
jungle-horror (Philippine export genre), 123, 129
jus sanguinas (right of blood), 26
jus soli (right of soil), 23, 26, 44n15, 167
Just Around the Corner (film, 1938), 135

Kael, Pauline, 162n10
Kant, Immanuel, 105
Kauanui, J. Kehaulani, 142, 143
Kauffmann, Reginald Wright, 81
Keitel, Harvey, 174
Kelljan, Bob, 144, 149
Kennedy, John F., 176
Kennedy, Robert, 176
Kenya or Kenyan, 232
Kermit the Frog (Muppet), 15
Khomeini, Ayatollah, 33–4, 37
Kickstarter, 222
Kier, Udo, 113, 182
Kierkegaard, Søren, 159
Killer of Sheep (film, 1977), 144
Kindred: The Embrace (series, 1996), 226
King, Martin Luther, Jr., 176
King, Stephen, 197
Kiosk (band), 35
Kipling, Rudyard, 108
Kiss in the Dark, A (film, 1904), 62
Kiss of the Vampire (film, 1964), 112
Klimt, Gustav, 172
Klinger, Barbara, 230
knowledge, categories of, 23–4
Kohner, Paul, 85, 88
Konvitz, Milton, 96
Kramer, Paul, 124
Kramer, Stanley, 137
Ku Klux Klan, 44n12
Kurosawa, Akira, 33

273

Laal Rang (film, 2016), 31
labor, 16, 33, 42, 56, 64, 116–17, 121, 130, 138, 139, 142, 174, 176, 179, 189, 200, 236
  cheap, day, stoop, or unskilled, 31, 57, 88, 123, 144, 158, 163, 173, 194
  contract or flexible, 102
  dead, 130
  domestic, free, slave, or unpaid, 84, 96, 109, 124, 154, 156, 205, 235; *see also* braceros *and* sakadas
  organized or unionized, 55, 58, 75, 123
Laemmle, Carl, 51
Laemmle, Carl, Jr., 68
Lamarr, Hedy, 74
land allotments, 30
Land, The (film, 1941), 60
Langella, Frank, 149, 170
Laos or Laotian, 161, 177
Last of the Mohicans, The (film, 1992), 170
Late Show with David Letterman (series, 1993–2015), 198
Latham, Rob, 6
latifundios (landowners), 118
Latin Lovers (stereotype), 61, 65, 69, 81–2, 91
Lau, Koon-wai Ricky, 203
Lautner, Taylor, 167
Lawrence of Arabia (film, 1962), 170
LBGTQ populations, 23, 141, 164, 165, 214, 225
  gay marriage, 212
  homophobia, 70, 90, 101, 159, 212, 215, 225
  homosexuality, 89, 112
  lesbians, 89, 113, 179, 202, 205, 225
  queerness, 7, 31, 42, 61, 64, 70, 84, 89–91, 101–2, 112, 134, 156, 182, 188, 214, 224–5
  transgender, 36, 220
Lean, David, 170
Lebanon or Lebanese, 14
Lederer, Francis, 58–9
Lee, Bruce, 104, 144
Lee, Christopher, 7, 100–1, 104, 106, 110–11, 113–15, 132nn2–3, 135, 172
Lee, Quentin, 204
Lee, Robert, 154
Lee, Spike, 159
LeFanu, Joseph Sheridan, 24, 34, 201, 204, 205, 224–5
Legend of the Seven Golden Vampires, The (film, 1974), 110, 111
Leigh, Vivien, 91
Leone, Sergio, 103–4
Let Me In (film, 2010), 159
Let the Right One In/Låt den rätte komma in (film, 2008), 158–9
Lewis, Bernard, 166
Lewis, Fiona, 112
Lewis, Juliette, 174
Lim, Bliss, 12–13, 123–4, 125, 129
Lincoln, Abraham, 44n12, 60
Lincoln, Abraham (character), 19, 229–32, 234–7
Linke, Uli, 43–4n11

Live Evil (film, 2009), 189
Living Corpse, The/Zinda Laash (film, 1967), 147
LOLcats (meme), 229
Lollywood, 2, 20n1
London, 27, 30, 35, 48–51, 64, 66, 69, 78, 82, 85, 87, 89–93, 96, 100, 113, 128, 145, 171, 190, 194, 215, 219
lonelygirl15 aka *lg15* (series, 2006–8), 221
Longinović, Tomislav, 172
López, Ana, 86
Lord of the Rings (film franchise, 2001–3), 163
Lorde, Audre, 164
Loren, Sophia, 104
Lorentz, Pare, 60
Los Angeles, 5, 18, 35, 47, 63, 69, 87, 134–6, 163, 199, 205, 208, 222
Lost Boys, The (film, 1987), 18, 173
Lost Boys: The Thirst (film, 2010), 195
Lost Boys: The Tribe (film, 2008), 195
Lost Cause (ideology of southern nationalism), 91
Lost Planet (videogame franchise, 2007–13), 226
Lotz, Amanda, 197
Love at First Bite (film, 1979), 150
Loves of Count Iorga, Vampire, The (film, 1970), 149
Loving v. Virginia (legal case, 1967), 156
low-budget cinema, 3, 115, 123, 144, 202
Lowe, Lisa, 14, 141, 143
Lowe, Todd, 214
LPC (likely to become a public charge), 98n3
lucha libre (professional wrestling), 1, 116, 119, 120, 219
Lugosi, Béla, 3, 4, 13, 15, 16, 22, 45, 64–5, 69, 71, 75–6, 78–83, 87, 93–4, 96, 98, 99n11, 104, 115, 132n3, 149, 154, 196, 232
Lynch, David, 37, 39

McClelland, Bruce, 7, 43n2, 228n5
McDaniel, Etta, 91
McDaniel, Hattie, 91
McIntosh, Peggy, 148
MacLeod, John T., 124
McNally, David, 31
McNally, Raymond T., 170
Maddin, Guy, 201
Maid in Morocco (film, 1925), 62
Majithia, Sheetal, 192n9
"Make America Great Again" (Republican Party slogan, 2016), 234
Making an American Citizen (film, 1912), 17, 50, 52, 53, 54, 56, 57, 69, 80
Making of an American, The (film, 1920), 57
Malarkey, Michael, 194, 210
Malaysia, 199
Malcolm X, 148–9, 176
Maltby, Richard, 69
Manganiello, Joe, 194, 212
Manhattan, 51, 58–60, 64, 81, 157–9, 191, 217
Manhattan Project, 158
Manifest Destiny, 34, 48, 52, 124, 170, 173, 187

INDEX

Manila, 127–8
"March of the Flag" (speech, 1898), 124
Marin, Cheech, 174
"mark of the vampire" (impressions of fangs on the neck), 46, 69, 71, 80, 82, 83, 159
Mark of the Vampire (film, 1935), 17, 93–4, 197
Mark of the West see Curse of the Undead/ Mark of the West (film, 1959)
Marr, Wilhelm, 99n10
Marsters, James, 182
Martin (film, 1976)
Marvel Comics, 180
Marx, Anthony, 130, 136, 155, 165
Marx, Karl, 31, 190
Mary Shelley's Frankenstein (film, 1994), 170
masala, 1, 114
mashups, 221, 227–31, *231*, 237
Matheson, Richard, 191
Mayall, David, 27
Mayans (1551–1697), 119, 175
Mbembe, Achille, 166
meat processing, 176, 184
Meatballs (film, 1979), 201
media convergence, 196–9
Media Studies *see* Film, Television, and Media Studies
Meek, Donald, 94
Melford, George, 17, 65, 68, 85
melodrama, 45, 55, 57, 76, 78, 84, 107, 202–3
 as safety-valve, 10
 miscegenation, 17, 47, 61–4, 68–70, 88
 reactionary, 38
 sensational, 52
Melting Pot (nationalist myth), 4, 18, 46, 58, 67n1, 73, 77–9, 82, 90, 92, 96, 105, 155
memes
 anti-Obama memes, 232–3
 Barakula, 232–4, 237
 internet memes, 14, 19, 227, 229–34, 237
memory, 39, 90, 154, 184, 218; *see also* amnesia
Méndez, Fernando, 117, *118*
Mendieta, Eduardo, 105
Merhju'i, Dariush, 73
mestizo (colonial Spanish caste), 44n15, 97, 124, 125, 155
Metro-Goldwyn-Mayor (MGM), 60, 68, 93, 111, 203, 232
México or Mexican, 3, 4, 9, 18, 30, 42, 44n16, 47, 85, 87, 88, 96, 102, 103, 114–23, 126, 130, 131, 189, 201, 207, 214, 216–19
Mexican American borderlands, 121, 159, 167, 173, 237
Mexican American War/La Intervención Norteamericana (1846–8), 63
Meyer, Stephanie, 167, 169, 187, 191–2n7
Miami, 69, 116, 215–17
Micheaux, Oscar, 144, 148
middle class *see* class
Middle Passage, 134, 149, 160; *see also* slavery
Mignolo, Walter, 105
Miranda, Carmen, 104
Mis-Directed Kiss, The (film, 1904), 62

mise en corps ("putting in the body"), 117
miscegenation, 10, 23, 25, 29, 53, 76, 78–9, 128, 139, 145, 155–7, 212
 criminalization of, 61, 82, 155, 185
 melodramas, 17, 47, 61–4, 68–70, 88
 PCA prohibition of, 100, 143
misogyny, 8, 49, 138, 156, 225
Mitchell, Timothy, 39
Mittell, Jason, 199
mixed-blood populations, 19, 23, 28–9, 78, 87, 156, 166, 183–4
mixed-blood children, 29, 70, 78
mixed-race in individuals or relationships, 155–6, 166, 203, 212
model minority (nationalist myth), 143, 154, 204
Modern Vampires (film, 1998), 228n7
modernity, 25, 27, 38, 43–4n11, 88, 90, 105, 115, 119, 125
modernization, 37, 38, 119
Mohanty, Chandra, 105, 166
Molina, Natalia, 88
monster mashes, 2, 94, 219, 229
Montréal, 10, 197, 202
Moonlight (series, 2007–8), 207, 228n6
Morayta, Miguel, 117
Morgan, Brit, 214
Morgan, Joseph, 210
Morgan, Ralph, 92
Mormonism, 52, 168, 186–7, 191n1
Morrisett, Lloyd, *15*, 196
Morrissey, Paul, 102, 112–13
Moth Diaries, The (film, 2011), 201
Mother, May I Sleep with Danger? (film, 2016), 202
Motion Picture Association of America (MPAA), 130, 172
Motion Pictures Exports Association of America (MPEAA), 103
Move On (film, 1903), 51, 67n4
Movie Macabre (series, 1981–93), 197
Movie, A (film, 1958), 229
Moyer, Stephen, 209
Mr. Vampire/Goeng si sin sang (film, 1985), 203
MTV (network), 195, 199, 223
Mughal-e-Azam (film, 1960), 126
mulato (colonial Spanish caste), 62, 71, 74, 90, 97, 155–6
Mulvey, Laura, 10, 64, 122
mummies, 119, 184, 207
Mummy, The (film, 1932), 48
Munsters, The (series, 1964–6), 2, 197
Murnau, F. W., 22, 33, 72, 75
Murphy, Eddie, 148
Murphy, Jimmy, 97
Murphy, Peter, 186
Murray, K. Gordon, 116
Muse Entertainment (Canadian production company), 202
music, 35, 38, 51, 61, 91, 93, 97, 126, 140, 154, 203, 204
 musical scores, 113, 215–16
 music videos, 157, 230
 musicals, 127, 128, 237

275

Musidora (Jeanne Roques), 24, 43n4
Musser, Charles, 79
Musser, George, 124
My Darling Aswang (series, 2010–11), 199
Mysterious Mr. Wong, The (film, 1934), 79
Mystery Science Theater 3000 (MST3K), 122–3

Nadja (film, 1994), 21
Naficy, Hamid, 75
NAFTA *see* North American Free Trade Agreement (NAFTA) (1994–present)
national belonging, 10, 104, 105, 141; *see also* social belonging
National Broadcasting Corporation *see* NBC
national cinema, 5, 11
national exceptionalism, 8, 9, 12, 14, 19, 23, 31–2, 42, 44n18, 48, 55, 58, 93–5, 104, 131, 141–2, 154, 161, 207–8, 213–14, 232, 238
National Film Board of Canada (NFB), 200
nativism, 13–14, 23, 27–8, 30, 61, 63, 69–70, 75, 77–8, 81, 88, 138–9, 142, 150–1, 181, 201, 212, 215, 232
naturalization, 18, 46, 59, 63, 69, 75, 86, 92, 103
Naturalization Act of 1790, 44n15, 75, 78
Naturalization Act of 1795, 30
Naturalization Act of 1879, 132n14
Nazism, 96, 112, 184, 208, 213, 218–19, 228n7, 236
NBC (network), 3, 193, 194, 198, 202–3
NBCUniversal, 195, 198
Neale, Steve, 122
Near Dark (film, 1987), 18, 152
Negra, Diane, 137, 142
"negroes" (as racist term), 135, 152, 232, 235
Neill, Sam, 190
Nellie the Beautiful Housemaid (film, 1908), 62
neoliberalism, 19, 31, 158, 161, 163–9, 176, 179, 188–91, 197, 217
Netflix, 3, 198
New Deal (1933–6), 59–61, 75, 98n3, 197
New Latin American Cinema, 145
New Moon (film, 2009), 186
New Woman, 24, 64, 90–1
New World, 8, 80, 236
New World Pictures (Hollywood production company), 123
New York, 3, 9, 10, 30, 48, 54, 56, 58, 60, 66, 69, 85, 90, 95, 112, 158, 167, 182, 203, 215, 217–18, 228n4; *see also* Manhattan and Brooklyn
New York City "Ghetto" Fish Market (film, 1903), 51
New Zealand, 9, 163, 174, 177, 184
Newman, Kim, 170
Ngũgĩ, wa Thiong'o, 145
niche market, 196
Nick Knight (series 1989)
nickelodeon, 48, 51, 81
Niemöller, Martin, 236
Nietzsche, Friedrich, 159
Nigeria, 20n1, 20n2

"niggers" (racist term), 144, 220
Night of Dark Shadows (film, 1971), 140
Nightmare Classics (series, 1989), 204
Nighy, Bill, 184
Niles, Steve, 222
Nixon, Richard, 136, 239n8
No One Knows about Persian Cats/Kasi az gorbehaye irani khabar nadareh (film, 2009), 39
Nocturna: Granddaughter of Dracula (film, 1979), 228n4
Nodier, Charles, 24
Noli me tangere/The Social Cancer (novel, 1887), 133n18
Nollywood, 2, 20n1
nomads or nomadic culture, 27–8, 207
noncitizens, 30, 40, 58, 62, 116, 124, 132n14
Noreiga, Chon, 63
Nornes, Abé Mark, 114
North American Free Trade Agreement (NAFTA) (1994–present), 122, 163, 164, 173–9, 181, 195, 215, 217
Nosferatu: A Symphony of Horror/ Nosferatu, eine Symphonie des Grauens (film, 1922), 17, 19, 22, 33, 45, 46, 72, 75, 107, 109, 132n10, 157, 167, 169, 171, 230
Not Without My Daughter (film, 1991)
Nowell-Smith, Geoffrey, 79
Nurmi, Maila, 197
Nussbaum, Martha, 105

Obama, Barack, 14, 229, 232–5, 237
offshoring, 9, 18–19, 165, 174, 195–7, 199–200, 215
oil, 5, 13, 33, 36–7, 140, 177–8, 190, 194–5
Old Dracula/Vampira (film, 1974), 145, 146
Old South, 12, 91, 135, 152, 156, 182, 205, 209
Old World, 8
Oldman, Gary, 32, 33, 170
Olson, Scott Robert, 142
On the Origin of the Species (book, 1859), 156
Once Upon a Time in the West/C'era una volta il West (film, 1968), 103
One Million B.C. (film, 1940), 128
one-drop rule, 30, 155
Only Lovers Left Alive (film, 2013), 151
Ono, Kent, 205
opossums, 47, 76, 94, 101
Oprah Winfrey Show, The (series, 1986–2011), 198
Organization of the Petroleum Exporting Countries (OPEC), 32, 110
orientalism, 17, 27–8, 32, 32, 39, 43, 62, 110–11, 154, 170–2, 184, 187, 189, 202–3, 232
Oriente es Occidente/East Is West (film, 1930), 88
Originals, The (series, 2013–present), 13, 19, 163, 209–11
Originals: Awakening, The (series, 2014), 223
Orlok, Graf or Count (character), 22, 46, 72, 157, 232

Other, 8, 32, 42
Ottoman Empire or Ottomans, 27–8, 33, 171–2, 195, 224
outsourcing, 3, 16, 164–5, 199, 221, 231

Pahlavi monarchy (1925–79), 21, 37
Pahlavi, Mohammad Reza, 32
Pahlavi, Reza Shah, 32
Painlevé, Jean, 72
Pakistan or Pakistani, 106, 147
Palestine or Palestinian, 37, 67n1, 218
Panamá, 235
Panama Canal Zone, 130
Paquin, Anna, 212
Paramount Decree (1948), 103, 197–8
Paramount Pictures (studio), 3, 103, 148, 197, 205
Park, Reg, 121
Parker, Lara, 140
parkour, 37
particularity, 138
Partido Revolucionario Institucional (PRI), 118–19
Passage to India, A (film, 1984), 170
Passing of the Great Race (book, 1916), 174
passing, 22–4, 43n1, 67n12, 73–4, 101, 138–41, 155–7, 204, 208
Passport Husband (film, 1938), 86
Pathé-Frères (studio), 51
patriarchy, 1, 7, 29, 33, 80–1, 84, 101, 138, 204, 206
patriotism, 6, 14, 18, 30, 33, 58, 60–1, 79, 98, 141, 159, 164, 167, 169, 174, 178, 182, 214, 217
Pattinson, Robert, 167
PBS (network), 15, *15*, 196
Peace at Westphalia (1648), 28
Pease, Donald, 42
peninsular (colonial Spanish caste), 88, 97, 117
Penny Dreadful (series, 2014–16), 10, 19, 194, 215, 219, 221
"People Are Strange" (song), 173
peplum (sword-and-sandal films), 120–1
Perlman, Ron, 178, 183
Perry, Imani, 12, 155
Persepolis (film, 2007), 38
Persepolis (graphic novel, 2000), 38
personhood, degrees of, 30, 44n14
Peterson, Cassandra, 197
Philippines or Philippine, 3, 9, 12, 16, 18, 30, 40, 44n13, 44n17, 48, 63, 94, 102, 115, 123–31, 133n20, 133n22, 142, 199, 215, 237
Pickford, Mary, 9, 62, 99n4
pied-noir, 132n7
Pilgrim, The (film, 1923), 174
Pirate Bay, 198
Pitt, Brad, 156
Pizarro, Francisco, 216–17
Pizor, Irwin, 123
plagues, 72, 110, 189, 210, 217, 219
Planché, James, 24
Plec, Julie, 209, 223
Poe, Edgar Allan (character), 235
Polański, Roman, 102, 111

Poland or Polish, 43n8, 44n13, 56, 90, 94, 161n5, 218, 225
Polidori, John, 24–5, 43n6
political agency, 8, 12
political correctness (as anti-equity expression), 139, 183, 206, 233
political economies, 5, 11, 16, 40, 42, 105, 116, 120, 123, 130–1, 167, 215
political representation, 11, 18, 29–30, 40, 71, 102, 128, 131, 136, 138–9, 142, 149, 168
politics, reactionary, 31–2, 63
Pollock, Sheldon, 105
polygamy, 26, 60, 82
Ponti, Carlo, 112
Porky's (film, 1982), 201
Port Charles (series, 1997–2003), 197, 215
Porter, Edwin S., 62
Portillo, Lourdes, 178
Portugues, Catherine, 111
Portrait of Dorian Gray, The (novel, 1890), 219
Posey, Parker, 183
postcolonialism, 80, 107, 151
 and cosmopolitanism, 105
 and migration, 48, 111
 postcolonial condition, 30, 41
 postcolonial terror, 125
 theory and scholars, 12, 25, 30–1, 41, 238
 Postcolonial Studies, 40
 United States, 43, 158, 237
postfeminism, 7, 8, 138, 179, 206; *see also* feminism and "girl power"
Prana-Films (studio), 17, 45
Pratt, Mary Louise, 26, 33, 41
Preminger, Otto, 117
Presidential Monsters (action figures), 238n3
Pride and Prejudice and Zombies (novel, 2009), 230
primitivism, 26, 62, 80, 90, 149
Production Code (1930–68), 48, 61, 68, 70, 87, 89, 100, 137, 138
Production Code Administration (PCA), 70, 89, 101, 131, 143, 183
production values, 9, 141, 170, 200, 202–3, 216, 219
Proposition 187 aka Save Our State (SOS) (1994), 150, 181
pseudoscience, 29, 30
Public Broadcasting Service *see* PBS
public-health crises, 110, 168, 188, 217
Puerto Rico or Puerto Rican, 30, 44n17, 124, 142, 149

Queen of the Damned (film, 2002), 157
queerness, 7, 31, 42, 61, 64, 70, 84, 89–91, 101–2, 112, 134, 156, 182, 188, 214, 224–5; *see also* LBGTQ populations

race
 and blood, 31, 92, 236
 and bodies, 52, 108, 152, 155, 184, 207, 209
 and borders, 95, 102, 107–8, 121
 and colonialism, 14, 28, 31, 124–6, 128–9, 135, 147, 181, 234
 definitions, 5–6, 12, 30, 69, 71, 142

277

race (*cont.*)
   nativity/nationality, 5, 12, 17, 23, 42, 71
   racial blindness, 138, 141, 161
   racial oppression, 19, 144, 183, 233
   racial profiling, 15, 96, 136, 142, 164, 182, 185, 208
   racial segregation, 51–5, 66, 68–9, 78, 86, 112, 130–1, 137–8, 140, 143, 145, 155, 178, 171, 217
   racial stratification, 130, 137–8, 143, 145, 148, 159, 236
   skin color, 4, 6, 12, 23, 207, 232, 237
   social company, 5, 12
   see also miscegenation
Radio Tehran (band), 35
Radway, Janice, 43
Rafael, Vincente, 126
Ramona (film, 1910), 62–3
Ramona (novel, 1884), 62
Rank Organisation, 132n2
Rapid (film, 1977), 201
Rapping, Elayne, 202–3
Rasputin the Mad Monk (film, 1966), 107
rats, 45, 76, 94, 172, 191
Reagan, Ronald, 159, 229
Real Girl's Guide to Everything Else, The (series, 2010), 221
redface, 188, 207
"redskins" (racist term), 220
Reeves, Keanu, 32, 33, 171
Reeves, Matt, 159
regional cinema, 5
relationality, 12
relationships, same-sex, 19, 70, 227
religion, 10, 12, 14, 23, 27, 32, 42, 52, 71, 89, 112, 141, 144, 164–9, 173, 206; *see also* Christianity; Islam; Judaism
Remy, Ronald, 115, 125, 233–4, 236
Republican Party, 6, 44n12
Retrofit Films (videogame developer), 223
Return of Count Yorga, The (film, 1970), 149
Return of Dracula, The (film, 1958), 59, 96
Return of the Vampire, The (film, 1943), 96
Return to Salem's Lot, A (film, 1987), 197
Revolutionary War (1775–83), 152, 235, 237
Rhines, Jesse, 144
Rice, Alex, 187
Rice, Anne, 28, 156–7, 169, 192n8
Rice, Condoleezza, 14
Rise: Blood Hunter (film, 2007), 228n4
River, The (film, 1937), 60
Rizal, José, 125, 133n18
RKO (studio), 3, 58, 60, 99n9
Robinson, Bill "Bojangles," 135
Roques, Jeanne *see* Musidora
Rodríguez, José Luis ("el Puma"), 216
Rodriguez, Robert, 174–5, *175*
Rogers, Ginger, 58, 74
Rohmer, Sax, 110
role playing, 225–7, 234
Roma, 27, 43n8, 72
romance, 158, 204, 206, 220
   interracial, 82, 87
   interspecies, 167

romance (genre), 1, 5, 203
   assimilation/immigration, 10, 17, 46, 52, 55–66, 68–9, 93
   courtly, 80
Romance in Manhattan (film, 1935), 58–60, 64
Romania or Romanian, 9, 51, 150, 161n5, 162n6, 195, 218
Romantic poetry, 10
Romero, Eddie, 124
Romero, George A., 154–5
Roosevelt, Franklin D., 98n3
Roosevelt, Theodore, 44n13, 60, 79
Rose Hobart (film, 1936), 229
Rosencrantz & Guildenstern Are Dead (film, 1990), 231
Rosencrantz & Guildenstern Are Undead (film, 2009), 230–1
Rosewater (film, 2014), 38
Ross, Steven, 51
Roxy Theatre, 69
rudo (wrestling figure), 119
runaway productions, 9–10, 18, 94, 101, 103, 111, 123, 127, 200
Russia or Russian, 27, 32, 43n8, 47, 51, 53–4, 69, 90, 107, 112, 125, 172, 178, 179, 183
Ryder, Winona, 33, 170
Rymer, James Malcolm, 24, 219
Rymer, Michael, 157

Sade, Marquis de, 220
Said, Edward W., 32, 38, 172
sakadas (contract laborers from Philippines), 102, 124, 128, 130–1
Salazar, Abel, 117
Salem's Lot (miniseries, 1979), 197
Salem's Lot (miniseries, 2004), 197
Salem's Lot (novel, 1975), 197
Salt of the Earth (film, 1954)
Samson versus the Vampire Women (film, 1963), 117, 120, *122*
Santa Barbara (series, 1984–93), 198
Santo and Blue Demon versus Dracula and the Wolfman/Santo y Blue Demon contra Drácula y el Hombre Lobo, El (film, 1972), 119–20, 191n5
Santo contra las mujeres vampiro, El (film, 1962), 117, 120, 125
Santo in "the Treasure of Dracula"/El Santo en El tesoro de Drácula (film, 1969), 119
Sartre, Jean-Paul, 159
Satanic Rites of Dracula, The/Count Dracula and His Vampire Bride (film, 1973), 110, 111
satire, 25, 32–4, 104, 140, 148, 150, 157–8, 174, 205
Satrapi, Marjan, 38
Saudi Arabia or Saudi, 37, 199, 228n8
"savage" or "savages," 28, 62, 123–4, 129, 166, 169, 176, 186, 212
Savini, Tom, 155
Scanners (film, 1981), 201
Schatz, Thomas, 34
Schreck, Max, 45, 72, 232
Schumacher, Joel, 173
science fiction, 1, 5, 10, 88, 184, 201

Scorpio Rising (film, 1964), 229
scorpions, 18, 47, 101
Scott, Allen, 197, 200
Scott, Gordon, 120
Scott, Ridley, 178, 189
Scott, Tony, 151
Scream, Blacula, Scream (film, 1973), 144
Seale, Bobby, 239n7
Second Amendment *see* US Constitution
Second Life (social-networking platform), 230
Section 481 tax incentive (Ireland), 219
secularism, 18–19, 23, 27, 40, 73, 108, 126–7, 141, 164–5, 167, 170
Sembène, Ousmane, 145, 234
Senf, Carol, 24
servitude, 12, 14, 16, 44n15, 84, 142
Sesame Street (series, 1969–present), 6, 15–16, 196
Sex and the City (series, 1998–2004), 221
sexism, 13, 25, 70, 83, 90, 102, 131, 152, 157–8, 168, 184, 221, 225, 230
sexual abuse, 6
sexual relations, 29, 90, 159, 230
sexuality, 22, 23, 29, 62, 64, 71, 84–91, 112, 118, 137, 151, 153, 170, 172, 204, 205; *see also* LBGTQ populations
sexually transmitted diseases, 23, 25, 81
    gonorrhea, 25
    HIV/AIDS, 23, 24, 159
    syphilis, 23, 25, 26
Shaw Brothers (studio), 110–11
Sheik, The (film, 1921), 17, 64–5, 69
Shelley, Mary, 219
Shivers (film, 1975), 201
Shohat, Ella, 12, 74, 82, 153
Shopping for Fangs (film, 1997), 204
Showtime, 10, 151, 194, 204, 205, 219
Shum, Mina, 204
Sikh, 172
SIMS (videogame), 230
Skal, David, 48, 85, 86–7
Skarsgård, Alexander, 212
slash (fan fic), 188, 225, 230
slasher film, 7, 181, 205
Slave Ship, The (painting, 1840), 220
Slayer/Mexferatu Mexico (film, 2006), 189, 227n1
"Sliding Scale, The" (short story), 124
Smallville (series, 2001–11), 200
Smith, Angela, 29, 84
Smith, James Blair, 51
Smith, Joseph, 187
Smith, Shawnee, 223
Smith, Will, 191
Snipes, Wesley, 179–80
social belonging, 1, 6, 11, 12, 15, 21–3, 35, 52; *see also* national belonging
social networking, 226, 229–30
social oppression, 13
socialism, 77, 233
soil, 6, 22–3, 26–7, 29, 72, 75, 78, 89, 92, 107, 118
Sollors, Werner, 141
Somerhalder, Ian, 209
Son of Dracula (film, 1943), 2, 17, 89, 91

Sony, 195
Soundlab (studio), 116
South of the City/Jonoub-e Shahr (film, 1958), 37
South, post-bellum, 91, 204
South Africa or South African, 9, 174, 175, 195, 227n1
South Korea or Korean, 20n1, 143, 199
Southern Strategy, 233, 239n8
Soviet or Post-Soviet, 113, 215, 232
Spadoni, Robert, 78
Spaghetti Westerns, 35, 220
Spanish–American War (1898), 124
species extinction, 164, 166, 184, 186, 238
speciesism, 13, 25, 168, 184, 214, 234
spectacle, 23, 33, 50, 120–1, 126, 158–9, 208
spiders or spider webs, 72, 84, 94, 101, 120, 170
Spierig Brothers, 189
Spigel, Lynn, 221
Stagecoach (film, 1939), 48, 94
Stake Land (film, 2010), 189
Stam, Robert, 74, 82, 153
Stanwyck, Barbara, 74
Statue of Liberty, 50–5, 58, 61, 66, 96, 208, 232
Steakly, John, 176
stereotypes, 42, 55, 64, 66, 69, 87–8, 103, 115, 138, 143, 174
    African American, 47, 135, 204; tragic Mulatta, 74, 90, 156; slave, 240
    Arab or Arab American, 61, 64–5, 82, 182, 183; Arab Sheik, 64–5, 65, 93; Arab- or Muslim- looking "terrorist," 164, 182, 215
    Asian or Asian American, 164
    Chinese or Chinese American, 61, 63–4
    Eastern European, 50
    Filipina/o or Filipina/o American, 62; dog-eaters, 131
    Hungarian or Hungarian American, 69; hunky, 54, 69
    immigrant, 55, 75–6, 79, 153, 180
    indigenous nations or Native American, 43n1; blood-thirsty Indian, 181; Indian chief, 93
    Italian or Italian American, 55, 79, 93
    Irish or Irish American, 55, 79
    Latin American, 182; "lazy peasants and wily señoritas," 86; machismo, 87
    Latin Lover, 61, 65, 69, 81–2, 91
    Mexican or Mexican American, 69, 88, 123, 174; greaser, 69, 123, 173; "lawless Mexican bandito," 96
    Muslim or Muslim American, 182
    national, 16, 66, 79
    Northwestern European (English, French, German), 79
    orientalist, 154
    queered, 61
    Russian mafia, 183
    savage/primitive, 62
    and Westerns, 93, 181
    white-female privilege, 180
Stevenson, Robert Louis, 95, 219
Stewart, Booboo, 169

279

Stewart, Jon, 38
Stewart, Kristen, 167
Stewart, Robin, 111
stigma, 121, 139, 142, 149, 151, 155–6, 165, 173, 189, 212, 233
Stoker, Bram, 14, 22–34, 43n7, 124, 225, 230; see also Dracula (novel, 1897)
Story of a Three-Day Pass, The/La Permission (film, 1968), 144
Strain, The (series, 2014–present), 19, 201, 215, 217
Strange Case of Dr. Jekyll and Mr. Hyde (novel, 1886), 219
Stranglers of Bombay (film, 1960), 107
Stratton, Jon, 206
Streeby, Shelley, 52
Stromgren, Dick, 64
structural inequalities, 13–14, 191, 209, 233–4
studio system, 9
subtitling, 85, 102–3, 114–16, 131
Sullivan, Shannon, 71, 98n1
Sundance Film Festival, 34–9
Supernatural (series, 2005–present), 196
supernaturalism, 12–13, 211
superstition, 23, 29, 89, 91, 93, 155
surrealism, 72
Sweet Sweetback's Baadasssss Song (film, 1971), 144
Syria or Syrian, 14, 183
Székelys, 27, 78

Tales from the Crypt (series, 1990–2000), 196
Tarantino, Quentin, 123, 174, 176
Taste the Blood of Dracula (film, 1970), 110
tax incentives, 9, 10, 194, 200, 219
Taylor, Lili, 159, *160*
Tea Party, 233–4
técnico (wrestling figure), 119
Tehrangeles, 5, 17
Telecommunications Act (1996), 197
telefilms, 203
telenovela, 1, 2, 215–16
Television Studies, 221; see also Film, Television, and Media Studies
Templesmith, Ben, 222
tent-poling, 198
Teo, Stephen, 111
Țepeș, Vlad see Vlad Țepeș (aka Vlad the Impaler)
Terminal Reality (videogame developer), 226
Terror is a Man (film, 1959), 124
Terror of the Tongs (film, 1961), 107
terrorism, 6, 14, 29, 38, 235
 corporate terrorism, 188
 New York City (2001), 1, 38, 182, 217
 Oklahoma City (1995), 182
 terrorist vampires, 163–91
 War on Terror, 12, 19, 166, 170, 214
Thailand or Thai, 174, 177, 195
Thirst (film, 1979), 192
Thirteenth Amendment see US Constitution
three-fifths Compromise (1787), 44n14, 149
Tilly, Meg, 204
TNT (cable network), 197

To Die For (film, 1989), 150
Todorova, Maria, 28, 172
tolerance, 8, 16, 63–4, 136, 196, 234, 236
Tomb of Dracula, The (comic book, 1973), 180
Toronto, 10, 197, 199, 200, 202, 203, 215, 217, 227n1
Tourneur, Jacques, 95
Tovar, Lupita, 85, 87, 88
tragic mulatta (stereotype), 74, 90, 156
transborder migration, 116, 120–2, 164, 166–7, 176; see also border
transgender, 36, 220
transgenre, 5, 9, 10, 11, 100
transhuman, 16
Trans-International Film (production company), 130
transmedia, 5, 9–10, 194
transnational media corporations, 9, 230
Transportation Safety Administration (TSA), 185
transspecies, 16
Transylvania, 18, 22, 25–8, 34, 47–51, 75–6, 78, 82, 84, 87, 91, 98, 107, 109, 111–12, 134, 149, 165, 171–2
travel writing, 27
Treaty of Berlin (1878), 27
Treaty of General Relations (1946), 133n22
trespass, 23, 43n1, 139
Trinh, T. Minh-ha, 115
True Blood (series, 2008–14), 2, 15, 19, 165, 188, 193, 194, 209, 211–15, 216, 232, 233–4
"Tu vuò fà l'americano" (song), 104
Tuck, Jessica, 211, *213*
Turkey or Turkish, 27, 32, 38, 51, 171–2
Turner, Frederick Jackson, 44n18
Turner, J. M. W., 220
TV Globo (production company), 215
Twilight (franchise, 2008–12), 2, 19, 22, 39, 75, 163–4, 167–9, 184, 186–8, 199, 225, 231; see also Breaking Dawn, Part 1 (film); Breaking Dawn, Part 2 (film); Eclipse (film); New Moon (film); Twilight (film)
Twins of Evil (film, 1971), 225
Twitter, 212, 224, 230

Under the Old Apple Tree (film, 1907), 62
"Uncle Tom" (racist term), 183, 208
underground cinema, 112
Underground Railroad, 236
Underworld franchise, 2, 19, 163, 184–5
 Underworld (film, 2003), 184
 Underworld: Awakening (film, 2012), 185
 Underworld: Blood Wars (film, 2016), 185
 Underworld: Rise of the Lycans (film, 2009), 184
undocumented immigration, 131, 142, 165–7, 174, 176, 181, 189
unions see labor, unionized
United Artists (studio), 3, 48
United States v. Bhagat Singh Thind (legal case, 1923), 14
Universal Pictures (studio), 1, 3, 30, 45–53, 56, 58, 61, 66, 68, 73, 75–6, 79, 85, 87–8,

91–2, 94, 96, 101–2, 105–6, 117, 143, 149, 165, 194–8, 203
universalism, 9, 14, 104–5, 138
universalization, 7, 14, 30, 34, 40, 42, 49, 74, 84, 101, 122, 139, 141
Unknown Island (film, 1948), 128
UPA Productions of America (production company), 130
UPN (cable network), 192n8, 197, 205, 207
urbanization, 38
US Constitution, 212
  First Amendment, 232
  Fifteenth Amendment, 137
  Second Amendment, 233–4
  Thirteenth Amendment, 209
US invasion and occupation of Haïti (1915), 220
US invasion of Iraq (1990–1), 17, 33–4, 170
US invasion of Iraq (2003), 33, 173, 182
US Steel Corp., 56–7
user-generated content (UGC), 10, 19, 222, 231

Vadim, Roger, 103
vagrancy, 23, 27, 235
Valemont (series, 2009), 19, 194, 223
Valente, Joseph, 25
Valenti, Jack, 130
Valentino, Rudolph, 64–5, 65, 83, 149
Vamp (film, 1986), 152–4, 203
Vampira Show, The (series, 1954–5), 197
Vampire, The/El Vampiro (film, 1957), 117, 118
Vampire, The/Le Vampire (film, 1945), 72
Vampire Circus (film, 1972), 111
Vampire Diaries, The (series, 2009–present), 2, 19, 39, 163, 194, 209, 223
Vampire Diaries: Bloodlines Revealed, The (videogame, 2010), 223
Vampire Hookers (film, 1978), 133n20
vampire hunters, 7, 11, 18–19, 22, 25–30, 33–4, 80, 100–4, 107–11, 136, 164–6, 172–7, 207, 209–10, 222–3, 227, 229, 235–7; *see also* vampire slayers
Vampire in Brooklyn (film, 1995), 148
vampire slayers, 7, 138, 143, 158, 164, 166, 177, 179–84, 205–6; *see also* vampire hunters
Vampire-Westerns, 96, 98
Vampire's Coffin, The/El Ataúd del vampiro (film, 1957), 117
Vampire's Kiss (film, 1989), 157
Vampire$ (novel, 1990), 176
Vampires (film, 1998), 19, 176, 177
Vampires, Les (film serial, 1915–16), 43n4, 196
Vampires Suck (film, 2010), 188, 231, 234
Vampires: Los Muertos (film, 2002), 176–7
Vampires: The Turning (film, 2005), 177, 195
Vampyre, The (film, 1819), 24
Vampyros Lesbos: Die Erbin des Dracula (film, 1970), 132n10
Van Helsing (film, 2004), 165, 194, 227
van Peebles, Melvin, 144
Van Sloan, Edward, 78, 89, 104
Vancouver, 10, 193, 200, 202, 227n1

Varney the Vampire, or the Feast of Blood (serial novel, 1847), 219
Vasey, Ruth, 66
veiling, 38–9
versatility, 8, 20n3
video mashups, 221, 227, 229–31
video-on-demand (VOD), 198
videogames, 10–11, 19, 194–5, 223, 225–7
  first-person shooter (FPS), 195, 226, 227
  hack-and-slash (H&S), 195, 226
Vidor, King, 60
Viet Nam or Vietnamese, 123, 160, 175–7, 228n4
Vietcong, 125
Vietnam War (aka American War, 1955–75), 123, 174–6
vigilantism, 41, 80, 97, 107, 109, 164, 172, 174, 176, 177, 180–2, 205, 234
Villarías, Carlos, 13, 45, 69, 71, 75, 79, 85, 87
virginity, 14, 84, 113–14, 168, 187, 225
virtual reality (VR), 226
Viswanathan, Gauri, 41
Vlad Țepeș (aka Vlad the Impaler), 14, 33, 161n5, 170, 172
von Count, Count (*Sesame Street* Muppet), 6, 15–16, 196
von Sternberg, Josef, 74
Voting Rights Act (1965), 137, 239n8

Walken, Christopher, 160
Walter, Mary, 125, 126, 127
Wanger, Walter, 48
War on Drugs, 12
War on Terror, 12, 19, 166, 170, 214
Warner Bros. (studio), 3, 106, 110, 197, 205
  Columbia-Warner (subsidiary), 110
  Warner-Pathé (subsidiary), 110
  WB (cable network), 192n8, 197, 205, 223
Way of the Dragon, The/Meng long guo jiang (film, 1972), 104
Web 2.0, 226
Weeds (series, 2005–12), 151
Week-end in Havana (film, 1941), 86, 104
Weine, Robert, 157
Wells, H. G., 124
werewolf, 31, 167, 184–6, 206, 209–14, 220
Werewolf, The (film, 1913), 185–6
Wesley, Paul, 209
Wesley, Rutina, 214
Westerns (genre), 11, 18, 33–6, 47–9, 52, 70, 80, 83, 88, 96–8, 152, 173, 176–8, 181, 186–8, 220
Whale, James, 48, 220
What Happened in the Tunnel (film, 1903), 62
Whedon, Joss, 179, 205
White, Jack, 62–3
White, Luise, 31
White Lies (band), 35
"White Man's Burden" (poem, 1899), 108
whiteface, 74, 154, 206
whiteness
  and death, 74–5
  "good white people," 71
  multicultural whiteness, 18, 136, 138–41, 143, 145, 149, 158–61, 204

281

whiteness (cont.)
  not-quite-white-ness or white-but-not-quite-white-ness, 3, 11, 23, 46, 52, 54, 69
  Whiteness Studies, 73
  transient and unsettled whiteness, 152–5
  unnatural whiteness, 4, 18, 46, 52, 55, 66, 71, 75, 79, 93, 139, 141, 143, 238
  white-identified-ness, 11, 18, 136, 139, 141, 237
  white privilege, 18, 71–3, 83, 98n1, 136–42, 148, 150–1, 154, 158, 169, 173–4, 181, 188, 209, 212
  white-savior complex, 7, 34
  "white trash," 18, 71, 150–2, 233
  white-upon-arrival, 4, 56, 65, 69, 87, 101–2, 115, 149
WikiLeaks, 198
Wild West, 152, 219
Wilde, Oscar, 219
Williams, Clara, 54
Williams, Raymond, 194
Williams, Spencer, 144
Williamson, Kevin, 209
Willis, Leo, 54
Willis, Sharon, 137
Wilson, Natalie, 187
Wizard of Mars, The (film, 1965), 128
"wog" (racist term), 220
Wolf, Leonard, 170

Wolf Man, 93, 95, 188, 219, 229
wolves, 76, 111, 112, 135, 169, 172, 185–6; *see also* werewolves
Woods, James, 176
world cinema, 5, 8, 11
World Trade Organization (WTO), 163, 178
wuxia, 1

X-Files, The (series, 1993–2002), 196, 200
Xbox 360 (videogame platform), 226
xenophobia, 30, 32, 34, 70, 79, 139, 196, 202, 204, 217

Yellow Dogs, The (band), 37–8
yellowface, 63, 207
"yellow peril" (racist term), 88, 110, 124–5
"Yes, We Can" (Democratic Party slogan, 2008), 233
You'll Find Out (film, 1940), 79
Young, Elizabeth, 47
Young, Robert J. C., 29, 41, 111

Zananeh/The Ladies' Room (film, 2003), 37
Zanger, Jules, 151
Zangwell, Israel, 46, 67n1
Zimmermann, Patricia R., 230
zombies, 24, 119, 120, 135, 155, 167, 195, 206, 208, 230–2

EU representative:
Easy Access System Europe
Mustamäe tee 50, 10621 Tallinn, Estonia
Gpsr.requests@easproject.com

www.ingramcontent.com/pod-product-compliance
Lightning Source LLC
Chambersburg PA
CBHW070752020526
44115CB00032B/1681